A House on Fire

A House on Fire

The Rise and Fall of Philadelphia Soul

John A. Jackson

OXFORD
UNIVERSITY PRESS
2004

OXFORD

UNIVERSITY PRESS

Oxford   New York
Auckland   Bangkok   Buenos Aires   Cape Town   Chennai
Dar es Salaam   Delhi   Hong Kong   Istanbul   Karachi   Kolkata
Kuala Lumpur   Madrid   Melbourne   Mexico City   Mumbai   Nairobi
São Paulo   Shanghai   Taipei   Tokyo   Toronto

Copyright © 2004 by John A. Jackson

Published by Oxford University Press, Inc.
198 Madison Avenue, New York, NY 10016
www.oup.com

Oxford is a registered trademark of Oxford University Press

Library of Congress Cataloging-in-Publication Data
Jackson, John A., 1943–
A house on fire : the rise and fall of Philadelphia soul / John A. Jackson.
        p. cm.
Includes bibliographical references and index.
ISBN 0-19-514972-6
1. Philadelphia soul—Pennsylvania—Philadelphia—History and criticism.
2. Gamble, Kenny. 3. Huff, Leon. 4. Bell, Thom. I. Title.
ML3537.J33 2004
82.421644'092'2—dc22
2004015648

Design and typesetting: Jack Donner, BookType

1 3 5 7 9 8 6 4 2
Printed in the United States of America
on acid-free paper

For all those
who helped to create
the Sound of Philadelphia
who are no longer with us

Contents

Preface

DURING THE 1970S, KENNY GAMBLE, LEON HUFF, AND THOM BELL collectively produced at least twenty-eight gold- or platinum-certified record albums and thirty-one million-selling gold- or platinum-certified singles.[1] They have also written more than one thousand songs between them. In doing so, they made superstars out of Harold Melvin and the Blue Notes, the O'Jays, Teddy Pendergrass, the Spinners and the Stylistics and injected new life into the career of Jerry Butler, among others. Among Gamble and Huff's biggest hits are "Back Stabbers," "Cowboys to Girls," "Drowning in the Sea of Love," "If You Don't Know Me by Now," "The Love I Lost," "Love Train," "Me and Mrs. Jones," and "You'll Never Find Another Love like Mine." Thom Bell has collaborated on, among others, "Betcha by Golly, Wow," "Didn't I (Blow Your Mind This Time)," "I'll Be Around," "I'm Stone in Love with You," "La-La Means I Love You," "The Rubberband Man," "You Are Everything," and "You Make Me Feel Brand New." Gamble and Huff produced most of their music for their own Philadelphia International record label, while Thom Bell worked mostly as an independent producer.

Philadelphia International Records was pop music's last great independent "hit factory." As such, it influenced not only the recording industry, but also American culture itself. Never again would such a provincial cadre of writer-producers wield power and authority as did Gamble, Huff, and Bell. They were the masters of Philadelphia soul, a multilayered, bottom-heavy brand of sophistication and glossy urban rhythm and blues, characterized by crisp, melodious harmonies backed by lush, string-laden orchestrations and a hard-driving rhythm section. For a brief period of time, Gamble, Huff, and Bell were able to overcome the country's racial divisions and make skin color irrelevant. One of the most important messages conveyed by Philadelphia soul was that blacks and whites could get down with the very same music.

Gamble, Huff, and Bell were among the most influential and successful music producers of the early 1970s. They used their black inner-city neighborhood as a metaphor for the struggle for human dignity and developed a black-owned recording empire. For the better part of a decade, the City of Philadelphia became pop music's epicenter (as it had done a decade earlier, during the first era of Dick Clark's *American Bandstand*). Philadelphia soul also developed an international appeal to the extent that three decades later it is a revered genre around the globe.

Much of Philadelphia soul remains musically pertinent, and classic hits from its golden era continue to be reinterpreted. Such was the case with the blue-eyed soul singer Simply Red's 1989 version of Harold Melvin and the Blue Notes' "If You Don't Know Me by Now," which reached the top of *Billboard*'s Hot 100 and earned a Grammy nomination for its composers, Gamble and Huff. In 2002, Patti Labelle's 1981 recording of "Love, Need and Want You," written by Gamble and Bunny Sigler, was sampled by the rapper Nelly in his song "Dilemma." Sung by female R&B vocalist Kelly Rowland (of Destiny's Child), "Dilemma" reached number one on *Billboard*'s R&B charts that summer and remained at the top of the charts for ten weeks. "It was wonderful," Sigler told me in 2002, with the song still on the charts. "It's really exciting . . . to be [heard] on the stations that [play] songs that the kids listen to." Nelly's update combined "the old and the new, and it made it better than before," added Sigler, who made his first recordings in the early 1960s. "We dealin' with a new generation!"[2]

Sigler told me that Gamble, too, "was excited for the recognition" garnered from "Dilemma." Two years earlier, Gamble had waxed enthusiastically about how new artists "are taking a lot of our old stuff and recycling it and bringing it back in different forms. They can take four chords off of one of our songs and write a whole new song to it."[3] Now, said Sigler, Gamble appeared even more enthused than his writing partner. "He was so busy bein' excited, I had to put my excitement on hold!"

"I MUST CONFESS, I NEVER GET TIRED OF HEARING SONGS that my partner Leon Huff and I have written," said Gamble two years earlier to the delegates to the 2000 Republican National Convention, in Philadelphia. When it comes to *discussing* that music, however, Gamble can sing a different tune. "He'll never talk to you," Thom Bell adamantly told me during my research for this book. "Gamble will not talk to you."[4] Since I began working on this project five years ago, several people who knew and/or worked with Gamble told me essentially the same thing. Still, I had reason for hope. While conducting research for my history of *American Bandstand* several years ago, I was assured by Dick Clark's own publicist, among others, that Clark would not speak with me. Clark surprised us all when he consented to be interviewed.

Through an intermediary who knew Gamble well, I sent him a letter of introduction and copies of my two previous books. Gamble could see for himself the style and quality of my writing. (Both books won literary awards.) Then, for a year or so, Weldon McDougal, who grew up with Gamble and at one time worked for Philadelphia International Records, pleaded my case directly to him. One day, McDougal enthusiastically informed me that Gamble had instructed him to give me Gamble's personal telephone number. When I called, Gamble said he would do the interview the following week. When that date passed and I did not hear from him, I called again. He told me he was sorry for not calling as promised, but he had misplaced my telephone number. Besides, added Gamble, he had changed his mind about doing the interview. He had talked things over with Leon Huff and the two of them decided against "giving away" their story. (Leon Huff's secretary subsequently told me over the telephone that Huff did not wish to speak with me.)

About a year later, during the winter of 2003, I met Gamble face-to-face at a function in Philadelphia. I introduced myself to him and told him that I hoped he would reconsider his decision and consent to do an interview. Without committing himself, Gamble wrote his number on a piece of paper, handed it to me, and told me to call him. My subsequent phone messages went unanswered. Thom Bell had been on the money from the start. He explained to me how Gamble derives satisfaction out of demonstrating to others that he is the one in control of a particular situation. "He just strings people along like that. I've seen him do that year in and year out." I did not have to be convinced.

It was "destiny [that] pulled us all together," said Kenny Gamble (not to me), when asked how the success of him, Leon Huff, and Thom Bell came about. "The music just happened." To Gamble's way of thinking, the coming together of such a diverse and talented group of people could not have been planned. "It all fell into place, because it was meant to be. So much music was produced and created. You wonder how all that happened."[5] And how it all ended. By then I realized that another visit to Philadelphia was in order.

Stand on Broad Street, about half a dozen blocks south of Penn Square and City Hall, and squint your eyes just enough to blur the images of six lanes of traffic whizzing by. It is easy to imagine the scene as it was three decades ago, when Philadelphia soul was at its apex. Although that particular section of Broad Street has been renamed the

Avenue of the Arts and the new home of the Philadelphia Orchestra—the gleaming $265 million Kimmell Center for the Performing Arts—looms to the left, William Penn's statue still stands preeminent astride City Hall's rooftop. And a hard look to the right reveals the three-story Philadelphia International Building, its logo gracing the structure's brick facade and its glass-paneled doors. The pulsating strains of Philadelphia soul classics such as "Ain't No Stoppin' Us Now," "Back Stabbers," "Only the Strong Survive," "The Rubberband Man," and "Then Came You" readily come to mind. But a closer look at the famous building brings the musical hit parade to an abrupt halt. Taped to the inside of Philadelphia International's locked doors is a tiny handwritten notice stating that the only person inside the building is the company attorney. Warner-Chappell Music now owns the lucrative song-publishing catalog of Kenny Gamble, Leon Huff, and Thom Bell. The trio's music is reissued by companies located in cities other than Philadelphia. The empty rooms that once housed Philadelphia International offer one of the last remaining vestiges of the vibrant musical empire that for a time surpassed Berry Gordy's Motown as the leading black-owned recording company. Fortunately, the remembrances of those involved with making the music also remain.

Pioneering Philadelphia record producer Morris Bailey (who helped to start the career of Patti Labelle) thought that Gamble, Huff, and Bell "just put Philly back on the map. . . . The rest of us might not have been any less talented, but [they] took it to the top. If it wasn't for Kenny Gamble we would be workin' at Horn & Hardart's, servin' apple pie and milk!"[6] Along with Bailey, many others expressed a willingness to share their recollections of this particular slice of Philadelphia's musical history. Some of those individuals are comfortably retired, while others, some down on their luck and nearly forgotten, continue to scratch out a living in and out of the music business. A growing number have passed on. Each of them recounted the part they played in the development of Philadelphia soul, as well as a desire to see that story documented. What I discovered is revealed in this book.

Spring 2004   John A. Jackson

Acknowledgments

Thanks to Pat Baird at Broadcast Music International; *From Out of the Past* editor and publisher Bob Belniak; Robert Bosco; the Philly Archives' Dave Brown; Capitol-EMI's Tom Cartwright; radio personality Harvey Holiday; The *Philadelphia Daily News*'s Al Hunter, George Nettleton, and Dan Nooger; radio personality Ed Osborne; the *Doo Wop Corner*'s Frank Pellicone, Leo Sacks, Andy Schwartz; Joel Selvin; attorney Michael Silver; Buffalo Bob Skurzewski; L. Carl Tancredi; Leon E. Taylor III; and everyone who consented to be interviewed for this book. Thanks also to the library staff at the Philadelphia Public Library, Temple University's Urban Archives, and the New York Public Library.

Special thanks to the "Forrest Gump of Philadelphia Soul, " Weldon Arthur McDougal III. If it happened, chances are good that Weldon was there or close by. Special thanks to Val Shively, a walking encyclopedia of Philadelphia pop music history. If Val cannot supply the answer, he knows who can. Without the help of these two good friends, this book might never have been completed.

Thank you to Oxford University Press music editor Kim Robinson, who believed in this project and saw it through. Thanks also to my literary agent, Nancy Love.

A House on Fire

Philadelphia was a one-horse town,
and Gamble, Huff, and Bell were
the horse.

—Carla Benson,
the Sweethearts of Sigma Sound

1

"I'll Get By"

(1942–1962)

T HE NIGHT OF AUGUST 29, 1964, was supposed to be a typical one at
the Uptown Theater. Local radio personality Georgie Woods ("the
guy with the goods") emceed a rhythm and blues stage show, just
as he had done many times before at the crumbling, cavernous arena
squatting in the heart of the North Philadelphia ghetto. Headliners that
evening included B. B. King and Gladys Knight and the Pips. It was a
"big show," recalled Woods, who was not only a popular disc jockey on
one of the city's two black-oriented radio stations, but also a civil rights
activist and a leading voice of the black community. Suddenly, a telephone call came in from the city's race-baiting chief of police, Frank
Rizzo. Trouble was brewing a few blocks north of the Uptown, where a
routine traffic stop was in the process of escalating into mob disorder.
The police were rapidly losing control of the volatile situation. Rizzo,
who nine months earlier had arrested Woods and threatened to run him
out of town after the activist-deejay turned up in the midst of a racial
disturbance, now begged for his assistance. Turning over command of
the Uptown to his understudy, Woods disappeared into the night. "I
was the only one in town who could talk to the people," he recalled.
"They believed what I said."[1]

Friday nights in the city were routinely fraught with minor neighborhood incidences, but this time, said Woods, "the people nearby were
in an uproar." By the time Woods arrived at the scene, in a car hastily
outfitted with a portable p.a. system and a rooftop speaker, he recalled
that "all hell was breakin' loose." It took Woods and other peacemakers
three sleepless days and nights to quell the unruly masses. They could
not envision that not only Philadelphia, but also all of America, was
about to embark on a torturous journey of racial strife.

Four miles south on Broad Street, the city's major north-south artery,
another denizen of Philadelphia's blighted ghetto could be found. But

twenty-one-year-old Kenny Gamble had things other than riot and mayhem on his mind. Gamble was an aspiring singer-songwriter who had recently become an apprentice to one of the city's pop music movers and shakers. He had just recorded an album for Columbia Records, and his prospects were so promising that visions of owning his own record company danced in his head.

It was easy to dismiss Gamble's dream as idealistic and naive. Berry Gordy's success at Motown notwithstanding, in the early 1960s, institutionalized (and in many areas, legalized) segregation was still the law of the land in America. Furthermore, since the beginning of the year, when Dick Clark opted for California cool over Philadelphia working-class grit and moved his televised *American Bandstand* west, the city had become a pop music wasteland. On top of that, the entire music industry was being ravaged by the Beatles-led British Invasion. Local writer-producer Morris Bailey told how a producer "couldn't get arrested with a Philadelphia record" back then. Bailey said that whenever he or one of his colleagues ventured to New York to promote a record, "they would actually laugh at you."

For Kenny Gamble to scale the heights he envisioned, he would need help. Faced with Philadelphia's low standing within the pop music business, as well as the bloody English rockers, Gamble already had two strikes against him. He was also hindered by his own shortcomings. Gamble, whose musical talents were sometimes exceeded by his ambition, was a fine singer and an improving songwriter. But his musical prowess was limited to the rudimentary strumming of three chords on a guitar. Nor could he read or write music. But Gamble also possessed a knack for turning daunting circumstances to his favor. He secured the technical assistance he lacked by forming alliances with the disparate piano players Leon Huff and Tommy Bell.

Leon ("Fingers") Huff could barely read music himself when he and Gamble met, but he could play a mean piano. It was Huff's musical passion that supplied the soul for the dissimilar trio. Tommy Bell, a classically trained pianist who could play eighteen other instruments as well, was its delineator. He could read and write music, talents developed out of a desire to preserve the precise melodies that constantly played in his head.

In the face of America's growing racial chasm, no one could foretell that the musical accomplishments of this unconfirmed trio of young inner-city blacks would someday exceed even their own fertile imaginations.

THE CITY OF PHILADELPHIA comprises numerous small towns or, more precisely, a group of ethnic neighborhoods. When William Penn arrived in 1682, to lay out his "great towne" on the shore of the Delaware River, just north of where the Schuykill River empties into it, he was influenced by the long narrow tract of land available to him.[2] Rejecting the cramped patterns of European cities, Penn constructed a symmetrical grid centrally anchored by two-hundred-foot-wide streets: Broad, which runs north and south, and High (later renamed Market), which runs east and west from river to river. The surrounding area came to be known as Center City. By 1800, with most of Penn's large tracts already chopped up by a network of narrow alleys and tenement rows, Philadelphia was the largest city in the United States.

Philadelphia's black community is as old as the city itself and accounted for about 5 percent of the total population until World War I. Then, northern industrial employers facing a labor shortage opened their factory doors to thousands of unskilled Southern blacks. Between 1900 and 1920, Philadelphia's black population more than doubled. Thousands of additional blacks, seeking work in the city's shipyards and factories, arrived in the city during the 1940s. With a lack of low-rent housing in all of Philadelphia prior to 1952, blacks were forced to live in the most blighted neighborhoods. Strained beyond capacity, these bustling black enclaves spilled over into unsightly old red brick row houses in North and West Philadelphia and in southern sections of the city.[3]

It was in South Philadelphia that Kenny Gamble was born on August 11, 1943. Gamble's mother, Ruby, a religious woman, raised her three sons (Charles was older and Carl was younger) without a father. They lived in the rear of a first-floor row house on Christian Street until 1956, when Ruby Gamble moved her family to West Philadelphia. The Gambles' new neighborhood, which contained pockets of integrated housing in the otherwise mostly segregated city, defied America's entrenched pattern of residential isolation. But West Philadelphia was generally in worse shape than the area they had just vacated. It was in this ravaged neighborhood that Gamble would first express a compelling interest in music.

Music has traditionally played a formative role in America's black urban communities. By the beginning of the nineteenth century, Philadelphia, with its rich musical heritage, was the cultural and intellectual center of black America. The city was home to the nation's first black concert singer, former slave Elizabeth Taylor Greenfield, who was known professionally as "The Black Swan." Greenfield was largely responsible for making Philadelphia the leading venue of the black concert stage. During the early 1800s, Philadelphia was also the home of Frank Johnson, the first black musician to win wide acclaim in America and overseas. In several ways, Johnson was the antecedent to

Kenny Gamble, Leon Huff, and Tommy Bell. Like that talented triumvirate, Johnson was a prolific composer and arranger. The trumpet-playing "Black Master of Melody" was responsible for a remarkable string of ground-breaking accomplishments: Johnson was the first person to develop a school of black musicians, as well as the first black to appear with white musicians in integrated concerts. He also employed exotic instruments, including a harp and a bell harmonium, in his concerts. (This was a practice Tommy Bell would emulate some one hundred years later.) Johnson was also the first American— black or white—to take a musical ensemble to perform overseas. But, as Eileen Southern noted in *The Music of Black Americans*, Frank Johnson's death "cut off a fascinating experiment in breaking through the rigid walls of segregation."[4]

To cope with the city's intensifying racism, Philadelphia's blacks steeled themselves in various manners. One of the most universal was the pursuit of music. Racial segregation put an end to Frank Johnson's pioneering musical efforts, but it had the opposite effect on another of Philadelphia's musical resources, its black churches. Over the next two hundred years, a great deal of black social and cultural activity centered around their houses of worship, which became powerful institutions that sustained every socioeconomic level. In this setting, the gospel sounds and styles of the South, brought to Philadelphia by the two great black migrations, flourished. One prominent sound was that of the gospel quartet. Philadelphia was home to two of the most famous and innovative (and sometimes controversial) aggregations; the Clara Ward Singers and the Dixie Hummingbirds.

In a flight from the abject poverty and racism of the South, the Ward family arrived in Philadelphia in 1930. The following year, Clara's mother formed the Ward Singers trio. (The group was soon expanded into a quartet.) Throughout the 1930s, the Ward Singers, who sang the latest religious compositions in an impassioned manner, routinely brought down the house in the city's Baptist churches. By 1943, the quartet was nationally known and soon laid claim to the title of world's greatest gospel group. The Ward Singers were the prototype of the forthcoming secular rhythm and blues groups in several ways: They were the first gospel group to forgo traditional robes for colorful sequined gowns. In addition, they performed in fancy, high-piled wigs and brandished ornate jewelry. The Ward Singers' flamboyant style ensured that the quartet was dogged by controversy. While purists hated their act, the group, which utilized four active vocals and a "switch-lead" tactic borrowed from the male shouting (as opposed to the softer, "sweet sounding") quartets, literally took gospel out of the church and into the nightclubs.

The Dixie Hummingbirds were Philadelphia's most famous and exciting male gospel quartet.[5] Generally regarded as one of the finest groups in gospel history, the Hummingbirds, a leading force behind the evolution of the modern gospel quartet sound, were renowned for their imaginative arrangements, progressive harmonies, and general versatility. The group incorporated many traditional a cappella performance techniques into its act. Among them were the bending and stretching of individual notes, the use of counterpart harmony weaves, carrying the rhythm along in the bass voice, and, like the Ward Singers, switching leads.[6] One vocal convention popularized by the Hummingbirds—the use of dual tenor leads and soaring falsetto ornamentation—was to have a significant impact on the development of Philadelphia Soul.

Formed in South Carolina by James B. Davis in 1932, the group made its first recordings in 1939. Three years later the Hummingbirds moved to Philadelphia, where their popularity continued to grow. The group's star attraction was baritone phenom Ira Tucker Sr., who had been with the group since he was thirteen years old. Tucker, who originally joined the Hummingbirds as a baritone before assuming the lead tenor role, eschewed the traditional flat-footed stationary stage stance. In its place, Tucker adopted the mannerisms of a Southern preacher, running up and down the aisles, rocking as if in prayer, and even jumping off the stage as he sang. His emotion-drenched singing and dramatic stage presence never failed to wow audiences. "By the 1940s, rocking soulful gospel had spread west and north, becoming the prevailing fashion in both rural and urban congregations," wrote James Zolten in his history of soul gospel music.[7]

While the Clara Ward Singers and the Dixie Hummingbirds remained at the vanguard of gospel music, a parallel, secular sound began to develop in Philadelphia and in other cities with large black populations. Most early black secular vocal groups performed in a manner that suggested combinations of spirituals, blues, and the remnants of barbershop harmony. This style would later be classified as pop, with its most famous practitioners being the Tin Pan Alley–styled Mills Brothers, whose smooth harmony sound attracted black and white audiences alike.

The first secular black group to have a major impact on the national development of rhythm and blues was the Ink Spots. About the same time that the Ward Singers were getting their start, the Ink Spots, led by Bill Kenny's soaring falsetto, had already developed a style that would be adapted by the seminal rhythm and blues "bird" groups (Ravens, Orioles, Swallows, et al.). The Baltimore-based Orioles, who specialized in love ballads, leaned toward a more blues-oriented sound rather than the style of the Ink Spots. In 1948, after their first hit, "It's Too Soon to Know," they became the most influential of all the early rhythm and blues groups. Lead singer Sonny Til was widely regarded as the "black Sinatra." He became a sepia sex symbol by making every woman in the audience believe he was singing only to her. Aroused women in the audience inevitably sought to tear the clothing from the provocative singer's back. (This would also occur some thirty years later with Teddy Pendergrass, one of Gamble and Huff's recording artists.)

Sonny Til's sexual appeal was universal, but for some reason, his lofty lead had its greatest concentrated effect on the development of secular rhythm and blues in the Philadelphia area. Most likely, that city's embracement of the falsetto lead stems from the large number of black gospel groups that called Philadelphia home in the early 1940s. Because of the city's large and expanding black population, Philadelphia radio stations began to regularly broadcast Sunday morning programs of black gospel music. Initially, such programs were broadcast on a network and heard in cities such as Philadelphia on the network's local affiliate. The success of these nationally syndicated black gospel radio shows eventually created a market in Philadelphia and other cities for programs of local origin. Philadelphia thus became the de facto capital of black gospel. More so than before, the prominent falsetto melodies of the genre were widely heard in all quarters of the city.

By the time Kenny Gamble arrived in West Philadelphia, young black vocal groups throughout the city were approximating Sonny Til's crying first tenor lead. Such vocal flattery developed into a harmony so peculiar to the area that it became known as the "Philly Sound." Its origin is credited to a West Philadelphia vocal group known as the Castelles (and specifically to lead singer George Grant). The Castelles' complex five-part harmony, which blended a falsetto lead with equally high first and second tenors, borrowed extensively from the Dixie Hummingbirds' dual tenor lead. The Castelles' exaggerated emphasis on the wavering lead tenor made their sound, which was usually supported by minimal instrumentation, a top-heavy one. Other local practitioners of the Philly Sound included the Buccaneers, the Capris, the Dreams, the Dreamers, and the Marquees. Each of them helped the distinct falsetto sound spread quickly throughout the city's black neighborhoods.

Most of Philadelphia's singing groups were associated with neighborhood recreation centers, where they performed at dances and other functions. Numerous group members attended West Philadelphia High, where, between classes, makeshift sets were formed in the hallways. For instance, it was not unusual to see and hear George Grant, George Tindley (lead voice of the Dreams), and Weldon McDougal (bass for the Larks) improvising together. Each neighborhood had its own favorite group. In what amounted to a cutthroat "battle of the groups" competition, some of them were invited to perform at other recreation centers throughout the city. During those years, scores of recordings sung in the parochial Philly style were made for several local labels. A few of the falsetto-led ballads even appeared on the city's rhythm and blues charts.[8]

Kenny Gamble's early musical stirrings may have been most influenced by a local rhythm and blues group called the Turbans, who were formed in Gamble's old South Philadelphia neighborhood in the spring of 1955. None of the Philadelphia groups adhered strictly to the high-tenor sound. For variety, they opted to record straight ballads or up-tempo rhythm and blues numbers. Other groups, most notably the Turbans, incorporated a touch of the Philly falsetto into particular songs. In doing so, they managed to surpass their local predecessors in terms of national success. That fall, the group's rendition of "When You Dance," a mambo novelty that featured Al Banks's intermittent falsetto, counterbalanced by a vocal bass hook, became the first record by a Philadelphia rhythm and blues group to make the Top 100 singles chart of *Billboard* (the industry's leading music trade publication).[9]

The national success of the hometown Turbans intensified the notion that singing in a vocal group conferred the ultimate form of prestige. This was especially true for someone raised on unforgiving inner-city streets, such as Billy Jackson. Jackson was a senior at West Philadelphia High in 1955 and a member of the popular North Philadelphia group, the Re-Vels. Because of his presence in the Re-Vels, Jackson, who would gain international status in the 1960s as producer of the Tymes vocal group, was regarded as a neighborhood hero. Lee Andrews (of Lee Andrews and the Hearts), who attended John Bartram High, in the southwest section of the city, was similarly acclaimed by his peers for being in a popular vocal group. Doing so was a heady experience, said Andrews. As a high school youth, "what else could you possibly do?" Of course, besides ego massaging, there were more practical reasons for a ghetto youth to join a singing group. With inner-city turf parceled out by local gangs, it was risky for a young male to venture outside his home territory. (West Philadelphia remained an integrated neighborhood at that time, and a preponderance of its gangs was formed along racial lines.) But a member of a singing group was granted a sort of neutrality. "As long as I was in a singing group I could go to North Philly, South Philly, everywhere," said Weldon McDougal.[10]

By 1956, Kenny Gamble was smitten by the desire to sing. But he was more enamored by the Chicago-based Dells, who scored a national hit that year with the ballad "Oh What a Nite," than he was with any Philly falsetto. (A decade later, Gamble would try in vain to sign the Dells to his own record label.) The thirteen-year-old, who enjoyed "singing in the bathroom" at Sayre Junior High, according to one of his classmates there, dedicated himself to learning all he could about the music business. This was mostly accomplished through silent observation, a technique that Gamble would employ throughout his career. His first professional study was with Cincinnati native Robert L. "Bobby" Martin, a veteran musician and music arranger, who had settled in Philadelphia a few years earlier. By 1956, Martin was a well-traveled vibraphonist with the Lynn Hope Quintet jazz combo, which he joined in the late 1940s. (Martin can be heard on Hope's 1950 R&B Top 10 hit, "Tenderly.") When not on the road, Martin spent much of his time writing musical charts and songs for promising young talent. "Groups came to my house and I was always rehearsin' them, trying to get something going," he explained. Martin's house thus became a popular haunt for various would-be singers and musicians. The traffic sometimes grew so thick that he was unaware of the wannabes lurking about. Yet the ubiquitousness of one silent thirteen-year-old did eventually draw the musician's attention. The youngster was a frequent visitor to Martin's house, but because he always appeared to be with a group of people, Martin never addressed him. But after the youth continued to show up on a regular basis, Martin finally asked, "Who is that guy who's always listening?'" The name Kenny Gamble meant nothing to Martin, and it quickly passed from his mind.[11] But Gamble did not forget Bobby Martin, who was to play an important role in the development of Philadelphia Soul.

GAMBLE'S FRIEND, TOMMY BELL, was born in Kingston, Jamaica, on January 27, 1943. When he was four years old, Bell's parents and their ten children moved to West Philadelphia. There, the industrious immigrant couple was determined to provide their offspring with a sound, practical upbringing. In the process, Bell's father, who worked in a local fish store while studying to be an accountant, instilled a healthy work ethic in his children. In addition, the Bell clan was taught civility, politeness, and correct, distinctive speech—Jamaican patois notwithstanding. Music was always a very important part of the Bell family's activities. Tommy's mother was an accomplished classical pianist. Her son has stated that until he was a teenager, classical music was the only form of music he was familiar with. Tommy's father, who played the pedal steel guitar and accordion, also became a rhythm and blues devotee in the mid-1950s. Tommy, who routinely observed his mother and father playing music around the house, soon joined in. "Everybody played, and I played right along with the rest of them," he recalled.

Tommy began to play the drums almost as soon as he arrived in the States. This musical expression stemmed from more than a childhood desire to bang on his mother's pots and pans. For as long as Bell can remember, he had heard music in his head, which seemed like a perfectly normal occurrence in the music-friendly environment he grew up in. But at five years of age, Tommy learned that outsiders did not share his musical gift. His first-grade teacher was in the middle of a lesson one day when she noticed Tommy was not paying attention. Recalling that day, Bell explained how he was "hearing music and I was humming what I heard." The teacher decided to make an example of her inattentive student. She questioned Tommy about something she had just told the class. When he did not know the answers, the teacher asked him why. Tommy innocently replied that he had been listening to music. He quickly realized he had made a big mistake in being so honest. The teacher then asked him to stand up and sing to the class whatever it was that he had heard in his head. Tommy rose dutifully, and proceeded to sing it all, "the violas and the cellos . . . the violins . . . the percussion," he recalled. The flustered teacher then sent Tommy to the school psychologist, who arranged a conference with the boy's mother. When informed of her son's transgressions, Mrs. Bell calmly asked the teacher whether her son had sung to her any of the music he claimed to have heard in his head. She said he had. Tommy's mother then said to the startled educator, "Well, then that's what he heard. Case dismissed!"

Not a day goes by during which Tommy Bell does not hear music in his head. And once he hears it, he does not forget it. Bell also does not forget the painfully embarrassing first-grade lesson about subjecting himself to the ridicule of others. "What a jackass I was," he lamented. "Too stupid to keep my mouth shut!"

Another tenet of the Bell family was that each of the children took piano lessons. Bell said his mother believed that "if you learned piano the correct way, then you could play any instrument." Accordingly, when Tommy turned six, his mother informed him that it was his turn to begin piano lessons. Tommy, who was content to bang on his drums, wanted no part of the daunting keyed instrument. At that point, the family piano teacher turned psychologist and informed Tommy that he would have the privilege of being the only pupil of the instructor to have a "double major" of drums *and* piano. The young lad bought it. Tommy began to practice vigorously on the family piano. "I was ready to jump, Jack," he recalled. "Tell Miles Davis and the boys to move over, here I come!"

Despite Bell's musical enthusiasm and talent, it did not occur to his parents—or to Tommy, for that matter—that music was a viable career choice. In 1956, at the insistence of his parents, Tommy enrolled at North Philadelphia's Dobbins Technical Vocational High School to study lithography. In any event, Dobbins was ill equipped to contribute to Bell's extraordinary musical talents. Wendell Pritchett, who began teaching music at Dobbins in 1957, said that the school lacked "the kind of emphasis in music" for which he had hoped. For one, there was no "formal program instrumentally," explained Pritchett. The only musical requirement for graduation from Dobbins was a student's participation during the senior year in what Pritchett described as an informal "choral group" of about four hundred. The group, which was open to students in all grades, met at seven each morning, before regular classes began. "Some of the students were conscientious, but it was hard for kids to really get up that much earlier," said Pritchett. "Tommy, to my knowledge, was there." Pritchett, however, could offer no other recollection of the participation of his now-famous student. "Tommy was on his own in terms of the formal courses offered there."

Bell was "on his own" musically and still strictly attuned to the classics, but he recalled how those interests were beginning to change. This was not as a result of anything Bell learned from Wendell Pritchett or the wanting music program at Dobbins Vocational, but because of Bell's classmates. It was they who provided the unsuspecting Bell with his first dose of rhythm and blues music. Bell said he found artists such as Fats Domino and Little Richard interesting, but the rudimentary, "preschool chords" of the classic vocal harmony groups left him cold. Only a few groups, such as the Platters, the Flamingos, and Little Anthony and the Imperials ("all the ones that went past the standard three-chord songs"), aroused his interest.

Tommy Bell made another important musical discovery while attending Dobbins. He learned that his budding musical prowess could be used as a source of income. Bell's epiphany occurred as he played piano for his sister Barbara's ballet recitals. Before long, other dance pupils began to request his services. Bell was soon earning a nickel per dancer for a thirty-minute performance. Now a teenager, Bell "was as happy as a termite in a lumberyard! Right then and there, I became an entrepreneur."

It was obvious to Tommy Bell's ghetto peers that the polite, well-spoken youth who studied classical piano was not their typical neighbor. Weldon McDougal, who saw him frequently around the neighborhood, recalled how Tommy "was very studious. Tommy was like a square. Every time I'd see him he had a book with him." Bell may have appeared square to his peers, but he was simply living up to the immigrant credo instilled by his parents: "You're different. In order to succeed, you're going to have to work ten times harder than the black man and a hundred times harder than the white man."

DURING THE SUMMER OF 1957, Philadelphia's pop music business was the benefactor of an unimaginable occurrence, one that would have repercussions—both positive and negative—on the local and national pop music landscapes for years to come. It began when the American Broadcasting Company, looking for some cheap programming to flesh out its barren afternoon television time slot each weekday afternoon, began to broadcast a Philadelphia-based teenage dance show called *American Bandstand*. Hosted by the congenial and sharp-looking Dick Clark, the program's format was simple: Clark spun the latest rock and roll records and a flock of teenagers danced in front of the cameras. To everyone's surprise (except Clark's), *American Bandstand* was an instant success that drew millions of viewers to ABC each afternoon. As host of the only nationally televised disc jockey show in the country, Clark wielded unprecedented clout in the record business. In the past it had taken weeks—if not months—of promotion in various test-market ("breakout") cities around the country to build a hit record. Dick Clark could now accomplish that feat in a single afternoon. Overnight, Philadelphia's unassuming pop music trade became the lodestar of the national industry. It also inspired the hopes and dreams of every street-corner singer in the city.

The Holy Grail was a nationally televised appearance on *American Bandstand*, which originated in a cavernous West Philadelphia ware-house studio that stood starkly in the shadows of the Market Street elevated train line. One of the first local benefactors of Clark's show was Lee Andrews and the Hearts. Beginning in 1954, Andrews and his group had recorded half a dozen ballads for several small labels, but they had little to show for their efforts. Then their next release, "Long Lonely Nights," happened to coincide with the debut of *American Bandstand*. Boosted by a late-summer promotional appearance on the trend-setting show, the Hearts' plaintive ballad became a national pop hit. *American Bandstand* helped to transform the hometown heroes into national celebrities, and the sky became the limit for all of Philadelphia's young singers. Later that year, Little Joe and the Thrillers' recording of "Peanuts" introduced those who had missed Al Banks's 1955 rendition of "When You Dance" to the Philly falsetto. Then Andrews and the Hearts surpassed "Long Lonely Nights" with the release of "Teardrops," a similarly styled ballad. As 1958 began, the City of Brotherly Love scored an unprecedented pop music exacta. Two *Bandstand*-driven hits, Danny and the Juniors' "At the Hop" and the Silhouettes' "Get a Job," reached number one on the pop charts.

In spite of *American Bandstand*'s "Happy Days" aura, the show gener-ated a more sinister quality, one that went unnoticed to viewers outside the Philadelphia area. It was no chance occurrence that during *American Bandstand*'s early years an overwhelming majority of its "regular" dancers were Italian-Americans from South Philadelphia.

American Bandstand was guilty of propagating a quasi–de facto discrimination that was designed to exclude most blacks. The show originated in 1952 and was called *Bandstand*. It was shown only in the Philadelphia area, and featured white pop music and an audience to match. (Most of the young dancers attended a nearby Catholic high school.)[12] "And," said Tommy Bell, "they made sure to keep it that way." Over the years, as rhythm and blues and rock and roll gained popularity among teenagers, *Bandstand*'s music reflected that change. But at the behest of the show's sponsors and station management, both of whom were reluctant to slay their televised golden goose by attaching a black face to its sponsor's wares, *Bandstand*'s teenage dance contingent remained almost lily-white.

Kenny Gamble and Tommy Bell lived only blocks from *Bandstand*'s studio. To them, Clark's show provided bitter evidence of the kind of treatment a black youth who dared to venture beyond the ghetto could expect. Gamble watched *American Bandstand* each day on television—all the better to scrutinize the singers, who lip-synched to their latest records. He recalled going, along with some of his black friends, to the *Bandstand* studio several times, where he discovered that "they wouldn't let too many black kids" on the show. Bell occasionally witnessed racial violence outside the *Bandstand* studio, "something the papers kept quiet all the time," he maintained. Viewers may have occasionally spotted a black male and female dancing together on the show, but "you'd never see him dancing with a white girl, oh no!" said Bell. Mostly, blacks were not seen at all. Weldon McDougal, who informally tended the *Bandstand* entrance door during the show's early years, claimed the show's producers "kinda kept the camera away" from any blacks who managed to make it to the dance floor. Such tactics were successful to the extent that when *American Bandstand* made its debut in August 1957, viewers around the country had no inkling that any blacks at all lived in Philadelphia.[13]

The exclusionary measures of *American Bandstand* were most likely not Gamble and Bell's first brush with racism. But occurring so close to home, they struck a particularly personal chord and helped to steel the two black youths to the racism they would encounter beyond the ghetto, particularly in the music business. Gamble and Bell's musical interests also provided them with a unique opportunity. By the time the two were teenagers, black stars such as Fats Domino, Joe Turner, and Ruth Brown, who were previously known only to predominantly black audiences, were idolized by millions of white adolescents.

KENNY GAMBLE ENTERED THE NINTH GRADE at West Philadelphia High in the fall of 1957, just as *American Bandstand* began to dominate afternoon television. According to music instructor Wendell Pritchett, who transferred from Dobbins Vocational to West Philadelphia High in 1959, Gamble displayed more interest in his school's formal music instruction than did Tommy Bell at Dobbins. At West Philadelphia High, Pritchett was in charge of a jazz band that, of course, was of no interest to Gamble, who could not read a musical note. But Pritchett also conducted a "specialized choral group, a choir." Gamble was not part of that, either. But Pritchett maintained that the choral group "did a tour one year [in which] Kenny participated." Mostly, recalled Pritchett, like Tommy Bell, Gamble "was doing his own thing" musically.

Georgie Woods remembered how Gamble "always had a thing for music." Ensconced in the familiar surroundings of the ghetto, Gamble tried his callow hand at creating songs and dreamed of crossover stardom as a singer. Woods told of how the earnest teenager used to hang around the WDAS studio to "run errands for us, get us sandwiches and things." Woods chuckled as he recalled how Gamble naïvely brought the Philadelphia radio personality records he had made at a penny arcade, in hopes that Woods would play them on the air.

Gamble showed signs of lyrical deftness in his songwriting, but his musical limitations continued to hold him back. Recognizing the need to work with someone that could read and write music, Gamble set out to find such an individual. Stephen Kelly, who lived just around the corner from Gamble, was the type of person Gamble was searching for. Kelly, who was instrumental in forming the Volcanos singing group in the 1960s, recalled those high school days, when Gamble's love of music "was just boomin.' Kenny knew my love for music, so he used to come around my house and bang on my mother's piano and say, 'Stephen, listen to this!' And he sang these songs he had written. I would say, 'Kenny, Kenny, Kenny, I'm not interested. I don't want to be a songwriter!' Dumb me!" he recalled with a laugh, some forty years later.[14]

Gamble was energized, yet all the more frustrated, by the neighborhood talent he continued to see crack the big time. (The latest to do so was West Philadelphia's own Billy Scott, who appeared on *American Bandstand* early in 1958, to promote his hit recording, "You're the Greatest.") Patsy Holt was a friend from the neighborhood, who would one day garner her own share of fame and fortune as Patti Labelle. She recalled how, back then, neither she nor Gamble "had a clue what the future might hold."[15] Gamble's future, at least, was about to be shaped by the formation of a consequential, lifelong friendship. Unbeknownst to Gamble, this individual lived almost as close to him as did Stephen Kelly.

NOT LONG AFTER GAMBLE ENTERED THE ELEVENTH GRADE at West Philadelphia High, his head was turned by an attractive young classmate named Barbara, who happened to be Tommy Bell's younger sister.

(The Bell family had recently moved to a new West Philadelphia location, closer to where Gamble lived.) Over the next few months, Kenny and Barbara's interest in each other blossomed. Tommy continued to work in his father's market and tend to his studies at Dobbins. Then one day in early 1960, Gamble paid a visit to Barbara's house, purportedly to seek help with his homework. As he entered, he was taken aback to see a young man about his own age, practicing the piano. Barbara introduced the two, and almost at once Gamble's attention shifted from her to Tommy. "So you're a piano player, huh?" queried Gamble. "I'm a songwriter. Maybe some day we'll get together." "It'll be my pleasure," replied Tommy, who had never written a song in his life. "Gambs found somebody who could play that piano," said Bell as he recalled that serendipitous meeting.

About two months after the two met, they began writing together. They spent a lot of time at Gamble's house, writing songs and talking about music. Bell recalled how Ruby Gamble ("Miss G") came home every day from her job as an x-ray technician and fixed dinner for them. "We would be over there singing and playing the piano and stuff," he said. "She would fix us sandwiches and things. Whatever little food she had, she would share. She took really good care of us." Although it is difficult for a musician to work with a nonmusician, Bell said he and Gamble "just clicked." Bell's ground rules were simple. "Don't tell me how to play this piano and I won't tell you how to write your lyrics," he instructed Gamble. "'Cause I can't write lyrics and you can't play the piano!"

By the spring of 1960, Bell, who then supported himself by working in the family fish store and by gigging at night with various bands, realized that studying lithography was "a waste of time." He dropped out of high school to pursue his budding musical aspirations. Kenny Gamble remained in high school. He also began a paid internship at nights and on Saturdays in the cancer research program at South Philadelphia's Jefferson Medical Tech, where he was in charge of administering injections into laboratory rats and caring for the animals. Bell, who often assisted his buddy there, laughed as he thought back to those days. Gamble "was studying to clean out rat cages!" he exclaimed. "Most of the time he didn't go to work, man. He paid somebody to do the job for him while we rehearsed."

Wendell Pritchett spoke of the "creative forces" that drove Gamble and Bell as teenagers. "Both of them were very talented and they were both very active in music." Indeed, the musical fires burned brighter than ever for Gamble and Bell, in what was a heady time for most blacks in America. Aided by overwhelming minority support, John F. Kennedy had just been elected president. Under the leadership of Dr. Martin Luther King Jr., the civil rights movement was about to enter a gratifying era of demonstrations and civil disobedience. In *One Nation under a Groove: Motown and American Culture*, Gerald Early observed that "at no time in their history did blacks feel more optimistic about the future. . . . [I]t was quite possible, at least, to think of entering the world of whites without going through the back door of the culture."[16]

It may have been possible to *think* that, but as Tommy Bell was about to learn, the "back door" was still very much in existence in the risky, cutthroat business to which they aspired. Bell, who still took piano lessons to improve his talent, aspired to be a musical conductor who worked with such pop luminaries as Sammy Davis Jr., Lena Horne, Judy Garland, and Billy Eckstine. "I was gonna be on Broadway!" he ruefully recalled. In 1961, Bell ventured to New York to take a music conductor's test. He breezed through the exam, only to be told there was no work available for "his kind." Dumbfounded in his naïveté, Bell demanded a fuller explanation for his rejection. He was then bluntly informed that they did not hire "colored" people to work on Broadway. That "cooled my nose real quick," he recalled. Bell was steered uptown to Harlem's storied Apollo Theater, where he dejectedly took a job playing the piano. Bell soon decided that if he were destined to be a pianist in a black theater combo, he could just as soon fulfill that destiny in his hometown. Bell returned to Philadelphia that summer and took a similar job with the Uptown Theater's house band.

Fortunately, another opportunity for Tommy Bell to advance himself soon arose. Luther Dixon, a New York writer/producer, most notably for the Shirelles, a female R&B quartet, was constantly on the lookout for studio musicians who could read and write music. During one of Dixon's occasional trips through Philadelphia, he happened on one of Bell's gigs. Bell's prowess on the Wurlitzer electric piano, then a relatively new instrument, drew Dixon's attention. When he found out that Bell could read and write music, Dixon offered to take the talented keyboard player under his wing and show him the music business. Bell jumped at the offer. He returned to New York and proceeded to follow Dixon on his usual rounds throughout the city. In doing so, Bell said he learned a number of things, including the true meaning of R&B ("rhythm and *business*") and the evils of drugs ("the first time could be your last time"). Bell wrote some songs with Dixon, and he also struck up a professional relationship with Dixon's musical contractor, legendary saxophonist King Curtis.

By 1962, Bell was well schooled in the ways of the music business. He returned to Philadelphia, where he gigged with a local band while he looked for steady work. Told that Cameo-Parkway Records, then the country's hottest independent label, was looking for studio musicians, Bell sought them out, only to find that the doors (literally) were not open to a black man. "They stopped me at the front door, man," he recalled.

After this latest racial snub Bell began to look to his friend Kenny Gamble, who had graduated from high school the previous June, for career assistance. Gamble and Bell not only resumed writing songs together, they began singing together. Bell recalled that the two "blended well as singers," so Gamble suggested they form a vocal duet. Bell had no interest in becoming a singer, but he "went along with the program" simply to please his friend. A singing duet known as Don and Juan was then riding high on the charts with a popular ballad called "What's Your Name." Gamble and Bell became Kenny and Tommy. With Bell's rejection by Cameo-Parkway fresh in mind, they headed instead to Swan Records. It was a sweltering summer day, and temperatures in the city rose to well over 100 degrees. The air-conditioning at Swan worked overtime, but not to the benefit of Kenny and Tommy, who were kept waiting outside on the sidewalk for several hours. Ultimately, the duo realized that things at Swan and Cameo-Parkway were pretty much the same. Kenny and Tommy did not even get an audition. After this latest encounter with closed doors, Gamble and Bell felt as if they were on a treadmill to nowhere. Several months earlier, Gamble had met Jerry Ross, a white man and one of Philadelphia's budding pop music mavens. It was time for Gamble to cash in on his acquaintance with Ross.

Twenty-eight years old and a graduate of Philadelphia's Olney High, Jerry Ross learned what he termed the disc jockey's "tricks of the trade" from managing an Armed Forces radio station in Alaska. After Ross was discharged from the Air Force in 1956, he became an announcer for WFIL radio and television in his home city. One of Ross's assignments was manning the announcer's booth of the newly minted *American Bandstand*. After he faced the fact that "there was already a Dick Clark," the affable and assiduous Ross eyed a career change. Ross diligently observed the nation's top record promoters strive to convince Clark of the hit potential of their platters, and he decided that he could do their job better than they could.[17] Ross left the broadcast booth in 1958 to promote records for a local distributor. Two years later, he became an independent promoter/producer and rented office space in the Schubert Theater Building.

If the Brill Building was the major league of America's pop music business, the Schubert Building, strategically located on Broad Street, about a quarter-mile south of City Hall, was its Triple-A echelon. The building's first two floors accommodated a theater, while the third to the sixth floors housed the marrow of the city's pop music industry:

talent agents, managers, voice coaches, songwriters, music publishers, record companies, and promoters. Ross Associates—Jerry Ross and his talented piano-playing songwriting partner Murray Wecht—was located on the sixth floor.

KENNY GAMBLE HAD HIS TICKET TO JERRY ROSS punched by Weldon McDougal. The amiable bass man of the Larks had formed the group in 1954, while still in high school. When he graduated the following year, the Larks were put on hold while McDougal spent three years in the Marine Corps. When he returned from the service, McDougal reformed the Larks. In 1961, the group auditioned one of their crowd-pleasing ballads, the haunting "It's Unbelievable," for Jerry Ross and Murray Wecht, who recorded the number on their own label. Ross also arranged for the group to lip-synch "It's Unbelievable" on *American Bandstand*. As the song developed into a national hit, the Larks soared, particularly in their West Philadelphia stomping grounds. Everywhere McDougal went, people wanted to know with whom he did business. It was then that McDougal ran into Kenny Gamble. "Hey man," queried Gamble, "How'd you cut that record? Who put it out?" McDougal told him about Jerry Ross.[18]

At a time when Tommy Bell was in New York, Gamble appeared at Jerry Ross's door and told him that "he wanted to write and he wanted to sing." Ross, who had heard similar words countless times from starry-eyed novices, promised Gamble an audition at a later date, when he was not so busy. But Gamble persisted. He began hanging around Ross's office "all the time," said the producer. "And every time I saw him he would say, 'I can sing! I can sing!'"

It was 1962 by the time Ross auditioned Gamble. When he did, Gamble's smooth baritone brought to mind Brook Benton (then a noted pop-oriented rhythm and blues singer). Gamble "was singing the kind of lyric and the kind of song that attracted my attention," he said. Ross was "very much impressed" and wanted to sign the novice singer as a solo act. But Tommy Bell was the only person who could play what Gamble sang, and Gamble would not sing without him—which was precisely how Kenny and Tommy came to record "I'll Get By," a straight rhythm and blues ballad written by the duo.[19] Kenny and Tommy made no subsequent recordings, perhaps because "I'll Get By," which was too derivative of Don and Juan's "What's Your Name," turned out to be a colossal flop.

Murray Wecht's departure from Ross Associates set the stage for an alliance between Jerry Ross and Gamble. (The circumstances of the Ross-Wecht split are uncertain. When queried about Wecht, who died several years ago, Ross was uncharacteristically taciturn.) The piano-playing Wecht had been what Bell described as the "music man" of the songwriting team. His departure put Ross in a bind. Meanwhile, Gamble, who still harbored singing ambitions, spent more and more time with Ross. "When he'd finish his gig at Jefferson, which was just down the street from me, he'd be at my office," said the producer. It was then that Ross discovered that Gamble "not only could sing, he could write." Ross signed the aspiring singer to a songwriting contract. Still, songwriting remained incidental to Gamble's singing. "In the back of his mind," said Bell, "a songwriter was not what he wanted to be. He wanted to be a singer. And, oh yes, he *can* sing!"

Gamble and Bell continued to frequent Ross Associates on a daily basis, where they wrote and sang together. Meanwhile, Gamble and Ross began to write together more frequently. (That, said Bell, is "what Jerry really wanted.") "Lo and behold," said Ross, "I discovered that Kenny had the ability to take poetry and make it sing."

It was crunch time for Tommy Bell, who was then twenty-three years old and newly married. His bride was not particularly enamored of his nomadic and unpredictable life as a studio musician and struggling composer. Bell vowed to her that if he did not make it in the music business by the time he was twenty-five, he would find another profession. Gamble's flowering association with Jerry Ross made it clear that if Bell were to fulfill his musical ambitions within his self-imposed time frame, he would have to do so without his friend.

Looking back on that pivotal event, Bell explained how there are people in life "who just don't fit you." In Bell's eyes, "something just was not quite right" about Jerry Ross. "But for Gambs, he was just right. Jerry was gonna teach him the whole thing."

Bell told Gamble about his inability to work with Ross and was not surprised when his friend replied that he had already cast his lot with the writer/producer. In recalling the difficult split, Bell waxed philosophical. "In your coming up you add and you take away until you finally come up with the right combination," he explained. At that particular time, he and Gamble "were taking away." In effect, Jerry Ross substituted Kenny Gamble for Murray Wecht, leaving Tommy Bell as the odd man out. But Ross and Gamble had a fundamental problem to solve; they lacked a piano player. "And," said Tommy Bell, "that's where Leon Huff came into the picture."

WHEN YOU LEAVE CENTER CITY TRAVELING EAST over the Benjamin Franklin Bridge, headed for the morass of urban mismanagement, decay, and corruption known as Camden, New Jersey, the first building of significance to the left that you see is Riverfront State Prison. Riverfront is an apt metaphor for Camden, itself a prison to the overwhelming majority of poor blacks and other minorities who live there. Leon Huff, who formed the third angle of the Gamble-Huff-Bell triumvirate, was one of those fated Camden residents. But Huff, aided and abetted by his musical talent and determination, successfully made it over the wall.

Camden was already perched on the precipice of decline when Leon A. Huff was born there on April 8, 1942. The son of a local barber, Huff grew up in one of the city's austere and foreboding housing projects, in its Centerville section. Huff told writer Eric Olsen that his father played blues guitar and his mother gospel piano, but his own musical style seems to have evolved from the rough street corners of Camden and Philadelphia. In 1976, Huff told writer Tony Cummings, that when he was about ten or eleven years old there was a teenager in Camden, called Sugar Cane Robinson, who "played a thing called the boogie-woogie" at the Earl Theater in Philadelphia. Whenever Sugar Cane played the Earl, Huff was in the audience. By observing Harris and listening to music on the radio and from records, Huff developed a rudimentary musical understanding. From that, he taught himself how to play the piano, later pointing out that there "wasn't really no schooling involved."[20]

According to Eric Olsen, Huff played drums in the Camden High band, and perennially made the All-City Orchestra, before graduating in 1960. By his own admission, Huff said he was not "thinkin' about no record business then."[21] But Huff's ambitions grew after he began work at a neighborhood clothier, where he met Dickie Burch. Jules "J.J." Johnson, who recorded for Polydor Records in the early 1970s, attended Camden High when Huff was there. Johnson said that besides selling clothing, Burch was "into workin' with vocal groups" in the area, many of whom were accompanied by Huff's piano.[22] Most likely it was Burch who got Huff thinking about the music business. Huff, who played piano for the 19th Street Baptist Church choir, but could cut a mean boogie-woogie on the keys, gravitated to the Schubert Building, in hopes that somebody was in need of a session pianist. One such person was Weldon McDougal, who, while singing with the Larks, had also begun to produce music. Whenever McDougal asked whether the enterprising sideman wanted to play on a particular session, Huff said yes. But no matter how many sessions Huff worked, he always seemed to be short on cash. Unable to secure enough work in Philadelphia to sustain him, Huff rode a Greyhound up the New Jersey Turnpike to New York and headed for the Brill Building. He began frequenting the offices of various production and talent heads there until they agreed to listen to him play. Huff finally landed some session work, and he began to acquire a reputation around town as a crack rhythm and blues pianist.

But Leon Huff's destiny did not lie in any New York recording studio. Rather, it was back in Philadelphia, in the Schubert Building. As Huff shuttled between sessions in New York and Philadelphia, he signed on for additional studio work with Ross Associates, just about the same time that Kenny Gamble was beginning to write with Jerry Ross. In one particular session for Ross in 1962, Huff fronted a Camden group called the Lavenders, during which he pounded the keys for an up-tempo dance number called "The Slide." Huff "banged that piano like it was coming out of the wall!" exclaimed Ross. "They had to tune it three different times during the session." "The Slide," which was typical of the dance fad genre so popular during that era, was a commercial failure, but it is a fine anticipatory example of Huff's rollicking, staccato-like boogie-woogie piano groove.[23] Moreover, "The Slide" demonstrated Leon Huff's musical potential to the receptive Kenny Gamble.

2

"Who Do You Love"

(1963)

BY THE END OF 1962, KENNY GAMBLE, LEON HUFF, AND TOMMY BELL had each made their initial recordings. The fact that those records were commercial disappointments was of little consequence to Huff and Bell. There would always be another session for Huff, and a fresh tune in the head of Bell. Only Gamble, who continued to harbor the notion of a singing career, had cause for discontent. Gamble faced a more formidable problem than any suffering brought about by one failed recording. The pop music moguls courted by Gamble were preoccupied with recording innocuous white teen idols.

With the advent of rock and roll, black recording artists of the 1950s were afforded an opportunity—albeit a brief one—to appeal to the burgeoning white teen market. Elvis Presley's national breakthrough in 1956 marked the beginning of black retrenchment in pop music, but then Elvis himself was deemed "too black" for mainstream America (especially for adolescent white girls, who purchased most of the pop records sold). Beginning with Ricky Nelson there commenced a parade of Elvis clones, each more benign than the last. The unprecedented popularity of *American Bandstand* ensured that the teen idol trail passed through Philadelphia—to be more precise, South Philadelphia, where virile Italian-American darlings such as Frankie Avalon, Fabian Forte, and Bobby Rydell resided.

As the 1960s began, Philadelphia became ground zero for the teen idol explosion. The independent record label to capitalize most on this phenomenon was Cameo-Parkway, which had been formed in 1956 by musician/bandleader-turned-songwriter Bernie Lowe (Lowenthal). Cameo (the Parkway label was added two years later) produced its first hit early in 1957, with Charlie Gracie's (Lowe's answer to Elvis) "Butterfly." The company entered the teen idol sweepstakes in earnest in 1959, when Bobby Rydell single-handedly kept Cameo-Parkway afloat for two years with a string of hits. The year 1959 was also the one in which Bernie Lowe literally struck gold. "The Twist," recorded by South Philadelphian Chubby Checker, ushered in an era of open dancing, in which partners became superfluous. "The Twist" also became the prototype for Cameo-Parkway's hit-making formula. The first order of business was to write a song about a particular dance, a move often prompted by Lowe's bosom buddy Dick Clark. (Former Re-Vels lead singer and Cameo-Parkway producer Billy Jackson said that Clark "would come in and tell us what was happening" in regard to any new dance he saw being done on *American Bandstand*.) The next step was to recruit some local low-budget talent. Then, said Jackson, "like a factory, we'd go in and make that kind of record." All that remained was for Dick Clark to promote the song on *American Bandstand* and for Cameo-Parkway to reap the profits.[1]

For Bernie Lowe, who perfected this particular modus operandi, the pop music sweepstakes became effortless and infinitely rewarding. During the early 1960s, Cameo-Parkway, which adhered to the axiom that dance records were consistent best sellers, sizzled. Chubby Checker, Bobby Rydell, the Dovells, the Orlons, and Dee Dee Sharp—all products of the streets of Philadelphia—compiled an impressive string of hits, each one celebrating one dance step or another. By 1963, Cameo-Parkway was the hottest independent label in the world, bar none.

Unbeknownst to the general public, and to the label's brass, Cameo also served as an incubator in which several individuals key in the development of Philadelphia Soul received their baptism into the music business.

The insiders at Cameo-Parkway had a good thing going, but it was nearly impossible for those on the outside to enter the company's inner sanctum.[2] Even Jerry Ross, by then a local hotshot who would soon produce significant hits for the likes of Spanky and Our Gang, Jay and the Techniques, and Bobby Hebb, was not able to breach Cameo-Parkway's fortress mentality. Ross said that Bernie Lowe suffered from "tunnel vision. [He] did not reach out for other artists and writers and producers who could have contributed tremendously to the growth of that label. He turned 'em all down and they went on to become successful elsewhere."

Lowe's shortsightedness began to haunt him in 1963, a year when significant changes in popular music, and in American society in general, began to occur. A change in music was heralded that summer by an intense ballad titled "Cry Baby," sung by Garnet Mimms and the Enchanters (actually the Sweet Inspirations), which became one of the hottest records in the country. Mimms (who was raised in Philadelphia) and the other singers were black, but they did not sing in the traditional black vocal group style.[3] Instead, as Mimms sang his impassioned, forgiving appeal to a former lover who had jilted him, only to be forsaken herself, the Sweet Inspirations mournfully screeched the song's title in the background. "Cry Baby," a stunning amalgamation of pop and black gospel, became a rhythm and blues chart-topper and a pop hit as well. It was a harbinger of the music that would soon be called "soul."

The year 1963 was a transition one for the civil rights movement and for the development of soul music. At about the same time that "Cry Baby" was released, the American civil rights movement adopted Martin Luther King's new, aggressive strategy of "coercive nonviolence," which was designed to garner broad white sympathy for the movement. When King and his protesters appeared in Birmingham, Alabama—the most stringently segregated American city of that era—to integrate the city's public facilities, they were met by savage resistance, including fire hoses, nightsticks, and attack dogs, all used indiscriminately on women and children alike. King's strategy worked. After a transfixed nation witnessed the event on television, the civil rights movement gained the sweeping national support it had previously lacked, and countless blacks were inspired to assert their grievances in their own cities and towns.

The genre of soul music broadly conveyed the essence of being black in America.[4] Both a catalyst for and a product of a new black consciousness that combined music with political and capitalistic measures, soul mirrored the increasingly militant struggle of America's blacks to find their own destiny. Beginning around 1959, when Ray Charles cut his seminal "What'd I Say," an indiscernible transition between traditional rhythm and blues and the new soul music, which roughly paralleled the civil rights movement, began to take place. By the time Charles uttered the bellwether phrase "just a little bit o' soul now" in a 1961 recording, the genie was already out of the bottle.[5] That year, America discovered the rich, vibrant baritone of Philadelphia's own boy-preacher Solomon Burke, who, by proffering a string of moody and intense ballads, beginning with "Just Out of Reach (of My Empty Arms)," paved the way for the coming soul storm. By then, blacks and whites were familiar with the likes of William Bell, the Impressions, Wilson Pickett, Otis Redding, Ruby and the Romantics, Carla Thomas, and the aforementioned Garnet Mimms.

Soul music was a work in progress that was bursting at the seams with passion. It was fired mostly by two independent record companies, Atlantic and Stax, and a number of tiny independent labels. Atlantic Records, based in New York City, was founded in 1947 by Ahmet Ertegun and Herb Abramson. Atlantic was a white-owned company yet historically sensitive to changes in black music preferences. The label soon became the eight-hundred-pound gorilla of rhythm and blues recording. Through its stalwart recordings by black pioneers such as Lavern Baker, Ruth Brown, Ray Charles, the Clovers, the Drifters, Clyde McPhatter, and Joe Turner, during the 1950s, the thriving independent label helped to facilitate rhythm and blues' transition to rock and roll. In the 1960s, producer Jerry Wexler assumed a more prominent role in Atlantic's operation. He worked with Ray Charles, Solomon Burke, Wilson Pickett, and others to help make Atlantic a leader in the development of soul.

Stax Records, of Memphis, Tennessee, was formed in 1960 by two white sibling bank clerks, Jim Stewart and Estelle Axton. The sign at the company headquarters proclaimed: "Soulsville, USA." Stax, which soon entered into a five-year national distribution deal with Atlantic Records, was not yet the font of impassioned creativity it would come to be. But by the middle of 1963, through recording artists William Bell, Booker T and the MG's, Carla and Rufus Thomas, and a twenty-two-year-old grainy-voiced Georgian named Otis Redding, the label had gained a name for projecting a gritty, black sound. For Stax, the best—and the worst—was yet to come.[6]

As Atlantic, Stax, and other lesser labels spread the gospel of soul music, back in Philadelphia, Kenny Gamble and Jerry Ross were writing together on a steady basis. In less than a decade, Gamble would have a hand in lifting rhythm and blues, and pop music in general, to new heights. But his first chart hit, co-written with Ross, was sung by the quintessential white teen idol Freddy Cannon. After Ross and Gamble were snubbed by Cameo-Parkway, the duo turned to Swan Records, which was a weak, distant cousin of Bernie Lowe's potent homegrown label. Formed in 1957 by Dick Clark and two partners, Swan (even more so than Cameo-Parkway) enjoyed an inside track to airplay on *American Bandstand*. Accordingly, the label had no trouble turning out hit records. But the broadcasting payola scandal of 1959–60 forced Clark to sell his interest in Swan to its other owners, and the label's gravy train became derailed. By 1963, Swan, bedeviled by poor management, bad luck, and the want of Clark's promotion, struggled to stay afloat. ("Those guys should have been selling shoes instead of records," said Jerry Ross with a sneer.) All the while, the talents of Jerry Ross and Kenny Gamble looked more and more attractive to the impoverished Swan. That summer, a Ross-Gamble teen dance opus called "Everybody Monkey," recorded by Cannon, became the duo's first collaboration to appear on the nation's best-selling record charts.[7]

Kenny Gamble's true songwriting potential was first exhibited via the Sapphires, a two-woman, one-man trio from New Jersey, first produced and recorded by Jerry Ross. That summer, after the Sapphires' debut record flopped, Ross turned to his new writing partner to help get the group on track. Together, Ross and Gamble wrote a shuffling mid-tempo number called "Who Do You Love," which eventually reached number twenty-five on *Billboard*'s Hot 100 chart. The song might have fared even better had not Swan, that fall, turned all of its overtaxed promotion to the Beatles'"She Loves You," causing "Who Do You Love" to become lost in the shuffle. While Jerry Ross was dismayed over the fate of "Who Do You Love," Kenny Gamble had reason to be pleased. The song represented Gamble's biggest chart success yet, and, as such, his name began to circulate among Philadelphia's pop music mavens. Furthermore, when the Sapphires followed "Who Do You Love" with an obligatory album, Gamble did the vocal arrangements for it and also sang the background vocals. Perhaps most important, Gamble and Ross became the principal songwriters for the Sapphires.[8]

As Jerry Ross trusted Gamble to rehearse other groups, Gamble began to expand his musical parameters. Ross recalled how his partner "would go into the studio and teach them some of the harmony parts and what have you." Ross also began to take his young protégé with him when he visited various New York music publishers, thereby opening valuable industry doors to Gamble. But there were limits to Gamble's responsibilities. Ross was reluctant to let Gamble try his hand at music production. Although some sources credit Gamble with having coproduced "Who Do You Love," Ross maintained that his writing partner and understudy did no production for Ross Associates "other than to observe and catalog for himself. In those days he was just writing with me and going through the learning process, watching what I was doing in the studio and being very open-minded."

OPEN-MINDEDNESS AND FORESIGHT WERE COMMODITIES in short supply at Cameo-Parkway, where the tunnel vision of the nation's principal purveyors of its adolescent dance ditties went persistently about their business. By this time, Leon Huff, who had played piano on some of the Ross-Gamble recordings made for Swan Records, had developed his own interest in writing music. Huff signed an exclusive song-writing contract with John Madara and Dave White, two young white songwriter/producers flush with a production deal with a major record label.

It was during the summer of 1963 that Madara and White set up shop in the Schubert Building, several floors below Ross Associates. Madara, twenty-seven years old, and White, three years younger, were local prodigies. Madara had quit school in 1955 to support his fatherless

family. He also became a would-be teen idol who, over the next few
years, cut a string of records that were never heard outside Philadelphia. Dave White spent his early years as part of his family's circus
balancing act. In 1956, White formed a singing group called the Juvenairs. Madara and White met after the former heard the Juvenairs
rehearsing on a street corner near his West Philadelphia home. Thus was
a friendship kindled, borne out of their mutual musical interests.
Madara and White then collaborated on a song that, after a convoluted
process, was recorded by White's group, which had been rechristened
Danny and the Juniors. "At the Hop" jump-started the career of Danny
and the Juniors, but the group never did live up to its smashing debut.
Over the next five years, Danny and the Juniors' chart success diminished steadily.

During the summer of 1962, Madara and White formalized a partnership and began writing and producing music for Philadelphia's
Jamie-Guyden Records. A year later the pair stepped up a notch, signing
an exclusive production deal with Mercury Records. When Mercury told
Madara and White to get their own office, they headed straight to the
Schubert Building. That summer, and into the fall, Madara and White
wrote and produced several chart hits for Mercury, their crown jewel
being Lesley Gore's "You Don't Own Me." After that, their reputation
and workload expanded enough to warrant taking on a hired hand.

John Madara first met Leon Huff at a nightclub, when the pianist was
performing there with the Lavenders. Huff's piano playing "just stood
out," he recalled. "I had him come down to our office and we signed
him to a writing and production contract. We made sure we used him
on every [recording] session so that he would have additional income
. . . and we wrote songs with him. We really gave him his head and he
fine-tuned his chops right there with us. . . . Leon was so talented . . . and
I think he learned a lot from us." Dave White remembered how Huff
"would go into his little cubicle and play the piano all day and come up
with songs." Unbeknownst to Madara and to White, their new "exclusive" songwriter was soon "coming up with songs" for other people in
Philadelphia.[9]

TWO FLOORS ABOVE MADARA AND WHITE, twenty-year-old Kenny
Gamble, through impromptu appearances about town, continued to
hone his craft as a singer. Bobby Eli, who was to become a top-notch
session guitarist and producer in the 1970s, was gigging in a West
Philadelphia bar where Gamble "used to walk in and do a guest spot"
every now and then. Gamble "practically lived around the corner, and
he used to come in there all the time to get up on the stage and sing a
number," recalled Eli. "There were like two or three that were his

favorites, that he would sing all the time" (they included Marvin Gaye's "Can I Get a Witness" and Jerry Butler's "He Will Break Your Heart"). Gamble particularly liked the fact that Eli "could do all the songs and knew all the changes." All Gamble had to do was announce his next song. "He did that so much," said Eli, "that we started hangin' out." The guitarist and the aspiring singer struck up a friendship that would blossom into a fruitful working relationship. Thanks to Jerry Ross, Gamble even landed a one-off recording deal that summer.[10] But because of Columbia's inept promotion of black music in general, the record flopped.

THE YEAR 1963 ENDED WITH AMERICA TRAUMATIZED by the assassination of President Kennedy. Nowhere was that loss felt more deeply than in the black communities across the country. Although Kennedy was cowed by Southern political influence and thus did not produce striking material results for the civil rights movement, most blacks at least regarded him as some form of kindred spirit. It was ironic, then, that Kennedy's successor, Lyndon B. Johnson, a Southerner of some suspect among blacks, presided over the most sweeping civil rights legislation since Reconstruction.

When it came to integration in America, the pop music charts set a model example. By 1963 they became the most integrated ever in terms of race and gender. So much rhythm and blues and soul music appeared on the heretofore white-dominated pop charts that *Billboard* discontinued its rhythm and blues singles chart that November, because it had become so similar to the publication's prestigious Hot 100 pop chart.

WHILE AMERICA'S POP MUSIC CHARTS GREW MORE INTEGRATED, Kenny Gamble, Leon Huff, and Tommy Bell remained trapped within an exploitative, white-controlled industry. As the talented trio strove to absorb everything they could about songwriting, arranging, and production, they continued to gaze forlornly at Cameo-Parkway Records. That company, with its tried and true formula—not to mention Dick Clark's assistance—remained the hottest independent record company in America. But during the coming year, two significant events occurred that not only affected the fortunes of the young and energetic trio of would-be music men but also wrenched from Philadelphia its grip on the pulse of the country's pop music. On February 8, 1964, *American Bandstand* made its debut from its new home in Hollywood, California. The following evening, the Beatles made their American television debut on *The Ed Sullivan Show*. After that historic weekend, nothing that had previously held sway in the country's pop recording industry was assured.

3

"Mixed-Up Shook-Up Girl"

(1964)

I
N SOME WAYS, THE 1960S DID NOT BEGIN UNTIL 1964. For the most part, the earliest years of the decade were merely an extension of the conventional cold war 1950s of the Eisenhower years. As late as 1963, there was little if any cause to think that radical changes were brewing. But by the end of the year Kennedy was dead at forty-three and the winds of change that brought both excitement and strife to America began to blow. The country's pop music industry did not escape the coming social upheaval.

By the spring of 1964, *American Bandstand* was ensconced in California. The Beatles and other English acts monopolized America's Top 10. In Philadelphia, the songwriting team of Jerry Ross and Kenny Gamble was in danger of losing its chief customer, Swan Records. Recent hits by the Sapphires and the Beatles offered only a brief respite to the company's eventual demise. Cameo-Parkway, too, was reeling. With the loss of Dick Clark's promotion, as well as heightened competition from the English Invasion artists, Bernie Lowe's once-mighty company was losing ground (and market share) to onrushing rivals. Cameo-Parkway's stiffest competition came from the Detroit-based Motown Records, which was the first label to successfully groom, package, and market the music of black artists to white America.

Berry Gordy Jr., a former prizefighter and aspiring songwriter who had worked on a Detroit auto assembly line during the 1950s, founded Motown in 1959. After trying his hand at songwriting (for Jackie Wilson, among others), Gordy began to produce his own recordings. In 1958, he recorded a rhythm and blues group from Detroit called the Miracles and also kindled a deep personal and professional relationship with the group's leader, William "Smokey" Robinson. It was Robinson who convinced Gordy to form his own record label. With the goal of producing music that appealed to blacks and whites alike, in 1960,

Gordy secured a loan from his family and formed the Motown Record Corporation. The company's first Top 40 hit (the Miracles' "Shop Around") was released late that year. In 1961, Motown had four more Top 40 hits. The following year, during which a sign proclaiming "Hitsville, USA" appeared in the front window of Motown's modest Detroit headquarters, Berry Gordy's figure rose to nine. Although Motown's Top 40 total reached fourteen in 1963, Gordy's company was not yet the slick pop juggernaut it would soon become.[1] Motown, which still functioned under a dissimilar group of producers, responsible for a myriad of vocal styles, lacked a distinct sound, let alone a broadly commercial one envisioned by Gordy. After a twelve-year-old blind harmonica player named Steveland Morris (as Little Stevie Wonder) came up with the aberrant, chart-topping "Fingertips—Part 2" that year, Gordy set out to revamp his company's sound. He cunningly called it "The Sound of Young America."

Gordy's new sound, a form of racially indistinct pop, emerged in 1964. It enabled Motown to prosper alongside the English Invasion artists at a time when other independent labels could not. The principal architects of Motown's new sound were Lamont Dozier and Brian and Eddie Holland, three blacks who comprised the label's lead songwriting and production team. "H-D-H," as the trio quickly became known in the business, employed driving baritone saxophone riffs and a rhythm section powered by James Jamerson's chest-thumping bass in their productions. Their method worked like a charm. That year, H-D-H produced eight of Motown's twenty-one Top 40 hits. In the words of rhythm and blues historian and music critic Nelson George, the revitalized Motown was ready to "change black music's position in the record industry and in American culture."[2]

MOTOWN'S INCREASING PROSPERITY was alarming to Bernie Lowe. Popular Philadelphia disk jockey Hy Lit was in Lowe's office one day in 1964, when the Cameo president "went nuts." "Look at this Motown, startin' to come on with unbelievable hit records!" exclaimed Lowe.[3]

In spite of its troubles, Cameo was in no danger of going out of business. Not yet, anyway. Profits were down for the first time, but the publicly owned company, which had always been better financed and managed than Swan, continued to make money. Yet even the parsimonious Lowe had to admit that for his once proud label to survive, drastic measures were in order. Lowe gave it his best shot. He acquired the small uptown record company that recorded Patti Labelle and the Blue Belles (then one of the city's hottest black groups). He also cut a deal with a British recording company to issue its records in the States on Cameo-Parkway. Most emendatory, Lowe opened Cameo-Parkway's doors to

outsiders. One of the first to take advantage of this change was the opportunistic Jerry Ross. He entered into a writing and production deal with
Cameo-Parkway, similar to the one he had with the dying Swan label.

Like Jerry Ross, Tommy Bell also profited from Cameo-Parkway's new
openness. One day Bell, who was then twenty-one years old, noticed an
ad for lead sheet writers placed in a local newspaper by Cameo-Parkway.[4]
Bell, who was playing piano at the Uptown Theater at the time, still
sought a steady job within the music business. Having already been
rebuffed by Cameo, Bell thought he might stand a better chance this time,
since lead sheet writers, who performed the "grunt work" of the pop
music industry, were not easy to come by. The work was boring and
uncreative, "the bottom of the barrel!" he exclaimed. "Nobody wants to
write lead sheets." But at a dollar-and-a-quarter per song, Bell was soon
writing lead sheets "that came out of your ears, man!"

Once inside Cameo-Parkway's previously unreachable confines, Bell
discovered that "because Motown was kickin' their pants," Bernie Lowe's
company sought to form its own black rhythm section. One day, Lowe
summoned Bell to his office. "You know a couple of colored guys that can
play instruments, don't you?" he asked the flabbergasted lead sheet
scribe. "Go get us a couple of them and put together a rhythm section!"

Bell laughed as he recalled the incident. "Here was a guy thinking'
that all you had to do was blow a whistle and the best musicians were
gonna walk in off the street!" Bell, still studying to become a concert
pianist, knew nothing about rhythm sections, black or white. "But they
didn't know that," he recalled. So he did as he was told.

Bell first approached two brothers, Roland and Karl Chambers, with
whom he had grown up in West Philadelphia. Roland, who turned
twenty in 1964, was two years older than Karl. They came from a family
steeped in musical tradition. Their great-grandfather had been the
leader of a South Philadelphia marching band and their mother still
marched as a majorette in local parades. Both brothers took an early
interest in music.[5] Roland, or "Roll," as his friends called him, was quiet,
humble, and observant. But he sprang to life whenever he held a guitar
in his hands. In fact, that is how Roland came to be involved with Bell to
begin with. Sometime in 1962, Chambers was walking on the streets of
West Philadelphia carrying his guitar. This prompted Gamble, who saw
him by chance, to ask whether he could play the instrument. When
Chambers said yes, Gamble invited him to his girlfriend Barbara's
house. It was then and there that Chambers met Tommy Bell.

Besides playing drums, the rail-thin Karl (known in the studio as
"Slim") demonstrated a propensity for street distractions, including
drug abuse. (The general consensus of those interviewed was that Karl
drew Roland in that direction.) By the time Roland was sixteen, he was

playing guitar for various artists in and around Philadelphia. He and Kenny Gamble, who was a year ahead of him at West Philly High, used to sing R&B harmony in local subway stations, the best public echo chambers in the city. After high school, Roland studied music at the Philadelphia Conservatory of Music for a short time. In 1962, he became the Orlons' road guitarist and toured the country with them (he would subsequently play guitar for the group for several years).

Tommy Bell said that even the Chambers brothers' impoverished inner-city neighbors regarded them as poor. Most blacks in West Philadelphia were raised "in fallin'-down houses," said Bell, but the Chambers's house was in such bad shape that the city condemned it. Beyond the abject poverty, Bell saw that Roland and Karl were talented musicians and obvious choices for his Cameo-Parkway recruiting campaign. Roland and Karl both jumped at the chance to join the rhythm section Bell was putting together.

Bell now had a guitarist and drummer to go along with his own piano and organ playing. All he lacked was a bass player. Bell happened to know a "great" one, named Win Wilford (known to those in Philadelphia as Winney). Wilford, who hailed from Baton Rouge, Louisiana, had just been mustered out of the Air Force. He sought to break into the music business and was drawn to Philadelphia by an uncle who lived there. In Philadelphia, Wilford played bass with various bands. As "one band led to the next one," Wilford crossed paths with Bell,[6] who told him about the new black rhythm section Cameo-Parkway was putting together. Wilford auditioned as the bass player and came away with the job. He characterized his addition to the newly minted group as "a good fit." They called themselves The Romeos (The Romeos nicknamed Wilford "Fret," because of the prominent frets on the instrument he played. Bell said all of the Romeos were good musicians who "had great ears.")

Cameo-Parkway then held auditions to recruit black vocal talent, "as if the next Supremes were walking around right outside our door!" exclaimed Tommy Bell. As ludicrous as this practice seemed to Bell, the novice arranger benefited greatly from it. Bell went to school at Cameo-Parkway's expense, "learning myself, how to work with a rhythm section," he explained.

BERNIE LOWE'S NEW OPEN-DOOR POLICY also boded well for Kenny Gamble, who had grown restless writing pop-oriented Sapphires tunes and increasingly dated rhythm and blues numbers for Swan. The new songwriting alliance between Ross Associates and Bernie Lowe's company finally secured Gamble access to Cameo-Parkway (which had recently moved to 309 South Broad Street, located diagonally across from the Schubert Building). Even so, the resourceful Gamble had already concocted his own scheme to gain entrance to the company. Gamble's plan was to win the heart of Dee Dee Sharp, one of Cameo-Parkway's hottest recording stars. "That's how his butt got in there in the first place," recalled Tommy Bell.

Dione LaRue (who declined to be interviewed for this book) was sixteen years old and not yet out of Overbrook High School in north-west Philadelphia when she was hired by Cameo-Parkway in 1962 to sing the backing riffs on Chubby Checker's "Slow Twistin'." After hearing LaRue sing, Bernie Lowe and Kal Mann decided that the young thrush would make a great choice to record a new dance song that Mann had just written. At Cameo-Parkway's insistence, Dione LaRue became Dee Dee Sharp, and her debut record, "Mashed Potato Time," became a million-seller that spring. "Mashed Potato Time" and its followup, "Gravy (for My Mashed Potatoes)," propelled Dee Dee Sharp to stardom. She became America's first black teen idol, and adolescent-oriented magazines rushed out stories about her. Some, such as the one that linked her romantically with Chubby Checker, were spurious. In real life, Kenny Gamble had become Dee Dee's number-one admirer.

Gamble wanted to meet Sharp "in the worst way," said Tommy Bell. Bell had observed the teen idol's demanding behavior in the recording studio (he diplomatically described Sharp's behavior as that of "a little star") and thought she would mean trouble for his friend. "You don't want to meet this girl," he cautioned Gamble. "She's not the girl for you." "C'mon Bell," pleaded Gamble, "you gotta introduce me!"[7] Bell did, after Gamble's relentless entreaties eventually wore him down.

After that, it was not unusual to see Gamble, who still worked part time at Jefferson Hospital, headed down Broad Street to the Cameo-Parkway building each day, clad in his white lab technician's coat. Once inside, he made small talk with Sharp, "tryin' to get in with some of his songs," said Weldon McDougal. Indeed, Gamble was successful there, too. He wrote several songs that Sharp recorded.

Another of Gamble's strengths was his ability to take stock of prevailing conditions and use them to his advantage. Now that he had access to Cameo-Parkway, Gamble called on that attribute. As a singer without a regular backing band, Gamble experienced difficulty in booking gigs. When he discovered Cameo-Parkway's new black rhythm section, Gamble envisioned the group as his own band. In short order they became just that. Gamble accomplished this feat in such an unas-suming manner that nobody in the group realized (or cared) what was going on. "We were in the studio every day, and we used to see Kenny there," said Win Wilford. "He was writin' some songs, and then, of course, Dee Dee was there." Gamble, who was already friends with three-fourths of Cameo-Parkway's new instrumental group, easily ingratiated himself with them. "It was the Cameo-Parkway house band," said Wilford, "but it wasn't long before we started gigging, playing as a band" behind Gamble. "Singers have a tendency to, in some ways, become the leader. That's what basically happened," explained the bassist for the group. Whatever activity the group was involved in, Gamble "was in charge of it," remembered Wilford. "When we got to the studio to do something, it was already basically laid out" by him. Still, Gamble relied heavily on the Romeos whenever he wrote. He "always would rely on the other talented people to help bring something together," said Wilford. If somebody else came up with a suggestion that Gamble liked, "that's the direction he would go in." Gamble would expand on this practice as his songwriting career progressed.

Gamble and the Romeos rehearsed for about six months and were then ready for their first gig. It was a testament to Gamble's adept social skills that the group's billing as Kenny Gamble and the Romeos did not bother any of them.

"We all got the same pay," said Wilford. "During the day, we were in the studio . . . [and we were] gigging all the time. It was a great arrangement." Wilford pointed out that he played with a lot of good groups around Philadelphia, but it was only when he got with Kenny and the Romeos that he realized "the potential of it."

Gamble described the Romeos as "basically a show band—good harmonies, excellent musicians—but not great singers." Like most local bands, they made a living covering the most popular dance numbers of the day. In 1963 and 1964, that included a hefty dose of Motown, a company that appealed to Gamble on two levels. First, it was black-owned (although Berry Gordy did install whites in several key positions). Second, its music appealed to all races. Gamble recalled that when he heard Marvin Gaye, David Ruffin, or Eddie Kendricks sing, he thought, "Now those guys are singers." Backed by the Romeos, Gamble could now tear into Motown tunes, such as "Can I Get a Witness," with newfound energy and tight accompaniment. "We did the top songs and we thrived on doing them like the records," said Win Wilford. Tommy Bell said he and the other members of the group "learned a lot just being in that unit. It was a great experience, a growth period. Everyplace we worked we packed them in." After gigging at small clubs in Philadelphia and in New Jersey, the Romeos eventually became the house band at Lauretta's Hi Hat, a popular Camden area night spot that catered to the rhythm and blues crowd. "We used to go there and sing our songs in our sharkskin suits," recalled Gamble. "It was beautiful."[8]

Georgie Woods remembered the Romeos as a "nice little group," but the activist/disc jockey perceived Kenny Gamble as "more of being in a managerial position than being a singer onstage." So did Leon Huff, who would soon replace Bell in the group. Huff later claimed that no one in the Romeos had "the disposition to be an entertainer." Huff said that while he and Gamble were members of the Romeos, both of them recognized that "control" was what counted most. "Decision-making on all creative levels, the *power*, you understand, to say yes or no."[9] Gamble and Huff would one day acquire that decision-making status. It would serve them well on the creative level, although the same could not be said for some of the duo's business decisions.

Besides gaining a regular backing band, Kenny Gamble eagerly befriended Joe Tarsia, the crack recording engineer who presided over Cameo-Parkway's spanking new recording studios. They met on a day when Jerry Ross brought the Dreamlovers in to record.[10] Kenny Gamble was there, behaving like "a person on fire," recalled Tarsia. "He was just a driven personality, stickin' his nose in wherever he could." Tarsia's professional expertise was critical to the long-term success of both individuals. As early as the loquacious Tarsia can remember, he had a fascination for all things electronic—why they worked and how he could repair them when they ceased to function. In 1952, after graduating from a technical high school in Philadelphia, Tarsia landed a job as a lab technician in the research department of electronics giant Philco. At night he moonlighted as a TV repairman. Tarsia said he "got the bug" for sound recording during the time he helped to rebuild Swan Records' tiny studio, and subsequently took a part-time job as an engineer there. The job was "exciting, and I loved it," he recalled. "I really learned by the seat of my pants." Tarsia was hired by Cameo-Parkway in 1962.[11]

Soon after that Dreamlovers session, Kenny Gamble was afforded yet another opportunity to advance his career. After Jerry Ross formulated a deal to have a major New York record company issue his Sapphires productions, Gamble often accompanied the producer when he commuted to the Big Apple, where Ross recorded the group. Also, sometime in early 1964, Gamble received his first label credit, for coarranging the Sapphires' "Let's Break Up." Embodied with prominent percussion and a style that drew heavily from the Drifters' Latin-tinged "On Broadway," "Let's Make Up" failed to catch on. But that did not matter to Gamble, who became preoccupied with New York's sophisticated recording facilities and studio techniques. While in New York, Gamble observed the process of multitracking, a relatively new method of recording, which involves recording vocals and various instruments on several different tracks, and then combining them on a master tape. (This process eventually became Gamble's modus operandi in the studio.) While in New York, Gamble also worked with the up-and-coming talent Ross surrounded himself with there, including writer/ arrangers Joe Renzetti and Jimmy Wisner.[12]

Jerry Ross spoke figuratively of Gamble's evolution as a producer. "At first we collaborated as writers and he stood by me side-by-side, interning, learning, watching, listening," he said. "I was the maestro, he was the student. And eventually the student became the maestro." That would take some time, however. At that point, recalled Gamble, he and Leon Huff "were just writers trying to be producers, trying to find out what a producer does."[13]

NEW YORK CITY WAS A CRUCIBLE FOR LEON HUFF, as well as for Kenny Gamble. As Gamble continued to look over the shoulder of Jerry Ross, Huff played the piano wherever and whenever he could land a session. He worked with some of the top people in the recording business in New York, including eminent producer Phil Spector.[14] Working for the demanding and eccentric Spector was also physically exhausting. Joe Tarsia laughed as he described how Huff, earphones on his head, fell asleep seated at the piano during one of Spector's legendary sessions.

Huff maintained his grueling pace despite his impromptu catnaps. It was as if he could not get enough work. Although tethered to John Madara and Dave White by his exclusive writing deal with them, Huff was free to play piano and record with whomever he chose. This he did for Frank Bendinelli and Leroy Lovett, of B&L Productions.

That April, Lovett introduced Bendinelli to an unnamed group from Camden, New Jersey, who wanted to record two songs that were written by their piano player, who happened to be Leon Huff. A week later the group recorded "Mixed-Up Shook-Up Girl," a number to which Huff's piano "really added spark," recalled Bendinelli. The group was christened Patty and the Emblems, and "Mixed-Up Shook-Up Girl" was released on a nationally distributed label out of New York. Had this fruit of Huff's moonlighting been released inconspicuously, no one would have been the wiser. But the pianist-turned-songwriter was far too talented for his work to go unnoticed. That summer, "Mixed-Up Shook Up Girl" became a Top 40 hit and blew Leon Huff's cover.[15] It was then, recalled Dave White, that he and John Madara first realized Huff was writing "on the sly" for Bendinelli and Lovett.

Bendinelli and Lovett were just as surprised as Madara and White. Bendinelli recalled how Huff was "absolutely stone broke" when "Mixed-Up Shook-Up Girl" hit, and how the hard-working pianist was then hired as a regular session player for B&L (where he earned fifteen or twenty dollars per date). Huff played "the funkiest keyboards you ever laid ears on" for at least fifty B&L productions (including thirty that he wrote), recalled Bendinelli. But Huff failed to mention to them that as a writer, he was contractually bound to Madara and White. Since Madara and White were paying Huff seventy-five dollars a week to write songs exclusively for them, "we should have gotten publishing" for "Mixed-Up Shook-Up Girl," said White. By the time the mess was sorted out legally, Madara and White owned half of that song—and half of everything else Huff had written for B&L.[16]

(It is notable that around the time of the brouhaha between Bendinelli and Lovett and Madara and White, the ubiquitous Kenny Gamble cut a demo for B&L, called "What Am I Gonna Tell My Baby." Gamble "came in with a little group [apparently it was Cameo-Parkway's black rhythm section]," recalled Bendinelli, "and Leroy put together a head arrangement [for the song]. Kenny did a great job."[17])

DURING THE SUMMER OF 1964, as "Mixed-Up Shook-Up Girl" blared from radios, black frustrations boiled over across America even as the civil rights movement continued to make landmark gains.[18] That July, President Johnson signed into law legislation that, among other things, protected voter rights and prohibited discrimination in all public facilities. It was the most sweeping civil rights act since the Civil War and marked the high-water mark for black-white cooperation in America's civil rights movement.

It is ironic that at this pinnacle of black-white cooperation, America stood on the doorstep of an era of widespread inner-city violence. On the first anniversary of Dr. Martin Luther King's "I Had a Dream" speech, in which he warned that America would be buffeted by the "whirlwinds of revolt" if true change in race relations did not occur, black rioting in Philadelphia and other cities broke out.[19] This volatile mix of hooliganism and genuine frustration, beyond the control of any black authority, portended troublesome times for Kenny Gamble, Leon Huff, and Tommy Bell. As the three were about to achieve their dream of musical autonomy, a yawning chasm between whites and blacks began to develop, not only in Philadelphia, where the defiant Frank Rizzo and his police force sustained one of the most confrontational racial policies of all, but also throughout America.

STILL, KENNY GAMBLE HAD PERSONAL CALL to feel fortunate. Almost a year after his first record flopped, Gamble received a second chance. That summer, Jerry Ross secured an independent production contract with Columbia Records in New York. As part of the deal, Ross brought three of his acts to record for Columbia. One of them was Kenny Gamble, who, said Ross, "had great potential" to be a star.

Gamble's debut album was released on Columbia Records that fall. The first single from the album was the Ross-Gamble composition, "You

Don't Know What You've Got until You Lose It." Gamble's dramatic reading of the song—about a man who tells his former girlfriend he will love her forever, but will never forgive her for forsaking him—was tinged with bitterness. But the single and the album failed to generate much, if any, airplay. In hindsight, Jerry Ross accused Columbia of "just not pushing Kenny as an artist," when, in fact, the problem was more complex.[20]

Columbia's idea of a black singer was pop balladeer Johnny Mathis, who the giant company was adept at promoting to white radio stations. Accordingly, Gamble's album, overburdened by Jimmy Wisner's onerous string arrangements, was more closely related to Mathis's type of pop than to rhythm and blues or soul. But most white radio stations balked at playing an untested black singer such as Gamble, even a singer with a pop-laden style. Airplay on black-oriented stations, which did not have any interest in hyping the next Johnny Mathis or Brook Benton, was nonexistent.[21]

As Kenny Gamble's singing career foundered, so did the fortunes of Bernie Lowe. Despite Lowe's new openness to black personnel, Cameo-Parkway had gone the entire summer without a Top 40 record. As Lowe eyed Motown's growing share of the pop marketplace, he called on the Ross-Gamble songwriting team to help stem the tide. The result was an up-tempo dance number called "The 81," which was recorded by a New York girl group called Candy and the Kisses. The song was inspired by a new dance performed at one of the local record hops Ross and Gamble frequently visited in order to keep their pulses on the latest trends in the pop marketplace. Produced by Jerry Ross and arranged by Jimmy Wisner, the decidedly Motown groove elicited a more blues-oriented gospel style not unlike that of Martha and the Vandellas. Record buyers could be forgiven for thinking "The 81," released that fall, was Berry Gordy's latest musical effort.[22]

Ultimately, "The 81" did little to ease Cameo-Parkway's woes. The song was a hit in the Philadelphia area, but nationwide it failed to crack *Billboard*'s Top 40. "The 81" did affirm the future songwriting partnership of Kenny Gamble and Leon Huff. Gamble has stated that his desire to write with Huff began about the time "The 81" was composed, when the two of them "were grinding out songs on different floors" of the Schubert Building. Huff would sometimes play piano when some of Gamble's songs were recorded (as he did on "The 81"). According to Huff, shortly after "The 81" session, he and Gamble were on the Schubert Building elevator when the inquisitive and opportunistic Gamble asked the reticent piano player if he wrote songs. Huff said he did and invited Gamble to his house. It did not take Gamble and Huff long "to realize that the producers we were giving our work to didn't know much about music, or sound, or style," recalled Gamble. "You name it, they didn't know it. . . . They couldn't see the potential in our music. So I got together with Huff." "That's when it really started," agreed Huff. "He came over to my house that night, and we sat down in my little music room and it sounded good from the beginning. We just started writing songs every day after that."[23]

Disharmony between Gamble and Jerry Ross apparently began to develop around the time that "The 81" was recorded. Although writing credit for the song went to Ross and Gamble, in 1976, Gamble claimed that he and *Huff* actually wrote the song. About the same time that Gamble made that claim, Huff contradicted it, maintaining he had simply been hired to play piano on "The 81." Huff said it was after that session that he and Gamble "started talking about collaborating on songs." Whatever Gamble's motives were for disparaging Jerry Ross, by the time "The 81" was released, Gamble was in the market for a new writing partner.[24]

As Kenny Gamble grew restless writing Motown knockoffs with Jerry Ross, and Leon Huff began to look beyond his writing for Madara and White, soul music continued to mature and take on various regional styles. In the case of Philadelphia Soul, the distinct falsetto lead popularized in West Philadelphia a decade earlier was assimilated into a cornucopia of flourishing local styles indigenous to the neighborhoods in which they developed. The situation was similar to what had occurred a decade earlier, during the development of rock and roll. In both instances, there were no icons to imitate or emulate and no patterns to follow. The principals involved in the development of Philadelphia Soul did not realize they were formulating a specific musical genre. They were happy to be doing what they loved, which was making music that interested them.

EACH SECTION OF PHILADELPHIA had its own singing groups and record labels, and, in some cases, recording studio. The city's handful of mom-and-pop recording facilities were the domains of producers who wielded an unwitting hand in the grass-roots development of Philadelphia Soul. One such locale was Tony Luisi's Sound Plus studio, where Frank Bendinelli and Leroy Lovett held sway. "Mixed-Up Shook-Up Girl" was Bendinelli and Lovett's biggest claim to fame, but the two of them also served up an early slice of Philadelphia Soul, called "Pretty One," which was recorded by an unnamed studio group. That gem remained unreleased, however, proof enough that the pioneers of Philadelphia Soul really were flying blind. Not long after "Pretty One" was recorded, Luisi and Len Stark produced "King of Love," by the Allures, an early example of a rhythm and blues number that served as a bridge to Philadelphia Soul.[25]

Another small recording studio responsible for several Philadelphia Soul precursors was Tony Schmidt's Impact Sound. That studio, also located in northeast Philadelphia, was the home territory of producer Phil Gaber, one of the city's greatest unsung producers. Around the time that "The 81" became Philadelphia's latest dance craze, the former jazz drummer recorded a prototype Philadelphia Soul ballad, "This Is Magic," sung by the Ballads. When it came to Gaber's style of music, he and his colleagues around town had no grand design. Gaber insisted that he "never really considered [the music] Philly Soul," that he was simply improvising, "just doing what [he] thought was happening at the time."[26]

For all the enthusiasm and regional sounding recordings generated by studios such as Sound Plus and Impact, those settings were mainly responsible for recording a caliber of artists that Philadelphia pop music chronologist Robert Bosco said were "known only to their mothers."[27] The true fountainhead of Philadelphia Soul, and the crucible for the rapidly developing professional relationship between Kenny Gamble and Leon Huff, was Frank Virtue's studio in North Philadelphia. Born in Philadelphia in 1933, Frank Virtuoso, during various stages in his life, was a musician, bandleader, car salesman, and recording engineer. Virtue became proficient on the violin and guitar while still in his teens. After serving in World War II, he formed his own trio to play at wedding-type functions. When rock and roll arrived, Virtue updated his act and, in 1956, formed a five-man combo called the Virtues, which he fronted on lead guitar.

After recording the Virtues and other local artists in a tiny studio Virtue built in his basement, in 1959 the electronics maven opened a professional recording studio, located over a North Broad Street storefront near Temple University.[28] Virtue settled into a comfortable routine of playing local gigs and running his tiny, yet vibrant, business. Stephen Kelly, who, as a member of the Volcanos (one of Philadelphia's seminal soul groups), recorded numerous sessions at Virtue's, laughed as he recalled toting the band's instruments up three flights of stairs, "a thousand-and-one steps, climbin' to the top," to reach the lofty studio. One of Virtue's earliest clients was Jerry Ross, who made Gamble and Bell's Kenny and Tommy recording there. Virtue's, which had one of only two three-track recording boards in town, was Philadelphia's "cookin' independent studio," recalled Ross. The room's technical proficiency, combined with its liberal mood-setting policy—including all night sessions enhanced by wine and other substances such as marijuana, which many musicians indulged in—made it a popular choice among local producers, recording artists, and musicians.

Gamble and Huff received their initial schooling from Jerry Ross and Madara and White, respectively, but when they began to play hooky

from their day jobs in order to put into practice what they had heretofore only been permitted to observe, they headed for Frank Virtue's
place. Their introduction to Virtue's turned on a chance meeting with
Weldon McDougal. After enjoying a brief fanfare with the Larks' hit,
"It's Unbelievable," McDougal continued to sing with the group and to
produce their records, as well as the records of other artists. Like
numerous other Philadelphians with similar musical ambitions,
McDougal gave Cameo-Parkway a try. The Orlons and Dee Dee Sharp
put in a few good words for him, but Bernie Lowe's closed-door policy
was still in effect, and McDougal remained unwelcome there. Then, in
1963, McDougal ran across old friend Johnny Stiles, one of the musicians
who played on "It's Unbelievable." As McDougal and Stiles reminisced,
a plan was hatched to start a record label and production company, the
latter to be named Dynodynamics.[29] (Luther Randolph, an associate of
Stiles, was also included in the deal.) McDougal had recently befriended
a hot young disc jockey named Jimmy ("make your liver quiver and
your knees freeze") Bishop, who worked at local rhythm and blues
station WDAS. The way McDougal saw things, if Bishop was made a
partner in Dynodynamics, "we could get our records played" at WDAS.
(Bishop is now a preacher somewhere in the southern United States, and
could not be located for an interview.)

Jimmy Bishop, who played an important part in the early success of
Gamble and Huff, was born and raised in Alabama. After attending
college, Bishop became a chemist. But in the late 1950s, he opted for the
more alluring job of radio disc jockey. By the early 1960s, Bishop had
made a name for himself on St. Louis radio. He had also befriended
Leroy Lovett, who then introduced him to McDougal. After a brief stint
on New York City radio, Bishop moved to Philadelphia in 1962 and
became the understudy to WDAS's headliner, Georgie Woods. (Bishop
also began to produce records that, he later admitted, "were lousy."[30])
Not long after Woods left Bishop in charge of the Uptown Theater show
at the start of the North Philadelphia riots in 1964, McDougal extended
the offer of partnership in Dynodynamics to the enterprising young disc
jockey.

Bishop "had an in with all the record companies," said McDougal.
After the disc jockey convinced Atlantic to release one of Dynodynamics's recordings nationally, McDougal was certain he had made the
right decision in inviting Bishop aboard.[31] Things looked even better in
December, when Arctic Records was formed in conjunction with the
owner of a local record distributorship, ostensibly to release Dynodynamics's productions. But McDougal, Stiles, and Randolph would rue
the day they decided to recruit Jimmy Bishop.

THE YEAR 1964 ENDED WITH GAMBLE AND HUFF poised to make a significant breakthrough in the pop music business. Gamble was no longer set on a singing career. Although he still recorded with the Romeos, he and Huff itched to try their hands at production. They would soon get that opportunity at Frank Virtue's studio, courtesy of the Dynodynamics crew. But they were not to do so in an era of domestic tranquility. Despite the landmark civil rights gains that culminated in 1964, the rioting in Philadelphia and other American cities was a grim warning of what lay ahead. Increasing U.S. troop strength in Southeast Asia and the disproportionate number of inner-city minorities—and casualties—there exacerbated black disaffection. But to many whites, the black rioting did not express legitimate grievances. Their alarm over the civil disturbances, a sharply rising crime rate, and rising black power rhetoric gave rise to a white backlash. America was headed for an era of civil strife and cultural upheaval that would have a profound effect on its society. For the moment, this festering racial divide was effectively obscured by the country's pop music. Mainstream tastes grew more attuned to Motown's Sound of Young America, and the Southern Soul sound pioneered by Atlantic and Stax continued to gain in popularity.[32] But the country's homogeneous pop audience, much like its black-white civil rights coalition, was about to split asunder. That was a reality Kenny Gamble and Leon Huff—who still chafed under their white bosses—were not able to ignore.

4
"Expressway to Your Heart"
(1965–1967)

I N 1965, AS PRESIDENT JOHNSON'S GREAT SOCIETY moved to bring blacks into the mainstream, more and more blacks moved in the opposite direction. Heightened tensions between blacks and whites, and among blacks at odds over how to deal with white racism, became obvious. That August, President Johnson signed into law the Voting Rights bill of 1965, which, along with the Civil Rights Act of 1964, marked the culmination of a decade-long drive. But resistance to civil rights legislation persisted, in the North as well as in the South. Additional battles loomed over more volatile issues, such as open housing, that did not have broad white support. Complicating matters was the murder of black leader Malcolm X, whose death created a void in black leadership able significantly to address the dispossessed masses. For many blacks, especially younger ones, Martin Luther King's policy of nonviolence in the face of violence seemed hypocritical, and the black community's position of tolerance could no longer be counted on to hold. Just five days after the Voting Rights bill became law, a black uprising in which thirty-four people died began in the South Central Los Angeles ghetto called Watts. A wary America heard the first ominous strains of "get whitey" and "burn, baby, burn," as a distinct pattern of summer violence began to emerge in black ghettos. While this growing division of black and white was more vividly reflected in areas that included the nation's education system and public housing, it was also evident in America's pop music. (That January, a year after *Billboard* eliminated its R&B chart because the listings were so similar to its Hot 100 chart, the music trade paper began publishing it again.)

It was in 1965 that American popular music split to a degree not witnessed since the pre–rock and roll era of a decade earlier. This musical gulf was more greatly influenced by black, and not white, sentiments. This year, rock and roll became, for the most part, music made by whites. Nelson George wrote that blacks increasingly viewed rock and roll (or rock, as it was beginning to be called) as "white boys' music that didn't reflect their musical taste or cultural experience. The ties between . . . rock and roll and its original black audience were being severed, and black America didn't seem to care."[1] On the other hand, black music's popularity among many young whites remained strong. When they danced, they did so to the sound of Motown, as exemplified by the extremely popular Temptations, Supremes, and Four Tops. With the support of numerous whites, soul music was able to move into the pop mainstream. That summer, Wilson Pickett's "In the Midnight Hour" and James Brown's "Papa's Got A Brand New Bag" hit the pop charts.

It was on the cusp of this era of racial discord and the uneven divergence of white and black popular music that Kenny Gamble and Leon Huff began to collaborate in earnest. The first step was taken when Huff, who had occasionally sat in with the Romeos, became a full-time member of the band. Tommy Bell's wife was pregnant at the time and did not want her husband working the clubs any longer. "It was just time to leave that single life behind," explained Bell. When he left the Romeos, Huff stepped in. Shortly thereafter, Huff and Gamble wrote together for the first time. They came up with "seven or eight songs," said Huff, "and decided to keep doing it."[2]

Because Gamble and Huff were disparate in personality and behavior, they seemed unlikely candidates to become partners. Teddy Pendergrass, who later achieved stardom under Gamble and Huff's tutelage, called the pair "a study in complementary talents." Pendergrass viewed the oft-brooding Gamble, who was a reserved and philosophical spiritual person, as a "deep thinker . . . [who was] in tune with what was really happening in the world around him." Pendergrass was particularly struck by the fact that no matter how successful Gamble became, "he never seemed to care about material possessions; he never even wore a wristwatch."[3]

Unlike the outgoing Gamble, Huff was gruff and taciturn in nature. Jim Gallagher, a former recording engineer who worked with Huff in the studio for many years, said that Gamble's partner "had like a hard kind of street attitude . . . [and] would almost never speak to anybody. He was all about the music in the grooves and he only talked to other musicians." Gallagher and his colleagues in the studio "used to kind of kid each other about how if we got Huff to grunt at us, that was a really social day" with him. Sensitive to his diminutive stature, Huff exuded flash and competitiveness. Gamble was disinterested in his wardrobe, while Huff was fastidious about his appearance. Pendergrass recalled the time he proudly drove up in a new Cadillac he had purchased with royalties from his first hit record for Gamble and Huff's company: "So you got your own Cadillac," sniffed Huff. "Just remember: For every one you can buy, I can buy ten."[4]

Despite their personal differences, when it came to musical collaboration, Gamble and Huff were a perfect match. Gamble said that the two "just had the feeling—the second sense—that told us we had something special to give each other." Tommy Bell called Gamble "the engine, [while] Leon put fuel in the tank." Morris Bailey, who observed the two at work in the studio, said Gamble and Huff "believed in one another." Gamble would say, "Let's try this!" If that did not work they would laugh at each other. "Oh man, you punked out again!" If Huff said, "Hey man, wait, wait, wait. Let's do this," they would try it. "They would try anything," said Bailey. "I've never seen two people who were more together in the studio."[5]

Still, before Gamble and Huff were able to write together on an unencumbered basis, their professional obligations to Jerry Ross and Madara and White needed to be addressed. As it was, Gamble had an easier time gaining his autonomy than Huff did. Jerry Ross's production agreement with Columbia Records, which demanded that he spend an increasing amount of time at the company's New York studios, pretty much put an end to the Ross-Gamble songwriting team. But no such imminent escape from Madara and White was in the cards for Leon Huff. As a result, Gamble and Huff's informal writing sessions created an urge of a different sort. "We had to take the initiative," explained Gamble. "Nothing much else was happening for us. Once we wrote together we just knew we had to produce together."[6]

Thanks to Weldon McDougal, the pair soon took a significant step in that direction. The Dynodynamics crew was recording at Virtue's one day when McDougal stepped out to get a bite to eat and ran into Gamble. Sensing an opportunity to "brag and boast," McDougal told Gamble he was in the midst of a production session and invited him to come on up. The musically insatiable Gamble did not have to be asked twice. When Gamble arrived at Virtue's, he and the Dynodynamics crew hit it off instantly. The sight of four black men working independently infused Gamble with a desire to do likewise. He was especially keen on Jimmy Bishop, who was then the program director at WDAS. As such, Bishop had final say on what records the station played.

With Jerry Ross preoccupied in New York City, Gamble began to spend an increasing amount of time at Virtue's, where a series of landmark productions by the Dynodynamics crew did not escape his mindful eyes and ears. Gamble soon injected himself into the mix, singing background on Barbara Mason's "Yes, I'm Ready," which, in the spring of 1965, became the first Philadelphia Soul record to gain national prominence. While at Virtue's, Gamble also witnessed the production of several other cornerstones of Philadelphia Soul: the Volcanos' "Make Your Move" and "Storm Warning," as well as Eddie Holman's "This Can't Be True (Girl)."

Thanks to the Dynodynamics productions on Barbara Mason, the Volcanos, and Eddie Holman, Philadelphia Soul began to gain focus. The Temptations-like "Storm Warning," on which lead singer Gene Faith lamented over having lost his love ("Stormin' in my heart since we've been apart . . . rainin' every day since you've been away"), was released just after "Yes, I'm Ready" and was the most soulful offering yet out of Philadelphia. Weldon McDougal, who was instrumental in developing the Volcanos' sound, described how the Dynodynamics crew's prominent use of vibes and "the way the strings sweetened things without getting in the way of the beat" differentiated those seminal recordings. "All the rhythm sounds started coming together on those records," said the producer.[7] Pumped by heavy airplay on WDAS, "Storm Warning" became a local hit, as well as the second Philadelphia Soul record (along with "Yes, I'm Ready") to appear on the national rhythm and blues charts.

Gamble and Huff were further impressed after McDougal and his Dynodynamics crew recorded Holman's "This Can't Be True (Girl)," a dreamy ballad about a man who cannot believe he has found his ideal love. While "Storm Warning" presaged the up-tempo dance side of Philadelphia Soul, the nineteen-year-old Holman's effort (on which McDougal's Larks sang behind Holman's penetrating falsetto) became the archetype on which much of the genre's "sweet" sound was based. Released on Parkway Records that summer, "This Can't Be True (Girl)" became another milestone in the genesis of Philadelphia Soul.

Up to that point, most up-tempo black records that emerged from Philadelphia were based on Motown licks. Now Gamble and Huff, exhibiting a proclivity for the evolving Philadelphia Soul genre, began to develop their own soulful groove. An early example of Gamble's writing was the Casinos' "Everybody Can't Be Pretty," a song that espoused his personal disregard of worldly things. In it, Gamble's advice to potential listeners was for them to be satisfied with who they are, because not everyone can be rich or beautiful. Powered by a prominent bass line, the high-pitched lead singer concludes by telling his sweetheart that even though she is not Miss America, she will be loved as long as she has "soul, soul, soul."

Gamble also spread his songwriting wings in a more personalized manner. Stoked by a combination of his own pointed advances, Dee Dee Sharp's adolescent curiosities, and an easygoing accessibility between the two, Gamble and Sharp had become romantically involved by then. But at the same time, the teen idol's career had fallen on hard times. Like so many American recording artists, Sharp's chart success became a casualty of the English Invasion. Although Sharp's records became more soul-oriented, her old fans did not accept her new direction. The songs that Gamble began to write for Sharp reflected his personal involvement with her. Perhaps goaded by rumors of an amorous fling between the teenage star and heavyweight boxer Cassius Clay (soon to be Muhammad Ali), Gamble wrote the ballad, "I Really Love You" for her.[8] That fall, the song became Sharp's biggest hit in over two years.

Gamble also drew closer to Jimmy Bishop, who, by then, had parted company with his partners in Dynodynamics. Bishop, in conjunction with the owner of a local record distributorship, had recently started his own record label, called Arctic Records (on which the Barbara Mason and Volcanos recordings had been released). In the spring of 1965, Bishop signed Gamble and the Romeos to a recording contract with Arctic, and the group proceeded to wax the double-sided Philadelphia Soul dandy, "The Joke's on You" and "Don't Stop Loving Me" (the former written by Gamble and Huff).[9]

As Gamble and Huff recorded together in the Romeos, their working relationship intensified. While Huff remained under contract to Madara and White as a songwriter, he and Gamble were free to work together in other areas. Billy Jackson was the former lead singer of the Re-Vels and, later on, Cameo-Parkway's first black producer. Jackson recalled how frustrated Gamble, Huff, and Bell had grown from their failed attempts to gain entrance to white-owned record companies around town, who "all had white teams and . . . did not want to bring in the black guys." Just as disheartening to Gamble and Huff were the nation's current events, which offered no hint of improvement in black-white relations. But after their crash course in record production—courtesy of the Dynodynamics crew—Gamble and Huff felt they were ready to form their own record company.

It was hardly the most expedient time for two inexperienced, under-capitalized young black men to think about doing so, and, accordingly, Gamble recalled how he and Huff "scuffled around trying to raise some capital to start the venture." They received some welcomed assistance from Philadelphia-born and -bred Solomon "Kal" Rudman. The short, stocky Rudman, a schoolteacher in neighboring Bucks County, Pennsylvania, was also a part-time disc jockey in Camden, New Jersey. It was the bombastic air personality's outgoing self-promotion as radio's next great thing that caught the attention of Kenny Gamble.[10] After securing a reported seven-hundred-dollar loan from Ben Krass, the South Street clothier to Philadelphia's entertainment community, Gamble, Huff, and Rudman were in business. They called their new label Excel.

Over the years, Gamble and Huff's most successful recording artists were already veterans of the studio by the time the producers got their hands on them. This pattern was established in 1965, when Gamble and Huff signed a local R&B group called the Intruders to a contract. The Intruders were led by the now-deceased Sam "Little Sonny" Brown, whose distinctive, straining voice "sounds flat, but it's not really flat," according to fellow group member Phil Terry. Recording for Gamble and Huff, the Intruders became one of the more successful soul acts of the late 1960s and early 1970s, and single-handedly kept the two producers afloat during their early years in the record business.[11]

The Intruders' roots extend back to the street corners of Philadelphia in the early 1950s, a time when the city's signature falsetto sound was just beginning to coalesce. Little Sonny, Eugene "Bird" Daughtry (deceased), and Robert "Big Sonny" Edwards were then members of a gospel quintet that traveled the widening path from religious music to secular rhythm and blues. The group's new name stemmed from the unruly lifestyle of its members. "We crashed a party and they said, 'Oh, the Intruders!'" explained Daughtry. In 1960, the Intruders met Phil Terry, who was then singing with his own rowdy bunch of street-corner friends. When Terry's group broke up, he joined the Intruders, making them a quartet. They cut their first record near the end of 1961, but it went nowhere. In fact, nothing of significance happened to the Intruders for the next three years. Then, in 1964, they came under the management of Leroy Lovett, who took the group into Sound Plus studio. The Intruders, who had previously known Leon Huff from the group's appearances at record hops with the Lavenders, were reacquainted with him there. By the time the Intruders left Sound Plus later that day, they had recorded about half a dozen songs for Frank Bendinelli and Leroy Lovett. Two of those songs were leased to a major label, but as had happened with the group's first record, their latest release went unnoticed. Nevertheless, Huff was convinced that the Intruders had potential. So was Kenny Gamble, who said that after the Intruders' B&L release flopped, the group was without a deal, "so we pursued them."[12]

The chase began at Lauretta's High Hat, where Gamble's Romeos backed the Intruders during one of their appearances there. After the show, the Intruders "went straight up to Leon's house in the projects in Camden," said Bird Daughtry. "And that's when we started to get our stuff together."[13] The Intruders spent months working with Gamble and Huff. Then, halfway through 1965, the producers booked studio time at Cameo-Parkway, where the Intruders recorded "Gonna Be Strong," a measured ballad that highlighted Little Sonny's peculiar nasal lead over an airy, Flamingos-like backing. Released late that summer, on the heels of the extensive black rioting in Watts, "Gonna Be Strong" made for a curious blend of traditional rhythm and blues harmony and soul.

The fact that Kenny Gamble was tight with Jimmy Bishop gave him and Huff a leg up in the difficult process of getting a record played on the air. Bishop was "one of the few people that really supported Kenny" by playing his music, recalled Georgie Woods. For that, Gamble and Huff could be thankful. Starting a record label was easy—dozens of new ones popped up each week. But most of them disappeared just as quickly, not so much for lack of a good record but for the lack of exposure and distribution of the product. On its own merit, the Intruders' "Gonna Be Strong" might not have survived the harrowing winnowing process of new releases received daily at WDAS. But Jimmy Bishop played it faithfully, and the song reportedly sold about 20,000 records locally. "It was no big thing," said Huff, "but it got us away."[14]

By 1966, THE AMERICAN CONSENSUS ON CIVIL RIGHTS had disappeared. Fired by younger, more militant leaders and punctuated by the slogans "Black Power" and "White Backlash," the movement entered a new phase. During a demonstration for housing desegregation in a Chicago suburb, Martin Luther King Jr. and his marchers were jeered and assaulted. In Congress, the most recent civil rights act, which would have banned discrimination in private housing, was defeated. Black rioting continued, and Atlanta and other American cities fell victim to the summer conflagrations. As the country's black-white coalition frayed, Muhammad Ali claimed status as a conscientious objector and defied his draft notice. Ali stated that he had no quarrel with the Vietcong, because none of them ever called him "nigger." Having articulated what countless young blacks were thinking, Ali's words helped to set off a firestorm of white protest and made the Vietnam War another target of black frustration.[15]

Unlike the outspoken Ali, Berry Gordy had managed to garner a broad-based racial constituency for Motown Records by diligently sticking to music of an apolitical theme. Likewise, the Gamble and Huff–penned "Gonna Be Strong," which dealt with a failed love affair, was decidedly apolitical. But the unfolding events in American society guaranteed that such a noncommittal stance would be increasingly difficult for them to maintain. Thanks to Bob Dylan, white rock had begun to address social issues. What would soon be categorized as soul music assumed a political bent of its own. This first occurred in 1964, with the Impressions' recording of "Keep on Pushing," and continued into the next year with Sam Cooke's "A Change Is Gonna Come" and Joe Tex's "The Love You Save (May Be Your Own)." The inclusion of social commentary in black music became so prominent that it was spuriously whispered that Martha and the Vandellas' summer blockbuster, "Dancing in the Streets," was a veiled message for blacks to riot.[16]

While Gamble and Huff eschewed the growing voice of black protest, they encountered trouble of a different nature. Not long after the Intruders' "Gonna Be Strong" was issued, the label owners discovered that another record company owned the rights to the Excel name. Perhaps influenced by the Motown steamroller, which now included its founder's eponymous Gordy label, Gamble and Huff renamed their fledgling enterprise Gamble Records. They also moved their company into Jerry Ross's former Schubert Building offices. Then they took the Intruders back to Cameo-Parkway, where the group recorded "(We'll Be) United," which was slated to be the first release on Gamble and Huff's rechristened label. In the song, Little Sonny's quivering falsetto told the story of starry-eyed lovers who were about to be united in marriage. "United," which appeared on *Billboard*'s Hot 100 and R&B chart that summer, fared considerably better than "Gonna Be Strong." That was enough to convince Gamble and Huff that they were headed in the right direction.

Music critic Nelson George wrote that, just as Gamble and Huff's music "echoed Motown[,] in its use of bass, strings, and overall ambiance of upward mobility . . . so did their ambitions." But Gamble and Huff had a considerable way to go to match Motown's formidable stable of recording stars. Seeking to expand their meager artist roster, Huff said that he and Gamble began "hanging out a lot at the clubs every weekend."[17] Gamble and Huff's talent quest netted them a local street-corner group called the Knights and King Arthur, who were responsible for Gamble Records' second release. Remembering those early days, Georgie Woods pointed out that "a lot of guys didn't believe in [Gamble and Huff] at the time, and it was difficult" for Gamble to get his music played anywhere other than on WDAS. That was obviously the case with the Knights and King Arthur's platter, which unceremoniously sank like a stone.

WHILE GAMBLE AND HUFF STRUGGLED TO GAIN A FOOTHOLD in the pop record business, Tommy Bell, as he wrote lead sheets for Cameo-Parkway, continued to hear those original melodies course through his brain. Bell was soon given the opportunity to commit those tunes to wax. It began when Chubby Checker hired Bell to be his musical director and keyboard player. Then, in the spring of 1965, Bernie Lowe, who was dogged by increasingly debilitating poor health, succumbed to a dearth of hits and a sea of red ink and sold his controlling interest in Cameo-Parkway. When Checker and Bell returned from a tour in England, Cameo-Parkway's new management named Bell as the company's resident producer. The title was fools' gold. In-house production at Cameo-Parkway had just about ceased by then, and Bell had scant opportunity to produce anything at all.[18] Bell continued to audition black talent for Cameo-Parkway, but his opinion was not held in high esteem by its new management. "Believe it or not," he recalled, "some good people came through there, but Cameo just wouldn't take 'em." Among those good people were the Delfonics, a vocal group whose soft, sweet, soul sound and Philly falsetto paved the way for Blue Magic, the Chi-Lites, the Moments, the Stylistics, and other tenor-led groups of the early 1970s.

Bell was at Cameo-Parkway one day during the summer of 1966 when he received a telephone call from an unidentified party who wanted to know whether Bell could produce records. "Of course I can!" replied the studio novice. "I got these guys who I'd like to pay you to listen to," announced the caller. Bell told him he did not want to be paid; he would listen to the group and determine whether they had recording potential.[19] The caller was Stan Watson, who was both a product and a survivor of Philadelphia's mean streets. Bell called Watson "a street hustler . . . [who] didn't know anything" about music. Watson derived a good portion of his income from a tow truck, which he used to pursue automobile wrecks pinpointed by surreptitiously listening to police radio calls. But he also owned a small record shop in West Philadelphia. If, indeed, Stan Watson did not know anything about music, he certainly knew enough to seek out someone with pop music experience to pass judgment on his novice vocal group.

The five-member group was called the Orphonics. Recalling their audition, Bell said that one member played guitar, one played bass, one was the drummer, "and the other two sang." Bell was not the least bit impressed after hearing the group's two singers, so he decided to listen to the voices of the other group members. In doing so, Bell discovered that the guitarist, William "Poogie" Hart, had a naturally high soaring tenor startlingly similar to that of Anthony Gourdine, lead singer of Anthony and the Imperials. Bell told Poogie to forget about his guitar, "from now on you're the lead singer." Several other Orphonics, angered over Bell's decision, threatened to leave the group. But Bell would not be cowed. He informed Watson that "the only way I can do anything with these guys" was with Poogie Hart as the lead singer. Watson then turned to his rebellious charges and said: "All you motherfuckers who don't want to do it his way, get the fuck out of here!" Two members of the group did exactly that, leaving Poogie Hart, his brother Wilbur, and Randy Cain to become the Delfonics.[20]

That summer, Bell took the trio into the Cameo-Parkway studio and cut the Poogie Hart–penned "He Don't Really Love You," a medium tempo ballad in which the group's high-pitched harmonies style was introduced. Because Bell did not have enough money to hire any musicians, he played all of the instruments on the record. In doing so, Bell overdubbed each instrument, making a separate recording of each one and then combining the recordings on the master tape. Such a procedure decreased the sharpness of the master recording each time it was repeated, and at one point Joe Tarsia, who engineered the session, told Bell, "Man, if you do this one more time we're not gonna have any sound!" But when "He Don't Really Love You" was finally completed, Cameo-Parkway declined to release it. In a bind, Stan Watson was forced to issue the song on a tiny label that was poorly equipped to promote the record. "He Don't Really Love You" sold well locally, but hardly anybody outside the Philadelphia area heard the song.[21] Bell, whose sparkling studio work with the Delfonics would eventually produce some of the finest examples of Philadelphia's newly evolving sweet soul sound, was downcast over Cameo-Parkway's rejection of "He Don't Really Love You." He "acted like he'd been fired" from the company, said Weldon McDougal.

Stymied in his efforts to produce records, Bell instead began to concentrate on arranging music. Weldon McDougal said Bell had a talent for arranging, "like nobody else. Tommy could write down the string arrangements, the horn arrangements, everything!" (McDougal was so impressed with Bell's skills that he hired him to arrange some sessions for the Larks.) Also appreciative of Bell's arranging prowess was producer Billy Jackson, who, like McDougal, was not a musician. Jackson recognized that Bell had what the producer needed to "translate my music, my ideas" and hired Bell to arrange some of his productions for Columbia Records. Then, as Bell expanded on his budding musical arrangement career, Cameo-Parkway, impressed by the strong local response to "He Don't Really Love You," asked him to produce a new recording by the Delfonics. Bell jumped at the chance. The resulting song, called "You've Been Untrue," got off to a promising start. But the record's strong initial showing was ultimately undermined by Cameo-Parkway's promotional shortcomings and failed to catch on.[22]

As 1967 began, Gamble and Huff endeavored to develop what Gamble described as the "right blend" in their music, something "more sophisticated" than old-school rhythm and blues. They spoke constantly "about how we hoped one day we'd be able to make our living in the music industry. And we dreamed of the day when we could wake up and come to a piano and a tape recorder and write all day long, every day."[23]

Someday, perhaps, but not just yet. For now, Gamble and Huff needed to hustle just to stay afloat, let alone achieve their dream. Huff continued to log an inordinate amount of studio session work, while Gamble opened a modest record shop on South Street. They continued to write and produce music together, and to operate Gamble Records out of their spartan offices in the Schubert Building.[24]

After a somewhat rocky start, Gamble Records, thanks to the Intruders, had achieved a state of fragile equilibrium. The Intruders' "Together," released early that year, actually flirted with *Billboard*'s Top 40. Val Shively, who grew up in Philadelphia and today is one of the world's foremost authorities on vintage R&B records, first met Kenny Gamble around that time. Shively, then in his early twenties, worked for the distributor from whom Gamble purchased the records for his store. "Kenny used to come in each day and pick up the records for his store and we talked about the Intruders' stuff," recalled Shively. He estimated that, by the time "Together" was released, sales on the Intruders' records had progressed to the point where a new release could be expected to sell thirty or forty thousand copies, "just in the eastern corridor." Best of all for Gamble and Huff, almost no promotion work was required from them. Records by the Intruders virtually sold themselves. "I'll take that all day long," Gamble told Shively. "This is my kind of thing, this is very comfortable. I don't want hit records; I just want these things. I can control this."[25]

GAMBLE AND HUFF MAY HAVE BEEN CONTENT with things as they stood, but events would soon conspire to blow the roof off their limited sphere of influence. Having built Gamble Records into the modest success that was envisioned from the outset, Gamble turned his attention to securing a steady production gig. Sometime after the release of "Together," he and Huff were hired as independent producers by a new label in town called Crimson Records. Gamble allegedly offered to sign himself and Huff on as exclusive producers for Crimson. (If so, he should have consulted Huff about the pitfalls of exclusive contracts.) "Put me on the payroll and I'll work just for you," he reportedly told the label owners.[26] But Crimson was not interested in any long-term deal with Gamble and Huff. They were out to capitalize on the musical genre called blue-eyed soul (soul music sung by whites). In an attempt to emulate the success of acts such as the Rascals, the Righteous Brothers, and Mitch Ryder and the Detroit Wheels, the label signed a group of white street punks from New York and Philadelphia known as the Soul Survivors. Radio and TV personality Jerry "The Geator with the Heater" Blavat, who was also one of Crimson's owners, considered the group to be "the blackest white act" in town. The Geator thought that the Soul Survivors and Gamble and Huff were a "perfect pairing," yet all Crimson wanted from the production team was one single.[27]

Gamble later recalled how "people couldn't understand . . . a white artist being produced by so-called 'black' producers." But he and Huff knew the score before they accepted the challenge. Wherever the Soul

Survivors played in Philadelphia, they drew lines of people onto the sidewalk—quite an achievement for a band that had not yet made a record. "That brought our attention," said Gamble. He and Huff were convinced that all the Soul Survivors lacked was a decent song. The recent opening of an expressway through Philadelphia's Center City was still enough of a hot topic of conversation around town to inspire Gamble and Huff to come up with a ditty called "Expressway to Your Heart" for the group. Then they took the Soul Survivors into the Cameo-Parkway studio to record it. Joe Tarsia, who manned the studio board that day, quickly realized that this would not be any run-of-the-mill session. "The whole group mooned me through the control room glass!" he exclaimed. Then, backed by the Romeos (and guitarist Bobby Eli), the Soul Survivors got down to business. As "Expressway" was being recorded, Karl Chambers hammered out a drum beat so pronounced that it could be danced to by anyone with *three* left feet, causing Joe Tarsia to categorize the song as "the closest thing to rock and roll" he ever did. To Gamble, "Expressway to Your Heart" was "soul-influenced pop."[28]

Before "Expressway" was released, the resourceful Tarsia rummaged around the studio and discovered an old sound-effects record that contained honking automobile horns, which he overdubbed onto the master recording. The Soul Survivors' recording—on which the love-struck lead singer pleaded and shouted like the Four Tops' Levi Stubbs about being unable to reach his girlfriend because he was stuck in a traffic jam, was released amid the sweltering heat of August. "Expressway to Your Heart" took off like a shot. By the time the song ran its course, it reached number four on *Billboard*'s Hot 100 and number three on the R&B chart. As the producers of such a blockbuster hit, Gamble and Huff received attention "in the whole industry and not just in the soul market," said a surprised Gamble. If, indeed, Gamble had offered himself to Crimson Records on an exclusive basis, he must have heaved a deep sigh of relief over having narrowly escaped the fix into which he almost put himself and Huff. As the independent producer of a major hit record, a variety of opportunities were certain to come their way.[29]

John Madara and Dave White also profited from the good fortunes of "Expressway to Your Heart." Because of Leon Huff's exclusive song-writing contract with them, Madara and White continued to receive a share of any song that Huff wrote with anybody else. "Expressway" was one such composition of Huff's "that didn't get away," recalled White. When Madara and White parted company in the fall of 1967, citing irreconcilable differences over where their musical interests were headed, most of the duo's publishing went to Madara, who chose to keep Huff on the payroll as a writer. (White got their record company.[30])

It was fortunate for Madara that he kept Huff around. Just before the breakup, Madara and White had produced a medley of "Let the Good Times Roll" and "Feel So Fine" for local singing sensation Bunny Sigler. Released by Cameo-Parkway that summer, the record became a strong crossover hit. That prompted the struggling record company to demand an album from Sigler as soon as possible. With Dave White suddenly out of the picture, Madara turned to Leon Huff to help produce it. Released that September, Sigler's album was one of the last projects Madara and Huff worked on together. After the success of "Expressway to Your Heart," Gamble and Huff finally had enough money to buy out Huff's contract from John Madara.[31] And when they did just that, Gamble and Huff were beholden to nobody but each other for the first time in their young careers.

"Expressway to Your Heart" demonstrated Gamble and Huff's ability to reach pop music's mass audience. What made this feat even more impressive was that it was accomplished during a time when America's racial composition came precariously close to fracturing. Problems of race and war continued to preoccupy the country throughout 1967, as the rate of black progress—too slow for blacks and too fast for whites—satisfied almost no one. In addition, the Vietnam War was now a part of the black agenda. (In New York City, Martin Luther King Jr. led a march of 400,000 to protest the escalating conflict.) America's open racial wounds were brought into focus by Muhammad Ali, who was at the vanguard of the opposition to the controversial war. After Ali was convicted of draft evasion, sentenced to five years in prison, and stripped of his heavyweight boxing title that year, most whites unsympathetically viewed him as a loudmouth shirker who got what he deserved. On the other hand, most blacks saw Ali as a martyr to the cause. White America grew even edgier as the summer rioting—which now seemed to be an annual ritual—was more destructive than that of the previous year. And it did not help matters when the militant Black Panther party began to receive its first national attention in the media.

This volatile mixture of black pride and growing militancy was largely responsible for the development of a new type of music called funk.[32] Funk first began to take shape in James Brown's one-chord work-outs of the mid-1960s, as black artists strove to reclaim their music from invasive white forays, such as the "blue-eyed soul" phenomenon. In an iconoclastic effort that attacked soul's increasing commercialism, funk artists deliberately developed a type of music with rough edges, one inspired more by its inherent value than its monetary reward. Brown's "Papa's Got a Brand New Bag" became funk's archetype. The following year, in 1966, the singer's "I Got You (I Feel Good)" topped the rhythm and blues charts and served notice of the arrival of the genre. Funk was formally categorized early in 1967, with the release of Dyke and the Blazers' "Funky Broadway." That summer, around the same time that James Brown provided another funk milestone with "Cold Sweat," Wilson Pickett enjoyed a huge crossover hit (one that appealed to whites as well as to blacks) with a polished-up version of "Funky Broadway." Ironically, while funk was an attempt by blacks to "darken" their music beyond the grasp of whites, whites took an instant liking to its sound. All of the previously mentioned songs (save for that of Dyke and the Blazers) made the top ten of *Billboard*'s Hot 100 chart—a lofty position that was unattainable without broad white sales.

As funk continued to develop, Gamble and Huff were poised to reap the benefits from the surprise success of "Expressway to Your Heart." Around that time, notable Chicago soul singer Jerry Butler said that he began to take notice of Gamble and Huff, "because they were making interesting music."[33] Working with Butler, that music would soon become far more interesting, interesting enough to enable Gamble, Huff, and Tommy Bell to assume the mantle of command in the development of Philadelphia Soul.

BORN IN 1939, IN SUNFLOWER, MISSISSIPPI, to sharecropper parents, Jerry Butler was three years old when his family moved to Chicago. Years later, while Butler was singing with the Northern Jubilee Gospel Singers and with a secular group, he met fellow-singer Curtis Mayfield. Butler left the groups he was in and, with Mayfield, joined a different vocal group. In 1957, that group became the Impressions. One year later, they signed with Vee Jay Records. Singing with the Impressions, and later on his own, Butler's rich baritone voice garnered no less than eight Top 40 hits between 1958 and 1964. But by 1966, he had gone two years without revisiting the Top 40. To make matters worse, Vee Jay Records was in the throes of bankruptcy.

Butler's luck seemed to take a turn for the better when, that spring, he signed with Chicago's Mercury Records. However, during the recording of the singer's first album for Mercury, he had a falling-out with the producer assigned to work with him on the project. To complete the album Mercury turned to one of its hottest properties, none other than Jerry Ross (who had recently produced Bobby Hebb's million-selling hit, "Sunny"). Butler's album, titled *The Soul Artistry of Jerry Butler*, was released in January 1967, but there was little optimism in the singer's camp when the album's first two singles failed to chart. Butler and Ross returned to the studio and that summer recorded the singer's next single, "Mr. Dream Merchant." But when "Mr. Dream Merchant" languished near the bottom of the sales charts, Jerry Butler's prospects with Mercury seemed no brighter than they had been with Vee Jay. It was then, as Butler and Ross labored to complete the singer's forthcoming album (also titled *Mr. Dream Merchant*), that Gamble and Huff entered the picture.

Gamble and Huff had known Butler since the spring, when the singer visited Philadelphia to perform at Pep's Show Bar. "Kenny and Huff came to the club one night and caught the show," he recalled. "They said, 'Why don't we get together and write some songs?' That was how it started." About the same time that "Mr. Dream Merchant" was recorded, the three of them found time to write a pair of songs together. Recorded in New York and produced by Gamble and Huff, both songs were included on Butler's *Mr. Dream Merchant* album when it was released that November. One of the tunes, "Lost (but Found in the Nick of Time)" was also released as a single just after the album came out. Meanwhile, the "Mr. Dream Merchant" single, which had become the title song on Butler's latest album, belatedly reached *Billboard*'s Top 40. Although this late-blooming hit overshadowed the release of "Lost (but Found in the Nick of Time)," the latter song, one of Jerry Butler's best, had great significance. While writing it, Gamble, Huff, and Butler discovered a creative spark among them. For the moment, Jerry Ross remained as Butler's producer, but Gamble and Huff's time was almost at hand.

While Gamble, Huff, and Butler were discovering that they had a future together, Tommy Bell was taking significant strides of his own. First, he heeded the suggestion of Chubby Checker's road manager and retired the name Tommy in favor of the statelier Thom.[34] Bell thought his new name sounded "kinda cool," but insisted the change "was no big deal. I always felt if somethin' was gonna happen, it wasn't gonna happen because I changed my name, it was gonna happen because I did something good!" And Thom Bell was about to do something exceptionally good.

Near the end of 1967, Cameo-Parkway announced it would soon close its doors. (The company's final records were issued the following January.) That development threw Bell and Stan Watson into a quandary over what to do with the Delfonics. Meanwhile, Bell took the group back to Cameo-Parkway in December, for another recording session. (Despite the demise of the record company, Cameo-Parkway's recording studio remained open to independent producers.) There, the Delfonics recorded the Poogie Hart–Thom Bell composition called "La-La Means I Love You," a dreamy ballad that featured Hart's falsetto lead in front of the Delfonics' high harmony backing. Once again, Bell played most of the instruments on what was essentially a rhythm and strings arrangement. Furthermore, as Bell would do on most of the recordings he produced for the Delfonics, he enhanced the group's sound with additional background voices. When the master recording of "La-La Means I Love You" was completed, Bell knew he had produced something special.

So did Stan Watson, who had enough confidence in "La-La Means I Love You" to form his own record label, Philly Groove, on which the song was released in the Philadelphia area as 1967 ended. In a flash, the record "started exploding" and drew the attention of several large record distributors, recalled Bell. "Everybody was clamoring for it." New York's Amy-Mala-Bell recording and distribution complex came away with the prize, and behind that company's potent national distribution and promotion, "La-La Means I Love You" shot to number four on both the pop charts and the R&B charts. The song became the biggest record that Thom (or Tommy) Bell had ever produced, but he received no satisfaction from the fact that, in terms of sales, his production eclipsed Gamble and Huff's "Expressway to Your Heart." "No, we never had that," maintained Bell. "All the time we were together, we never had any jealousy thing goin' on. Because we all started together, we were all helping each other. There were times that they helped me with a song and times I helped them. . . . We just got down and hustled and did what we loved to do—make music."

Despite such averred camaraderie, Gamble and Bell had not formally worked together on a music-related project since their Kenny and Tommy recording. And when they finally did, Gamble's deep-seated desire to control his relationships and Bell's oppositional passion for independence ensured that there would be speed bumps along the road of success for the lifelong friends.

5
"Cowboys to Girls"
(1968)

I F THERE WAS ONE PARTICULAR YEAR IN WHICH AMERICAN SOCIETY
threatened to disintegrate, that year was 1968. Mired in a increasingly
unpopular war in Vietnam, with any signs of a negotiated settlement
dashed by the Communist-led Tet Offensive in January, President
Johnson told the nation that he would not seek reelection that fall. Weeks
later, a white gunman assassinated Martin Luther King Jr. in Memphis,
igniting black rioting and violence in some 125 cities and causing more
than thirty deaths and thousands of injuries and arrests. That June,
Robert Kennedy—perhaps the only white politician with an enthusiastic
black following—was murdered in Los Angeles. Over 100,000 blacks
and whites marched together in Kennedy's processional, but many
wondered whether nonviolence itself was at an end as subsequent
rioting left forty-six dead. The Democratic Convention, held in Chicago
that summer, symbolized the country's internal bleeding, as antiwar
demonstrators, in full view of the mass media, were beaten mercilessly
by police. That fall, Republican Richard Nixon eked out a narrow victory
over his opponent. To many blacks—90 percent of whom voted
Democratic—Nixon's victory signaled the perpetuation of institutional
racism. While America had always been racially divided, the situation
had not engendered such direct conflict for over a century.[1]

As usual, the composition of the country's popular music reflected
the alienated social state of the nation. All the more remarkable, then,
that, during this antagonistic time, Kenny Gamble and Leon Huff, and
Thom Bell on his own, managed to achieve new heights of commercial
success. Bell was first to accomplish his breakthrough, with "La-La
Means I Love You," but as the year began, Gamble and Huff were yet to
have a significant hit on their own label. The national success of
"Expressway to Your Heart" was an eye-opener of sorts for Gamble and
Huff. The Intruders may have been selling a respectable amount of

records along the Eastern corridor, but when it came to national success, they—and Gamble Records—continued to fly below the radar. If Gamble and Huff could scale such lofty heights on the charts with an unknown pack of brash white boys, why not with a talented R&B group such as the Intruders? The group "could really sing," said Leon Huff. "They could harmonize—it wasn't really hard for us to rehearse them, once they got the parts, they knew the parts. They had the harmony. . . . And Little Sonny had such a unique voice."[2] What the Intruders did not have was a unique song, one to which the masses could relate. "Expressway to Your Heart," based on the universal frustrations of being stuck in traffic and in love, was just that kind of song. The flip side of the Intruder's previous release was "A Love That's Real," a song that made mention of the popular "Jack and Jill" nursery rhyme. For the group's next record, Gamble and Huff expanded on the concept of cherished childhood memories. Focusing on the all-embracing theme of the rites of passage from childhood games to adult love, they wrote a song called "Cowboys to Girls." Believing it to be the ideal vehicle with which to achieve the Intruders' breakthrough, Gamble and Huff pulled out all the stops. In the past, Joe Renzetti (a.k.a."J. Renzy") arranged most of the Intruders' songs. Renzetti was Jerry Ross's man, dating back to the Sapphires and the Dreamlovers productions. Renzetti was also a musician (he played on "The 81"). But he had since become preoccupied with writing arrangements for Jerry Ross's pop productions for Mercury Records (including Bobby Hebb's "Sunny," Jay and the Techniques' "Apples, Peaches, Pumpkin Pie," and Spanky and Our Gang's "Sunday Will Never Be the Same"). To bump the Intruders up another notch, Gamble and Huff now sought a more soulful arranger.

Bobby Martin was astonished to get the call. He knew that Renzetti handled the Intruders' arrangements. What is more, Martin had recently been rebuffed in his quest to get Kenny Gamble to release some recordings that Martin had produced. After Gamble's rebuff, Martin did not expect to hear from him again. Nevertheless, there was Gamble on the telephone: "Martin, I got some work for you," he declared. "I'm recording the Intruders and I want you to do some arranging." "What about Renzetti?" asked Martin. "He's not with me anymore," said Gamble. "Come on over!"[3]

To a degree, the officious Gamble had stalked Martin for the past eight years, beginning when Gamble first appeared as an anonymous teenager at Martin's house in the 1950s. In 1961, Jerry Ross signed a R&B group called the Dreamlovers to a recording contract and hired Martin to arrange what turned out to be their biggest hit, "When We Get Married." Sometime after that, recalled Martin, he began to encounter a "young fella" at the Schubert Building who always made it a point to greet him with an enthusiastic, "Hello Bobby Martin!" The young man's persistence intrigued Martin, who finally asked someone who that "young fella" was. Kenny Gamble, he was told. Because of Gamble's association with Jerry Ross, he was then able to keep a close tab on Martin's professional activities and summon him at the appropriate time.[4]

GAMBLE'S CALL WAS THE BIG BREAK in Martin's lengthy but unheralded career. After touring with Lynn Hope's combo in the 1950s, Martin was hired as artist and repertoire director for Philadelphia's Newtown Records in 1961. Ably assisted by Morris Bailey and Johnny Mobley, he produced Patti Labelle and the Blue Belles' first recordings. But Martin received no production credit from Newtown, and he left there in 1963. Meanwhile, he continued to play his vibes at local gigs and to write arrangements for various artists about town. Martin "had a style" recalled Bailey. "He was really a great arranger and producer . . . probably the greatest horn part writer on the whole planet." Those who worked around Martin were already aware of his considerable talents. After "Cowboys to Girls," the rest of America would know.

"Cowboys to Girls," which was recorded at Cameo-Parkway, afforded Kenny Gamble a chance to demonstrate his resourcefulness in the studio. Joe Tarsia recalled how, at the start of the session, Gamble aimlessly walked by the studio's electric piano and switched it off. As the instrument shut down it made an unusual electrical sound. Gamble took notice of this seemingly innocuous occurrence and incorporated his accidental discovery into "Cowboys to Girls." At a certain break near the end of the song, "where there was a drum fill," said Tarsia, Gamble "turned the piano off and you can hear the sound that it made." Tarsia claimed that was the "first sort of synthesized psychedelic sound" Gamble ever put on a recording.

From the outset, "Cowboys to Girls" was one of those distinguished records destined for greatness. Philadelphia soul chronologist Tony Cummings wrote that Little Sonny's "eccentrically meandering lead was as special a sound as heard in soul that year." The lighthearted romp, released just weeks before the murder of Martin Luther King Jr., offered a stark contrast to the grim days that lay ahead for most blacks. In a matter of weeks "Cowboys to Girls" edged onto *Billboard*'s pop and R&B charts. Perhaps most important, the song was added to the coveted playlist of New York's WABC, which, at the time, boasted the largest radio audience in America. Hundreds of stations across the country routinely waited for WABC to add a record to its playlist before they did likewise. Consequently, the inclusion of a record on ABC's playlist meant guaranteed sales of tens of thousands of records in the metropolitan area alone. Nationwide, the numbers could be expected to reach hundreds of thousands, if not millions.[5] That is exactly what happened to "Cowboys to Girls, which eventually reached number one on *Billboard's* Hot 100 and sold over a million copies.

Gamble, Huff, and Kal Rudman finally had a blockbuster hit on their own record label. Rudman's reported share of the profits (including a buyout he received from Gamble Records) was almost $100,000. He then quit teaching and began to publish a national music industry tip sheet for radio programmers, called the "Friday Morning Quarterback." The FMQ not only became a remarkable moneymaker; it eventually cast Rudman as one of the most influential figures in pop music. For a time, Gamble and Huff profited from their close association with such an eminent music business authority. In time, the cozy relationship would raise eyebrows, but for now Gamble and Huff were in clover. Not only did they finally command a sizable bankroll; to a large extent, the irksome comparisons to Motown's Berry Gordy abated. "Now they accepted what *we* were doing," said Gamble.[6]

"Cowboys to Girls" was also a turning point in the career of Bobby Martin. "Ever since then," he pointed out, "I was [Gamble's] number one arranger." (Martin did not work exclusively for Gamble and Huff; he did so on a freelance basis.) The unassuming Martin slipped effortlessly into Gamble and Huff's harmonious working relationship. The producers would present Martin with a taped demo of an artist, usually accompanied by Huff's piano. Martin then wrote the charts, whereby he "sketch[ed] out the rhythm section, all the breaks and everything. And then, when they went into the studio, I would conduct and Kenny and Huff would fill in what they wanted." During the actual recording, Martin's job was "to keep the beat going, to make sure it was in the pocket. After we'd get the rhythm cut—and we cut some real hot tracks—then Kenny and Huff would put the voices on there." It was then Martin's job to add strings and/or horns to the recording.

WITH THE INTRUDERS AS THEIR SPOKESMEN, and Bobby Martin as their principal arranger, Gamble and Huff now had the power to project their music from their own label rather than from somebody else's. The next step was to corral the musicians needed to develop some kind of signature sound. Up to now, Gamble and Huff had used the Romeos for instrumental accompaniment on most of their productions. Lately, however, with the group members focusing on their individual agendas, the Romeos had become an afterthought to them. By the end of 1966, Win Wilford had moved to New York to pursue a career in modeling and acting. He then commuted to Philadelphia whenever the Romeos recorded. But clearly, the end of the Romeos was near. "The band was just about breaking up," recalled its bass player, whose final gig with them was on "Cowboys to Girls."

Around that time, said Gamble, "we'd begun to settle on a regular bunch of musicians" to use in the studio. They were "the guys who were beginning to mean something in Philly."[7] Those "guys" whom Gamble spoke about were basically the regulars at Frank Virtue's (and sometimes Universal Distributors' 919 studio, which opened up in North Philadelphia early in 1965). Those half-dozen musicians had played on countless recording dates around Philadelphia, dating back to Weldon McDougal's early 1960s' sessions with the Larks. Even Gamble and Huff had used them sporadically. (One of the first records the group cut for Gamble and Huff was an instrumental version of the Intruders' hit "(We'll Be) United." Credited to the "Music Makers," the record was released on Gamble Records in the fall of 1967.)

Oddly enough, it was the musicians' participation in a session for another local producer that convinced them to put Gamble and Huff at the top of their preferred client list. As "Cowboys to Girls" was still climbing the charts, local producer Jesse James and his arranger, Bobby Martin, took singer Cliff Nobles into Virtue's to record a song called "Love Is Alright." When James entered the studio that day he possessed less than the barest of necessities to cut a two-sided single. James had only one song written out. At least he had the *words* written out. The musicians on call for the session quickly worked up a melody for James's lyrics.

After Bobby Martin ran through the countdown, "we just started jammin,'" said guitarist Bobby Eli. Eli's counterpart, Norman Ray Harris, came up with the lead guitar figure, and bassist Ronnie Baker showed drummer Earl Young the changes by nodding his head. As Harris's hypnotic guitar line was brought to the fore, the forceful Young had to restrain his drumming. As would occur so many times in the future with this group, once the rhythm track jelled, a melody was created. And in time, a suitable take of "Love Is Alright" was recorded. Jesse James was so confident the song was a hit that when Frank Virtue asked him about recording a flip side, James replied, "I don't give a shit, man. Use the backing track."[8] Then he left the studio. With that, Bobby Martin and Frank Virtue began to tweak the instrumental track to "Love Is Alright," eventually creating a bass-driven B side they called "The Horse" (named for a popular dance). Both sides of the record were credited to Cliff Nobles and Co.

Not long after "Love Is Alright" was released, the song began to die an undistinguished death. Then a disc jockey in Tampa, Florida, flipped the record and played "The Horse." Within a week, it sold ten thousand copies in Tampa alone. Then "The Horse" broke nationwide, and

Nobles—who did not play an instrument and was not even in the studio when "The Horse" was completed—soon had a two-million-selling hit. The song was a godsend to the absentee vocalist (and to Jesse James), but the same could not be said for the anonymous sidemen who created and played on it. All they received was their modest session fee. "None of us got a dime [extra] for that," recalled vibraphonist Vince Montana Jr.[9] This did not sit right with Bobby Martin. "Cliff and Jesse weren't even there!" he exclaimed. Martin said he "tried to get some [additional] bread" for the actual creators of "The Horse," the band members, but James "wouldn't give me anything."

Although the musicians who created and played on "The Horse" collected only their session fee, they were suddenly in great demand about town. "From then on, we sort of were the guys, the lucky pieces [who were] sought out to play" on most every record recorded in Philadelphia, recalled Montana. "'The Horse' really started it." Jesse James may have gone to the bank on "The Horse," but he "made a bad mistake," said Bobby Martin. After that, "we all swore we wouldn't work with that guy again. Instead of sticking with [James] we went with Gamble and Huff, who dealt straight."[10] (Ironically, it was not Jesse James who was hurt most by the realignment of Virtue's studio musicians to the Gamble and Huff and Bell camps, but rather the Dynodynamics production crew that suffered most by that development. Dynodynamics producer Johnny Stiles recalled how, "once the Philly thing really got under way, the musicians we had been using almost exclusively were being used" by Gamble and Huff and by Bell. "We had to line up and wait our turn."[11])

Guitarist Roland Chambers was the first member of that noted rhythm section to meet Kenny Gamble, but the catalyst in organizing the players into a cohesive unit was Bobby Eli. (Eli can be heard playing guitar on literally hundreds of Philadelphia R&B and soul sessions, and he also produced several notable soul tracks in the 1970s). He was born Eli Tatarsky, to a Jewish family in North Philadelphia, in the early 1940s. When that rapidly changing section of the city became predominantly black, the Tatarskys, unlike most of their white neighbors, chose to stay put. "All my buddies were black," said Eli. "All my experiences were black. And when I started getting into music [his father played the mandolin], that was black, too." Barely into his teens, Tatarsky played guitar for a neighborhood vocal group. Since the name "Tatarsky" was "kinda on the ethnic side," he decided to change it. Tatarsky took Eli as his surname, and then went searching for a new first name. It was the dawn of the 1960s, when young Italian singers were in vogue, especially in Philadelphia. And most of them seemed to be named Bobby something-or-other. From that day on, said the guitarist, "I was known as Bobby Eli."

When Eli turned fifteen, he began writing songs with the father of one of his friends. It was just a matter of time until the guitarist's passion for music led him to the recording studio. Eli's first major gig came in 1961, when Jerry Ross recruited him to play on the Dreamlovers' "When We Get Married." That same year he met Leon Huff at Camden's Roxy Ballroom (Huff was playing with the Lavenders, Eli was in the audience). That night, after the show, "we befriended each other," recalled Eli, who, every so often, would pay a visit to Huff's home in the Camden projects. Eli met Gamble in 1963, but neither Gamble nor Huff realized they both knew the guitarist until 1965. Eli was at Huff's place one evening, rehearsing a vocal group, when Gamble happened to call on the telephone. Huff enthusiastically told his partner about "this bad white dude over here playin' a guitar" and advised Gamble to "check him out." When Gamble discovered who the "bad white dude" was, he and Huff "elected me to be part of their eventual rhythm section," said Eli.[12]

Eli recalled meeting bassist Ronnie Baker "on a gig," at about the same time that the portly guitarist met Gamble. Baker appeared at one of Eli's gigs, "said he was a bass player, and we started to talk." Then they began to hang out at Eli's house, practicing their licks. Those closest to the lighthearted Baker (who died of cancer in 1990) say he was second in stature only to his idol, Motown's famed bass player, James Jamerson. What set Baker apart from other bass players was his peculiar way of playing a bit behind the beat, "to give it a little bit of a pull," explained Eli. Baker "actually made up those bass lines on all the songs" he played on, added the guitarist. "All of them were gems of his." Baker was also the humorist of the group, who "always kept people laughing," recalled Eli. "At the same time, he was studious and dedicated to his craft." It was Eli who secured Baker's first session dates, for local producer Bob Finizio.

Norman Ray Harris (who succumbed to a lifelong heart ailment in 1988) was born in Virginia. (His cousin was soul singer Major Harris.) After moving to Philadelphia, Harris developed an interest in jazz and learned how to play the guitar. Meanwhile his sister began dating Ronnie Baker. When Baker mentioned that he was looking for a guitar player, she suggested her brother. Bobby Eli recalled that Harris had his initials on his guitar. Eli and his friends ribbed him, claiming that the initials actually stood for "No Reading Harris," because, at that time, Harris could not read music. No great matter—in time, Harris would make his mark in the music business, not only in Philadelphia, but the world over. Harris "introduced the jazzy, Wes Montgomery sound to R&B music," said Morris Bailey. Joe Tarsia thought he was "the most soulful guitar player Philadelphia ever had, without question." Sadly, Harris was also plagued with a lifelong heart ailment. "Norman had a bad heart, and yet he had a heart of gold!" exclaimed drummer Charles Collins. "He was one of the greatest people that I've ever met." Norman Harris, Bobby Eli, and Ronnie Baker first played together some time in 1963, on a Dynodynamics-produced session for the Tiffanys. Eli called that session "the starting point" of the renowned Philadelphia rhythm section.

Gamble and Huff's signature sound was rooted in that rhythm section. It began with the masterly thrust and bracing high hat of Earl Young, who came of age on the tough streets of North and West Philadelphia. Young literally drove the vaunted Philadelphia sound. "There was nobody quite like Earl, man," reminisced Bobby Eli. "Nobody!" Eli recalled how the sinewy drummer got so into the music he was playing that he actually grunted in time to the beat. Young received his big break while hanging out at Virtue's studio. When Karl Chambers failed to appear for the recording of Barbara Mason's "Yes, I'm Ready," Young sat in on drums for that historic session and never looked back. "Earl really started sharpening his tools," recalled the Volcanos' Steven Kelly. "Every time he turned around he had a pair of drumsticks in his hands." Young even taught himself how to read music. Young's beat and Baker's bass lines anchored what became Gamble and Huff's rhythm section. Joe Tarsia told how, when Baker played, he wanted to sit right next to the drums "so he could watch Earl Young's foot and lock in with the kick." Young recalled how he, Harris, and Baker "used to play in different little clubs around Philadelphia. We developed our own sound and went on from there." Bobby Eli thought the first gig they played on collectively was a Volcanos session at Virtues, in 1965 (he could not remember which session, but said it was not "Storm Warning").[13]

Rounding out the talented core of rhythm players was percussionist Vince Montana Jr., who was born in South Philadelphia in 1928 and became the elder statesman of the musical contingent. (He was also the last to join, because the Dynodynamics crew, for whom the other members first played, used Jack Ashford whenever they needed a vibraphonist.[14]) Montana's musical career began when, at six years old, he was convinced by his teacher to play the orchestral bells in a school play. From then on, Montana was hooked on music. By the time he was sixteen, Montana attended South Philadelphia High during the day and played the vibes at local dance clubs at night. During the early 1950s, he gravitated to jazz venues and played behind such legends as Charlie Parker, Sarah Vaughan, and Stan Getz. Montana then moved to Las Vegas, where he worked as a vibraphonist and percussionist in the city's big show rooms. Montana returned to Philadelphia in the mid-1950s and started his own dance band. He also began to do a lot of session work. (In 1958, he played vibes on Frankie Avalon's "Venus.") At an early 1960s session for Leon Lovett and Frank Bendinelli, Montana met Leon Huff. He met Kenny Gamble at Cameo-Parkway, while he was doing session work and Gamble was wooing Dee Dee Sharp. In the late 1960s, Montana put in a stint with Mike Douglas's television show band. Then, while doing a session at Frank Virtue's studio, Montana met the other members of the rhythm section and became the final piece to the puzzle. Baker, Roland, Chambers, Eli, Harris, Montana, and Young: "We were the band," recalled the vibraphonist. "We were the guys!"

IN THE SPRING OF 1968, when "Cowboys to Girls" was released, Gamble and Huff began working in earnest with Jerry Butler. The opening came when Jerry Ross, after a dispute with Mercury over creative control of his productions, left the company. Butler informed Mercury that he wanted Gamble and Huff to produce his next album. Mercury agreed, and Gamble, who thought Butler was "a great singer," did not have to be asked twice. Still, Gamble realized that working with Butler on a full-time basis would be a challenge. As he later noted, Butler "was cold, man," and Jerry Ross and his arrangers, Jimmy Wisner and Joe Renzetti, "weren't really getting anywhere with him."[15]

One reason that Gamble and Huff were so adept at reviving the careers of veteran recording artists such as Jerry Butler was that they did not fall into the trap of trying to replicate the artists' past recordings. Gamble and Huff took stock of Jerry Butler's penetrating vocal delivery and wrote to this strength. They also considered Thom Bell's stellar debut with the Delfonics and brought him and Bobby Martin aboard as freelance arrangers. Bell, who, at that point, was a comparative novice at arranging, said that he learned a great deal from Martin about the techniques of employing violins, violas, cellos, and such on recordings. Between them, Martin and Bell freed Jerry Butler from the cloying, overly dramatic productions the singer had been saddled with in the past.

The combined talents of Gamble, Huff, Martin, Bell, and Butler yielded a string of eloquent soul ballads that not only revived Butler's career but also elevated it to new heights. Furthermore, it was on the Butler recordings that the talented producers and arrangers established the components of their hallmark sound: a driving rhythm section replete with potent bass lines, rich, layered arrangements, lush strings, and a distinct female chorus.

The way the three worked together was "like magic—a magic moment for us," said Gamble. "We laughed a lot. We had a lot of fun. We would talk about situations that people would get themselves into in their love life and whatever, and we would write about it." They resumed their erstwhile collaboration and wrote "Never Give You Up" in Gamble and Huff's office. As Huff played the piano, Gamble and Butler worked on the lyrics. Then, said Butler, "Huff and Kenny would come up with concepts and play some chords, and I started singing." Butler claimed that, because the three of them were all fire signs (Butler a Sagittarius, Gamble a Leo, and Huff an Aries), "something fierce [was] ignited" among them. Gamble and Huff, with whom Butler wrote "Hey, Western Union Man," "A Brand New Me," and "Never Give You Up" in one sitting, "brought out my best, when I thought I was giving my best," said the singer.[16]

The three were "perfectionists," said Gamble. They "wouldn't allow one note to be wrong."[17] Bobby Martin, who arranged "Never Give You Up," said it took an entire day to cut that one song. The following day was spent recording it again, because Gamble "wasn't satisfied. He was searchin' for something that we weren't getting," recalled Martin. "I don't know what he was lookin' for, because it all sounded the same to me. But he finally got exactly what he wanted." And what Gamble wanted, the public also seemed to want. "Never Give You Up," Butler's first release of 1968, became the singer's biggest solo hit in almost six years. His follow-up, "Hey, Western Union Man," sold even better.

Jerry Butler was not the only artist with whom Gamble, Huff, and Thom Bell (the latter as a freelance arranger) had success with in 1968. One night that spring, a young Texan named Archie Bell and his group, the Drells, performed at Lauretta's Hi-Hat. At the time, Bell (who is no relation to Thom Bell) and the Drells had a monster dance hit called "Tighten Up" on the charts. Gamble and Huff were in the audience that night, feeling charged by their recent accomplishments with Jerry Butler. After the show, the pair approached Bell in his dressing room and told him that "they would like to produce somethin' on us," recalled the singer. Bell just happened to be in the market for a new song to record.[18] "Tighten Up" had been recorded a year ago. Since then, Bell had been drafted into the army and sent to Germany. (He was currently home on a thirty-day pass.) Meanwhile, "Tighten Up" rose to the top of the pop charts and the R&B charts. But Atlantic Records did not have a follow-up record by the group to release.

Bell said he "didn't know anything" about Gamble and Huff, so he called his manager, who checked with Atlantic Records. Atlantic gave Bell the okay to work with Gamble and Huff, but by the time the producers finished writing Bell's next single, called "I Can't Stop Dancing," Bell had returned to Germany. Gamble and Huff sent a demo of the song to Bell, who listened to it and thought, "Wow man, this is really nice!" With that, he hopped an army transport plane and headed for Atlantic's New York studios to record the song.

Leon Huff considered it an honor to produce at Atlantic's venerable New York studio and admitted to being "thrilled to death" the first time he walked into the legendary room. Huff was aware that he and Gamble "were going into some heavy territory in terms of black music."[19] Accompanied by Gamble and Huff's new rhythm section, Archie Bell laid down the lead vocals to "I Can't Stop Dancing." But when it came time to add the backing vocals, the Drells were nowhere to be found. Instead of using the group, Gamble and Huff became the Drells and sang the backing tracks. (Ostensibly, this was done because of time constraints, which prohibited waiting for the Drells to arrive from wherever they were on the road. Whatever the reason for the Drells' absence, this would not be the last session on which Gamble and Huff chose to forgo a group's backing singers in favor of their own vocals and/or those of other session singers.)

"I Can't Stop Dancing," arranged by Thom Bell, became a Top 10 hit during the summer of 1968, requiring Archie Bell to shuttle back and forth between Germany and New York on three-day passes in order to complete his second album for Atlantic. Gamble and Huff produced several of the tracks (mostly those designated for single release), and the album was then fleshed out with cover versions of recent soul and rhythm and blues hits. As they did on "I Can't Stop Dancing," Gamble and Huff provided the background vocals for the album tracks they produced. That was fine with Archie Bell, who thought Gamble and Huff "were right into the flavor of what the Drells were doin'." Bell's second single off his latest album was the Gamble and Huff–penned "Do the Choo Choo," a Bobby Martin–arranged dance novelty based on a Texas line dance. Later that year, Gamble and Huff produced some tracks for Archie Bell and the Drells' third album, titled *There's Gonna Be a Showdown*. Its title track became Archie Bell and the Drells' third Gamble and Huff-penned dance hit. (The *Showdown* album also contained one of Kenny Gamble's earliest stabs at sociopolitical commentary. "Green Power" was a reminder to children everywhere about the importance of getting an education.)

The association of Archie Bell and Gamble and Huff proved beneficial for both camps. If not for Gamble and Huff, Bell thought he might have been remembered as "one of those artists who had [just] one hit." As for Gamble and Huff, they solidified their relationship with Atlantic Records, a company that would soon send some of its biggest artists to Philadelphia to record under the aegis of the blossoming production duo.

Like Gamble and Huff, Thom Bell was just beginning to hit his stride. Had it not been for "La-La Means I Love You," however, Bell's career would have ended then and there. Some years earlier, Bell promised his wife Sylvia that he would leave the music business if he did not accomplish something significant by the time he turned twenty-five. "La-La Means I Love You" just happened to be released the month Bell reached the quarter-century mark, thus ensuring his continued presence in the music business. The success of "La-La" also caused Amy-Mala-Bell to foot the bills for future recording sessions by the Delfonics. No longer would Bell, in an effort to keep production costs down, have to indulge in copious overdubbing in order to achieve the sound of an entire orchestra.

Just as Jerry Butler clicked at writing songs with Gamble and Huff, Poogie Hart paired nicely with Thom Bell. After the release of "La-La Means I Love You," Bell and Hart became the Delfonic's regular songwriters. Hart said that Bell "was elated" with the songs Hart had written and that the two "developed a relationship." Working together in Stan Watson's tiny office or at Hart's house while Hart's mother fed them, Hart supplied the words to their songs and Bell furnished the melodies. "And that's how we would write," recalled Bell, "he and I at the piano."[20]

Ever since Bell first worked with the Delfonics he had a certain sound in his head that he wanted to duplicate in his arrangements for the group. That sound did not include "blaring trumpets and crap," he emphasized. "I wanted to hear those brassy notes, [but] I wanted to hear them *strong* but soft at the same time.... I kept fooling around and studying and studying and studying, and finally I came up with the French horns." Bell introduced that instrument on the Delfonics' next single, called "I'm Sorry."[21] The song was too similar in tempo and style to "La-La Means I Love You," however, and failed to match the phenomenal success of the Delfonics' first hit. "I'm Sorry" also suffered when the Delfonics' first record, "He Don't Really Love You" (which had been rejected by Cameo-Parkway) was rereleased to capitalize on the popularity of "La-La Means I Love You." "He Don't Really Love You" sold better the second time around, and its reappearance confused enough people so as to diminish sales of the Delfonics' new recording.

For the most part, after Thom Bell recorded "La-La Means I Love You," he began to employ the same musicians on his recordings as Kenny Gamble and Leon Huff did on theirs. But Bell's sessions could not have been more dissimilar to those of Gamble and Huff. They were like "night and day!" exclaimed Joe Tarsia, who engineered those early studio dates. Bell ruled his sessions in the manner of a benevolent dictator. Before he went into the studio to record, he wrote out every note he wanted played. "And it had to be played exactly like it was written," emphasized Bobby Eli. "You dared not deviate," seconded Tarsia. "When the clock struck twelve, it was downbeat, and the charts were all there and people played the music." Earl Young was well aware that playing a session for Bell meant "you read every note on the paper." During one session a fly landed on Young's music sheet and the intensely focused drummer "read the fly as being a note, thinking it was part of the music!" recalled Bobby Eli with a chuckle. That is not to say a Thom Bell recording session was devoid of levity. On the contrary, Bell was a natural jokester, who would continually interrupt the intense proceedings with a joke or two. He also had humorous nicknames for everyone in the studio (such as the short, squat horn player Bell referred to as "Basketball").

Gamble and Huff's sessions were far more inclusive than Bell's. Since they could not write music, they would "essentially come in with chord charts and work out the arrangements with the musicians," said Tarsia. Gamble and Huff sometimes had the musicians write out the charts for a particular song. As the players ran down the charts, they sometimes contributed different figures, such as bass lines and drum patterns. "There was a lot of experimentation going on," said Eli. "Sometimes a song was built entirely around a riff that the rhythm section originated." The first time Archie Bell went into the studio with Gamble and Huff, he was amazed to discover that they "didn't have any basic structure, no music or anything! They would go in there with [some] chord changes written on sheets, [and] slap the stuff down." Norman Harris often worked out his guitar parts as Ronnie Baker developed the bass line. Then, after Earl Young came in on the drums, "they would run it down, trial and error, trial and error, until Gamble heard what he wanted," recalled Tarsia. The musicians in the studio sometimes went through as many as twenty versions of a song before the tape began to roll. (There was, of course, a downside to Gamble and Huff's laxness in the studio. Bobby Eli recalled how when a session was called for ten o'clock in the morning, "by the time everybody started loosening up and getting into the swing of things you probably didn't get going until about twelve or one." Then, said the guitarist, "Gamble and Huff started being late, so, little by little, the musicians sorta wound up coming in later and later, sometimes two or three hours later." Joe Tarsia told how Gamble, Huff, and the musicians would "talk and smoke a cigarette and 'kibitz' a little bit. Then they'd run a tune down and would break for lunch.")

Although Gamble made most of the calls in the studio, Leon Huff and his piano was essential to the recording process. Huff "was very proficient in being a *groove* master," said Bobby Eli. "He came up with a lot of figures that were integrated into his chord patterns, and sometimes I, or Ronnie or different people, would latch onto those figures." (Archie Bell said that when Huff played the piano, "you could hear the whole orchestra.") Huff's creativity aside, it was Gamble who drove the sessions. "Huff set the groove, Gamble set the mood," was how Joe Tarsia saw things. "I always said that Kenny Gamble was a born psychologist. He knew how to get the best out of people. He made everybody *feel* good. He never got mad. He used to sit on a stool in the middle of the studio and say [to the musicians], 'Yeah, yeah, yeah, play that!'" Tarsia said that Huff was "sorta like the bandleader." At Gamble's urging Huff would occasionally "take the reins," but when he did, he tended to "get lost in his creativity."

THE HEADWATERS OF 1960S SOUL HAD, for the most part, been located at Atlantic Records in New York, Stax-Volt in Memphis (Stax formed the Volt label in 1963), and Fame in Muscle Shoals, Alabama. Now Kenny Gamble, Leon Huff and Thom Bell, who recently acquired status as producers who packed a commercial punch, served notice that Philadelphia was a new player in the soul game. Three of that trio's Philadelphia Soul productions appeared on *Billboard*'s Top 40 during the summer of 1968. The Intruders' "(Love Is Like a) Baseball Game)" ("three strikes and you're out!") reprised their breakthrough theme of childhood memories combined with adult experiences. The Delfonics scored with "Break Your Promise," and "Hey, Western Union Man" became the first up-tempo hit of Jerry Butler's career. But at this point Gamble, Huff, and Bell's elegantly tinged urban pop was not readily categorized, which led some critics to doubt the merits of this form of Philadelphia Soul. Morris Bailey called such detractors "one track mind" critics who said that Gamble and Huff's music wasn't "funky enough" and Bell's was "too pretty."

Pretty or not, Thom Bell commanded total artistic control over the Delfonics' blossoming career. With or without the critics' approval, the group's lush ballad sound would soon establish them as reliable Top 40 hit makers. When it came time to record the Delfonics' second album, Amy-Mala-Bell spared no expense, enabling Bell to act like the proverbial kid in a candy shop. Bell brought an entire forty-piece orchestra into the studio, including an odd assortment of oboes, bassoons, flugelhorns and a harp. The album, titled *The Sound of Sexy Soul*, offered a more opulent sound than heard on the Delfonics' debut album. The first single from the new album, "Ready or Not Here I Come (Can't Hide from Love)," contained a lyric that Poogie Hart had written around the familiar childhood phrase, and the song quickly reached the Top 40 ranks.

The Delfonics' new album was recorded at Cameo-Parkway studios. At that time no one was certain how many more recordings would be made there. Cameo-Parkway's new owner, Allen Klein, having engineered the company's takeover the previous year, proceeded to lock

Cameo-Parkway's master recordings in a vault in New York and shut the record company's doors. Klein kept Cameo-Parkway's recording studio open for outside business, but its employees remained at the mercy of its ruthless and predatory owner. Nobody recognized the precariousness of the situation more clearly than did Joe Tarsia, Cameo-Parkway's chief engineer for the past six years. For Tarsia, crunch time arrived with the demise of Cameo-Parkway Records. He quit his job at the studio and set out on his own, without an inkling that this bold move would one day ensure him of a steadfast link not only to the musical legacy of Gamble, Huff, and Bell, but to all of Philadelphia Soul.

Fortunately for Tarsia, the venerable Reco-Art studio, located on the top floor of a two-story building on North Twelfth Street, in Center City, was standing idle at the time. Sound Plus studio had taken over the facility in 1964, but after that studio ceased to function, the entire building became vacant. During the summer of 1968, Tarsia secured a lease on the premises. It is a misconception that the studio Tarsia acquired was second-rate. Granted, the building's primitive steam heating system caused a violent hammering in the pipes, which played havoc with recording sessions. And an air conditioner in the control room wall allowed bothersome outside noises to leak in. Furthermore, an electrical grounding problem with the building's soda machine created a buzz in the electrical system whenever the machine dispensed its product. (Tarsia rigged a red light to the machine, which came on when a recording was being made. The soda machine was not to be used when the light was on.[22])

On the other hand, professionals "liked the sound" obtained at Reco-Art recalled Bobby Eli, who played on many sessions there. "The room itself had a [good] reputation. A lot of hits were recorded there." The studio's vaunted sound was partially a result of its forty-foot-long makeshift echo chamber, which ran alongside the room, parallel to a hallway. The chamber "was part of the charm of the place," said Eli. "You can hear [it] very prevalently on a lot of the early Gamble and Huff productions recorded there, especially on the strings." Reco-Art was a strictly monaural (one-track) facility. In fact, it was that studio's pristine mono recordings that piqued the interest of Tarsia, an ardent advocate of the open, ambient, roomy sound quality Reco-Art so precisely captured.[23]

Joe Tarsia was about to turn thirty-four. Any fear of the risk he was about to undertake was negated by his now-or-never situation. With a paid-off house and car, and a wife and two kids to support, Tarsia said he "rolled the dice" and secured a lease on the entire building. He called his new enterprise Quaker Sound, but quickly decided that that name sounded "too provincial." While he dined at a restaurant one day, Tarsia noticed the Greek alphabet printed on the placemats. The letter Sigma reminded him of a college fraternity atmosphere, and it "sounded high-tech," said the engineer. Tarsia rechristened his studio Sigma Sound. He completely renovated the room, installing an eight-track tape recorder—double what he had worked with at Cameo-Parkway—and a fourteen-input mixing console, which placed Sigma on the cutting edge in sound recording technology. That August, Sigma Sound opened for business.

Years later, Gamble credited Tarsia with being "a tremendous part of our team, [who] was with us from the beginning." But Gamble was not so effusive in 1968. Before committing to use Sigma Sound, he and Huff ran a sound test at the refurbished studio. When it was concluded, they matter-of-factly told Tarsia: "Oh yeah Joe, it sounds good. You got something here. I think we'll give it a try."[24] The opening of Sigma was the final ingredient in the development of Philadelphia Soul, as the studio's eight tracks provided a cleaner, more open quality to the forthcoming recordings of Gamble and Huff. Billy Jackson called Tarsia "the glue that held everything together" for Gamble and Huff. Sigma, said the producer, "personified what black music turned out to be in Philly." Jackson said that Tarsia was Kenny Gamble's "second ear," one of the few people who could say to Gamble, "Hey man, that doesn't sound right. I think you ought to do it again." (Tarsia recalled how "sometimes Kenny would listen to me, sometimes he wouldn't.") Jerry Butler said Tarsia was an "acoustical genius [who] was as much a part of the Philly Sound as any of the writers and producers." (Tarsia modestly insisted that he was simply "in the right place at the right time.")[25]

As HOT AS GAMBLE AND HUFF WERE IN 1968, the Intruders remained the only bankable artists on their record label. The most scrutinized addition to Gamble Records' artist roster that year was Dee Dee Sharp. After her troublesome transition from teen idol to soul diva, Sharp moved from Cameo-Parkway to Atlantic Records in 1966, which turned out a handful of quality rhythm and blues and soul recordings on the company's Atco subsidiary. But Sharp's timing could not have been worse. When she arrived at Atlantic, the company was preoccupied with their other recently signed female soul singer, Aretha Franklin. Accordingly, Sharp's career suffered immeasurably from a lack of promotion by Atlantic. She began to concentrate on her live performances and became one of the first rock and roll singers to play venues such as Las Vegas and Tahoe. After venturing to Europe and the Far East in 1967, Sharp married Kenny Gamble. Then when her recording contract with Atlantic expired, she signed with her new husband's record label. Sharp's debut single (as Dee Dee Sharp Gamble) for

Gamble Records was a strong up-tempo dance number called "What Kind of Lady." Given her recent string of failed releases, however, it was no surprise when that record, which was released during the summer of 1968, did not chart. This latest disappointment did not bode well for Sharp's singing career—or, for that matter, for her marriage to the company's boss.

As Dee Dee Sharp Gamble attempted to return to America's pop charts, the country's black-white rift continued to widen. Martin Luther King's murder had sparked passage of the Open Housing Act, which expanded the antidiscrimination principles previously won to the sale or rental of residential property. But rather than strengthen the movement, this final piece of civil rights legislation of the 1960s helped shatter it. To many whites previously sympathetic to the civil rights movement, it was one thing to allow blacks to vote and to use public facilities. Allowing them to live in white neighborhoods was something else. King's death resulted in a wave of black uprisings and the ascendance of black revolutionaries. (During the Olympic Games in Mexico City that September, some black athletes conducted a "black power" protest by raising gloved fists and bowing their heads on the victory stand as the American national anthem played.)

As America's pop music continued to reflect the nation's divisive mood, the number of pop songs advocating black pride increased, and black music in general developed a harder edge. At Stax, now under the direction of former disc jockey Al Bell, the company's first black executive, artists such as Eddie Floyd and Johnnie Taylor adopted a funkier and grittier sound. The same held true for Atlantic's soul artists, including Sam and Dave, Aretha Franklin and Arthur Conley. But the most dramatic change in black sound occurred at Motown, when Holland-Dozier-Holland acrimoniously left the company in the midst of an ongoing dispute over royalties. It was then that Norman Whitfield, the brash and confident understudy to Holland, Dozier, and Holland, seized his mentors' vacated authority.

Under the tutelage of Whitfield and his writing partner, Barrett Strong, Motown's music became edgier than Smokey Robinson's was and funkier than Holland-Dozier-Holland's was. In October, the pop music world was shocked by the release of the Temptations' latest single. At first listen, the words and the energetic drug rush–simulating instrumentation of "Cloud Nine" seem to indicate a paean to drug use. But a closer listen revealed ambiguous lyrics that neither celebrated nor condemned drugs. A week after "Cloud Nine" hit the streets, Marvin Gaye's "I Heard it through the Grapevine" was rush-released as a single (after a disc jockey played the cut on the radio and it caught on). Ostensibly written about the breakup of a relationship, "Grapevine" had a much deeper meaning. The song was "highly political in its implications [and captured] the late-sixties obsession with rumor, paranoia," wrote Craig Werner in *A Change Is Gonna Come*. Sound of Young America, indeed. Even the judicious Motown had been overtaken by the tumultuous times.[26]

The quaint hippie ethos of love, peace, and harmony managed to linger on in some musical quarters, however. The growing popularity of integrated musical groups such as the Chambers Brothers and Sly and the Family Stone (the latter not only racially integrated, but sexually mixed as well) was viewed by some as a portent of—or perhaps even a vehicle for—eagerly anticipated changes in the broader pattern of race relations. As Martin Luther King was buried and James Brown was branded an Uncle Tom by radical blacks, Sly and the Family Stone offered a panacea: "Dance to the music," they implored, backed by a groove that made it impossible to remain still. Despite the underlying chaos of the Vietnam War, the "Summer of Love," the Black Power movement, and its white backlash counterpart, Sly and the Family Stone managed to evoke high (if naïve) aspirations. "Certainly," Craig Werner wrote of the group, "no musical act presented a more exhilarating image of what America might become."[27]

With this smidgen of newfound optimistic spirit swirling around them, Kenny Gamble, Leon Huff, and Thom Bell spent their days (and a good portion of their nights) at Sigma Sound, working to complete Jerry Butler's *The Ice Man Cometh* album.[28] "Are You Happy," which was intended to be the final single from Butler's album, was released in November and barely edged into the Top 40. At that point, everyone involved in making *The Ice Man Cometh* thought that the album had run its course. But they were seriously mistaken. That bountiful collection of songs contained one more hit, a pop music masterpiece that obliquely promoted the growing black pride movement. The tune was destined to sell a million copies, surpass "Cowboys to Girls" as Gamble and Huff's best-selling composition, and become the biggest hit of Jerry Butler's career. Most significant, it would come to define Gamble and Huff's brand of Philadelphia Soul.

6

"Only the Strong Survive"

(1969)

Kenny Gamble, Leon Huff, and Thom Bell got off to a spectac-
ular start in 1969, when Jerry Butler's "Only the Strong Survive"
sold over a million copies. It was a song that would not have been
written had Butler not heard someone utter the title phrase in a conversation. Butler thought it would make a great topic for a song, and
Gamble and Huff agreed. In what Butler called "one of the most
productive and inspiring writing sessions" the three ever had, they sat
down and wrote the million-seller "Only the Strong Survive."[1]

Thirty-five years since its inception, the unforgettable "Only the
Strong Survive" remains a pop masterpiece, exhibiting all of Gamble and
Huff's musical trademarks. (Amazingly, the song was captured in a
single take. "We went into the studio and Butler had to sing two vocals
and get to the airport and be on a plane in two hours," remembered
Thom Bell. "Man, that joker said, 'turn on the tape.' He knocked out both
the songs in about twenty minutes and was gone!")

The song opens compellingly, with Earl Young's thumping bass drum,
Roland Chambers's cloying guitar work, Vince Montana's ringing vibes,
a crescendo of strings, and, finally, a female chorus. All of this before
Butler even begins to sing his sad tale about the demise of his first
romance—and about his mother's advice that "only the strong survive."
It is a full minute before the Thom Bell/Bobby Martin–arranged song
gallops into its uplifting chorus. The delicate counterplay of strings,
vibes, and guitar during the song's instrumental bridge flaunts Sigma
Sound's cutting-edge capability and Joe Tarsia's penchant for spacey,
elegant sound. Gamble, who throughout his career favored a strong
rhythm backing, was not satisfied employing the standard four or five
musicians here. Instead, he used almost a dozen players, including two
percussionists, two keyboard players, and three guitarists. Tarsia cited
Gamble's penchant for exploiting Sigma's expanded capabilities to their

fullest as he created his diligently layered productions. "It was just massive," exclaimed the Sigma engineer, whose philosophy was that "more" was not necessarily better. (Tarsia, who constantly preached that dictum to Gamble, admitted that Gamble "didn't listen to me much.") Fortunately, Tarsia was able to spread out the final mix of "Only the Strong Survive" across eight tracks.

"Only the Strong Survive" was released as a single in January 1969. It quickly rose to number one on *Billboard*'s R&B charts and to number four on that publication's Hot 100, selling well over a million records in the process. All the more inexplicable then, that the crown jewel of Butler's *The Ice Man Cometh* album was not even slated for single release.[2] Asked how such a gem could be considered mere album filler, Butler laughed. Everyone involved with the song considered it "just an album cut," he revealed. Everyone except the singer's wife, who told her husband in no uncertain terms: "That's a hit song!" Butler laughed harder as he remembered the incident. "Shows you what geniuses we are!"

As Butler's *The Ice Man Cometh* album neared completion, Archie Bell—his military obligation fulfilled—reappeared in Philadelphia, in need of a new album. It was here that Bell got his first taste of Sigma Sound. He said he was "in heaven" recording there. "Those cats were . . . an awesome team!" The results spoke for themselves. Bell's *There's Gonna Be a Showdown* album, released that spring, was arguably the best of his career.

Gamble and Huff had talked the talk. Their work with Archie Bell, the Intruders, and particularly with Jerry Butler showed they could also walk the walk. (Gamble and Huff were nominated for a Grammy Award for their production work on *The Ice Man Cometh* album, and Butler received nominations for Best R&B Song, for "Only the Strong Survive," for Best Album, and for Best R&B Vocalist.) But while there seemed to be no limit to Gamble and Huff's impressive production work for outside artists, the same could not be said of their success with artists signed to Gamble Records. The problem was exemplified by the label's leading artists, the Intruders, who, after their blockbuster hit "Cowboys to Girls," became mired in pop's second echelon. None of the other artists on the Gamble label even came close to *Billboard*'s Hot 100 charts.

This vexing situation became known as "the curse" to Gamble, Huff, and Joe Tarsia. Gamble and Huff "couldn't catch flies with their artists," exclaimed Thom Bell. "Garbage can catch flies, they could not. They just couldn't seem to hit 'em right." But the production duo "knew where they were going," said Tarsia. "If one record was not a hit, they thought the next one would be."

THE YEAR 1969 WAS ONE OF CONTRASTS FOR AMERICA. The country's technological prowess was demonstrated when the Apollo 11 astronauts landed on the moon, while in Cleveland, Ohio, the polluted Cuyahoga River caught fire. On the economic fore, the Dow Jones average plunged and the prime interest rate soared. Indicative of the country's pop culture, half a million young people at the Woodstock festival in upstate New York celebrated what was then hailed as a new musical era of peace, love, and understanding. But less than four months later, that optimistic era abruptly ended when a spectator was stabbed to death at a Rolling Stones concert in California. In addition, America's racial tensions continued to run high. "Black Power had entered every area" of black society, observed Craig Werner.[3] There were demands for the creation of black studies programs at universities across the country, and some civil rights organizations actually began to exclude whites from their ranks.

Little common ground remained for blacks and whites in America. While this rift, to some degree, affected the nation's pop music, a significant number of whites continued to embrace black tunes. At the time, this dynamic seemed irrelevant to Gamble and Huff, who remained on the fringes of the recording industry. The problem with Gamble Records was not so much the quality of the recorded music but what happened to that music *after* it was recorded. Kenny Gamble realized that he and Huff were novices at the business aspect of making and selling music and "really need[ed] a staff of people" to operate their record company successfully. But a paid staff of professionals was a luxury the two could not afford. Gamble and Huff's shoestring operation also fell victim to the evolving pop music business itself. Since the advent of "free-form" FM radio in the mid-1960s, record album sales continued to eat into what had traditionally been a singles-dominated market. But Gamble and Huff were even less successful with their album marketing than they were with selling singles. ("Cowboys to Girls" offered the most striking example of their plight. Although the hit single sold over a million copies, the album of the same title sold dismally.) Perhaps most vexing to Gamble and Huff was that, as black men in a white-dominated industry, they faced the unspoken problem of racism, one that could not be addressed for fear of reprisal. The early victories of the civil rights movement had done little to change the undue racial distribution of economic opportunity and power in the music business. Whites, some overtly racist, continued to own most of the record companies that produced and distributed soul music, and they gave short shrift to struggling young blacks such as Gamble and Huff.[4] With America's racial tensions on the rise, the problem was bound to grow worse.

In an attempt to get more of their records played on the air, Gamble and Huff decided to form a second label, which they called Neptune

Records. Because of the growing impact of album sales on the industry, they sought a well-established company to handle the distribution and promotion of the releases on Neptune. But the decision of which company to select for that task was not to be made in haste. A year earlier, when Atlantic Records' agreement to distribute Stax Records expired, Stax declined to renew the deal. Atlantic then referred Stax to the small print of the original distribution contract. To Stax's surprise, all of the recordings made by that company during the years that the distribution agreement with Atlantic was in effect reverted to Atlantic. Because of this nefarious deal, Stax was forced to begin again from scratch as a record company. Avoiding minefields such as this was an important consideration in Gamble and Huff's search for a distributor.

It was near the end of 1968 when Gamble and Huff ultimately signed a distribution deal with Chess Records, a Chicago-based independent with a long and successful history of marketing records by black artists to a mixed audience. Chess bypassed the industry's traditional distribution system and cobbled out one of its own. It was this distribution web that especially interested Gamble and Huff.[5]

Gamble and Huff were hip to the latest developments in R&B, including Norman Whitfield's weighty Motown productions and Sly Stone's psychedelic black rock. It was their hope that the artists signed to Neptune Records would counterbalance the Intruders' sweet-sounding efforts on Gamble Records. The first artists signed to their new label were a well-traveled trio from Akron, Ohio, called the O'Jays. Gamble and Huff had been interested in the group for a year now, after they were highly touted by the Intruders, who had observed the O'Jays when both groups appeared on the same bill at Harlem's Apollo Theater. Since that time, the O'Jays had become dissatisfied with their record company and invited Gamble and Huff to take in one of their shows. Gamble and Huff were so impressed by Eddie Levert's rugged, penetrating lead vocals and Walter Williams's easy tenor that they signed the O'Jays to a recording deal.

Eddie Levert and Walter Williams had known each other since elementary school in Canton, Ohio. In 1958, while still in high school there, the two began singing gospel tunes on the radio. Gospel soon gave way to rhythm and blues. Levert and Williams recruited William Powell, Bill Isles, and Bobby Massey and formed the Triumphs vocal group. After a name change to the Mascots in 1959, the group cut eight sides for Cincinnati's King Records. (None was released at the time.) The following year, Cleveland disc jockey Eddie O'Jay, a longtime admirer, took the group under his wing and infused their stage act with professionalism. Ostensibly out of gratitude, the group took the name O'Jays.[6] After continuous touring and sporadic recording, in 1963, the O'Jays—now pared down to the trio of Levert, Williams, and Massey—

experienced their first (albeit modest) national chart action with "Lonely Drifter." But it was not until two years later that the group was able to improve on that success (with a revival of Benny Spellman's "Lipstick Traces"). Another two years passed before the O'Jays hit again, this time with "I'll Be Sweeter Tomorrow (than I Was Today)." As in the past, however, the group was unable to sustain even this sporadic success.

The O'Jays' signing with Gamble and Huff did not call for much fanfare. The journeyman group had recorded for half a dozen labels over the previous decade, and with a dozen singles and three albums to their credit, the group had nothing to show for its efforts but one modest hit. The O'Jays' undistinguished recording history was of no concern to Gamble and Huff, however. Focusing instead on the group's revamped dynamic stage performances, they believed they had a winner in the fold.[7]

With Neptune's inaugural release set for the spring in 1969, Gamble and Huff summoned the O'Jays to Sigma Sound to record a tailor-made composition called "One Night Affair." Coarranged by Bobby Martin and Thom Bell, the song bore scant resemblance to the group's previous recordings. Eddie Levert's gritty vocal and Leon Huff's arresting piano dominated the song from its outset. The engaging background vocals deeply immersed in the mix left no room for—indeed, rendered unnecessary—any sweetening by Gamble and Huff's anonymous female studio singers. After hearing the final mix of "One Night Affair," which was one of the best dance records of the year, Eddie Levert said the O'Jays "knew Gamble and Huff were great."[8]

Three decades later, two things stand out about "One Night Affair." One is the now-quaint "free love" hippie ethos openly espoused in Gamble's lyrics. In the song, Eddie Levert, scarred from a broken love affair, tells another woman he has no plans to marry her or even to love her, for that matter. All he wants is a one-night affair. The song's other notable characteristic is the constancy of the up-tempo dance groove that became Gamble and Huff's forte.

Although almost everyone who had a hand in recording "One Night Affair" expected it to be an unmitigated smash, the song drew mixed results. "One Night Affair" appeared on the R&B charts, but handicapped by a ban on airplay imposed by most AM radio stations because of the song's lyrical content, the song failed to score high in *Billboard*'s Hot 100. Additionally, Chess's distribution system, while impressive for an independent, "didn't have the distribution power like Columbia or RCA" had, observed Marshall Chess, the son of label co-owner Leonard Chess.[9] Even worse, Chess Records was no longer the company Gamble and Huff had signed on with. About the same time the Neptune distribution deal was closed, the Chess Brothers sold their recording company to General Recorded Tape (GRT), a California-based company that specialized in manufacturing prerecorded tapes for recording companies such as Chess. GRT, whose primary interest in buying Chess was to enter the recording business itself through the acquisition of the company's back catalog and artist roster, was not the least bit interested in distributing a nondescript R&B label out of Philadelphia. Subsequently, Neptune became lost in the GRT shuffle. "Everything went haywire," said Kenny Gamble. "We were pushed to the side. . . . It was an unfortunate thing for us."[10] Gamble and Huff's disenchantment with Chess deepened after the O'Jays' next single, a more temperate dance number (sans politically incorrect lyrics) called "Branded Bad," failed to chart.

"Branded Bad" was simply a variation of Gamble and Huff's uptempo dance fare, but the single's flip side offered a more insightful example of Gamble's early songwriting. "There Is Someone Waiting Back Home" is set in Vietnam, where a black combatant is sustained each day by the thought of his sweetheart waiting for him back home. The singer tells of doing his "duty" as "a man," going to Vietnam "to defend my home land." While such hawkish sentiment was consistent with the first Vietnam-related pop songs played on AM radio, when "There Is Someone Waiting" was released in 1969, even mainstream rockers had taken to recording antiwar songs. Also, by this time, most blacks had finally recognized their disproportionate representation in the controversial war and become more actively opposed to it. In ghettos across America, the notion of a black man "defending his homeland" by serving in the military in Southeast Asia was not widespread. What, then, was Kenny Gamble, a proud young black man whose beliefs would eventually run closer to those of Elijah Muhammad and the Black Muslims than to Martin Luther King, thinking when he penned his conservative prowar ditty—one of the first black records to tackle the volatile subject of Vietnam?[11] Perhaps Gamble's lyric indicated how he and Huff, young entrepreneurs in an ultraconservative business, endeavored to avoid being labeled black firebrands. Also, beneath Gamble's pop demagoguery and sociopolitical bombast lies the heart and soul of a conservative black capitalist. Toss in the fact that Gamble's younger brother served in the military in Southeast Asia, and the lyrics of "There Is Someone Waiting" may well have reflected his feelings toward the controversial war.

Besides the O'Jays, another artist signed to Neptune Records was Walter "Bunny" Sigler, who had most recently recorded for the now-defunct Cameo-Parkway label. Sigler was born in Philadelphia in 1947, the day after Easter Sunday, with one protruding front tooth—which is how he acquired his sobriquet. Sigler began singing in Sunday school. By the time he was in high school he was already a local sensation, performing at various clubs around town. Sigler briefly joined a vocal group called the Opals, but he reverted to a solo career when the other group members failed to appear for a show one evening and he went on by himself. Sigler's histrionic, emotional style, which included falling to his knees and crying on stage, was a sight to behold. But it was no help to him in the recording studio. Consequently, Sigler, who had been making records since the early 1960s, did not gain national prominence until his "Let the Good Times Roll" and "Feel So Fine" medley, recorded for Cameo-Parkway, became a hit in 1967. But fortune was not yet on Bunny Sigler's side. A year later, Cameo-Parkway closed shop, "and everything stopped at one time," recalled the singer.

After several months of performances in Miami, Sigler, in an attempt to jump start his stalled recording career, returned to Philadelphia and sought out Leon Huff. (Huff had played on Sigler's Cameo-Parkway hit and also helped to produce the spirited singer's ensuing album.) But Sigler still did not control his own destiny. The remnants of Cameo-Parkway, including Sigler's recording contract, now belonged to Allen Klein. Huff, who was recently schooled by John Madara and Dave White on the sanctity of a signed contract, informed Sigler that he would have to wait until his Cameo-Parkway pact expired before he could be signed by anyone else. Despondent and frustrated, Sigler began to hang out in the Schubert Building's narrow halls, where he worked out his frustrations aggressively practicing his martial arts skills. When visitors came up to see Gamble or Huff, invariably they would observe Sigler, who, said the singer, was "out in the halls, kickin' . . . punchin' the walls and stuff." Alarmed over the anxious queries about the "crazy guy" practicing karate out in the hallway, Kenny Gamble told Sigler, "Look, why don't you go on in one of the rooms and try to write with somebody." In a flash, Sigler was inside Gamble and Huff's offices, writing. And when his Cameo-Parkway recording contract expired, he even cut a couple records for Neptune. But those records, like the Neptune label itself, had a limited future.

DESPITE THE DIM PERFORMANCE OF NEPTUNE RECORDS, Gamble and Huff continued to sign artists to their Gamble label, which remained independent of Chess Records. But the contrasting array of new singers signed to Gamble Records failed to raise the label's profile. Nor did the Intruders, who continued to blow hot and cold, equally likely to turn out a flop or a hit. One singer who would eventually make a memorable contribution to Philadelphia Soul was concealed among this stable of unproductive artists. His name was Paul Williams, and he was destined to record one of Gamble and Huff's most enduring hits. But for the moment, Williams was just another struggling young jazz singer. Born in Philadelphia in 1934, Williams gave his first public performance when he was just eleven years old. To avoid confusion with several other performers who shared the same name, when Williams turned sixteen, he changed his to Billy Paul. After gigging with sax luminary Charlie Parker, Paul's jazz-infused musical interests veered further in that direction. He made his first recording in 1955 and then joined the armed forces. Once out of the service, Paul's reputation as a jazz stylist continued to grow. (Bobby Eli likened him to "a combination of Oscar Brown Jr. and Al Jarreau.") In 1967, after Paul met Kenny Gamble at a local nightclub, the singer's career began to get on track. He signed a recording contract with Neptune in 1969, and a self-produced jazz-oriented album of show business standards was released later that year. But Gamble and Huff fared no better marketing Billy Paul's light jazz vocals than they did with their underachieving soul artists. His debut album went virtually unnoticed.

By now, the music of Kenny Gamble, Leon Huff, and Thom Bell (and a growing list of other producers) was recorded at Sigma Sound. This was a most fortuitous development for Joe Tarsia, who recalled that during his studio's first year of operation, "the whole thing literally exploded." Consequently, Tarsia eagerly constructed a second studio, on the ground floor of the building he leased. Intent on keeping Sigma on the cutting edge of recording technology, the sound wizard upgraded his capabilities to sixteen tracks.[12] Sigma's technological advances came just in time for Gamble, Huff, and Bell's next independent production. Atlantic Records, impressed with how the careers of Jerry Butler and (to a lesser extent) Archie Bell had been revived in Philadelphia, sent another of their artists to the City of Brotherly Love. But instead of a black R&B singer, Atlantic dispatched a white Englishwoman named Dusty Springfield, who already had eight Top 40 hits to her credit by the time she arrived at Sigma Sound. A year earlier, Atlantic had shuffled Springfield off to Memphis, where she recorded her soulful *Dusty in Memphis* album. Four singles from that collection charted in 1968, but when a fifth solo try failed to crack *Billboard*'s Hot 100, Atlantic realized it had overreached in milking hits from Springfield's *Memphis* album. After the company "hit the wall with Dusty," said Atlantic producer Jerry Wexler, it was decided to pair her with a new producer. Wexler said the powers at Atlantic "were respectful" of Gamble, Huff, and Bell's recent studio work and decided to "give them a shot."[13]

Springfield's first single cut in Philadelphia, "A Brand New Me," reached number twenty-four on *Billboard*'s Hot 100 that fall. The Thom Bell–arranged song was her biggest hit in a year. But Springfield's *A Brand New Me* album, released in January 1970, was, at best, a moderate success. While Gamble and Huff had a hand in writing all of the album's ten tracks, the pair ceded part of the album's production to some of the underlings in their growing musical organization.[14] Gamble and Huff also uncharacteristically altered their studio recording technique in order to accommodate Thom Bell, who co-wrote a song for the album and wanted to record it in his own preferred manner. "That was the first time Gamble had ever done a live session, with thirty-five, forty guys [inside the studio] all at once," said Bell. "He was scared to death!" Gamble repeatedly asked whether Bell was certain he had written the music correctly. (Bell did not blame Gamble for not trusting him because, at that point, "he actually didn't know how good I was or wasn't.") When the session was completed, Gamble recalled that it had "worked like magic." Remembering that session three decades later, Bell said, "That wasn't any magic, man! Just things I heard."

Jerry Wexler, who had produced some of the tracks for Dusty Spring-field's *Memphis* album (which is considered one of the singer's finest), thought the Philadelphia crew "did a pretty good record, but it was no *Dusty in Memphis.*" Wexler's qualified assessment was on the mark. There was no one outstanding song on *A Brand New Me*. The title track notwithstanding, the songs and mood of *A Brand New Me* bear a pallid sameness.

IN COMPARISON, JERRY BUTLER'S *ICE ON ICE* ALBUM, which the singer described as "our attempt to do another kind of *Ice Man Cometh*," fared much better. There were slight changes from its predecessor, however. The most significant was the prominence afforded the female backup singers employed on the sessions. This was a technique that Gamble, Huff, and Bell employed extensively on future recordings. From a commercial standpoint, it may have been unreasonable to expect *Ice on Ice* to outdo its forerunner, but the album came surprisingly close to doing just that. *Ice on Ice* got off to a fast start when its first single, the bouncy Martin and Bell–arranged "What's the Use of Breaking Up," reached *Billboard*'s top 20.

Despite Jerry Butler's protracted success, as 1969 drew to a close, Gamble and Huff could not rely on the increasing popularity of soul music to put them over the top. On one hand, the songs they had written with Butler (twenty in two years) represented the pinnacle of the soul singer's recording career. And the acceptance of Butler's two Gamble and Huff–produced albums amply demonstrated his crossover appeal to white audiences. Yet there were conflicting signs within the pop music pantheon regarding the future status of soul music. That summer, in deference to the genre's increasing popularity, *Billboard* changed the name of its "Rhythm And Blues" chart to "Soul." But by the fall, the latest word from *Billboard* was that the "stagnancy of soul music coupled with the rapid changeability of pop has left soul by the wayside."[15] As Gamble and

Huff faced the pop music industry's uncertainty about soul music's viability, their success with Jerry Butler also brought to mind "the curse." With albums beginning to exceed singles in terms of total pop market sales, Gamble and Huff were no closer to tapping into that success with their own tiny labels than they had been two or three years earlier.

As the 1970s began, the civil rights movement, in its successful battle to dismantle legal segregation, had inadvertently created new problems among blacks and whites. Advocates of Black Power asserted themselves, and certain factions called for varying degrees of racial separatism (the most extreme being the Nation of Islam, which demanded complete separation from the American mainstream). Black music was now recognized as a potentially revolutionary tool. No longer were record companies fearful of espousing social commentary and exploiting racial pride. In *Just My Soul Responding*, Brian Ward wrote of the coupling of "the new cultural politics of the black power era . . . with a shift in the funding base of the struggle from whites toward blacks." This union, wrote Ward, "meant that activists began to curry the support of soul stars and black music entrepreneurs in a far more systematic and sometimes highly aggressive manner."[16] In such rapidly changing times, Kenny Gamble's Vietnam opus now stood out as an embarrassing anachronism. Furthermore, Gamble found himself in a philosophical bind of sorts. Although he would eventually become increasingly enamored of much of the Nation of Islam's strident racial philosophy, the young writer/producer was not yet in a position whereby he could integrate his evolving social beliefs with his efforts to attract a multiracial audience to his music.

Accordingly, Gamble's fortunes, as well as those of Leon Huff, remained static. The Intruders, in a nether phase of their up-and-down cycle, failed to get their first single release of the year onto the charts. (The good news was that the group was now poised for a hit.) While the Intruders were inconsistent, Gamble and Huff's other artists were nonexistent. Neptune managed to turn out some masterful soul recordings, but none of them became hits. Although Neptune's subservience to GRT contributed to the problem, Gamble and Huff, whose business savvy did not begin to approach their writing talent and studio smarts, had to shoulder their share of the blame for the ineffectiveness of their own record labels. As Nelson George observed, "the balance of creativity and business skill needed to smoothly administer the operations would in fact always elude the pair."[17] At a time in which R&B and soul's traditional powers—Motown, Atlantic, and Stax—were ripe for the taking, Gamble and Huff were treading water as record company executives.

In a broader sense, Gamble and Huff had actually taken a step backward in attaining their goal of owning and operating a viable record label. The pop music business was undergoing a period of corporate consolidation, making it more difficult, if not impossible, for an independent record company to survive. Unlike the early 1960s, when independent labels could wheel and deal for airplay, five major record manufacturers (Columbia, Warner-Seven Arts, RCA Victor, Capitol-EMI, and MGM) now controlled more than half of the pop marketplace. Proof of Gamble and Huff's growing impotence within that structure was evinced by their attempt to boost Neptune's anemic album catalog. Although Billy Paul's second album, a jazz-oriented collection of songs with heavier orchestration and a decidedly more soulful sound than exhibited on his first album, managed to penetrate the R&B charts, it was doomed by Neptune's misfortune. By the summer of 1970, the label was history. Gamble concluded from his overtures to other distributors that "independent distribution was drying up." Unable to pay Neptune's artists, Gamble and Huff let most of them go. Leon Huff was philosophical about Neptune's demise, vowing that he and Gamble "knew there'd come a time when GRT would realize what they'd blown . . . so we just regrouped with what we had already. . . . We knew we could give artists hits if they'd have a little confidence in us."[18]

It was during this already traumatic period that Gamble and Huff's fruitful association with Jerry Butler came to an end. The circumstances surrounding this split remain uncertain. Butler has stated that when he signed a new five-year contract with Mercury in 1970, the record company sought to extend the production agreement they had with Gamble and Huff. However, Gamble and Huff "made the decision that they were not going to record any artists that weren't on their labels because they would be defeating what they would be trying to do," said Butler. Maintaining that he accepted Gamble and Huff's reasoning, Butler insisted they "parted amicably." But his claim that Gamble and Huff no longer wanted to produce artists other than their own is not supported by fact. Shortly after leaving Butler, Gamble and Huff went on to produce several other artists, most notably Wilson Pickett and Joe Simon.[19]

What appears to be more of a factor in Gamble and Huff's ambiguous split from Jerry Butler is plain old-fashioned money. In 1971, Butler's manager claimed that after the singer's two stellar albums with Gamble and Huff, the pair demanded an increase in their production fee from Mercury Records. "Mercury agreed to the first raise since the partnership had been very successful for all concerned," stated Butler's former manager. "But Gamble and Huff came back again and asked for another raise and Mercury refused." In 1974, Gamble told the *New York Times* that it was Butler who had left him and Huff, "for precisely the reason we left other people. He wanted to do his own production; it was a move the Brother felt he had to make. . . . We could dig where he was coming from." Obviously, the split was not an amicable one. In the *Times*'s story, Gamble felt it necessary to boast (truthfully) that Butler had "never been as successful on his own as he was with Gamble and Huff."[20]

Suddenly without the talented artist with whom they had achieved their greatest success, Gamble and Huff were fortunate that Atlantic was more enamored of their work with Dusty Springfield than were the music critics. Atlantic again called Philadelphia, this time wanting to know what Gamble and Huff could do for Wilson Pickett. Born in Alabama in 1941, the twenty-nine-year-old soul-screaming Pickett moved to Detroit in 1955. While residing in the Motor City he sang in various gospel groups before becoming the lead singer of the Falcons R&B group in 1961. When the group disbanded in 1963, Pickett began what turned out to be an impressive string of releases for a small label owned by singer Lloyd Price. In 1964, Atlantic purchased Pickett's contract, after which he reeled off an incredible string of R&B and soul crossover hits. From 1965 through 1967, Pickett had eight Top 10 R&B records (four reached number one), and all of them became pop hits as well. Smitten with this pop success, Pickett began to stray from his soul roots, and by 1969, he applied his screeching style to pop covers, including the Beatles' "Hey Jude," Steppenwolf's "Born to Be Wild," and the Archies' "Sugar, Sugar." The hits continued to roll on, but they no longer approached the blockbusters of his pure soul period. Then, after Pickett's 1970 *Right On!* album was a disappointment, Atlantic decided to move the singer back to his roots—but this time, with an urban edge.

Because Atlantic's recent focus on British rock acts left the company with too many acts to handle, it began employing outside producers. And despite the fact that Gamble and Huff lacked what Jerry Wexler termed Atlantic's "low-down, funky ethos," Wexler knew the producers "were making good records in Philly . . . [so] Kenny and Leon were obvious candidates" to produce Wilson Pickett.

Not long after "The Wicked Pickett" arrived at Gamble and Huff's Schubert Building offices to go over the game plan for his new album, the singer was introduced to Sigma Sound's spanking-new twenty-four-track board. After being told that Gamble and Huff's sessions were extremely relaxed, that the producers would, among other things, sit and tell jokes, the sparing Pickett demanded to know, "Who's payin' for this time?" Leon Huff calmed the excitable singer by assuring him that "we got a deal with the studio" (which, said Tarsia in retrospect, "was an exaggeration"). After that tense exchange, Huff "sat in the booth and stared at me for about three days . . . waiting for me to do something wicked!" said Pickett.[21]

Despite the indifferent results Gamble and Huff received after assigning much of the work on their Dusty Springfield album to their growing stable of subordinates, they did not hesitate to do likewise with Wilson Pickett's album.[22] Bobby Martin was called on to do the album's arrangements. Now a standard practice, strings and horns were added during the "sweetening" process. Although "The Wicked Pickett" accompanied by violins may seem to be a stretch, his Philadelphia album included two string arrangements. One, "Help the Needy," is a double-tracked vocal prototype Philadelphia Soul ballad. The other is the melodious "Days Go By." Lest the presence of violins on Pickett's album cast doubt on his manliness, the singer's familiar braggadocio shines through on the potent dance number, "International Playboy" (on which Pickett blusters how his name is known "in old Hong Kong," where he is "just as famous as egg foo yung.")

Pickett's Philadelphia sessions netted two standout tracks. One was the Gamble and Huff–penned "Engine Number 9 (Get Me Back on Time)," which was also the debut single from Pickett's album. If any particular song demonstrates the collectively creative exhibitionism of the Sigma rhythm section, it is this six-minute-plus gem. Unlike most Gamble and Huff sessions, during which the singers methodically overdubbed their vocals to prerecorded rhythm tracks, Pickett insisted on a bit of spontaneity as he sang. Just before attempting "Engine Number 9," the fidgety singer approached Earl Young and said to the drummer, "Look Earl, I want you to just *groove* with me!"[23] That was just what Young and his compatriots wanted to hear. Pickett is the type of singer "who has to have a good rhythm section," recalled Young. "He just likes to stomp on the floor and tell you to put the groove right there." The Sigma rhythm section was more than up to the task. "That's all you gotta do is tell us to groove with you," added Young. "I really had a good time when he came in."

"Engine Number 9" evolved just as numerous Gamble and Huff compositions had. It was "a spontaneous thing," recalled Joe Tarsia, who engineered the session. "After they got the nucleus they wrote the song, and boom, it was finished!" The rhythm section "sorta started jammin', and started to develop the music," continued Tarsia, and they soon realized they were on to something special. Less than three minutes into the song, Pickett can be heard to declare how he was going to "hold it just a little bit" and let "the boys" work out. That, of course, was the rhythm section's cue to jam. "Everybody was takin' a lead," recalled Tarsia. Bobby Eli contributed what the Sigma engineer called a "wild guitar thing" to the extended instrumental break. Eli, ever the gadget-freak who always had the latest in guitar technology, waited patiently during the recording for the moment he could immortalize the sound created by his latest equipment. Not the neatest person in the world, Eli was seated next to what Tarsia described as "a ball of wire, one thing plugged into another," when Pickett suddenly implored him to, "play that guitar, son!" Tarsia chuckled as he relived the moment. "It was the funniest thing," he said. Eli "literally dove into his pile of wires!" What followed was an almost four-minute improvisation, as the rhythm section, high-lighted by Pickett's guttural vamping, Bobby Eli's stinging fuzz guitar, Ronnie Baker's chest-hammering bass, and Earl Young's bedrock beat, collectively flew by the seat of their funky pants.[24]

The other standout song, which became the second single released from Pickett's album, was "Don't Let the Green Grass Fool You," a spir-ited mid-tempo number whose lyrics were contributed by staff songwriters. In espousing a homespun philosophy, "Green Grass" paid creative homage to "Only the Strong Survive."

When all was said and done, Pickett left Sigma Sound the way he arrived—worried about the recording bill. The final tab was around sixty thousand dollars, "which was unheard of at the time," said Bobby Eli. The hot-tempered soul man, who usually spent about fifteen thousand dollars per album, angrily told Gamble and Huff that he had "never spent so much money on an album before."[25] But if Pickett or Atlantic Records were unhappy with the album's cost, they were mollified by its fate. *Wilson Pickett in Philadelphia* became the artist's biggest album in three years and yielded two substantial hits. That summer, the impromptu "Engine Number 9" became Pickett's biggest hit since his waxing of "Funky Broadway" three years earlier. Then, the album's second single, "Don't Let the Green Grass Fool You," outdid "Engine Number 9." It also became Pickett's first million-selling single.

Gamble and Huff had done it again. This time they injected interest and renewed chart power into the career of Wilson Pickett. Perhaps the person least impressed by Pickett's latest effort was his former producer, Jerry Wexler. Wexler conceded that Gamble and Huff had indeed performed a "pull motor job" on Pickett's career, but he thought that *Wilson Pickett in Philadelphia* did not "compare in essence" to the singer's Muscle Shoals sessions. Perhaps it did not. But it was Leon Huff who offered a more exact opinion of Pickett's Philadelphia sessions, observing that the singer "needed a hit when he came to us, and we gave him a gold record."[26]

Gamble and Huff's memorable sessions with Jerry Butler and with Wilson Pickett showed that they possessed the talent necessary to write and produce commercially successful albums. "Little by little, piece by piece, they made the curve," observed Thom Bell. "And then the circle was complete"—well, almost complete. By the summer of 1970, all Gamble and Huff lacked were the requisite ties to a major record label and its associated marketing and distribution capabilities—provided, that was, that the center of American society held and that black-white relations somehow would begin to approach the level of fellowship exhibited inside the studios of Sigma Sound.

7

"Betcha by Golly, Wow"

(1970–1971)

A s Kenny Gamble and Leon Huff continued to struggle with their own record labels, Thom Bell experienced problems of his own. The bloom was coming off the rose as far as his affiliation with the Delfonics was concerned. The group's second album, released early in 1969, proved disappointing, in both sound and sales. *The Sound of Sexy Soul*, which was recorded at Cameo-Parkway, had to compete with the fuller-sounding arrangements that were now coming out of Sigma Sound and, as a result, sounded flat and outdated even before it was released. The album's lone single, "Ready or Not (Here I Come)," barely made *Billboard*'s Top 40. Bell rushed the Delfonics into Sigma to cut a new single, the up-tempo "Funny Feeling." But when that song fared even worse than did its predecessor, Bell decided to shake things up. Reverting to the familiar relaxed tempo of "La-La Means I Love You," he employed a new vocal pattern for the Delfonics, in which Wilbert Hart's baritone was heard first before it gave way to Poogie's familiar tenor. In addition, "You Got Yours and I'll Get Mine" utilized stronger background vocals than did its predecessors. The song cracked the Top 40 that fall, but Bell, who was also working with Gamble and Huff, was preoccupied with Jerry Butler's forthcoming *Ice on Ice* album and Archie Bell's *There's Gonna Be a Showdown* album. Furthermore, Bell and Bobby Martin were now involved in arranging and producing a local Philadelphia soul trio called the Intrigues (who scored a hit that summer with the falsetto-led ballad "In a Moment"). Consequently, no album of new Delfonics material emerged in 1969.[1]

The Delfonics' "Didn't I (Blow Your Mind This Time)" kicked off 1970 by selling a million copies (and netting the group a Grammy Award for best R&B vocal performance by a group). Nevertheless, Thom Bell's association with the Delfonics began to unravel. William Hart "got a little mixed up, thinking he was the star," recalled Bell. "He wanted to be

Poogie and the Delfonics, all that nonsense!" Things reached the point "where he wouldn't do anything unless it was done his own way." Bell's unhappiness extended beyond the Delfonics to label owner Stan Watson. Under Bell's original agreement with him, Watson's company received three-quarters of the music publishing royalties on the Delfonics songs, and Bell was supposed to receive the balance. But Bell claimed that not only did he never receive his rightful share of the publishing royalties, but Watson also took half of the production credit for the Delfonics' music, after Bell did "all the work." Watson "didn't do anything!" exclaimed Bell. "I don't even remember seeing him in the studio."[2]

The time had come for Thom Bell to move on. The Delfonics' self-titled album, released that spring, was his final collaboration with the group. Stung by his acrimonious experience with Stan Watson, Thom Bell did not produce another record for about a year, concentrating instead on arranging songs "for Gamble and Huff and anyone else who came along."

But despite the unpalatable breakup with the Delfonics, Bell's work with the group left an indelible mark on the sweet sound of Philadelphia soul. "No group in Philadelphia was copied as much as we were," said Poogie Hart, whose refined falsetto, manifested by Bell's sparkling production, enabled the Delfonics to lead the way for the tenor-dominated love ballad groups of the 1970s, including Blue Magic, the Chi-Lites, and the Moments.

BY ALL INDICATIONS, THE FORMATION of Kenny Gamble and Leon Huff's next record label was a product of synchronism. At precisely the time the producers began a quest for their own high-powered label, the music industry made a decision to cultivate the mother lode of American R&B and soul. During the first era of rock and roll, hundreds of independent record companies competed with the handful of major labels for radio airplay. But by 1970, the pop music industry, which had mimicked the American business trend of consolidation, bore a striking resemblance to the pre–rock and roll era. Five major record manufacturers now controlled more than half the market. An additional 35 percent of sales was divided among nearly one hundred smaller companies, while the remaining 10 percent or so was fought over by hundreds of other labels, including Gamble Records. That was not Gamble and Huff's greatest concern, however. Operating an independent record company in a climate of serendipitous immediacy, where product grew obsolete the day it became available to consumers, was akin to playing Russian roulette. Industry-wide, 81 percent of all single releases and 77 percent of all albums issued lost money.[3] In addition, with album sales having now surpassed those of singles, independent companies such as Gamble

Records were forced to focus on the more costly and complicated process of producing and marketing the long players.

At this point, Gamble and Huff needed affiliation with a major label more than ever. Fortunately for them, when it came to soliciting such a company, Gamble and Huff held some bargaining chips. To begin with, their masterful production ability had already resulted in a distinct, fully developed sound. Equally as important, the duo had begun to cultivate inroads to black radio, which was receptive to their unique brand of urban, sophisticated R&B. Finally, Gamble and Huff had managed to retain several of the most promising acts from their now defunct Neptune label.

Even so, Gamble and Huff's greatest advantage in their pursuit of an alliance with a major record company stemmed not from their own accomplishments but from the music industry's recent interest in black popular music. By the end of the 1960s, utilizing the long-play album format, rock had successfully merged with folk and jazz to become a major factor in pop music sales. The same could not be said of rhythm and blues and soul, which, despite a considerable white following, lagged behind rock in adopting the album as its main format. It was only after Motown, Atlantic, and Stax demonstrated that well-promoted black artists, supported by major labels, could deliver the goods—both in the grooves and in company profit margins—that the majors set out to enlarge their album share of the R&B/soul music pie.

In addition to the music industry's hard sales numbers, more sweeping forces motivated the American recording giants actively to pursue a music they had eschewed up to now. Most paramount of these influences was the country's emerging fixation on popular black mores. Although it might initially seem puzzling that America's dominant white society began to exhibit a preoccupation with black culture just when immoderately polarized race relations prevailed, the elements of pop culture suggest otherwise. Most significantly, America's white link to black music, which began during the 1950s, never totally vanished, even during the fractious late 1960s. That kinship was about to be strengthened by the nation's pop culture, a dynamic and revolutionary force that traditionally serves to remove society's traditional barriers, including class and custom.[4] In this case, a white avant-garde hippie counterculture made up of civil rights workers, antiwar demonstrators, and "rich kid radicals" sparked a rising interest in black refinement.

Compelling evidence of this "Black Renaissance" was advanced by network television, heretofore a bastion of white conservatism. In 1969, Bill Cosby employed his gentle sense of humor and philosophy to mollify his blackness and to become the first black to land his own weekly situation comedy. The following year, America first embraced a variety show headlined by a black performer. Comedian Flip Wilson broke Cosby's compliant mold by projecting himself through over-the-top racially stereotyped characters.[5] Wilson's intemperate black caricatures were then eclipsed by the character of George Jefferson, network television's sharp-tongued black neighbor of the bigoted blue-collar worker Archie Bunker, as seen in the groundbreaking comedy series *All in the Family*. The widespread countenance of Jefferson (who was soon given his own TV series) was indicative of society's acceptance of the growing self-esteem among blacks. *All in the Family*'s popularity also showed that whites and blacks were at least willing to admit that fundamental problems existed between the races.

Further indications of white fascination with black pop culture occurred in American film. The dominating image of blacks in cinema cast by Sidney Poitier's ultra-assimilated characters of the 1960s was shattered in 1971, with the release of the low-budget film *Sweet Sweetback's Baaadass Song*. The controversial film defied Poitier's positive-image precept and heralded the changing direction of black cinema and culture. *Sweet Sweetback's Baaadass Song*, which featured a sexy, powerful, and righteously angry black protagonist, paved the way for a series of early 1970s "blaxploitation" films that became extremely popular among blacks and whites alike.

It was no coincidence that around this time of growing interest in black culture, the record business began to view black acts as album artists. The increasing number of black albums that now appeared near the top of the pop charts suggested a growing white audience for black music that was topical, political, and outspoken. In 1969, the release of Stax songwriter/session musician Isaac Hayes's seminal *Hot Buttered Soul* cast the long-playing album as a creative force in R&B and soul. The following year, Stevie Wonder's *Signed Sealed and Delivered* revealed the singer's growing ambition, as well as a more socially relevant attitude for his record company, Motown. By offering extended album tracks on the Temptations' *Cloud Nine* and *Psychedelic Shack* albums, Motown producers Norman Whitfield and Barrett Strong challenged the industry-wide notion that a black album need be nothing more than a collection of singles and nondescript filler.

Rhythm and blues had traditionally been missing in action from network television. The music had endured imperfect representation on Dick Clark's quasi-integrated, nationally televised *American Bandstand* for over a decade, but Clark's show did not even feature black dancers on a regular basis until 1964. Beginning in 1971, however, a nationally syndicated black version of *Bandstand*, called *Soul Train*, appeared and became extremely popular in areas where large black communities existed.

Amid this climate of growing black pride and the increasing white

interest in black music, minority-owned record labels began to network
with black-oriented radio stations and other minority-focused media
outlets in order to build a powerful industry lobby. Then, with backing
from the federal government, blacks began to demand that large white-
owned companies seeking to traffic black cultural product hire more
black executives and workers. In some cases, companies hired entire
departments of minorities to work specifically with black music.
Taking stock of black music's growing crossover appeal, Kenny
Gamble proclaimed that "Philly soul records had the ability to break
big pop if only a company could recognize that situation."[6] It was no
surprise, then, when Gamble and Huff actively began to seek out a
large record company with the financial resources to deliver their
brand of Philadelphia Soul to a mass audience. Or that when the
writer/producers contacted Columbia Records sometime in 1970, that
company was all ears.

Columbia was then the country's leading record manufacturer, with
a history dating to 1889. Over the next fifty years, as Columbia weathered a variety of mergers, ownership changes, and bankruptcies, the
company developed into a dominating, yet vulnerable force in the
recording industry. Columbia emerged from World War II as one of the
big four of the recording business and then cruised effortlessly into the
1950s on an endless sea of middle-of-the-road pop songs, Broadway
show tunes, Hollywood film soundtracks, and a wealth of classical
music. Guided by the rock and roll–loathing head of A&R (artist and
repertoire) Mitch Miller, Columbia thrived as it disdained such lowbrow
music. Things looked even rosier for the company as the 1960s began.
Believing (or at least hoping) that the recent broadcasting payola scandal,
in which some disk jockeys were shown to have accepted bribes to play
certain records, had sounded rock and roll's death knell, radio programmers across the country retooled their formats to favor "good" music.
And for the first time in its history, Columbia garnered a major share of
the recording business sales.[7] But the new industry leader was caught
shorthanded when the Beatles and their British compatriots hit the States
in 1964 and upset the pop apple cart. Columbia then looked to its erudite
president Clive Davis to get the company back on track.

The Broooklyn-born and -bred Davis, who had joined Columbia in
1960 as a corporate attorney, seemed an unlikely candidate to undertake
such a task. Nevertheless, Davis was fortified by an avid personal
interest in the machinations of show business and pop music, which he
had cultivated from the required reading of the show-business bible
Variety for a college course. In 1961, the independent-minded, hard-
driving Harvard Law graduate was named as the company's general
attorney. Then, during an organizational shakeup in 1965, Davis was

Columbia's surprise choice to become administrative vice president. A year later, Davis was named vice president and general manager of the company. By 1967, Davis recognized that Columbia had to expand into rock music in order to survive. He began to stock the company's pop division with rock stars, and two years later, Columbia's sales of rock records jumped from 15 percent of the market to a whopping 60 percent. Still, Columbia lacked the strong black music presence it would need successfully to fend off the company's principal challenger.[8]

The Black Renaissance of the early 1970s and the surprising crossover success of Columbia Records' Sly and the Family Stone (not to mention Aretha Franklin's stunning ascendancy at Atlantic Records after six aimless years with Columbia) changed Columbia's opinion of rhythm and blues and soul music. By 1971, Clive Davis acknowledged "the explosive crossover potential of black music," as exemplified by the likes of Isaac Hayes, Curtis Mayfield, and the Temptations, and formulated a plan to get Columbia on board the soul train. The company would create a separate soul music division, it would sign black artists and producers, and it would seek manufacturing and distribution agreements with independent soul music firms. Late that year, Columbia appointed veteran music business executive Logan Westbrooks, a black, as Director of Special Markets (read "black") and ordered him to "create a black marketing staff to penetrate the black market." It was also around this time that Columbia commissioned "A Study of the Soul Music Environment Prepared for Columbia Records Group," commonly referred to as the *Harvard Report*.[9]

By this time, Columbia was well aware of Gamble and Huff, who had done some independent production work for the company in 1968 for the Vibrations R&B group. While none of the Vibrations songs became a hit, Ron Alexenburg, then head of Columbia's promotion, saw promise in Gamble and Huff. At staff meetings, Alexenburg began to refer to them as "guys who were really having success in the rhythm and blues area."[10] But perhaps because of Gamble and Huff's fruitless Vibrations sessions, Columbia displayed no interest in pursuing the production team. Likewise, Jimmy Wisner, hired by Columbia in 1968, was rebuffed when he suggested to Clive Davis that Davis should make a deal with Gamble and Huff. It was only after Jerry Butler's "Only the Strong Survive" broke big early in 1969 that Davis began to regard Gamble and Huff as a creative force from whom Columbia might benefit.

Although Columbia Records and Gamble and Huff were now mutually attracted to each other, after an initial meeting in 1970, the two parties found themselves at loggerheads. While Gamble and Huff sought to obtain their own record label, backed by Columbia's distribution, Columbia simply wanted to sign Gamble and Huff to a straight staff writing and production contract. But Kenny Gamble, sensing that

Clive Davis "was more excited about starting a relationship with us than we were with him," declined Davis's offer.[11]

The talks almost ended then and there. Ron Alexenburg, who was involved in the negotiations with Gamble and Huff, sensed that the only way the producers were going to make a deal "was through their own label." He lobbied Davis to reconsider his original proposal. On second thought, the concept of a black record company designed to mesh with Columbia's potent marketing and distribution system began to grow more attractive to Davis, who, in his autobiography, affirmed Gamble and Huff's intense dedication and competitiveness, as well as their "creative spark" and "passion." If Columbia signed Gamble and Huff to an exclusive production agreement as part of the package, the company could achieve its initial goal of adding some notable black producers to its roster. Clive Davis recognized that Columbia and Gamble and Huff "had the opportunity to do something great." Gamble and Huff "were ready to make a move," said Ron Alexenburg. "And we delivered!"

It was not exactly a deal made in heaven, but the compromise agreement worked out by Columbia and Gamble and Huff was one from which both parties stood to benefit. The producers' custom label was called Philadelphia International Records. Columbia guaranteed the cash-starved entrepreneurs an advance of $75,000 to produce fifteen singles and $25,000 for each album. Columbia, in turn, got its foot in the R&B and soul music door.

But not everybody thought Kenny Gamble and Leon Huff had made such a wise move throwing in with Columbia. Gamble said he and Huff were told by some that they were "crazy considering going to Columbia, what do they know about soul music?" But Gamble believed that there were "a lot of hip people" at Columbia, a company that was no longer "that old establishment Tin Pan Alley thing."[12] Besides, Gamble and Huff were now looking past the limitations of a strictly black audience. "Kenny wanted to have his music heard," said Ron Alexenburg, "and he didn't care who listened to it."

It was not until February 1971 that Columbia officially announced the creation of Philadelphia International Records (PIR). By then, Gamble and Huff, pressed for additional operating space, had expanded their offices to include the entire sixth floor of the Schubert Building. To tend to the everyday business of their new enterprise, they turned to Earl Shelton, the former administrative head of Cameo-Parkway Records. Shelton was a black man who had worked days at Cameo. To cover his back, Shelton took music education courses at Temple University at night. His schooling soon paid dividends. When Cameo closed up shop, Shelton began teaching music in Camden High School, which is what he was doing when Gamble and Huff offered him the administrative position at Philadelphia International.[13]

Thom Bell had worked at Cameo during the time that Shelton was there. He described the executive as a sharp individual who "knew his stuff." When Shelton ran something, "it was run correctly. You didn't have to worry about anything." Shelton was a loyal and dedicated employee. Bell used to see him "on Christmas Eve, Easter, all times, workin' his backside off" at Philadelphia International. "When everyone else was gone, he would be right there workin'!" Gamble's longtime friend Phil Asbury, also a black man, became Philadelphia International's in-house attorney, while Harry J. Coombs (also black) was named head of promotion. "To a degree," Gamble and Huff ran Philadelphia International as an independent label, qualified Ron Alexenburg. "They had their own creativity, they signed their own artists, they wrote and produced their own music and they came to us with the finished product. They handed it to us, we pressed the records, we distributed 'em, and we funded [promoted] them. They were the ones, with our staff, that got the records started on the radio."

Columbia and Gamble and Huff each displayed optimism over their recent agreement, but in an industry as racially categorized as the pop music business, both parties faced uncertainty. When it came to promoting black music, Columbia had limited experience and few connections within the business. The company placed Philadelphia International Records under the aegis of Logan Westbrooks's Special Markets Division. Columbia initially sought to develop a solid base for Philadelphia International product through black channels and then to broaden the music's appeal. In theory, at least, the plan was a sound one. But Gamble and Huff soon discovered that Columbia's merchandising acumen in promoting black music left a great deal to be desired.

CONTRARY TO COMMON BELIEF, Philadelphia International was not an immediate hit-making machine. The initial series of releases on the new label was decidedly unremarkable, if not immeasurably puzzling. That dubious string began in March 1971, with Philadelphia International's initial single release, a pop ditty called "Arkansas Life" sung by a white, long-haired hippie named Gideon Smith. For the next year, Gamble and Huff's fledgling label released a total of sixteen singles and one album. The songs were sung by a woeful array of unknowns (such as Smith), local shopworn veterans (Bobby Bennett), optimistic wannabes (Johnny Williams), a Tom Jones clone (Dick Jensen), and some familiar standbys (Bunny Sigler and Dee Dee Sharp Gamble). The only Philadelphia International artists to see any chart action during that stretch were the Ebonys, a gritty male-female group discovered by Leon Huff in his old Camden neighborhood. Their emotional thriller, "You're the Reason Why," made the lower half of *Billboard*'s Hot 100 that summer. "You're the Reason Why" was the only one of Philadelphia International's first sixteen releases to reach the white ears so eagerly anticipated by Gamble, Huff, and Columbia Records. (It is unknown whether anybody made the connection that the success of "You're the Reason Why" was because it was the only Philadelphia International single to manifest the Philadelphia Soul sound.) The only Philadelphia International album to generate any interest (or sales) during that span was Billy Paul's *Going East*, a jazz-infused collection of Gamble and Huff–produced songs that barely scratched *Billboard's* Top 200 album chart.

This unremarkable string of early Philadelphia International material was due in part to a lack of attention by Gamble and Huff, who were otherwise preoccupied when their deal with Columbia was struck. Much of their time and energy went to keeping alive their own faltering Gamble Records, which had not (and would never) become more than a promotional vehicle for the Intruders. Gamble and Huff also had a prior commitment to try to resuscitate the career of yet another R&B artist whose recording career had cooled considerably. This time, gospel-turned-soul singer Joe Simon was set to venture to Philadelphia, in hopes of reviving his recording career. Born in Louisiana in 1943, Simon, like so many of his soul brethren, began singing in church. By the 1960s, guided by the legendary Nashville disc jockey John Richbourg, Simon had switched to secular music. Between 1966 and 1970, the soul singer released fifteen singles, each one appearing on the pop and R&B charts. Simon's biggest outing came in 1969, with his number one R&B hit, "The Chokin' Kind." But after Simon's mournful 1971 hit, "Your Turn to Cry" was followed by two middling efforts, John Richbourg enlisted Gamble and Huff to rekindle Simon's lofty chart success.

When Joe Simon arrived at Sigma Sound late that summer, he felt right at home. It was "very nice" working with Gamble and Huff, and everybody "had a great time," recalled the singer.[14] Joe Tarsia, who engineered the sessions, had a different view. He said Simon's sessions seemed to bog down for various reasons. (The recording of "Drowning in the Sea of Love," for instance, began about seven o'clock one evening and continued past two the next morning.) Tarsia was not certain whether the difficulty stemmed from Gamble's exacting creative process or the singer's "inability to get the song." Tarsia and his coworkers also discovered that the Southern-bred Simon preferred the studio to be hot when he recorded. Philadelphia's stifling summer temperatures apparently were not hot enough for Simon, who requested that the heat in the studio be turned on. He then proceeded to don a scarf and overcoat! Meanwhile, jarred from the summer doldrums of inactivity, Sigma's steam heating system began to make a water-hammering sound in the pipes, which interrupted the sensitive recording process. "The studio must have been ninety degrees!" exclaimed Tarsia, who insisted that recording Joe Simon "wasn't an easy experience" for him.

"Drowning in the Sea of Love" was released as a single that September, and became Simon's second million-seller. When Simon's "The Power of Love" was released early in 1972, it became the biggest hit of his career. Triggered by those two singles (both of which evoked Gamble and Huff's standout work with Jerry Butler), Simon's Gamble and Huff–produced album became the biggest of his career.

JOE SIMON'S LATEST ALBUM contained two blockbuster hits, but it also illuminated a weakness of Gamble and Huff that no affiliation with a prestigious record company could remedy. Out of necessity or design, their albums generally produced a paucity of hit-quality songs. When it came to albums, Gamble and Huff's modus operandi seemed to be two tracks that were "killer" and the rest filler. Gamble and Huff occasionally demonstrated the capacity to write a catchy hit song, but that particular flair did not transmit to their overall body of songs. Other than the hit "Expressway to Your Heart," Gamble and Huff did not write (or produce) any of the songs on the Soul Survivors' debut album.[15] Furthermore, the Intruders' once-promising career slowly waned as Gamble and Huff saddled the group with lightweight, juvenile material, in an attempt to come up with another "Cowboys to Girls." Archie Bell's *There's Gonna Be a Showdown* album was arguably the singer's best effort ever, but, other than the title cut, it did not contain another standout track. The two albums Gamble and Huff did with Jerry Butler were anomalies, on which Butler greatly contributed to the quality of the songs. *The O'Jays in Philadelphia* album contained perhaps three memorable numbers (one being the Holland-Dozier-Holland homage, "Deeper in Love with You"), while Dusty Springfield's album tracks are strikingly similar in construction and mood, with nary a standout track among them. Wilson Pickett's *In Philadelphia* album provided yet another case of the producers' "two killer, the rest filler" approach. One of the album's two hits was not written by Gamble and Huff, while the one that was ("Engine Number 9") was ultimately brought to life by Pickett's vamping and the playing of the studio musicians, not by the song's lyric. Likewise, Joe Simon's album contained two outstanding hits and not much else. In a pop music landscape that increasingly catered to albums, Gamble and Huff had not yet demonstrated that, as songwriters, they were in step with the changing times.

While Gamble and Huff's ability to write an album's worth of quality songs remained suspect, their studio mastery continued to shine. As Joe Simon celebrated his return to the best-selling charts, Columbia exercised its right to the production services of their new studio whizzes. Gamble and Huff (and Thom Bell) were paired with the eccentric, Bronx-born singer-songwriter Laura Nyro. At Sigma Sound to record Nyro's *Gonna Be a Miracle*, the producers teamed the plump earth mother goddess with the Philly grit of the R&B/soul trio called Labelle (Patti Labelle, Nona Hendryx, and Sarah Dash). The result was a masterful album of delicately arranged soul covers that was released in the fall of 1971. *Gonna Take a Miracle* fared well enough on the charts to lessen the sting of Gamble and Huff's floundering Philadelphia International record label. But Columbia was about to discover that the Midas touch that Gamble and Huff had unfailingly displayed as they produced records for artists other than their own was not a sure thing.

While Columbia Records waited restlessly for its investment in Philadelphia International to return a dividend, the company presented Gamble and Huff with the most challenging assignment of their promising careers. They were selected to produce the Chambers Brothers, a floundering, enigmatic group that had Columbia at its wit's end. The Chambers Brothers—four gospel-singing blacks from Mississippi and an Irish-American drummer from New York—had been with Columbia since 1966. They had experienced a burst of fame in 1968, with the eleven-minute psychedelic gospel-folk-blues rocker, "Time Has Come Today." Powered by this acid-tinged freak-out song, the Chambers Brothers album from whence the song came became a late-blooming staple of FM rock stations. But since then, the genre-defying hybrid group had defied Columbia's vision of them as a traditional soul band. Meanwhile, black radio perceived the Brothers as condescending Uncle Toms and would not play their records, while the band's core following of white hippies was not large enough to sustain them commercially. Now, almost four years (and three disappointing albums) after their left-field hit, Columbia's patience with its black hippie band had worn thin. If Gamble and Huff were able to return the Chambers Brothers to the charts, the giant record company would feel somewhat exculpated for its as-yet barren Philadelphia International Records deal. So it was that, during the summer of 1971, the Chambers Brothers arrived at Sigma Sound to record an album of spirituals and self-penned message music, to be titled *Oh My God!*

It was a bad mix from the start. The last thing Gamble and Huff wanted was a band intent on singing its own songs and playing its own instruments. The Brothers' first rude surprise came when they were informed that the instrumental tracks for *Oh My God!* would be supplied not by the band but by the Baker, Harris, and Young contingent. Then they discovered that Gamble and Huff had no intention to use any of the songs the Brothers had written for the anticipated album. As anyone familiar with Gamble and Huff's production procedure could have told the Brothers, all the writer/producers wanted from the group were vocal tracks (which Gamble and Huff surely planned to augment, using their regular backup singers).

By the time fall arrived, Columbia did not yet have a Chambers Brothers album in the can. The pairing of Gamble and Huff with the Chambers Brothers "just didn't pan out creatively," recalled Joe Tarsia. The Sigma engineer who recorded those sessions believed that "the chemistry probably wasn't there"; the result was that "nothing happened." Only two tracks had been completed (which Columbia released as a single). The album was eventually completed but was never released in the United States. Soon after that, the group temporarily broke up. But hard feelings toward Gamble and Huff persisted, with Willie Chambers making the provocative claim that Gamble and Huff subsequently transposed many of the ideas they had gleaned from the Chambers Brothers to the O'Jays. "All the stuff the O'Jays did on their early recordings, the direction came from that particular album of ours," said Willie. "Around the time that 'Backstabbers' came out. That's when we were gettin' it in the back," added brother Joe.[16]

The calamitous Chambers Brothers sessions only intensified Columbia's impatience with Gamble and Huff. Columbia not only considered Philadelphia International Records a bust; it questioned Gamble and Huff's highly touted value as staff producers.

UNTIL THE FORMATION OF PHILADELPHIA INTERNATIONAL RECORDS, Thom Bell split his time between producing on his own and working on arrangements and productions with Gamble and Huff. This informal arrangement did not satisfy Kenny Gamble. "Kenny was really trying to get Tommy to be a part of the Philadelphia International team," said Joe Tarsia. If Philadelphia International Records was, indeed, a team, Gamble, who possessed a strong compulsion to orchestrate any and all of the business arrangements he was a party to, was its quarterback. Gamble finally asked whether Bell was interested in working at Philadelphia International on a more formal basis. Assuming that Gamble's offer meant a continuation of their informal working relationship, Bell said he would. To his surprise, Gamble handed him an employee contract to sign.

Thom Bell had not worked full-time with any particular artist since he parted company with the Delfonics. Gamble, who, according to Bell, sought "to tie everybody up, thought maybe I was needy to a point where I would jump at anything." But Bell would have none of Gamble's machinations. "Oh no," he exclaimed. "You don't have enough money for me to be exclusive to you!" But he left the door ajar, telling his longtime friend, "When you guys have a good deal, bring it to me, then we'll go from there."

Thom Bell's spirit of independence was reinforced by the fact that he was about to become the exclusive producer of a new singing group, one

with which he would eclipse the stellar musical milestones he established with the Delfonics. Early in 1971, Bell had received a telephone
call from seasoned record producers Hugo (Peretti) and Luigi (Creatore),
who had just acquired the master recording of a song titled "You're a Big
Girl Now." The song was a throwback to the 1950s style of group
harmony, sung by a new group called the Stylistics.[17] "You're a Big Girl
Now" had been released locally and sold well enough for Avco Embassy
Records to acquire the song for national distribution. When "You're a
Big Girl Now" became a national R&B hit, Avco purchased the Stylistics'
contract and handed the group to Hugo and Luigi. But when it came
time for the Stylistics to record a follow-up record, the group was unable
to come up with anything suitable for release. At that point, Hugo and
Luigi, who had little experience when it came to producing R&B, called
Thom Bell. Bell said he would "take a listen" to the group. During an
audition at Bell's office ("just me, them, at the piano, nothin' else"), the
gifted writer/arranger/producer was unimpressed with what he heard.
"I can't work with these guys," he told Hugo and Luigi. Out of desper-
ation, the Avco staff producers offered Bell carte blanche to do whatever
he thought necessary with the Stylistics. Only because Bell believed lead
singer Russell Thompkins Jr.'s distinctive, nasal high tenor falsetto
(similar to Poogie Hart's) showed great potential did he agree to
produce the group.

It was no coincidence that the Stylistics would record songs in a style
similar to that of the Delfonics. Thom Bell explained how, in order for
him to write or produce for any singer, he first had to be able to imitate
that artist in his mind. "Then I start writing and thinking like them. It's
only because I sing those kind of parts myself that I can do them quite
naturally." Since Bell sang in the same range as Russell Thompkins Jr.
and Poogie Hart, he could imitate them both.

Nevertheless, Thom Bell had his work cut out for him. Because the
Stylistics displayed a raw talent, the producer literally started at the
bottom in his approach to the group. Airrion Love recalled how Bell
initially treated them "like we were total newcomers in the business."[18]
The first thing Bell did was to lower Thompkins's soaring falsetto a
notch, explaining to the lead singer that if he started off high from the
very beginning of a song, "you can't go any higher." Recalling that
exchange many years later, Bell said that bringing Thompkins's voice
down prevented the delicate-voiced singer from straining to sing higher
than he was physically capable of doing.

Bell also recognized that Thompkins's peculiar tonal pitch and near-
frail delivery demanded novel accompaniment. The innovative maestro
thus expanded on the full orchestral arrangements he had utilized so
effectively with the Delfonics, continuing to experiment with instruments

not associated with R&B and soul music. Then, with Thompkins finally able to handle whatever lead vocals Bell threw at him, the producer turned to strengthening the overall sound of the Stylistics so that the group would not be overwhelmed by Bell's elaborate orchestrations.

But before Bell was able to create any music with the Stylistics he needed a new songwriting partner, able to concoct lyrics to his melodious compositions. Bell found that partner in Linda Creed, a twenty-year-old French Jew he met through one of the Delfonics in 1969. Linda Creed was born in Philadelphia in December 1948. She was raised on the confectionery early 1960s pop music of Connie Francis and similar singers, as promulgated by the hometown *American Bandstand*. Then, as a young teen, Creed "was prostrated on the floor" after seeing Smokey Robinson and the Miracles perform on television. "That's music!" she thought. Creed then realized that, musically speaking, she had a lot of catching up to do. Because Creed was about to enter a predominantly black high school, the R&B convert was assured a crash course in the music. Creed was also assured to create whispers among her friends, who, she recalled, "didn't quite understand" her obsession with black music and the people who made it. Creed said she "became very black-oriented, because to know something you have to experience everything and only through feeling that experience can you know what you're talking about." She pestered Delfonic Randy Cain (whom she knew because she cut a record for the same label the Delfonics recorded for) to listen to her poetry. Cain told Thom Bell about it. Bell had no interest in poetry, but, he said, "let me listen to her. Maybe I can turn her into a songwriter." When they first met, Bell asked Creed whether she could write lyrics "to an exact melody." She said she could, so Bell agreed to give it a try. Creed and Bell "just started clicking" as a songwriting team, recalled Stephen "Eppy" Epstein, who would marry Creed in 1972. Bell "really found somebody who could write lyrics to his music, and it was just such a perfect match." The first time the pair worked together, they wrote "(I Wanna Be a) Free Girl," a song Kenny Gamble liked so much that he had Dusty Springfield record it. (Bobby Eli remembered Creed "jumping for joy in the studio, knowing that one of her songs was being recorded.") In fact, the imperious Gamble was so impressed with Creed's work that he hired her as a staff writer for one of his and Huff's publishing companies.[19] Thus began Linda Creed's brilliant, but tragically short, songwriting career.

Despite the instant chemistry between Thom Bell and Linda Creed, their professional relationship initially required a bit of tweaking. When Bell had written with Poogie Hart, the two of them sat side-by-side at the piano as they worked. But that method was not an option for Creed. She "got bored sitting around the office with me working on the melody," said Bell. "She didn't like just sitting at the piano while I'm working out melodies." Bell told Creed to "go home and do what you're gonna do," until he finished the music. When it came to writing the chorus of a song, if Bell knew what he wanted, he would sing it himself. "If I didn't know what I wanted, I'd leave that blank." He then gave the music to Creed, who wrote the lyrics. "And that's exactly how we worked." Once the song was completed Bell introduced it to the Stylistics by singing it to them, as "a point of reference." He emphasized how he would "always sing the song to the artist, or else bring a tape or something. We did better doing it live. I'd sing all the parts and the background."

Thom Bell said that Linda Creed was regarded by her co-workers as "just one of the guys! We never saw her as a real live girl, a female that could be in love and could cry. She was just as rough as any one of us. No one ever called her 'Linda,' not around us. That didn't even *sound* right!" he recalled with a laugh. "She was 'Creed.'" Besides disregarding her gender, nobody who worked at the predominantly black record company ever considered Creed's skin color, either. "She'd been around us so long that no one paid any attention to her," said Bell. "She was just there! You didn't know whether she was white, pink or green! That was just Creed."

Stephen Epstein saw things from a different perspective. Although Bell and Creed did quickly develop a facile working relationship, Epstein said that the pioneering black-white songwriting couple (perhaps the industry's first) "got a lot of criticism, because everybody thought they were having an affair. A lot of people were jealous that here's this little white girl with this black guy." Epstein also claimed that when Bell and Creed traveled to New York City for business-related meetings, she was thought by many to be Bell's white girlfriend. Bell and Creed managed to get past this misperception "by the success of their songs," said Epstein, "And [eventually] everyone realized they really were partners."

As THOM BELL AND LINDA CREED PREPARED to scale new heights with the Stylistics, Kenny Gamble's offer to Bell of a Philadelphia International contract now seemed even more impertinent. In Bell's masterful design, Russell Thompkins Jr. *was* the Stylistics. On most of the group's hits Bell would have Thompkins sing virtually solo. The group then joined in on the chorus, almost as an afterthought. On Bell's initial Stylistics recordings he strengthened the overall group sound with the additional voices of Linda Creed (who aspired to be a singer) and Barbara Ingram. Apparently, the Stylistics countenanced Bell's recording studio design. Baritone Herb Murrell acknowledged that when Bell took the group under his wing, they were young and "didn't know much about the business." Thanks to Bell, the members "all grew," added Murrell, and the producer's experience and knowledge of music "passed onto the group." Tenor Airrion Love said that when the Stylistics first heard the sound that Bell was able to achieve with them, they "were really gassed." Thom Bell's makeover of the Stylistics resulted in "captivating" soul music "that neither excited the listener with deep intensity, nor left him marveling at his mellow coolness," wrote Tony Cummings in *The Sound of Philadelphia*. The music, said Cummings, "came from a remote ethereal world of love, sadness and purity."[20]

The first Creed-Bell composition recorded by the Stylistics was the ballad "Stop, Look, Listen (to Your Heart)." (Bell mixed Russell Thompkins Jr.'s lead vocal so high that the other voices were almost nonexistent.) Released in the spring of 1971, the song became the first in a string of Top 40 hits for the group. Bell's second session with the Stylistics was even more productive. Bell again employed Linda Creed and Barbara Ingram to sing background (while this time he anonymously joined in) on "You Are Everything." With the voices of Thompkins and the two women dominating, that ballad became a Top 10 hit on *Billboard*'s R&B and Hot 100 charts. When the Stylistics' self-titled album was released that fall, the next single, "Betcha by Golly, Wow," bested its predecessor in chart performance and also sold a million copies. The Stylistics' debut album was, in effect, an instant "greatest hits" collection and was ultimately certified gold in its own right. Russell Thompkins Jr.'s "delivery, shimmering style, and brilliant pacing and control temporarily rendered almost every other 'sweet' soul vocalist and group speechless," noted music critic Ron Wynne. "Pretty soon, the Delfonics, Blue Magic, Moments, and others would fight back, but in 1972, everyone was playing catch-up to the Stylistics."[21] Indeed, the group's string of heavenly love songs would eventually net the Stylistics five gold singles and three gold albums, making them the most successful love ballad group of that era.

As Thom Bell excelled with the Stylistics, Gamble and Huff continued to be haunted by "the curse." A full year after Philadelphia International Records was launched, they continued to wallow in the string of nondescript singles released on their Columbia-backed label. In the spring of 1972, the last of the group of fifteen singles for which Columbia paid $75,000 sank unceremoniously. With virtually nothing to show for Columbia's $100,000 investment in Gamble and Huff, the corporate bean counters took stock of the situation. Billy Jackson, who produced records for Columbia at the time, said that the recording company suspected that Gamble and Huff were "fillin' in their obligation" by releasing "all their old masters that they had [previously] made." Since Jackson was from Philadelphia and knew Gamble and Huff, Columbia said to him, "Billy, you gotta go down to Philly and talk to these guys and tell 'em ... [to] start bringin' out hits."[22] And that, said Jackson, was when Gamble and Huff "stopped bringin' that [old] stuff out ... and started makin' records."

In fairness to Gamble and Huff, it must be noted that Columbia Records' inept promotion of black music was part of the reason for the lack of hits on Philadelphia International Records. In fact, while the first series of PIR singles rolled off the production line (and off everybody's radar screen), Kenny Gamble became convinced that Clive Davis did not know the first thing about promoting black records. Gamble, who had a smattering of promotional experience from running Gamble Records, thought he knew what it took to play the game. Gamble "learned that to get your records played, you had to give up a little action," recalled the longtime columnist for Philadelphia's black press, Masco Young. Gamble thus began offering his promotional suggestions to Clive Davis, but the cocksure executive ignored him. At that point, Gamble and Huff demanded a meeting with Davis and attorney Eric Kronfeld. Kronfeld informed Davis that Columbia's vexing producers were frustrated by Columbia's inept promotion and wanted out of their Philadelphia International deal. Davis "was ashen," said Kronfeld. "It was the first time anyone had asked to leave Columbia."[23]

A stunned Clive Davis thus agreed to let Philadelphia International Records promote its own product. To help support the fledgling label's efforts, Davis okayed quarterly payments to Philadelphia International from Columbia Records' parent company, CBS, to be used to promote the releases of their custom label. Now Philadelphia International's promo man Harry Coombs, and his associate Edward Richardson, a colorful and flamboyant character who went by the sobriquet "Lord Gas," had free rein (and bundles of CBS's cash) to attempt to get Gamble and Huff's records played on the radio.[24]

As 1971 ENDED, PHILADELPHIA INTERNATIONAL RECORDS remained a recording company with no stars and no direction. But with Harry Coombs and Lord Gas now handling the floundering company's promotional chores, a dramatic change was in the wind. In just a few months, Philadelphia International Records would begin to produce huge crossover hits and would eventually sell more than ten million records. Gamble and Huff's company would begin to simulate the salad days of Motown itself. But as Kenny Gamble would discover, the cost of that success was very dear.

8

"Love Train"

(1972)

WHATEVER THE INITIAL PROBLEMS WITH PHILADELPHIA International Records were, the regular coterie of studio musicians that Gamble and Huff employed on their recording sessions was not included in them. The core of this endowed group was its rhythm section, "a family [that] worked together and played off of each other," said trombonist Fred Joiner.[1] By now, original players Ronnie Baker, Roland Chambers, Bobby Eli, Norman Harris, Vince Montana, Larry Washington, and Earl Young had been joined by pianist/organist Lenny Pakula and guitarist T. J. Tindall. While this talented group was free to work individually or collectively for whomever they chose, they came to be known as the house band of Kenny Gamble and Leon Huff. (Thom Bell simply regarded them as the best musicians available and hired them accordingly.) Because Gamble and Huff were now responsible for a preponderance of the recording at Sigma Sound, their approval became a prerequisite to playing with what had come to be regarded as Philadelphia's "A-team" of studio players.

The late Larry Washington was the group's percussionist and resident comic. Washington was "the clown, the guy you'd have around to keep everybody laughing," recalled Bobby Eli. The farcical percussionist took pleasure in showing everyone he met a picture of himself waving as he was being carried into an ambulance on a stretcher. "Poor Larry used to catch a lot of flack," said bandmate T. J. Tindall, who remembered Kenny Gamble remarking, "If fish is brain food, Larry ought to eat a whale."[2] Washington may have been the class clown, but he was an integral part of the rhythm section, "the glue that held it all together," thought Bobby Eli. It was Washington's rhythmic play on the congas and bongos that gave the music "that galloping effect, which is part of what made the Philly Sound." Besides being amiable and talented, Washington was always on call. Drummer Charles Collins told how

Washington kept a cot at Sigma Sound. "He'd do a session upstairs and then as they'd listen to the playback he'd come downstairs and play on another date!"

Unlike Larry Washington, Lenny Pakula and T. J. Tindall had to talk their way into the vaunted rhythm section. ("We were white and we had soul, man! That's what they liked about us," was Pakula's reasoning for why he and Tindall were accepted into the group.) The Philadelphia-born and -bred Pakula became proficient on the piano and the Hammond B-3 organ while putting in a stint with the Navy. By 1969, Pakula was looking for a job as a musician. Because Leon Huff, too, was a piano player, Pakula headed for the Schubert Building to talk to him about possible employment. Pakula said that he "didn't know [Gamble and Huff] from Adam," but he loved black music and he knew that the writer/producers had a couple of hit records to their credit by then. "The buzz around town was, these guys were the producers of the future," recalled Pakula. But Huff was reluctant to hire someone off the street, especially the long-haired Pakula, who looked more like he should be auditioning for a job with the Allman Brothers Band. "C'mon man," pleaded Pakula, "I'll play for ya." He did, and Huff liked what he heard. "I sounded black," said the organist. "I was just too in tune with R&B." Not only did Huff agree to use Pakula on some sessions, when Gamble learned that Pakula could read and write music he put him on staff, to write chord charts and do some arranging. "You'll have a future here," Huff told the enthusiastic young organist.[3]

Pakula played on the Intruders' *When We Get Married* album, as well as *Wilson Pickett in Philadelphia*. (He also arranged Pickett's million-selling single, "Don't Let the Green Grass Fool You.") Pakula also played on and arranged songs for Gamble and Huff's albums with Laura Nyro and Joe Simon. Thom Bell took him to California to play on a Nancy Wilson album he produced, and Pakula even produced the very first Philadelphia International single. During those heady first years he became a fast friend with Roland Chambers. "I just loved that life," the organist wistfully recalled three decades later. "What more could you ask for?" Quite a bit more, he would ruefully learn.

Thomas "T. J." Tindall was originally from Trenton, New Jersey. He played guitar in various bands while in high school. After Tindall graduated in 1968, he enrolled in college, but left after a brief stay in order to play his guitar "for a living." ("Basically, I just kind a knew I would end up doing that," he recalled.) In 1969, Tindall moved to Philadelphia, where he joined another band. After cutting an album in 1970, the group split up, leaving Tindall stuck in Philadelphia. One day, Tindall, who was a big R&B devotee, happened to be listening to Wilson Pickett's *In Philadelphia* album. As he usually did whenever he listened to music,

Tindall paid particular attention to the guitar solos. As he listened he thought, "Whoever's doin' this, I can do it better." That, said Tindall, "was kinda the inspiration" for him to go and "bug" Gamble and Huff, "until they gave me a shot."

In 1971, just before the formation of Philadelphia International Records, Tindall began frequenting the offices of Gamble and Huff. Lenny Pakula could have told him what to expect. Gamble and Huff "didn't even want to talk to me because they didn't see any need for a white kid with hair down to the middle of his back to be playin' in their music," recalled Tindall. Nevertheless, the guitarist "hung out for about six months and just kept buggin' 'em and buggin' 'em and buggin' 'em. I think they kinda got a kick out of my persistence, although they really didn't think that it would work musically." But the resolute guitarist eventually got his chance. One day while the Chambers Brothers were recording at Sigma Sound, Roland Chambers (no relation to the Brothers) called Gamble and Huff and said he would not be in for that evening's session. Tindall just happened to be there. He again begged Gamble and Huff for a chance to play. This time, the producers, caught in a pinch, had little to lose in giving Tindall a try. "All right, all right," they told him, "Go home and get your guitar!"[4] Tindall did the session, "and they were real happy with it," he recalled. "That's how it started. I pretty much had to push my way in. I just would not take 'no' for an answer."

With Norman Harris, Roland Chambers, and Bobby Eli already in the fold, the need for a fourth guitar player might be questioned. But each of the four "had a sort of job," explained Tindall. Norman Harris "was responsible for that big, open, like electric acoustic sound, and a lot of the melodies and things like that. Also the octave thing that he did, kinda like that Wes Montgomery sound." Bobby Eli "always had the new toys," continued Tindall. "He would do all the 'wah-wah' stuff, the sound effects, the sitar sounds, the 'chink-chink-chink' and all that stuff. My job was to do fill, like when Teddy [Pendergrass] would sing a line, somebody had to answer that with a melody. That was my job." Tindall thus became a part-time member of the famed Philadelphia rhythm section.[5] The guitarist characterized his tenure with Gamble and Huff as "a blast! Ten years of just one hit after another. How are you not gonna have fun doin' that?"

While the rhythm section was responsible for laying down the music over which a song's vocals would later be overdubbed, two other groups of musicians, playing the horns and the strings, were of equal importance to the Philadelphia Soul sound. Gamble, Huff, and Bell's horn section, which consisted of saxophones, trombones, trumpets, flutes, oboes, and French horns, numbered about ten players. Gamble and Huff's original horn contractor was Sam Reed, a black musician, who also played saxophone on forty or fifty tracks produced by them. Reed was born in South Carolina, but moved to South Philadelphia when he was six. He began playing saxophone in junior high school, and by the time Reed graduated from high school in the 1950s, he was frequenting the local bebop jazz scene, where he worshipped at the heels of Charlie Parker. Like many jazz musicians of that era, Reed moonlighted on R&B sessions to pay the bills. (He can be heard playing sax on the Silhouettes' number-one hit of 1958, "Get a Job.") In the early 1960s, Reed played in the house band at the Uptown Theater. In 1962, he became the leader of that congregation. A year later, when Jackie Wilson appeared in Philadelphia for Labor Day, Reed put together a backing band for him. "That started it," said Reed. He then became the horn contractor for Leroy Lovett and Leon Huff. He met Kenny Gamble and Thom Bell at Cameo-Parkway Records. Gamble "would be in the studio watching the engineers" do their job, recalled Reed. "He knew that I was basically the person to contact to get the horn players around Philly. . . . So I just happened to be in the right place at the right time." From then on, said Reed, whenever Gamble and Huff used horns on a session, "they would basically call me."[6]

"Everything that was played for the horns was pretty much written down," recalled lead trombonist Fred Joiner, who, during his memorable career, has worked with the likes of Count Basie, Duke Ellington, and Cab Calloway. But Gamble and Huff relied on Joiner's expertise to provide "the different nuances and things like that, sounds that they might have wanted [but] they couldn't explain." Joiner, who was born and raised in North Philadelphia, developed an interest in orchestral music in junior high school. After hearing members of the Philadelphia Orchestra play there, he began studying the trombone. Because Joiner "just loved music that much," every Saturday he toted his horn about twenty blocks to attend music lessons. After graduating from high school in the late 1950s, Joiner wanted to play in the Philadelphia Orchestra, so he began taking private lessons with a member of that notable symphony. Although an extremely talented trombonist, Joiner was advised by his tutor to look elsewhere to apply his musical "gift"—he would not be admitted to the orchestra because he was black. The eighteen-year-old Joiner was "shattered" to the extent that he put his beloved trombone aside and joined the military. But when his hitch was up, he returned to Philadelphia and began hanging around with "the cats that were playing jazz in the clubs." Joiner also landed a job in the Uptown Theater's band, where he met Sam Reed. Reed was "very instrumental" in getting Joiner started in the business, said the trombonist.[7]

Another regular trombonist of Gamble, Huff, and Bell was Richard Genovese, who proudly declared that he played on everything in Philadelphia "that was ever done with horns on it." Genovese has also been an executive in the musicians' local since the 1960s. Two major factors played a part in his decision to become a musician. The first was the high school he attended. Born and raised in Philadelphia, Genovese attended South Philly High, a font for pop music luminaries running the gamut from Mario Lanza to Eddie Fisher to Frankie Avalon and Fabian. But Genovese's foremost influence on his decision to become a musician was his family. His father and three of his eight siblings were musicians. "So that's how it started," he chuckled, "a family of musicians, livin' in a row home in South Philadelphia." Genovese began playing the trombone at South Philly High. After graduation, he attended Philadelphia's prestigious and exclusive Curtis Institute music academy. He then began a mix of Broadway gigs and studio session work.[8]

The horn section's lead French horn player was Joe DeAngelis, former teen idol wannabe Joe "Damiano" and younger brother of producer Peter DeAngelis. Joe DeAngelis "was *the* French horn player," exclaimed Richard Genovese. "Joe was *primo*, one of the best! We never heard Joe crack a note."[9] Jack Faith, who also arranged and produced for Philadelphia International, was the group's flute and (sometimes) alto-sax player. Leon "Zack" Zachary was the horn section's principal alto saxophonist. Zachary was the elder statesman of the group. He was a big band veteran who "played with Lionel Hampton [and] . . . sat in with Basie," attested Fred Joiner. "He's an excellent, master musician."

Sam Reed continued as Gamble and Huff's horn contractor after Philadelphia International Records was formed, calling on "the very same guys" he had been hiring for years. But in 1972, just as Philadelphia International was ready to hit its stride, Reed abruptly moved from Philadelphia to California, and Don Renaldo took over Reed's horn contracting duties.[10]

Don Renaldo (born Vincent Pignotti), a tough-looking Italian-American, also played first violin on Gamble and Huff's recordings.[11] "That cat was one of the best fiddle players in the country," said Thom Bell, a kindred spirit of sorts. (While attempting to break into the music business Renaldo and Bell had both been shunned because of their ethnic backgrounds. Renaldo experienced the vestiges of virulent anti-Italian sentiment that developed in Philadelphia during a massive influx of Italian immigrants to that city in the late 1800s.) Renaldo "was a fantastic musician, top shelf, number one chair, man," exclaimed Bell. "There were very few people that could outplay this dude." Exactly when Renaldo (now deceased) joined the local R&B recording scene is uncertain. Weldon McDougal claimed that he used Renaldo on Barbara Mason's historic recording of "Yes, I'm Ready," which was made at a time when Renaldo was primarily working the local club and wedding scene. According to McDougal, it was then that Kenny Gamble first heard Don Renaldo play, after which Gamble, too, began using the virtuoso violinist on his sessions. But Russell Faith, who overdubbed the strings on "Yes, I'm Ready," said that Renaldo did not play on that recording. (Faith said that he used string players from what was then called the "Jewish Mafia" on "Yes, I'm Ready.") He thought Renaldo did not enter the local R&B recording scene until sometime later, most likely when Sigma Sound opened in 1968.[12]

Don Renaldo was an excellent choice to become contractor for Gamble, Huff, and Bell's string contingent of about a dozen (including a harpist), many of whom played with the Philadelphia Orchestra. Not only was Renaldo a gifted musician, but like Richard Genovese, he was also a member of the executive board of the Philadelphia chapter of the musician's union. As such, Renaldo had primary access to all the city's musicians. He "became the man to contact if you wanted some string players," said Sam Reed.

Being a studio musician for Gamble, Huff, and Bell was a coveted job among Philadelphia's session players. When Philadelphia International Records was formed, union scale for session musicians was sixty-five dollars for a three-hour minimum. "Which, believe it or not, was very good money back then," declared Richard Genovese. "That really paid the most money for the least amount of time that you had to put in." It was more money then a musician could earn playing a three-hour theater or club gig. Furthermore, a heftier percentage of the musicians' session wages (as compared with theater or club wages) were contributed to the union retirement fund. And, added Genovese, the job "was prestigious. The studio musician was like the highest you went. It was the ultimate goal." Gamble, Huff, and Bell's players always had as much work as they wanted. In addition to the sessions of the Big Three producers in town, out-of-town producers would come into Philadelphia to make a record and would ask for the same musicians whom Gamble, Huff, and Bell used on their recordings. "There were times we were in that studio like maybe five days a week, or more, doing things," recalled Genovese. He and his fellow musicians often turned down theater and show gigs or took them only on the condition that they could be absent on days that they had a recording session to do.[13]

The full complement of rhythm, horns, and strings was "an interesting combination," said Bobby Eli. Members of the heterogeneous group were classically trained or self-taught and ranged in age from young to old. Some were streetwise, others staid. Some were slim, while others were paunchy. By the time Philadelphia International Records was formed, this elite group of studio musicians also comprised "a good mix" of black and white, noted Fred Joiner. In an era of pervasive racial disharmony, there was no antagonism among these musicians. "Not at all!" exclaimed Eli. "We were the tightest of tight!"

Leon Huff and Kenny Gamble in a rare shot, without their "game faces." (Photo courtesy of W. McDougal)

Thom Bell
in the 1970s.
(Photo
courtesy of
W. McDougal)

The Philadelphia International Records building, 309 South Broad Street, Philadelphia. (Photo courtesy of W. McDougal)

Thom Bell in the studio with the Stylistics, ca. 1972. Russell Thompkins is on the far right. (Photo courtesy of John A. Jackson)

Weldon McDougal, mid-1970s, with the logo he designed for Philadelphia International Records. (Photo courtesy of W. McDougal)

In the studio at Sigma Sound. *Left to right*: Owner/engineer Joe Tarsia, Leon Huff, Lou Rawls, Kenny Gamble. (Photo courtesy of W. McDougal)

MFSB: The musicians who made the music. Bass player Ronnie Baker is at the extreme left. Percussionist Larry Washington and guitarist Norman Harris are kneeling in front. Drummer Early Young is sitting on his drum. Bobby Martin is standing in the right foreground. Guitarist Bobby Eli is looking over Martin's right shoulder. Saxophonist Zack Zachary is fourth from the left. String contractor-player Don Renaldo is to Zachary's left. Trombonist Fred Joiner (wearing hat) is behind Renaldo. Producer-arranger Richard Rome is behind Bobby Eli. Ron "Have Mercy" Kersey is standing to the left of Rome. (Photo courtesy of W. McDougal)

MFSB guitarist Norman Harris at home, with some of his gold records. (Photo courtesy of W. McDougal)

The Sweethearts of Sigma Sound, ca. 1970s. *Left to right*: Carla Benson, Barbara Ingram, Evette Benton. Their voices were on just about every record that was produced in Philadelphia in the 1970s. (Photo courtesy of Carla Benson)

Dusty Springfield and Bobby Martin, in the Schubert Building, 1969. (Photo courtesy of Bobby Martin)

Linda Creed.
(Photo courtesy of W. McDougal)

Archie Bell (*front*) and the Drells "Can't Stop Dancin'" on Philadelphia's South Broad Street. City Hall is in the background, Philadelphia International Records to the extreme right. (Photo courtesy of W. McDougal)

Harold Melvin and the Blue Notes on stage. Melvin is on the far left. Teddy Pendergrass is in the center, Bernard Wilson is second from the right. (Photo courtesy of W. McDougal)

The O'Jays on stage. Eddie Levert is on the right. (Photo courtesy of W. McDougal)

Bobby Eli and Weldon McDougal at Sigma Sound. (Photo courtesy of W. McDougal)

"Sweetening" Philadelphia Soul with strings and horns. Don Renaldo is to the right. (Photo courtesy of W. McDougal)

The "Little Mighty Three," *Left to right:* Songwriter-producer Joe Jefferson, Charles "Charlie Boy" Simmons, Bruce Hawes. (Photo courtesy of W. McDougal)

A dapper
Leon Huff
at the keys.
(Photo
courtesy of
W. McDougal)

Leon Huff's desk at 309 South Broad Street. There was no doubt about whose office this was. (Photo courtesy of W. McDougal)

The dynamic Bunny Sigler
on stage. (Photo courtesy
of W. McDougal)

MFSB keyboardist-producer
Lenny Pakula. (Photo
courtesy of W. McDougal)

The Soul Survivors. Their 1967 hit "Expressway to Your Heart" proved to be Gamble and Huff's first big hit. (Photo courtesy of W. McDougal)

Left to right: Gene McFadden, producer-arranger Victor Carstarphen, Sigma engineer Jim Gallagher. (Photo courtesy of W. McDougal)

"Ain't No Stoppin' Us Now!" John Whitehead (along with Gene McFadden) was responsible for one of Philadelphia International Records' biggest hits. (Photo courtesy of W. McDougal)

Left to right: Don Renaldo, Bobby Martin, Leon Huff, promoter Mamadu (deceased), and the Intruders' Phil Terry. (Photo courtesy of W. McDougal)

Dee Dee Sharp and Kenny Gamble. (Photo courtesy of W. McDougal)

The Intruders, ca. late 1960s. Phil Terry is on the far right. (Photo courtesy of Val Shively)

The Mighty Three: A rare shot of (*left to right*) Leon Huff, Thom Bell, and Kenny Gamble. (Photo courtesy of Val Shively)

Recording for Philadelphia's top producers gave the musicians an extra burst of creative energy. When working with Gamble and Huff, in particular, they were called on to demonstrate their creativity, not to perform the music dispassionately as it was handed to them on a piece of paper. "We were the guys that did all the rhythm," asserted Vince Montana. "We were in there working and creating songs for Gamble and Huff." They were the kind of musicians "who could play for anybody," said Bunny Sigler, "from the O'Jays to Billy Paul to Johnny Mathis. They did everything, but they were still funky musicians." The rhythm section would generally roll into Sigma Sound around 10:30 or eleven in the morning and have their breakfast, "and everybody would be joking and carrying on," recalled T. J. Tindall. By twelve-thirty or one o'clock they were ready to work. "And by six we'd generally have three tracks done." Gamble governed the studio like "an empire," added Tindall. He "just wouldn't take no for an answer. . . . He knew how to get it done, man."

This did not make life easy for Sigma engineer Joe Tarsia, who usually had only the time it took for the musicians to learn a particular song and work out the arrangement before he was expected to be ready to record. "When we were done learnin' the arrangement, we were ready to cut!" explained T. J. Tindall. "And if you made us play it too many times, it just lost the spark." The rhythm sections "usually got it on the first or second take," added the guitarist, "so Joe was always under a lot of pressure to be ready in a hurry." Often Tarsia would claim that he needed an additional run-through before he was ready to record. "No you don't," Gamble and Huff invariably told him. "Cut it!'"[14]

It was Kenny Gamble's idea to sign these top-flight musicians to a recording contract and call them "MFSB" (which he and Leon Huff then copyrighted). Ostensibly, MFSB stood for the Philadelphia International "family," mother, father, sister, brother. Gamble and Huff "wanted to portray the message that although we were diverse people we were all connected musically," said Lenny Pakula. "That's what MFSB meant, as far as I could always tell. We *were* family!" Vince Montana chuckled when he was asked what MFSB signified. Mother, father, sister, brother was the "clean version," he said. "I don't think you want me to repeat the other version." The "other" version, of course, was "mother-fuckin' son-of-a-bitch." It was an expression common among musicians, comparable to saying someone "played his ass off," said Montana. At Sigma Sound, "all the guys" would use it, said the vibraphonist.

Once signed as part of MFSB, the musicians could continue to play on sessions for whomever else they wanted. But anything they recorded for Gamble and Huff would now be credited to "MFSB." Thus, with several strokes of a pen, Gamble and Huff created a new recording act for Philadelphia International Records.[15]

WHAT IS COMMONLY ACCEPTED AS THE TRUE BIRTH of Philadelphia International Records occurred late in 1971, with the signing of two acts that would provide Gamble and Huff's heretofore directionless company with its first legitimate stars. Their biggest successes to date had been achieved working with veteran recording artists in need of a career revival. True to form, the company's new artists fit that very mold. One of the acts, the O'Jays, had even recorded for Gamble and Huff's ill-fated Neptune label. The other group, Harold Melvin and the Blue Notes, was a lounge act whose members long ago had deemphasized their lackluster recording career to focus on their highly successful stage show. All told, the O'Jays and the Blue Notes had a combined thirty years of recording experience, with at least twenty different labels, and zero Top 40 hits. It was not surprising, then, that Philadelphia International's signing of these two shopworn groups created no buzz throughout the recording industry.

Harold Melvin and the Blue Notes were then in the midst of a meandering career that, for the past fifteen years, had produced a myriad of personnel changes and one minor hit record. The Blue Notes were "old men" by the time they signed with Gamble and Huff, noted Bobby Martin. Well, perhaps not that old, but not particularly coveted by their new record label, either. Gamble and Huff had actually wanted to sign the Dells, a venerable R&B group from Chicago.[16] "Gambs always loved the Dells," said Thom Bell. "He got 'em down there into Philly, into the office, to try and sign them." But Gamble could not convince the Dells to change record companies. So he decided he would create his own Dells, and signed Harold Melvin and the Blue Notes to Philadelphia International.

The original Blue Notes were formed as a quartet in North Philadelphia, in 1954. Two years later, the group added sixteen-year-old Harold Melvin, a self-taught piano player, who had been singing around town with his own group. As a quintet, the Blue Notes won a series of amateur night competitions at New York's Apollo Theater and also made their first recordings. But their record company was preoccupied with promoting the then red-hot Cadillacs, and the Blue Notes' recordings fell by the wayside. When the group disbanded in 1958, Harold Melvin approached Bernard Wilson and Lawrence Brown, who were then singing with a group called the Chord Steppers. "Y'all want to be the Notes?"[17] asked Melvin. "Why not?" said Wilson and Brown. Then the trio added John Atkins as the group's new lead singer.[18]

As 1960 began, with Harold Melvin at the helm, the Blue Notes managed to eke out a living on the road, playing small black clubs on the "chitlin' circuit" for ten dollars a night. "It wasn't easy but we managed," recalled Lawrence Brown. "We were doing okay despite having no records on the chart." Late that year, the Blue Notes incorporated John Atkins's soaring falsetto with a melody by Johann Strauss and backed it with an early Philly string arrangement. The ballad, called "My Hero," became the group's first hit. But, outside the Philadelphia area, falsetto leads such as Atkins's were still regarded as a mere novelty, and several excellent Blue Notes follow-ups, sung in the same vein as "My Hero," failed to catch on. For the remainder of the 1960s, the Blue Notes, caught between the fading classic R&B harmony style and the ascending soul sound, recorded with limited success for a variety of labels.[19] To survive, the group reverted to club work. To increase their meager earnings, they reinvented themselves as a "white act," said Bernard Wilson. Harold Melvin added some Broadway show tunes to the group's repertoire and they began performing in tuxedos as other group members shared the lead vocal chores. They were quite good at it, too. Bernard Wilson recalled how the Blue Notes "did all the top clubs in the country, Vegas and the Copacabana, and in the world."

Near the end of the 1960s, there occurred two crucial events that finally got Harold Melvin and the Blue Notes onto the fast track. First, John Atkins and his old-school falsetto left the group, and Harold Melvin temporarily stepped to the forefront.[20] But the fastidious and moody Melvin, who ruled the Blue Notes with an iron fist, knew his own limitations. His forte was managing and guiding the group, not fronting it. This led to the second crucial event: Harold Melvin's selection of a new lead singer.

In 1970, after playing a gig in Puerto Rico, the club owner wanted the Blue Notes to extend their set. Harold Melvin was not eager to overtax his already tired voice, especially after a night's worth of singing, but he obliged. By his account, Melvin then asked the musicians who comprised the group's traveling combo whether "they could play a couple of more tunes and they didn't mind. That's when I first heard Teddy sing." "Teddy," of course, was Theodore Pendergrass, the combo's twenty-year-old drummer. Melvin was shocked when he heard Pendergrass, whose hoarse, yet forceful gospel-drenched baritone bore a striking similarity to the Dells' lead, Marvin Junior. Whether Melvin recognized the similarity of the two voices is unknown. But, said Melvin, "I knew then that I had something."[21]

The crafty Melvin wasted no time in bringing his drummer to the forefront. Despite Pendergrass's tender age, the Philadelphia-born musician was no raw recruit. He had drummed for a time with the legendary James Brown Review and also sang with the Epsilons, a Philadelphia group. After Lloyd Parkes was added as the fifth member of the group, Harold Melvin and the Blue Notes were poised for an unimaginable run of chart success that would eclipse even their best live performances. But one problem remained for Harold Melvin: His group was without a record label.

Melvin and Kenny Gamble had known each other since the mid-1960s, when the Romeos and the Blue Notes both recorded for Arctic Records. Gamble "was connected with the Blue Notes really closely," said Leon Huff. Bernard Wilson agreed that Melvin and Gamble "were tight, pretty cool." Melvin "was always connected with good singing groups," explained Huff, "so sooner or later it was a natural thing for us to hook up." The first step in that direction took place in a Camden, New Jersey, club, when Gamble appeared there one evening to take in the show starring his longtime pal. Gamble knew that Melvin "had been constantly trying to find a lead singer," and as soon as he heard Teddy Pendergrass sing, he realized that the leader of the Blue Notes had finally found his man. And Gamble had found his Dells.[22] (According to Bobby Eli, the "whole group" of Blue Notes sessions recorded for their first Philadelphia International album "was originally meant for the Dells.")

Harold Melvin was at the very same hotel in Puerto Rico where he first discovered Teddy Pendergrass when Gamble called and told him that "he just made a deal with CBS and needed [Melvin] to get there as soon as [he] could." When the Blue Notes' gig ended a couple of weeks later, Melvin flew back to Philadelphia, sat down with Gamble, "and decided what we were going to do and I started to get to work," he recalled. Teddy Pendergrass remembered Melvin telling the group, "We did it! We've got a deal!"[23] It was some time before the then-euphoric Pendergrass discovered the disturbing details of that deal.

As the Blue Notes prepared to make their first recordings for Gamble and Huff, the group thought "they could make it" with Pendergrass "doing that soulful lead and Kenny and Leon allowing us the freedom to express ourselves," said Lawrence Brown.[24] But the Blue Notes soon discovered that Pendergrass's lack of recording experience initially precluded any of the freedom of expression of which Lawrence Brown spoke. As usual, Gamble and Huff spent "maybe a week or so" with their studio rhythm section, laying down the basic tracks for the Blue Notes album, said Bobby Eli. The producers had already conceived some of the tracks, while others were developed in the studio with Gamble and Huff and the musicians working together. Only then were the Blue Notes summoned to Sigma Sound.

When they arrived there, the first song Pendergrass attempted was the Gamble and Huff–penned soul ballad "I Miss You." This song, about a repentant husband who seeks reconciliation with his alienated wife, was intended to be the debut single off the Blue Notes album. But Pendergrass could not provide a satisfactory take. Pendergrass was clearly uncomfortable in the unfamiliar confines of the recording studio. The frustrated singer "couldn't feel it," recalled Harold Melvin, and was unable to "just open up his voice" to sing over the prerecorded rhythm track. ("We were a live group," exclaimed Bernard Wilson. "We were used to audiences!") A perplexed Kenny Gamble asked Melvin how to resolve the problem. "Well, let me cut him live," said the discerning group leader, recognizing that to feel relaxed, Pendergrass needed other people, especially young females, around him. [25] Sure enough, in a studio filled with female fans, Pendergrass came through.

Despite (or perhaps because of) the Blue Notes' previous recordings, the group could not survive unless they remained on the road, performing. Thus, explained Bernard Wilson, their first album for Philadelphia International had to be done "in sessions," with the Blue Notes traveling "in and out of town" until they had laid down the requisite vocals. Then, said Wilson, the group left town, "busy worrying about getting to where we were going" to perform next and giving nary "a second thought" to their just-completed album. Most likely, the Blue Notes had split before Gamble, Huff, Bell, and Bobby Martin returned to Sigma to "sweeten" the tracks by overdubbing strings and horns.

Only seven tracks appeared on the *Harold Melvin and the Blue Notes* album. The eight-minute-plus "I Miss You," with Lloyd Parkes supplying the Philly falsetto and Harold Melvin speaking the song's monologue, was issued as a two-part single in March 1972.[26] The combination of Teddy Pendergrass's raw, yet soulful voice, heard above the Blue Notes' smooth backing and a sizable orchestra, elicited definite thoughts of Marvin Junior and the Dells. The Thom Bell–arranged tune also stayed on the *Billboard*'s R&B chart for almost four months, nudging its way to number seven that summer. It had been over a year since a Philadelphia International single (the Ebonys' "You're the Reason Why") fared so well. But the Blue Notes (and Columbia Records), courting white record buyers, had hoped for an even broader response to "I Miss You." (The song made it only to number 58 on *Billboard*'s Hot 100.)

Nevertheless, Columbia, most notably Clive Davis, remained undaunted. Prior to the release of the Blue Notes' second single, Davis placed an ad in *Billboard* magazine. "By next week the whole world will be singing 'If You Don't Know Me by Now,'" the copy brazenly declared. And just as Davis had boldly predicted, the group's latest single—another longing soulful ballad (this one arranged by Bobby Martin), featuring Teddy Pendergrass's pleading over Lloyd Parkes's falsetto riffs—captured the white market as well as the black. "If You Don't Know Me by Now" spent four months on *Billboard*'s charts, reaching the top slot on the R&B list and number three on the Hot 100. (The song was eventually certified gold and received a Grammy nomination for Best R&B Group Performance.[27]) The mass popularity of "If You Don't Know Me by Now" also sparked sales of the Blue Notes' album and caused Columbia Records to feel more confident about their Philadelphia International deal.

As for the Blue Notes, they were shocked at the magnitude of their newfound popularity. "Oh, you wouldn't believe the surprise!" exclaimed Bernard Wilson. The group's giant hit dramatically increased the number and the quality of their bookings. Wilson said the Blue Notes "were ecstatic" when they began to play "the arenas, the stadiums, and [appear on] all the television shows. We were the *shit* now. We never looked back."

The surprise success of the *Harold Melvin and the Blue Notes* album stemmed from the stirring combination of the voices of the group, the arrangements of Bobby Martin and Thom Bell, and the production of Gamble and Huff. It was also due in part to Gamble and Huff's uncanny knack of recognizing what type of music a certain artist, and a particular set of circumstances, warranted. In this instance, it meant eliciting an entire album of ballads from a group that thrived on the varied repertoire of song styles offered in their stage act. "Imagine that!" marveled Bernard Wilson thirty years later. "We wouldn't have done it like that." We Blue Notes, he said, "didn't know we were a ballad group" and would have put several "fast tunes" on the album. Most surprising, Wilson claimed that if the group had chosen the album's songs, "If You Don't Know Me by Now" would not have survived the final cut. "Shows you how much *we* knew!" chuckled the singer.

GAMBLE AND HUFF RESUMED THEIR PROFESSIONAL RELATIONSHIP with the O'Jays at the same time they began working with Harold Melvin and the Blue Notes. The O'Jays were now a trio, consisting of Eddie Levert, Walter Williams, and William Powell. (Bobby Massey had left to try his hand at producing records.) When Neptune Records folded and the O'Jays returned to Cleveland, Williams said that the group "kept in touch with Gamble and Huff and they kept us informed about the Columbia deal." Meanwhile, the O'Jays received overtures from Norman Whitfield at Motown and from Holland-Dozier-Holland, but, said Williams, "those people make all the groups sound alike and we wanted our own sound." Gamble regularly spoke with Eddie Levert about signing with Philadelphia International, said Williams. But, said Williams, after receiving "no follow-up on the [Neptune] product that we had out with them," the O'Jays remained leery about rejoining their former producers. (At one point, Gamble and Huff reportedly suggested that Levert sign with them as a solo artist, but he declined to leave the group.[28])

In the end, Gamble's persistence paid off, as the O'Jays signed with Philadelphia International. Levert said the group "always felt that Kenny and Leon were more able than any producers to capture the group on record." The trio "just wanted to be the O'Jays" and believed they could "accomplish that better with Gamble and Huff." The trio had "good vibes" with the writer/producers, added Levert. "We knew we could go into the studio with them and . . . come up with something."[29] Then again, what Levert described as "big financial guarantees" made to the group by Gamble and Huff surely contributed to those good vibes.

Having re-signed the O'Jays, Gamble and Huff burned for a song that would make the group the superstars the producers had envisioned some three years ago. Miraculously, they were virtually handed such a song by two down-and-out locals in their early twenties who were looking for jobs. Back in the 1960s, Gene McFadden and John Whitehead (Whitehead was shot dead in Philadelphia by an unknown assailant in 2004) had sung with Otis Redding's touring band, the Epsilons. But when Redding was killed in a plane crash in 1967, the Epsilons were no more. By 1971, McFadden and Whitehead's most prized possession was the lyric to a song they had recently written. They headed for Gamble and Huff's offices in hopes of selling the opus there. Perhaps they might even be hired as songwriters. So as not to be thrown out of the producers' offices before they could make their desperate pitch, McFadden and Whitehead lurked about the soda machine located in the hallway near Huff's office. When a thirsty Huff showed up, McFadden and Whitehead began to speak the words of their song to him. So intrigued was Huff by the story of dishonesty and betrayal told in the lyric the young duo had christened "Back Stabbers" that he hired McFadden and Whitehead as Philadelphia International staff writers.[30] Then Huff went to the creaky upright piano in his office and put McFadden and Whitehead's words to music.

But when the O'Jays first heard "Back Stabbers," they balked. Kenny Gamble said he and Huff "had to almost force the O'Jays to sing it, they didn't like it." Unlike the Blue Notes, who had expected to record up-tempo songs but were (wisely) steered in the opposite direction by Gamble and Huff, Eddie Levert thought that "the slow love songs were our thing."[31]

Once the O'Jays had been persuaded to record "Back Stabbers," the task of arranging the song fell on Thom Bell's shoulders.[32] He thought that "Back Stabbers," which originally began with a lone, jazzy guitar, needed an immediate hook with a "grandiose" approach. "Edit me eight more bars in front of that thing and I'm gonna give you another beginning," he told Gamble. Utilizing, among other instruments, violins, a harp, and a French horn, Bell composed "a suite to the whole front of that thing," introduced by Leon Huff's stark piano tremolo. Songwriter/background singer Phil Hurtt, who was privy to the recording of "Back Stabbers," claimed that Gamble and Huff "must have cut that intro about fifteen or twenty times," because Huff wasn't satisfied. Once the intro was finalized, the producers turned to the rhythm track, and then the O'Jays' vocals were added. But it was not until "Tommy laid those strings down" at the song's sweetening session that they began to realize the magnitude of what had just been created. "We all stood there lookin' around at each other," recalled Hurtt. "Oh my God!" he thought. "What is happening here?"[33]

What was happening was a radical departure from anything the O'Jays' had ever recorded. "Back Stabbers," which author Nelson George described as "a dark, ominous meditation on treachery, highlighted by Bobby Martin's brilliant horn chart and the interplay between Levert's high-intensity vocal and the backing voices," was simply one of the best songs, best productions, to ever emerge from Philadelphia International Records. This was high praise, especially considering that that particular version of the monumental song came close to never being heard by the public. Bobby Eli, who played guitar on the session, said that when Kenny Gamble listened to the playback of the original rhythm track, he was not satisfied. "I don't know, guys, I don't know," said Gamble to the band. "Let's come back tomorrow and we'll try another one.'" They did, and recorded a second take of "Back Stabbers" that had what Eli termed "a harder drum feel."[34] To his everlasting credit, Gamble made the correct call and chose to release the first version of the now-classic song.

The album's ten tracks were finished during the winter of 1972. The O'Jays became ecstatic over the results. Gamble and Huff "knew exactly how to get us across," recalled Eddie Levert. "We couldn't believe how good the musicians were, the quality of the songs, everything was just fantastic."[35] The album, wisely titled *Back Stabbers*, was released just after the Blue Notes album. The title song became the O'Jays' first single for their new record company. While almost everyone involved in the creation of that song had positive thoughts about it, they did not dare imagine the blockbuster it would become. "You don't know," said Thom Bell. "What you do is, you do the best you can, and you hope that you got some goodies on it. But you really don't know. No one can tell a hit record in advance."

Bell and his colleagues had, indeed, done the best they could do. The "Back Stabbers" single reached number one on *Billboard's* R&B chart that summer. Of even greater significance, the song climbed to number three on the Hot 100 and became the first Philadelphia International single to be certified gold. ("Back Stabbers" also netted the O'Jays a Grammy nomination for Best R&B Song of the Year.) Years later, music writer and critic Alan Light called "Back Stabbers" "the defining moment" of the era, "where the terror that runs through many of those records meets a swirling, propulsive string arrangement and furious vocals." After "Back Stabbers," wrote Light, "there was nothing left to prove."[36]

The white crossover market drawn to "Back Stabbers," which

accounted for a preponderance of the record albums sold, was exactly what Columbia Records was looking for when they made the Philadelphia International deal almost a year and a half earlier. "You don't make money on singles," said Columbia executive Jim Tyrell, in 1972. What Columbia needed was a "hit single and then pump the album big-time, and after the album is out there and the hit single begins to flag, we come in with the second and the third single."[37] It had taken longer than expected for Philadelphia International to live up to Columbia's game plan, but the company's patience was finally rewarded. When "Back Stabbers" began to get airplay, "the wonderful rocket ship took off," said then president of Columbia's Epic Records, Ron Alexenburg.

The O'Jays' next single, "992 Arguments," may well have been titled "Back Stabbers—Part 2." The song fared well enough, considering the similarities to its predecessor, but it was the group's third single, issued in the fall of 1972, that became Philadelphia International's biggest-selling single up to that time. Leon Huff said he knew "Love Train" was "special" from the time he and Gamble were composing it on the raggedy upright piano in Gamble's office. Huff's recollection of that scene offers a rare glimpse of how he and Gamble worked together. With a portable tape recorder rolling, Huff would "just sit down and start playing. Gamble might say, 'Yeah, play that again.' It was like, as I played, he'd write in his mind—whatever came off the top of his head. And, because we talked all the time, we came up with some great titles or songs through conversation." Huff called their writing process "the perfect give-and-take. . . . The way I was playing it and the way Gamble was singing it, the words were just flowing out." Gamble said that when he and Huff wrote, they attempted to "stick basically to life-type situations—to something anyone could feel . . . [or] identify with." For example, "Love Train" was an attempt to write "about the world as we saw it. We felt that people all over the world should be at peace with each other. That was the message we were trying to relate."[38] The lyrics to "Love Train" were finalized in the studio, "as the rhythm track was being laid down and before the O'Jays even got their hands on the song," recalled Bobby Eli. Eli said the first time he heard the words "people all over the world," he knew the song "was gonna be an international hit." And it was. "Love Train" became a million-selling, number-one hit on the pop and the R&B charts in the States, and also made the Top 10 in England.

Song for song, the O'Jays' *Back Stabbers* album was arguably the strongest album Gamble and Huff had produced since Jerry Butler's *The Ice Man Cometh*. The "Back Stabbers" and "Love Train" singles helped to keep it on *Billboard's* album charts for forty-four weeks, resulting in Philadelphia International's first certified gold album. With "the curse" finally lifted, Columbia did not have to wait nearly so long for Gamble and Huff's next gold album. It came on the very next Philadelphia International release.

LIKE THE O'JAYS, BILLY PAUL ORIGINALLY RECORDED for Gamble and Huff's ill-fated Neptune Records. During that time, Gamble and Huff attempted to guide the languid, jazz-infused singer toward the mainstream (and to greater record sales), but the singer's wandering, unpredictable voice had precluded any such success. Thom Bell observed that, at times, Paul "would sing so flat it sounded like you could land a 747 [jet] on it." Gamble and Huff infused Paul's initial Philadelphia International album, *Going East*, with more of a soul flavor, but lacking a standout single, *Going East* went nowhere but south.

Now, a year later, the singer's *360 Degrees of Billy Paul* album was ready to be shipped to stores. This time, owing to the album's promising standout single, there was a hint of optimism from Paul, Gamble and Huff, and Columbia Records. "Me and Mrs. Jones," a soul ballad designed specifically for radio airplay, was a timeless tale of admitted infidelity. Composed by Gamble, Huff and Cary Grant "Hippie" Gilbert, Huff's longtime friend from Camden, the steamy number was arranged by Bobby Martin, who said he opted for "a big band sound, a bluesy sound, and it fit perfectly."[39] The public overwhelmingly agreed.

Imagine the surprise of the thirty-seven-year-old Paul when he "awoke one day and saw that "Me and Mrs. Jones" was number one on the charts, across the board.[40] "Me and Mrs. Jones" and the Blue Notes' "If You Don't Know Me by Now" had played tag with each other as they ascended the charts. Each song sold a million copies, giving Philadelphia International back-to-back gold singles. "Me and Mrs. Jones" ultimately surpassed the Blue Notes' classic as it went on to top *Billboard*'s Hot 100 and R&B charts that fall. ("Mrs. Jones" was nominated for a Grammy for Best R&B Song, and Billy Paul received a Grammy for Best Male R&B Vocal Performance.) Spurred on by the popularity of the single, Paul's *360 Degrees* album also attained gold status. The surprise success of "Mrs. Jones," in addition to bestowing widespread popularity on Paul, also afforded the singer a formidable platform from which to advance his suddenly charged career. But Paul's stunning success also presented a dilemma to Philadelphia International: Which song should be released next that would best capitalize on Billy Paul's newfound popularity? The decision was made by Kenny Gamble, who had been most astute in his selection of material for the Blue Notes and the O'Jays. But Gamble's choice of a follow-up to "Me and Mrs. Jones" was disastrous.

The past six months had been exhilarating for Gamble and Huff and Columbia Records. Philadelphia International now hummed like a well-oiled machine. Gamble and Huff's growing list of accomplishments included two certified-gold albums and four million-selling singles released on their own label. "The hits started coming, they started rolling," said Thom Bell. "Then they started rolling even more." Sigma Sound's Joe Tarsia, who engineered those hits, recalled how, during a Gamble and Huff session, "literally, the hair on my arms used to stand up when they'd get into a groove." But there was more to Philadelphia International's upswing than the quality of its music. "We were cuttin' hits, but a lot of people cut hits, and you never heard 'em again," said MFSB guitarist T. J. Tindall. "Somehow, Gamble figured out how to get that stuff sold. I guess between his promotion staff and the deal he cut with Clive Davis, or *whatever*, they managed to make it happen. . . . In order for it to be successful . . . you have to be sold properly. Gamble made it all come together."

To the delight of Columbia Records, Gamble and Huff finally had the horses to pull the Philadelphia International wagon. Ron Alexenburg was not surprised at the turnaround. Gamble and Huff "were solid producers and terrific songwriters," he said. But even Alexenburg was taken aback by Philadelphia International's sudden magnitude of record sales. "To think that you'd have [several] albums being recorded at the same time that were all gonna be multi-million-dollar earners, nobody planned that!" he exclaimed. Fellow Epic executive Rick Swig pointed out that black music "never sold any albums until Gamble and Huff and CBS created a more album-oriented music." When it came to albums, Columbia was now able to "pump heavy tonnage" out of Philadelphia International.[41]

December's *Jet* magazine pictured Gamble and Huff on its front cover. Inside the black-oriented publication was a two-page story, "Gamble and Huff: The Men behind the Record Stars." Accompanying the text were photographs of Gamble, Huff, Billy Paul, Harold Melvin, Wilson Pickett, and Jerry Butler. The article credited Philadelphia International with being "one of the most successful record companies in the music industry." In it, Kenny Gamble made no bones about the company's ambitious goals: "Now that we have gotten to this point we don't want to be branded as a company, for example, that pushes only R&B," he stated. "That's already been done and it's sort of an outmoded concept. . . . We work mainly with black artists, sure, but we're quite capable of working with pop acts." The article also mentioned mounting "rumors . . . that the dynamic duo will duplicate in Philadelphia a musical explosion similar to the one Berry Gordy brought about in Detroit (Motown) and the Stax organization in Memphis."[42] By the end of 1972, Detroit, Memphis, Muscle Shoals, and other established centers of soul music were hip to the fact that Philadelphia was a player to be reckoned with, as a potent hit maker and as the source of an entirely new soul sound.

9

"Am I Black Enough for You?"

(1973)

I N 1973, PHILADELPHIA INTERNATIONAL RECORDS became one of
America's most important record companies just one year after
asserting its influence on the pop music industry. The elimination of
Philadelphia International's initial promotional problems helped a great
deal, and once the hits began, a snowball effect was created. Whereas,
not long ago, Philadelphia International faced difficulty getting its
records played on the air, now, said disc jockey Georgie Woods, "If
Kenny Gamble came to the studio with a record that sounded like it
could be a hit, boom, we put it on the air and played it."

But not every artist signed to Philadelphia International was able to
ride the coattails of prosperity. Foremost among the unfortunate were
the Intruders, once the flagship act of the nascent empire of Gamble and
Huff. Having been supplanted as the company's leading act and beset
by the personal problems of lead singer Little Sonny Brown, the
Intruders had fallen by the wayside. Despite containing the hit "I'll
Always Love My Mama," the group's *Save the Children* album, released
early in 1973, rose only as high as number 133 on *Billboard*'s Top 200
album chart. The Intruders' next album for Gamble and Huff was their
last. Shortly thereafter, they disbanded.

On the other hand, Billy Paul, who was coming off his million-selling
"Me and Mrs. Jones" smash, seemed an unlikely candidate for diminished popularity. On the contrary, the singer's next single stood to
increase his newly acquired mainstream popularity. But Kenny Gamble's
choice for Billy Paul's follow-up single was the confrontational "Am I
Black Enough for You?" Written by him and Huff, the song was a defiant
paean to black pride and resolve. It coupled an oppositionist attitude
with a lyric that celebrated a growing number of black protagonists. All
of that, and the relentless refrain of the song's title, "Am I Black Enough
for You?" would not endear itself to the massive white audience that

awaited Billy Paul's next release. Paul said he specifically told Gamble not to release "Am I Black Enough for You?" as a single, because he thought the song would "turn off a lot of people." Thom Bell agreed wholeheartedly. "Why in the world would you release that?" he asked Gamble. Gamble's response was that he thought "Am I Black Enough for You?" was a "great" song. "That thing's not gonna draw flies," Bell warned his friend. Phil Hurtt also told Gamble that releasing the antagonistic song was a bad idea that will "shut some doors." But the final say "was CBS's and Kenny Gamble's," said Billy Paul, who was "very upset" with the decision.[1]

Those who knew Kenny Gamble well were not surprised by his decision. Thom Bell said Gamble had grown more and more interested in "political and religious dealings" by then. But if Gamble's decision to release "Am I Black Enough for You?" resulted from his fastidious and increasingly dogmatic outspokenness concerning black-white relations, it also exposed two paradoxical notions. Gamble was not antiwhite but extremely problack. He believed that most blacks did not take themselves as seriously as they should and were often their own worst enemies. But while he believed that blacks should recognize their worth, unite, and make themselves into a force to be reckoned with, Gamble also thought that blacks and whites should coexist peacefully (see the lyrics to "Love Train"). Gamble either thought—naïvely—that the release of "Am I Black Enough for You?" could somehow advance these two opposing social ideals, or else he brazenly chose to let the chips (and Billy Paul's career) fall where they may. (Paul was convinced that Gamble "thought it was more important to use my fame to get the word out than to help my career."[2])

"Am I Black Enough for You?" was released as 1973 began and "was a disaster!" exclaimed Epic's Ron Alexenburg. The song barely dented *Billboard*'s Hot 100 and failed to reach the R&B Top 20, an indication that blacks as well as whites were dissatisfied with it. "Am I Black Enough for You?" was the "wrong song to follow 'Me and Mrs. Jones,'" lamented Paul. After the song's release, the singer said he "never got back up" to where he had been. "It damaged me, and I was bitter about it for a long time."[3] In his desire to espouse his sociopolitical beliefs, Kenny Gamble fumbled away any chance Billy Paul had of sustaining his momentary crossover appeal. But that was the least in a series of problems Gamble was about to encounter.

DESPITE THE RUSH OF SUCCESS GENERATED by Harold Melvin and the Blue Notes and the O'Jays during the first half of 1973, Philadelphia International nevertheless reverted to its unsteady past. New recording activity became sporadic at best, as Gamble and Huff instead released a spate of recycled material.[4] The reason for this slack period of recording may have been Gamble and Huff's preoccupation with other aspects of their expanding company. At that point in time, Philadelphia International underwent a major overhaul, which included the formation of two new companies and a move to new headquarters. If that was not enough to engage Gamble and Huff, a disturbing development at CBS, the parent company of Columbia Records, certainly was. Not only were the young recording moguls on the verge of losing their Columbia godfather, Clive Davis, but, more traumatizing, Gamble and Huff were about to become targets in a major investigation of payola in the music business.

On May 29, 1973, the industry was shocked when Clive Davis, then president of CBS Records Group, was abruptly dismissed for alleged misappropriation of corporate funds. CBS president Arthur Traylor said the company had uncovered "meticulous records of wrongdoing" on the part of Davis, who was implicated by one of Davis's underlings, David Wynshaw.[5]

As these events unfolded, the record business was already under investigation ("Project Sound") by a federal strike force looking into alleged links to payola, drug trafficking, and other avenues of organized crime. David Wynshaw had recently been implicated in an unrelated drug charge. In hopes of gaining leniency, he decided to cooperate with federal authorities. Wynshaw told the strike force that Columbia spent over $250,000 a year on payola to black radio stations to promote black-oriented records. This practice reportedly began in 1971, at precisely the time Columbia entered into its production and distribution deal with Philadelphia International Records. Wynshaw also implicated Philadelphia native Kal Rudman, who, at the time, published a music industry tip sheet called "Friday Morning Quarterback." Because Clive Davis had instituted promotional agreements with Rudman and with Philadelphia International Records, virtually every employee of Columbia Records (right up to the president) and Philadelphia International Records was implicated.[6]

Prior to 1960, there were no statutes—federal or state—prohibiting payola (cash payments or other inducements to gain exposure of certain records). Until then, the practice was common among record distributors, who carried the payments on their books as a legitimate cost of doing business. Recipients of such payoffs were also guilt-free, providing they reported the income on their tax returns. But this deceptive practice unraveled in 1959, when, driven by a complex mix of political motives, business rivalries, and petty jealousies, the matter was brought out in the open. Federal hearings on payola held the following spring culminated in a statute that made the practice a federal crime. But for over a decade, no one had even been charged under the statute.

By the end of 1973, Project Sound was fully under way. Jonathan Goldstein, the tough and incorruptible U.S. Attorney in Newark, New Jersey, knew that during the payola scandal of 1959, prosecutors in New York (citing a dubious and little-known state commercial bribery statute) targeted the takers of the bribes (disc jockeys) and not the givers (record manufacturers and distributors). Goldstein was determined to nab the bribers this time around.[7]

Besides conducting the investigation of Columbia Records in New York, Goldstein's office initiated probes in four other cities: Newark (involving Brunswick Records), Philadelphia (Philadelphia International Records), Memphis (Stax Records), and Los Angeles (where the activities of a local promotion man were examined).

If Kenny Gamble had chosen to remain in his unassuming South Street record shop, comfortably hawking Intruders' records throughout the New York–Philadelphia–Baltimore–Washington, D.C., corridor, he would never have been in this position. But his and Leon Huff's coveted alliance with CBS Records, followed by a rush of promotion and, finally, gold platters, had changed everything. Gamble and Huff were two black men now running with the big dogs, and all eyes—some unwelcome, as it turned out—were on them. At this point, Gamble and Huff could do nothing to alter the outcome of the government's investigation. With the anticipated major overhaul of their burgeoning music empire at hand, the two embattled record executives shoved the payola distraction to the back of their minds and attempted to go about their business. But the disquieting situation did not go away.

Gamble and Huff had no control over the payola investigation, but when it came to their expanding musical empire they were still *the men*. With Philadelphia International Records finally on solid footing, Gamble and Huff looked to establish financial security. Furthermore, although the prospect remained unlikely, the pair tried again to get Thom Bell involved. Philadelphia International was on the verge of becoming "so big that you couldn't contain it," said Bell. What Gamble had in mind "was to consolidate the whole Philadelphia *sound*," he added. Gamble and Huff "had bought everybody else out but me. . . . I was the only one that wasn't part of anything."

With that, Gamble, who apparently still refused to acknowledge his longtime friend's aversion to being tied down to any record company, approached Bell about becoming a senior arranger and producer at Philadelphia International and told his friend he wanted to put him on salary. But Bell had not changed his mind. "No, no, no!" he exclaimed. "Not *pay* me!"

Some three decades later, Bell explained how he refused "to be tied down to anybody. Atlantic Records couldn't do it. Columbia couldn't do it. None of them could. If they gave me ten million dollars I wouldn't be workin' for them. All the money in the world was not gonna make me happy. What made me happy was producing records. You cannot be in a creative business and be doing what you don't like to do. That's the kind of stuff that drives you crazy."

Still, the idea of a business venture with Gamble and Huff that was unrelated to music and required none of Bell's creative energy was appealing to him. "If you put two good things together you should come out fantastic, and everyone benefits that much more," he explained. But this was not the most propitious time to be contemplating any new business, especially one involving the music industry. A national mood of uncertainty prevailed in 1973. Although U.S. involvement in the Vietnam War ended that year, America was fraught by other setbacks. For one, President Nixon was under increasing fire from the Watergate scandal. Then, Nixon's vice president came under investigation for allegedly receiving kickbacks when he was a public servant in Maryland. (The vice president resigned that October.) After three years of prosperity, the country had recently entered an economic recession, largely brought on by oil prices that soared because of an Arab oil embargo. Gasoline shortages spurred a domestic energy crisis, replete with long lines at filling stations. The Dow-Jones average continued to plunge as the country struggled under wage and price controls. Nowhere were the unsure feelings stronger than among America's nearly 24 million blacks. As they continued to experience limited gains without fundamental social change, as well as disproportionate economic woes, black trust in the government dipped to its lowest point since 1958.

WHEN VIEWED IN THIS DISMAL CONTEXT, the artistic and economic success of Kenny Gamble, Leon Huff, and Thom Bell was even more impressive. Their fundamental problem was not how to make a dollar but where to invest the bundle they already earned. Certainly, not in the stock market. There was gold, which had doubled in value after the U.S. dollar was devalued early in the year. And there was real estate, that hard asset that had defied even the Great Depression. Gamble, Huff, and Bell opted for the latter. The three formed a holding company with which to purchase real estate and into which they put equal amounts of capital. The trio called their new company Great Philadelphia Trading that, explained Bell, became the "umbrella or the shell to a whole bunch of other things that we had."

In one of life's soul-gratifying ironies, the first property acquired by Great Philadelphia was the aging structure located at 309 South Broad Street: the old Cameo-Parkway building, to which access had been

denied Gamble and Bell during the early 1960s. The plan was to reno-
vate the three-story building, located on the eastern side of Broad Street
at the corner of Spruce Street, and then lease the first-floor storefronts
and second-floor office space to local merchants as a means of generating
income. Philadelphia International Records would leave the Schubert
Building (located diagonally across Broad Street, to the north) and lease
the third floor of 309 South Broad from Great Philadelphia Trading.

There was one hitch in the plan. The three would have to take out a
loan to purchase the huge structure, which contained almost 40,000
square feet of space on each floor. Considering the country's adverse
economic climate and the fact that three young men—young *black
men*—who were in the *record business*, of all things, were asking for a
large sum of money, the odds did not favor Gamble, Huff, and Bell. "We.
went to every bank in Philadelphia," said Bell. They looked at us like
we were crazy. *Colored* guys in music!" Unable to secure a loan in
Philadelphia, the three, with the help of CBS, finally managed to do so
in New York, but only after putting up "all kinds of collateral, *and*
cash," recalled Bell.

The old Cameo-Parkway building "was a raggedy piece of nothin!'"
at the time, said Bell. "We put a lot of money into that building.⁸ How
are you going to have a classy company in a raggedy building?" Strange
as it may seem, one of the things that Philadelphia International Records
did not do was to erect a sign on the building. "All of those years, there
was never a sign!" exclaimed former Sigma Sound and Philadelphia
International Records engineer Jim Gallagher. "No one ever knew that
[Philadelphia International] was there." Gamble, Huff, and Bell "loved
their anonymity," recalled Gallagher. "It blew my mind that they could
live in town and work there on Broad Street, walk down the street and
no one—except for people they grew up with—would walk up to them
and say, 'Ooh hey, you're the famous record producers.'" Needless to
say, passers-by in front of 309 South Broad Street were occasionally startled to see a Jerry Butler or Teddy Pendergrass suddenly emerge from
the building.

Gamble and Huff soon shared with Bell their idea of creating a "big
publishing company" that would combine all of the song copyrights of
the three's then-considerable music catalog. Bell liked the idea. Their
new song publishing company was called Mighty Three Music. Its
motto became: "You'll Never Forget Our Tunes." Although Gamble and
Huff continued to pay Bell to occasionally arrange and produce for
Philadelphia International, his involvement in Mighty Three Music
allowed Bell to remain independent of that company.⁹

After 309 South Broad Street underwent extensive renovations to the
third floor, including installation of deep-pile blue shag carpeting—on

the walls as well as on the floors—the building became the new home
of Philadelphia International Records. It was "the situation we'd always
dreamed about," said Leon Huff.[10] He and Gamble then began to hire
additional staff and "set up the Gamble, Huff, Bell family." Each member
of that "family" had his own office. Thom Bell's was a lesson in utility,
the only prerequisites being a piano and a taste of Schubert Building
cacophony. "I could write much better when there's a lot of noise and
phones were ringing and things," he explained with a laugh. "If a place
is quiet, I can't write worth a darn." Just as Bell's office defined him, so
did those of Gamble and Huff. The inner sanctum of the height-sensi-
tive and gruff Huff was dominated by a large, oval-shaped, elevated
desk, on the front of which was the name "HUFF," spelled out in block
letters three feet tall. The omniscient Gamble did not have an ordinary
office chair behind his desk; he preferred to sit on a throne-like seat. As a
visitor walked down the third-floor hallway of the new headquarters,
the muffled sounds of piano and singing could be heard as writers
worked out their songs.

GAMBLE, HUFF, AND BELL'S NEW REAL ESTATE AND PUBLISHING ventures
took shape at about the same time that Philadelphia International
Records released a spate of albums during the fall of 1973. The success of
Harold Melvin and the Blue Notes' debut album for Gamble and Huff
had vaulted the group from obscurity to the forefront of R&B, and for
the first time in their long careers, the group held out promise for a
forthcoming album. Because the Blue Notes were now known as a
ballad group, it was not surprising that when the recording of their new
album began, the group was informed that the first single from the
album was another slow song. With that, "The Love I Lost" was
presented to the Blue Notes "as a ballad in the style of 'If You Don't
Know Me by Now," recalled Teddy Pendergrass.[11] But during two days
of rehearsal, the song morphed into an up-tempo dance number.

Bobby Eli remembered that "The Love I Lost," as originally written,
was "very much" like the Dells' "Oh, What a Night." He claimed it was
Leon Huff who, during rehearsals, exclaimed, "Oh man, it's too 'draggy.'
Let's pick up the tempo!" When the Blue Notes got their hands on the
revamped rhythm track, the group took an "unorthodox approach" to
adding their vocals, said Teddy Pendergrass. "Usually the lead singer
states the chorus, with the other vocalists harmonizing above and below
him. But in Gamble and Huff's arrangement, Harold, Bernie, Larry, and
Lloyd sang the full entire chorus in cool, seamless harmony, thus freeing
me to growl, shout, and riff around them."[12] The faster version of "The
Love I Lost" demonstrated that the Blue Notes were just as adept at
handling fast songs as they were at ballads. Their latest album, titled

Black and Blue, was a mixture of up-tempo dance tunes, ballads, and even a show tune, but the standout tracks were fast dance numbers.

The two-part single of "The Love I Lost" (sans the extended preaching of Pendergrass contained on the album track) quickly ascended to the top of *Billboard*'s R&B and the Hot 100 that fall. It sold a million copies, making the Blue Notes the third Philadelphia International act in less than a year to accomplish that enviable feat. For the group's second single, released early in 1974, Gamble and Huff hedged their bets on whether to continue to emphasize the Blue Notes' recent up-tempo success or to return them to the ballad style of their first album. The dance-oriented "Satisfaction Guaranteed (or Take Your Love Back)" was coupled with the ballad "I'm Weak for You." The faster side won out. "Satisfaction Guaranteed" became a Top 10 R&B hit that spring, and Gamble and Huff continued to promote Harold Melvin and the Blue Notes as an up-tempo group.[13]

The O'Jays' second album for Philadelphia International, *Ship Ahoy*, was released back-to-back with the Blue Notes album. There were those who doubted as to whether the O'Jays were capable of improving on the success of "Back Stabbers." As evinced by the release of Billy Paul's "Am I Black Enough for You?" as a single, Kenny Gamble began to demonstrate the essence of a proud and socially conscious black man.[14]

But for his messages to be carried forth, Gamble needed one of Philadelphia International's recording acts to serve as his mouthpiece. He found that act in the O'Jays, whose deft interpretation of censorious songs, such as "Back Stabbers," "Shiftless Shady Jealous Kind of People," "When the World's at Peace," and "992 Arguments," had already given the group an aura of social relevance. Now it was time for Gamble to expand on that theme.

Gamble and Huff had written a song called "Ship Ahoy," which was intended for the movie soundtrack of *Shaft in Africa*. But the stark tale about the treacherous, sardine-packed middle passage of captured Africans headed to the New World and a lifetime of bondage and servitude was not used in the film. Gamble and Huff not only decided that the O'Jays would record "Ship Ahoy," but they resolved that Philadelphia International's foremost group would record an entire album based on the theme of slavery. How long the project would take was anyone's guess. Sigma's Joe Tarsia noted that "on a real good day we would cut five rhythm tracks. On a bad day we would cut one. They would just be creative until they either got tired, or the musicians had another gig that they had to run to, or whatever." When it came time for the O'Jays to record the vocals, Eddie Levert said he "felt every drop" of Gamble and Huff's emotion-fused songs. "Kenny and Leon understood the human condition. They told the truth. I lived with every song of theirs, in every stage."[15]

The album's first single was the Gamble and Huff–penned "Put Your Hands Together," which featured poignant cry and response calls over an extended vocal break. After a slow start, in early 1974, the song reached number two on *Billboard*'s R&B charts and number ten on the Hot 100. Just as "Put Your Hands Together" began to lose steam, the African-derived polyrhythmic "For the Love of Money" was released as the next single. Bobby Eli, whose inflammatory "wah-wah" guitar permeates the song, recalled how New York bassist Anthony Jackson came up with the original concept of "For the Love of Money." Jackson "came in the studio with the bass line and Gamble and Huff wrote the song around that bass line," said the guitarist. "For the Love of Money" was the song that Joe Tarsia "had the most fun in being involved in." Tarsia's involvement demonstrates why he and his recording studio were considered an integral part of the sound of Philadelphia Soul. The recording of the *Ship Ahoy* album required the overdubbing of sound effects, "like the whips and chains and all the groans and backwards effects and everything," recalled Bobby Eli, who played guitar on the sessions. Because of the limited amount of channels on the mixing board in Sigma Sound's upstairs studio, Tarsia linked it to the board in the recently opened downstairs studio in order to add the special effects to the final mix of the album. Then the sound engineer really went to work. He took a tape of the O'Jays singing the chorus of the song and recorded it backward, onto the final master recording. He then conceived a recorded echo effect by leaving open one of the recording channels and then flipping the tape again, thus creating a "fade-in" chorus. "I think I should have gotten production credit," the studio wizard jokingly exclaimed as he recalled the incident. "For the Love of Money" was Philadelphia International's seventh million-selling single (and the third for the O'Jays).

Everything about *Ship Ahoy*, including its display of varying styles and lyrical content, Eddie Levert's leads, Walter Williams's and William Powell's harmonies, as well as Bobby Martin's arranging and Gamble and Huff's production, was astounding. It remained on *Billboard*'s album chart for forty-eight weeks; where it peaked at number eleven in the spring of 1974. Decades later, many still claim it to be the O'Jays greatest album ever. Pop music critic Ron Wynne, for one, called it a "masterpiece . . . [that] combined shattering message tracks and stunning love songs in a fashion matched only by Curtis Mayfield's finest material."[16]

Unfortunately, the recording success of the O'Jays and the Blue Notes did not extent to Billy Paul. The singer recalled that, after the "Am I Black Enough for You?" fiasco, "there was a lot of pressure" on him to record a follow-up album as quickly as possible. The result was *War of the Gods*, on which Paul, in an effort to court both his two distinct audiences, continued to tiptoe between jazz and soul. *War of the Gods* was on par with its predecessor (save for the fact that it lacked a two-million-selling single). The album's lone single did receive considerable radio airplay, "But it was too late by then," said Phil Hurtt. *War of the Gods* did not contain a song good enough to overcome the attitude of disapproval generated from the release of "Am I Black Enough for You?" and Paul's latest album failed to make *Billboard*'s Top 100 listing.

It was sometime during the fall of 1973 that Gamble, Huff, and Bell, now ensconced in their new headquarters, chatted with a reporter sent by the prestigious *New York Times* to conduct an interview that, when published, would confirm their arrival in the business. Speaking from behind a pale blue piano in his office, Thom Bell effusively pointed out how, despite the ado over Philadelphia's famous dance music, his work was created "for folks who listen as well as those who dance." Kenny Gamble, exuding his advancing paternal rationalism, explained how he, Huff, and Bell "work to give our audiences a number of different things to hear. It's all there," including strings, horns, multiple percussion lines, and strong voice fixtures, "if you want to listen to it," said Gamble. In keeping with his belief of setting a role model, Gamble said that "black kids need to know" about the ghetto beginnings of him and Huff and how the two are now "responsible for producing, dig that, producing something that can be sold proudly, anywhere in the world. The records we make project a call for harmony and understanding. Some people think it's hip to mock that, but we're just trying to live up to what this city is supposed to symbolize." Leon Huff caustically vented his feelings about the white press and how his and Gamble's "crossover" into the mainstream domain had drawn some negative criticism, mostly from white critics. Saying that the "rock critics [had not] been very receptive to our music," Huff, in a huff, declared that "the press is composed of mainly people who cannot really hear black music." Huff defiantly added that he and Gamble "hear the town better than anybody else, we know what it sounds like sweet, and what it sounds like going bad. People don't have to dig our music, we ask simply to be respected. Some whites have difficulty doing that—respecting black cats without patronizing us, and we don't need any disrespective kind of nicest-colored-guys-I-ever-met type of jive from anybody."[17]

In the *New York Times* article, Gamble also boasted how Philadelphia International's relationship with CBS "pays very solid mutual dividends," and Huff agreed that the arrangement was profitable all around. Indeed, thanks to the Blue Notes, the O'Jays, and Billy Paul, Philadelphia International was finally coming up with blockbuster albums, much to the satisfaction (and relief) of CBS. Gamble and Huff's company ended its banner year with the release of MFSB's second album, titled *Love Is the Message*. The first single from the album was the dance-oriented opus called "TSOP" (for "the sound of Philadelphia"). The song not only became Philadelphia International's third million-selling single to top *Billboard*'s R&B chart and the Hot 100, but it added another hit recording act to Gamble and Huff's roster.[18]

As AMERICA'S HEDONISTIC GENERATION REVELED in a dance explosion heretofore unseen in a decade, Philadelphia's soulful dance music, as demonstrated by the widespread popularity of "TSOP," exerted its influence on the R&B market. Kenny Gamble crowed that the Philly Sound "is the best kind of dance music there is."[19] Few argued the point. Relying on Philadelphia International's eminently danceable funk and lavishly soaring soul singles had resulted in the company's two biggest albums (*Ship Ahoy* and *Love Is the Message*), as well as the Blue Notes' million-selling dance-floor classic, "The Love I Lost." Ron Alexenburg said that Gamble and Huff's label was a "tremendous help" in Columbia's weathering the economic downturn in that it put CBS "right back in the black record business." At one of CBS's annual conventions, Harry Coombs handed Alexenburg a preview cassette of the O'Jays' "For the Love of Money." The Epic Records president stood up in front of the entire CBS Sales and Promotion department and introduced the song as the next release from Philadelphia International. Alexenburg then reminded the crowd that Gamble and Huff's company "has made you people nothing but"—at which point he sang the lyric, "money, money, money." The audience of over a thousand CBS people stood and cheered.

It was not just in America that Philadelphia International had taken the industry by storm. "It was obvious," remarked Kenny Gamble, "that what Philly had to give, the whole world wanted."[20] Recognizing that development, CBS established Philadelphia International labels in England and several European countries. As 1973 ended, Kenny Gamble, Leon Huff, and Thom Bell took their biggest acts to Europe in order to mine the global market that now existed for Philadelphia Soul.

10

"I'll Be Around"

(1974)

THOM BELL, THROUGH MIGHTY THREE MUSIC, was now affiliated with Kenny Gamble and Leon Huff, but the affable and strong-willed maestro, regarded by industry movers and shakers as one of its hottest creative talents in the business, continued his independent production work. The bulk of it was with the Stylistics, whose lush, sweet-soul recordings had, after just one album, established the group as the leading practitioners of that genre.

In the spring of 1972, just as "People Make the World Go Round," the final single from the Stylistics' debut album, was released, Bell took the group into Sigma Sound to record their second album, called *Round 2: The Stylistics*. In making that recording, Bell decided to add female voices that would "sing with a certain sound, an octave above whoever else I was recording."[1] His use of Linda Creed and Barbara Ingram to perform that function on his initial recordings of the Stylistics had been a transitional move. Now, Bell instituted his plan in earnest. "I need background singers," he told Barbara Ingram. "Can you get me some?" "No problem," she replied.[2] Ingram called her first cousin, Carla Benson, who was a music major at a nearby college, and asked whether she knew anybody else who could sing. "Well, [my friend] Evette is sittin' right here!" came the reply.[3]

Evette Benton and Carla Benson had been friends since kindergarten. Over the years the two had grown closer and closer, with Evette becoming "like the sister I never had," said Carla. The two attended Camden High together, and when it came time for college they became roommates. (Barbara, who was several years older than Carla and Evette, was already working.) At the time, Carla, who had been singing as long as she could remember, and began formal training at the age of twelve, was a classically trained lyric soprano who could flawlessly execute an Italian aria. While Carla never sang in church, Evette regularly sang in her church choir.

Evette recalled how she was "terrified" as the makeshift trio drove across the bridge from Camden to Philadelphia for an audition with Thom Bell. When the young ladies arrived at the assiduous maestro's office in the Schubert Building he sat down at the piano and, one by one, accompanied each singer on her choice of songs. But when Bell asked them to sing something together, the novice trio responded with a dumbfounded look. "We didn't even have sense enough to plan a song!" exclaimed Evette. They quickly put together a three-part harmony rendition of the chorus of the current pop hit "MacArthur Park." That was more than enough for Bell, who called Gamble and Huff into his office.

After Barbara, Carla, and Evette again sang "MacArthur Park," Huff growled, "Ya'll wanna sing on a session? Ya'll wanna make some money?" They said yes, and he told them to report to the studio at midnight. Why midnight, they wondered aloud. " Musicians "sleep in the day and work at night," he snapped as he left the room. "That's the business."[4] Thom Bell adopted a more paternal attitude with his new backup singers. "Once we start using you, you do know your lives are not gonna be the same, don't you?" he asked. "Yeah, we'll see," was the trio's sardonic reply. That night, they sang on their very first professional session: Joe Simon's "Pool of Bad Luck."

Their next assignment was *Round 2: The Stylistics*. Bell pointed out how, in every big recording studio, "just like with the musicians, there's always one set of background singers that are the 'A-team.'" "And I'll tell you, boy," Bell effusively recalled, "those mamas gave you a sound! They sang perfectly above the tops of the lead singers, without intruding." Barbara, Carla, and Evette quickly developed into Sigma Sound's A-team, and would back up a wide array of singers, on hundreds of songs, for years to come. "Tommy mentored us . . . the entire way through," said Carla. "He told us so many things. . . . If he said it, we did it." Bell also served as their protector. People "kinda learned not to mess with us, because if they did, Thom would take care of it." Initially, the trio was informally referred to as "Tommy's girls," but after Joe Tarsia christened them the "Sweethearts of Sigma," that sobriquet stuck.

Backed by the Sweethearts' vocals, the Stylistics maintained their torrid hit-making pace. That fall the group experienced their third million-seller, "I'm Stone in Love with You."[5] The Stylistics' second album actually contained two million-selling hits, but that striking achievement was overshadowed by the fact that Bell was already looking past the group.

IF THOM BELL POSSESSED ONE OTHER CONSTANT besides his knack for creating Top 40 hits for the Delfonics and the Stylistics (the total stood at eleven at this point), it was his propitious sense of knowing when to move on. "You see," he explained, "in the whole of my recording career my idea is to learn as much as I can about something, then use that as a stepping stone and go to the next thing, but still retain what's been learned. So when you move up you'll be wiser."[6] Bell had also grown bored with the Stylistics, much as he had while working with the Delfonics. Both groups had sterling lead singers, but the relatively weak background singers Bell had to work with put a damper on his ambitious compositions. It was all Bell could do to augment the supporting singers' rudimentary sounds, let alone experiment with new ideas. It was time for Bell to "move up" to a new challenge.

Just prior to the recording of the Stylistics' second album, Bell moved to exploit Atlantic Records' recently established conduit to Sigma Sound (Dusty Springfield, Archie Bell, and Wilson Pickett). Bell did so with the Detroit-based Spinners, who, like most of the reclamation projects that ended up at Sigma Sound, toted significant baggage in the form of previous recordings. Between 1972 and 1976, under Bell's tutelage and powered by the twin lead vocals of Phillippe Wynne and Bobbie Smith, the Spinners evolved into an integral part of the Philadelphia Soul sound. Their incredible run of hits during that stretch made them one of the most popular and successful vocal groups in the history of modern black music.

THE SPINNERS BEGAN AS THE DOMINGOS, five Detroit ghetto youths— C. P. Spencer (lead), Bobbie Smith (tenor), Henry Fambrough (baritone), Pervis Jackson (bass), and Billy Henderson (tenor)—who got together in high school in 1955. After winning the Top Amateur Vocal Group award in Detroit in 1957, the Domingos changed their name to the Spinners, and George Dixon replaced Spencer as the group's lead singer.[7] After developing a strong reputation around Detroit, their first record, "That's What Girls Are Made For," became a hit during the summer of 1961. But the meager distribution of their record label, owned by former Moonglow Harvey Fuqua, undermined the group's success. In 1962, Fuqua, then married to one of Berry Gordy's sisters, merged his label (and the Spinners) with Motown. By that time, Edgar (Chico) Edwards had replaced George Dixon in the group.

Beginning in 1964, the Spinners had five releases on Motown, with varying degrees of success. But it seemed as if Motown's best songs went to other artists. Meanwhile, in 1967, G. C. Cameron replaced Chico Edwards and became the Spinners primary lead singer. The Spinners were then moved to one of Motown's subsidiary labels, where, in 1970, they enjoyed their biggest hit up to that time.[8] However, several disappointing releases later that year brought the group back down to earth. Weary of shifting labels and producers and of receiving second-rate material, the Spinners were convinced they would forever be lost in the shuffle at Motown, and when their contract expired in 1971, they decided to move on. G. C. Cameron chose to stay with Motown to pursue a solo career. As his replacement, he recommended Philip Walker, a friend from Cincinnati who had recently been rejected in his bid to join the Contours. Walker, a troubled loner whose psychological problems would continually constrain the Spinners, joined the group and became Phillippe Wynne.

Longtime friend Aretha Franklin put the Spinners in touch with Atlantic Records, and the group signed a contract with that company near the end of 1971. Early the following year, the Spinners cut four tracks in Detroit that Atlantic subsequently deemed not worthy of release.[9] "They had spent $20,000 . . . and the stuff sounded terrible," said Thom Bell, who, at that point, was set to enter the picture. Atlantic president Henry Allen approached Bell about producing one of the company's artists. Bell told Allen to send him a list of those who were available. Among the artists on the list were Roberta Flack, Eddie Floyd, Aretha Franklin, Wilson Pickett, and Sam and Dave. Bell noticed that the typing on the last page was "crooked" and ran off the paper. On the very bottom line he could make out the letters "S" and "P," and a piece of an "I" and a little bit of an "N." He wondered whether these were the Spinners.

Bell had been aware of the Spinners since the summer of 1961, when the group came through North Philly as part of a package tour, singing "That's What Girls Are Made For" at the Uptown Theater. Bell, who was the house pianist at the time, was duly impressed by the group's rendition of the song.[10] Now, a decade later, Bell called Atlantic and asked whether the Spinners were, indeed, on the list he received. They were, but Atlantic discouraged him from selecting them, saying that the company was prepared to release the group from its contract. "Hold it, no!" exclaimed Bell. "I'd like to do them." Atlantic assured Bell that he really did not want to get involved with such an underachieving group. "I *know* who I want," exclaimed the producer. "I want those Spinners!"

When Bell and the Spinners finally met, however, they did not want him. "Motown did such a number on them that they never wanted to see a black producer again," revealed Bell.[11] But creative ideas were already in Bell's head, and he was not to be denied. The producer, who did not even possess a driver's license, challenged the Spinners with a curious wager. If Bell produced a number one record for them, they would buy him a Cadillac. If Bell failed, he would pay each Spinner $10,000. The group agreed, thus paving the way for an incredible run of hits that would overshadow Bell's productions with the Delfonics and the Stylistics. The first thing Bell did was institute a significant change in the Spinners lineup. Seeking to expand on his airy, string-laden style of soul, Bell reinstated Bobbie Smith as lead vocalist (his light tenor had heretofore been considered too weak to carry that position). The move was a stroke of genius, as Smith's voice proved a perfect match for Bell's leisurely arrangements.

That is not to say Bell did not encounter problems working with the Spinners. Because of the amount of money Atlantic had spent on the group's aborted sessions earlier in the year, the recording company authorized funds for only four new Spinners songs. "I'm telling you, you're gonna want and need an album, and I'm not gonna be able to give it to you because I'll be booked up doin' somebody else," warned Bell. But not only did Atlantic refuse to fund an album's worth of material for the Spinners, they also refused to pay the group's fare to travel to Philadelphia to record. So it was that, in the summer of 1972, working with the mainstays of the Philadelphia rhythm section, Bell laid down four tracks at Sigma Sound and then took a duplicate master of the music to Detroit, where the Spinners did their voice-overs. When Bell returned to Philly, he "put the girls on, and the strings and horns, and mixed it." The songs were four pop-soul masterpieces. The first single, "How Could I Let You Get Away," a lush Stylistics-type ballad, was issued that July, but radio deejays soon opted for its flip side. "I'll Be Around." The song, written by Bell and high school classmate Phil Hurtt (Linda Creed, preoccupied with planning her wedding, did not write any of the four Spinners songs), was a smooth, guitar-dominated dance number punctuated by Larry Washington's infectious conga-playing. Thanks to the deejays that flipped the record, Bell did not have to wait long for his new Cadillac. "I'll Be Around" became the Spinners first number-one R&B record and a million-seller to boot. (Hurtt laughed as he recalled how Creed, after returning from her honeymoon, chased him down the Schubert Building hallways, shouting, "You stole my song!" "I didn't steal your song," Hurtt playfully replied, "you got married!"[12])

Thom Bell was off to a fine start with the Spinners, and 1973 proved even more fruitful for him. While that year was the breakout year for Kenny Gamble and Leon Huff's Philadelphia International Records, it was simply another breakneck year for Bell. In some ways it was also a surprising one. Although Bell now routinely turned down requests to produce other artists, he was about to take on a group of which he wanted no part. Late in 1972, an acquaintance of Bell approached him and pleaded for him to write for and produce a group that he had under contract. Bell, who customarily listened to any artist before he agreed to work with them, uncharacteristically agreed to produce his friend's group without first hearing them sing. Linda Creed was still on her honeymoon, so Bell teamed up with writer Sherman Marshall for the project. Meanwhile, the group in question had just changed its name from Triborough Exchange to New York City. "Man, that's dumb!" thought Bell. "Just hearing those words doesn't mean anything. It doesn't cut through." Hearing New York City sing did not cut it for Bell, either. The lead singer "couldn't really sing," he recalled. But what was worse, "he'd get mad when someone tried to teach him how to sing." But a promise was a promise to Bell, so he spent several weeks in the studio with MFSB, laying down the rhythm tracks for an album. Then, Bell and Marshall, "doing the best [they] could possibly do" and employing "more tricks ... than the man in the moon," managed to complete the album (which Bell said he "hated"). The album and the single, both titled "I'm Doin' Fine Now," were released early in 1973. The song became a Top 20 hit, but Bell dismissed the group's accomplishment by saying, "Most people thought that was the Spinners."[13]

Besides his grudging work with New York City, Bell also found time, at the behest of the Spinners manager, to produce sessions for Ronnie Dyson, who first made his mark as the teenage star of the Broadway musical *Hair*. Dyson's "One Man Band (Plays All Alone)," produced by Bell for Columbia Records, became a hit early that year and opened the door for Bell to fulfill one of his most prized goals. He was able to produce an album for Columbia's melodious pop crooner Johnny Mathis, whom Bell had long idolized. Mathis was "the *crème de la crème*," thought Bell. "He has a fantastic voice, man." Bell had been angling to produce Mathis for over a year, but when he first contacted Clive Davis about doing so, "Clive didn't want to give him to me. He couldn't quite see this young black guy in Philadelphia, doin' the kind of music I do," produce Mathis. "What kind of music do I do?" wondered Bell, who thought perhaps Davis had him mixed up with Gamble and Huff, or somebody else in Philadelphia. But Mathis's recording career had taken a downturn as of late. "The black stations weren't playing him; the white stations weren't," said Bell. "Nobody was playing him at all." Bolstered by his work with Ronnie Dyson, Bell finally convinced Davis to let him produce Mathis.[14]

In one of Clive Davis's final moves before being fired by CBS, he set in motion the Mathis-Bell recording sessions. Bell recalled the first time he and Linda Creed "sat" with Mathis, and the awestruck producer told him to "just sing anything, man." After just ten minutes, Bell told Mathis, "That's all. I'll see you probably in two month's time with some songs." Mathis was taken aback by the short amount of time Bell had listened to him sing. "That's all I need, man," explained Bell. "In my mind, I'm imitating you. If I can imitate you in my mind I can write for you." (Mathis, on the other hand, recalled having "long conversations" with Bell and Creed about the projected songs for the album, during which "they took all my thoughts, all my little quirks and what have you and put them into songs."[15])

However it happened, Bell and Creed then wrote for six weeks straight, "nothin' but writing, two songs a day," recalled the producer. That was not good enough for a still-wary Columbia, however. Mathis's recording career had evolved to the point where he now sang mostly songs made famous by other artists. In keeping with that pattern, Columbia asked Bell to include a couple of "old songs" on the album. "Catch me while I'm young and fresh," protested Bell. "When I'm old I'll do old songs." But Columbia remained adamant, so a compromise was worked out. Mathis "loved" two of the Stylistics' hits, "Stop, Look and Listen (to Your Heart)" and "I'm Stone in Love with You," and wanted to include them on the album, said Bell. That was fine with Bell, who thought it was "keeping with old songs that were previously done, and kind of new at the same time."

That summer, Bell took the MFSB rhythm section into Sigma Sound and recorded the rhythm tracks for Mathis's new album, *I'm Coming Home*. (Playing for Mathis "was a different thing, really a challenge," recalled the heavy-handed drummer Earl Young, who had to tone down his act considerably for the occasion.) When the album was released, Bell hired his own promotion man to work it, seeking "to break out in areas that I [previously] couldn't break." Although the album's first single, the Burt Bacharach–inspired "I'm Coming Home," became a number-one adult contemporary hits for one week in the fall of 1973, that lofty plateau was mostly the result of heavy radio airplay, not record sales. While the release of "I'm Coming Home" returned Mathis to *Billboard*'s Hot 100 chart for the first time in over four years (and became his biggest chart hit since 1963's "What Will My Mary Say"), the song stalled at number seventy-five.[16]

Mathis's *I'm Coming Home* album was artistically satisfying for Thom Bell, who said that he "wanted the best that we could get, and we got the best," and for the esteemed singer, who called it "one of the best albums I've ever done." Such effusive praise served only to make the album's somewhat disappointing commercial fate a bitter pill to swallow. After failing to crack *Billboard*'s Top 100 Albums chart, *I'm Coming Home* quietly slipped from the charts. Mathis, who attributed the record's disappointing showing to the fact that Clive Davis, "the person who instigated the record ... wasn't really there to give it the emphasis," thought so highly of it that he asked Bell to become his road conductor.[17]

Bell spent a brief time on the road with Mathis in that capacity, but his immediate future did not lie with playing an endless string of one-nighters to aging concertgoers, no matter how appreciative they might be. Arranging and conducting for Johnny Mathis was self-indulgent gratification for Bell, but it was the Spinners who now loomed large in his mind. Working with the Delfonics and the Stylistics, despite their outstanding lead singers, had been more admonitory than inspirational.

But with the Spinners, Bell had the twin leads of Bobbie Smith and Phlilippe Wynne, plus three additional accomplished singers, with whom to challenge his creative genius.

In the fall of 1972, Atlantic released the last two of the four songs Bell had recorded with the group. When "Could It Be I'm Falling in Love" quickly equaled the popularity of its predecessor, becoming a number one R&B hit and selling a million records, Motown attempted to make hay with a hastily slapped-together "best of" album. And just as Thom Bell had predicted, Atlantic began to plead for an album's worth of new material from the group. Motown "tried to sneak out some product on the Spinners" recalled Bell with a laugh, "and Atlantic was hot with me because they didn't have an album."

Bell took the group into Sigma Sound in February 1973 and laid down six more tracks to fill out the Spinners self-titled debut album for Atlantic. The sessions were "very structured and detailed," remembered Joe Tarsia. "While Gamble's rhythm sections might take all day to do one song, Tommy would go in precisely with three or four songs and hand out charts with no spontaneous innovation asked for, or wanted!" Bell had painstakingly gone through his ritual of introducing the new songs to his artists. "I'd sing all the parts, sing the background," he explained. Each group member had a tape recorder. When Bell came in, he "started teachin' them the song. Bobbie would bring his tape recorder over and I'd sing all of his parts on that song. Then with Phillippe, I'd sing all of his parts. And Henry, 'bring your recorder over here.'" Each group member thus had his own parts to the song on his own recorder, "so that at their leisure they could rehearse those parts," explained Bell. "But I tell you, I was working day and night" to get the job done.

The Spinners was released in March, along with the single "One of a Kind (Love Affair)." Joseph Banks Jefferson, who became one of the Spinners' main writers, wrote the song. Jefferson, born and raised in Petersburg, Virginia, landed in Philadelphia some years earlier due to one of life's twists of fate. During the mid-1960s, Jefferson was the road drummer for the Manhattans R&B vocal group. While playing in Philadelphia, Jefferson came down with a foot infection so serious that he had to withdraw from the tour. He rented a small apartment in West Philadelphia for what he thought would be a couple of months. "I've been in Philly ever since!" he exclaimed in 2003.[18]

Early in Jefferson's career, he and three friends had formed a self-contained R&B group called the Nat Turner Rebellion. After Jefferson settled in Philadelphia, the group reformed and was signed to a recording contract by Stan Watson. The Nat Turner Rebellion toured with the Delfonics, whose road guitar player was Thom Bell's younger brother, Tony. Tony was sufficiently impressed with Jefferson's songwriting to introduce him to his brother, who was still the Delfonics' producer at the time. Thom Bell "liked a lot of the stuff I was writing," recalled Jefferson, and offered to sign Jefferson to a writing contract with his publishing company. Jefferson, who described himself as "kind of backwoods and young" at the time, jumped at the offer.[19] Soon after doing so, he received a call from Bell, who requested a song for the Spinners' first Atlantic album. As it was, Jefferson had recently broken up with his girlfriend. He proceeded to turn the words she wrote on a wall the day she left ("I'm leavin' you, I love you, I can't stay with you") into a song. When Jefferson began to sing the song for Bell, Bell abruptly cut him off at the second verse, telling the songwriter, "You don't have to play any more. That's a hit record, man!" With Bobbie Smith and Phillippe Wynne blending immaculately on a shared lead, "One of a Kind (Love Affair)" topped *Billboard*'s R&B charts (the third song on the Spinners' album to do so) and sold a million copies.

The Spinners album on Atlantic, which turned out to be a mini "greatest hits" album, also served notice that new group member Phillippe Wynne had few peers as a sophisticated soul singer. *The Spinners* remained on *Billboard*'s album chart for seven months. It reached number fourteen there and was eventually certified gold. Not that long ago, the Spinners had longingly eyed their peers at Motown. Now, supported by a newfound confidence, they rose above them. And despite the company's hastily released collection of old Spinners tracks, Motown suffered a serious case of egg-on-the-face.

AS THOM BELL BECAME MORE INVOLVED with the Spinners, it became increasingly difficult to juggle his time between them and the Stylistics. For a time in 1973, as the latter group released hit singles from their second album, there was no problem. "Break Up to Make Up," the Stylistics' first single of 1973, became the group's second consecutive million-seller (and fourth overall). "You'll Never Get to Heaven (If You Break My Heart)," released at the same time as *The Spinners* album, just missed the pop Top 20. And that summer, when the time arose for a new album and single by the Stylistics, Bell dutifully rose to the occasion, even though he realized this was his final album with the group. For some time now, Bell no longer believed he was able to take the Stylistics "to the next level. I always felt it wasn't right to take an act and just grind them into the ground," he explained. "My job is to do the creating and to give direction." Bell's yardstick for continuing to work with a particular artist involved a constant projection into that artist's future. When Bell listened to a particular artist he was producing, "if I can't hear them a year from now, if I can't make plans for them for a year from now, then, to me, I'm not doing my job. And if I can't do my job, what's the use of me being around? I'm just wasting your money and I'm wasting your time and I'm wasting my time." Bell told Avco Records that "a year from now I won't be doing any more product" on the Stylistics, thereby giving the record company time to find another producer. He then proceeded to rally the troops for one final effort.

The resulting album, called *Rockin' Roll Baby* (which was released about the same time as Bell's Johnny Mathis album), contained two exquisitely crafted hits. One was the album's up-tempo title song, the other a more typical ballad, called "You Make Me Feel Brand New," which was structured along the lines of "You Are Everything." *Rockin' Roll Baby* came about when, after finding success with "all these beautiful slow songs that Thom and Linda were writing," the Stylistics "thought it'd be nice if we could do a fast thing for a change," recalled Airrion Love. [20] Linda Creed and Thom Bell responded with the atypical, rollicking "Rockin' Roll Baby," which was driven by Thom Bell's relentless pounding piano riff. A stylistic change for the Stylistics, "Rockin' Roll Baby" became a Top 20 hit that fall.

"You Make Me Feel Brand New" was written a year earlier, during the time that Linda Creed was engaged to be married. She recalled being so happy as she wrote the song that "each line I was jumping up and down saying 'I love it!'"[21] On the other hand, Creed's writing partner "hated" the lyric to "You Make Me Feel Brand New" when he first heard it. "See, there are two things we never wrote about," he explained. "We stayed away from religion and politics," because you were "lookin' for problems" if you started writing about those topics. Bell had expected that axiom to endure when he handed his writing partner the melody for "You Make Me Feel Brand New." And he did not expect to hear anything out of the ordinary when Creed came in the next day and exclaimed, "Bell, I got it. I wrote it just for you."[22] "Yeah, okay Creed," he prosaically replied, "let's hear it."

Linda Creed began to sing, but when she got to the words "God bless you," Bell told her to stop right there. "What, are we goin' to church here or somethin' now?" he shouted. Creed broke down in tears. "I wrote it for you, Bell," she sobbed, "'cause you're my buddy, you're my pal."[23] As was her wont, Creed lamented to her parents how Bell refused to even listen to her song. Creed's father convinced Bell to at least listen to his daughter's work, after which Bell realized the song did have merit. "Okay, just this once we'll write somethin' about God," he told his distraught partner. "But if there's a bunch of a mess from this, just remember I told you not to do it."

Not only was the song topic of "You Make Me Feel Brand New" a change for Creed and Bell, so was the song's musical structure. On it, Bell introduced Airrion Love as a singer, pairing his baritone with

Russell Thompkins Jr.'s familiar tenor on a double on lead.[24] "You Make Me Feel Brand New" opens with Love singing the words, "My love, I'll never find the words, my love," as he quickly reaches his limited vocal range and his voice cracks. Only then does Thompkins Jr. (and the Sweethearts of Sigma, heard prominently in the mix) come to the rescue of Love (and the song).

Because "You Make Me Feel Brand New" was not issued as a single until 1974, by which time Bell had already split from the Stylistics, his association with the group appeared to last a bit longer than it actually did.[25] The song reached number five on *Billboard*'s R&B charts and number two on the Hot 100 that spring. (The song also added a fifth notch to the Stylistics' string of million-selling records.) In the end, "You Make Me Feel Brand New" became one of the biggest hits ever written by Creed and Bell. "So there you are," he said. "You never know, man!"

Despite the two hits contained on the Stylistics' *Rockin' Roll Baby* album, it did not fare as well as the group's first two collections and failed to break into the top half of *Billboard*'s Top 100 albums. This slightly diminished interest in the group was most likely due to the natural cycle of popularity that affects most artists, coupled with Thom Bell's growing preoccupation with the Spinners.

BELL'S ILLUSTRIOUS WORKING ASSOCIATION WITH THE STYLISTICS reached an end after just three albums (the same number he produced for the Delfonics). During that two-year span, a remarkable string of music was created. Bell's songs with the Stylistics stand as the supreme "sweet" soul productions of all time. Two of the group's albums produced by him were certified gold, and nine consecutive singles made *Billboard*'s R&B Top 10 and the pop Top 40. (Five were million sellers.) For Thom Bell, moving on was a welcome goal. But for the Stylistics, much as it had been for the Delfonics, the loss of their multitalented producer was traumatic. "Obviously," stated Airrion Love in 1974, the Stylistics owed Thom Bell "a great, great deal. And equally obviously, we want to record with Thom again." (They would, but not until the group was well past its prime, many years later.[26])

Working primarily with the Spinners, Thom Bell remained as busy as ever in 1974. More boisterous than the saccharine-sweet Stylistics, yet less tenacious than, say, Motown's Temptations, the Spinners, under Bell's tutelage, continued to evolve into one of the most popular and successful rhythm and blues vocal groups ever. Critics now hailed Bell as the "maestro of symphonic soul." If there was one surprising aspect of his success with the Spinners, it was that Linda Creed was not a significant factor in that achievement.[27]

Bell's vision of the Spinners involved a new songwriting team he had astutely assembled to write for the group's *Mighty Love* album in the fall of 1973. That team consisted of Joe Jefferson, Bruce Hawes, and Charles Simmons. Baldwin Bruce Hawes, the son of a Philadelphia minister, was a talented keyboard player who, like Jefferson, Bell signed as a staff writer for Mighty Three Music. Jefferson and Hawes each had a song placed on the Spinners first album for Atlantic; their first collaboration came on Bell's Johnny Mathis album.

The least experienced of this new songwriting trio was the street-savvy "Charlie Boy" Simmons. Joe Jefferson said that Simmons was "your resident tough guy. If you needed somethin' handled in the neighborhood, you'd give Charlie a call." The Philadelphia-born Simmons had known Kenny Gamble for many years and had even worked in Gamble's South Street record shop during the 1960s. Once Philadelphia International became established, the opportunistic Gamble was fond of telling acquaintances, "If you've got some talent, come by and see what you can do."[28] Simmons took Gamble at his word and stopped by 309 South Broad Street to see him one day. But it was Thom Bell who signed Simmons and wisely partnered him with Joe Jefferson and Bruce Hawes. Although Simmons was not a musician, "this guy could work a melody, man!" exclaimed Jefferson.

The first fruits of the Jefferson-Hawes-Simmons songwriting team had first appeared on the Stylistics' *Rockin' Roll Baby* album, in the form of three nondescript filler tracks. Writing for the Spinners was where the talented trio made its mark. Their true potential was first displayed on the group's *Mighty Love* album, for which the budding songsmiths wrote three tunes, including the title song. The song "Mighty Love" was begun by Joe Jefferson and completed by what Jefferson called "group effort." Bruce Hawes came up with the title, and Thom Bell added "that big introduction, which," said Jefferson, "really made it sing." But what truly made "Mighty Love" sing was Phillippe Wynne, who, for the final two and a half minutes of the song, stammered, stuttered, babbled, and scatted his way through an obsessive rampage, as the rest of the group repeated the song's title in the background. Released as the lead single off the Spinners' new album, "Mighty Love" became a number-one R&B and Top 20 pop hit. It also thrust Wynne to the forefront of the group.

The second single from the *Mighty Love* album was "I'm Coming Home," which was the title track of Bell's Johnny Mathis album. To the festive, driving rhythm of Thom Bell's keyboard and Larry Washington's congas, Phillippe Wynne displayed his gospel roots, and the song became a significant crossover hit. The third single from *Mighty Love*, released in the late summer of 1974, was the melancholy Jefferson-Simmons collaboration "Love Don't Love Nobody." That song originated spontaneously one day as Jefferson and Simmons sat in their office, lamenting over their recent failed love affairs. At one point, Jefferson told Simmons, "It takes a fool to learn that love don't love nobody." Simmons's eyes lit up. "Did you hear what you just said?" he asked his partner. Jefferson had not, but thanks to Charlie Boy's gut instinct, the two now had a song title to work with. "In an hour's time we had the song written," said Jefferson.[29] The seven-minute opus, released as a two-part single, is one of Phillippe Wynne's finest performances. It, too, became a significant crossover hit.

Thom Bell's idea to pair Bruce Hawes and Charlie Simmons with Joe Jefferson was a prescient one. The Spinners' *Mighty Love* album equaled its gold-selling predecessor and solidified the group's status as R&B stars. Furthermore, the Spinners now had a talented songwriting team behind them that would serve them well. "When we got together in a room it was magic, man!" crowed Jefferson. "As far as the Spinners go, we probably nailed some of the biggest songs that they had." Soon, "Jefferson, Hawes, and Simmons" began to be spoken as one word around the offices of Philadelphia International.

As smooth as things were going for Bell and the Spinners, when it came time to record his third album with the group, the producer employed a new rhythm section. While Gamble and Huff continued to rely on the MFSB rhythm section for their studio work, Bell had other ideas. "With Gambs and Huff, [the musicians] did a lot of creating," he explained. "And with me they just played what they saw on the paper." As the sound of Philadelphia grew in popularity and the city's session players—particularly those in MFSB—became more in demand by other producers, it became evident to Bell that his heretofore reliable studio talent "was just starting to spread out too much. They were doing sessions just to make money and then hurry to get out of there so they could do their own thing," he recalled. To Bell, this was intolerable. "They were handsomely paid at every session I ever did," he added. "When nobody was paying anything, I was paying double."

By the end of 1973, Bell had had enough. "You guys are too busy now and I need a fresh start," he told Baker, Harris, and Young. "And I thank you for all you've done." One of the disgruntled musicians allegedly told Bell that he would never have another hit record without them playing on it. "Never have a hit record again, huh?" fumed Bell. "I'll show you!" In preparation for the session with the Spinners, Bell recruited an entirely new rhythm section (except for Bobby Eli and Larry Washington). (It may not have been a slap at Baker, Harris, and Young, but Bell decided to call the next Spinners album *New and Improved*.) His determination to produce a hit the first time out with his new musicians was also fueled by the reactions of Gamble and Huff. "Gambs and Huff said, 'Man, you're never gonna be able to get hits with *these* guys!'" recalled Bell.

"No," he replied, "the difference between what I do with them and what you do with them is the difference between day and night." In March 1974, before Bell even began to work on the album (and its follow-up, *Pick of the Litter*, which was recorded at the same session), he sought to demolish the Baker-Harris-Young "never have another hit record" threat with the Spinners' next single. Pulling out all the stops, Bell teamed the Spinners with Dionne Warwick on a song called "Then Came You."[30] "That was why he kinda like rushed that record," claimed Jim Gallagher, who worked on the session. "He didn't even wait to do all the rest of the album."

Bell and Warwick had known each other since the mid-1960s in New York, when he played piano for "demos and things" and she sang background vocals on various recording sessions. For years, Warwick wanted Bell to produce her, but Bell said he "didn't have time" to work with her. "I was just too piled up, man." Bell now found the time. He suggested that Warwick sing a duet with the Spinners, who had been the opening act on her tour the previous summer. Thrilled at the prospect, Warwick agreed. Bell laid down the original rhythm track for "Then Came You" at Sigma, then took it to Los Angeles where he recorded Warwick's vocals at a "raggedy studio the Beach Boys had" there. When Warwick heard the playback, she "made a face," recalled Bell. "She didn't like it much, but I knew we had something. . . . So we ripped a dollar in two, signed each half, and exchanged halves." Bell told Warwick, "If the song goes number one you have to sign the thing and put "I'm sorry" on it and send me my half. If not, I'll send you my half." Then he brought the vocal tracks back to Philadelphia, overdubbed the Spinners' vocals, "and did the strings and horns and stuff." That summer, "Then Came You" topped *Billboard*'s Hot 100, and eventually sold a million copies. "She sent me my half of the dollar bill!" recalled Bell with a laugh. "There was an apology on it."[31]

The Spinners' *New and Improved* album (which contained "Then Came You") was released in the fall, along with the single, "Living a Little, Laughing a Little," a joyous, gospel-infused Creed-Bell ballad. That song became a Top 10 R&B hit, but it was also the first of the Spinners' Atlantic singles not to generate significant crossover sales. But the album's next single became a classic recording, owing to Thom Bell's masterly studio manipulation and to the obligations his artists felt toward him. That song, "Sadie," was a warm Jefferson, Simmons, and Hawes ballad, in which Phillippe Wynne reflected on the memory of the strong matriarchal figure in his life. Jim Gallagher, the assistant Sigma engineer on the session, said the bulk of "Sadie" was written by Charlie Simmons, "specifically for Phil Wynne, because in some previous conversation they had realized they had both lost their mothers when they were young."

When Simmons first brought the song to Bell, "everyone knew as soon as we heard it" that it had the potential to be an "emotionally packed" production, said Gallagher.

Gallagher first realized that Thom Bell had something special in mind for "Sadie" when Bell set aside an entire evening just to do that one lead vocal. That night, the only Spinner in the studio was Philippe Wynne. Bell gave the command to "roll tape" and Wynne sang the song, "from beginning to end, without a stop, without a punch-in, without anything," said Gallagher. When Wynne had finished the emotion-filled take, everyone in the studio was on the verge of tears. Everyone but Thom Bell, that is. "Phil, that was really good," coaxed Bell. "Let's try one more." Again, Wynne sang the song from beginning to end without stopping. At that point, "everyone was crying," said Gallagher (Thom Bell included, claimed the engineer, although Bell "will never admit it, but man, he was"). "All right Phil, that was really great," Bell told Wynne. "But I want you to do another one." At that point, the emotionally spent singer objected, saying he had poured his heart and soul out on the previous takes. "You can do it," Bell beguilingly cajoled the now-distraught Wynne. "Do another one.'" Wynne did a third take without interruption. With everyone still in tears, Bell beckoned Wynne to the control room. He then turned to Gallagher in a most business-like manner and said, "Okay, take number two is the one."

When Bell wrote the arrangement for "Sadie," he added a touch of horns to the song. But instead of strings, he added a pedal steel guitar, which projected a rural flavor about growing up poor that strings could not convey. Gallagher thought Bell's unorthodox use of the steel guitar in lieu of strings "was genius, . . . [especially] when everyone just imagined he would do a string chart."[32] Although "Sadie" did not become a huge crossover hit, it did make *Billboard*'s R&B Top 10. Perhaps most significantly, the emotion-charged song developed into a perennial Mother's Day favorite for blacks.

The widespread popularity of "Then Came You" almost single-handedly assured gold status for the Spinners' *New and Improved* album. The group was no longer "new," by any stretch of the imagination. But their evolving body of work now defined the meaning of the word "improved." Indeed, *New and Improved* became the revitalized group's third gold album and the biggest seller yet of their lengthy career. With Phillippe Wynne standing head and shoulders above his contemporary soul singers and with the Jefferson-Simmons-Hawes writing team hitting full stride, the fortunes of Thom Bell and the Spinners seemed boundless as 1974 drew to a close.

11

"TSOP (The Sound of Philadelphia)"

(1975)

By 1974, America was in a full-blown recession. The Dow-Jones average, after plunging 45 percent in less than two years amid the worst economic climate the country had experienced since the Great Depression, bottomed out. Inflation, unemployment, and oil shortages continued to rise. New York City, the financial capital of the country, was on the verge of going broke, and American industry appeared to be in an irreversible decline. There were predictions that the oil-producing countries, or perhaps the Japanese, would soon be able to buy America. The country finally extricated itself from the Vietnam morass, only to have its citizens' faith in the government shaken to the core by the Watergate scandal. In turn, America did what it usually did in the face of hard times: It danced in the face of its troubles. Given the bleak domestic climate and the fact that America was due for a dance fad (they usually occurred about every ten years; the last one involved the twist), disco was a phenomenon waiting to happen. Stressful times for the American people necessitated active physical releases such as athletics and sex. Disco dancing offered tens of millions of people a sublime blend of the two. As a result, dance clubs called discotheques became extremely popular.[1]

Disco music began to take shape in 1973. That spring, Manu Dibango's African-beat "Soul Makossa" (recorded in France) became the first dance-floor hit to emanate from the clubs to radio. It did not take the ever-hungry music industry long to discover that discos were a great way to expose its music to a whole new audience. This growing influence of the dance clubs was duly noted at 309 South Broad Street. Leon Huff said that he and Kenny Gamble sometimes hung out in the discos because "we loved to see those people dance off of our music." To Huff, disco's siren was not so much the musical form, but rather the "energy" it provided. "People wanted energy," he declared.[2] Gamble and Huff were particularly adept at injecting that energy into their up-tempo music, as evinced by the 1972 classics, "Back Stabbers," "Love Train," and "992 Arguments."

Philadelphia International was "heading the discotheque boom because the Philly sound is the best kind of dance music there is," crowed Kenny Gamble. The "discotheque boom" Gamble spoke of referred to the dance clubs, not to the music that was played inside them. Disco records per se did not yet exist in 1973. But even if they had, Gamble would not have classified his and Huff's dance-floor favorites as such. Perhaps out of fear of losing their identity in disco's onrushing flow, Gamble and Huff were reluctant to admit any complicity to the development of the genre. Huff flat-out denied that Philadelphia International ever produced "disco" recordings. He described the spirited music produced by him and Gamble as dance records that contained "a house on fire" within them. Joe Tarsia swore he "never" heard Gamble utter the word "disco"; it was simply "not a word in Gamble's vocabulary." Once Philadelphia International began rolling out the hits. Gamble "never set out" to make disco records added Tarsia. "Kenny and company made great up-tempo songs that were very danceable . . . [and] were absorbed by disco." Bobby Martin concurred. Gamble and Huff "were cuttin' what they wanted to cut, some good music, the kind of music that lasts, [that people] don't get tired of." But the producers could not deny that the energy in their records was derived from the beat. Huff claimed that he and Gamble were simply "giving people a beat they like," while Gamble said the pair's "funky dance records . . . dictated the beat."[3]

That beat emanated from Earl Young, whose steadily thumping four-on-the-floor bass drum and telltale hiss of an open hi-hat joining each beat brought him acclaim as the originator of the disco groove. (Young's 1970s drum kit is enshrined in Seattle's Disco Hall of Fame.) The powerful drummer was perfectly suited for the task. Guitarist T. J. Tindall called Young "a very simple drummer [whose] whole thing was just right in the middle of the groove. Some drummers play a little behind the beat, some drummers are a little ahead of the beat. . . . Earl was right up the middle, almost like a machine." While Young's repetition of four evenly weighted and evenly spaced pulses was just about the simplest rhythmic pattern possible, it is also one of the most versatile. Tindall said Young's straight on style "left room" in the music for Ronnie Baker's thunderous bass lines.

"I cut disco and they didn't even know they was cuttin' disco," said Young. "These are grooves that I made up in the studio. I just wanted to create my own sound as a drummer so that I didn't sound like anybody else. And I don't!" Young's defining moment occurred at Sigma Sound during the summer of 1973, while Harold Melvin and the Blue Notes recorded "The Love I Lost." Although that song began as a ballad, it evolved into an up-tempo dance classic. "I'm not particularly crazy about playin' slow songs," revealed Young. "I like to play fast songs." Young's preference for what he termed "dance music" apparently carried over into the studio that day. "The Love I Lost" did not take shape as a ballad. After Leon Huff decided that the song's slow tempo was not working, "right there on the spot, Earl came up with that hi-hat pattern that everybody started using, like for the disco records and everything," recalled Bobby Eli, who played guitar at the session. "Earl just started groovin' with that, and then I came up with that guitar figure at the very beginning, and it sort of evolved. It just came out of nowhere." "The Love I Lost" was the first record Eli could think of that had that "disco groove." Teddy Pendergrass, who sang the lead, called the song "perhaps the first disco hit."[4]

One of the strongest advocates of Earl Young's up-tempo beat was Thom Bell, who, with the help of Baker and Young, popularized a galloping rhythm that would, in time, be dubbed the "disco beat." An early incarnation of Bell's patented beat can be heard on the Spinners' "Mighty Love," which was cut not long after "The Love I Lost." "You hear that thing Earl did on the sock cymbal," said Bell, "and that basically is what started that whole disco thing, right there."

The codification of disco as a musical genre occurred with MFSB's recording of "TSOP (The Sound of Philadelphia)" early in 1974. That largely instrumental song, with its swirling strings, orchestrated heavy beat, and whispered female backing, originated as the theme for the televised dance show *Soul Train*. "TSOP" "is what the ingredients sounded like in the test tube," observed music critic Dave Marsh. "In another six months or so, they'd convert the beat and strings into a rigid formula called disco."[5] The disco formula consisted of an incessant beat (the standard tempo being 150 beats per minute), flavored with complex, sinuous Latin dance rhythms and flowery, romantic orchestrations mindful of the Big Band era of the 1940s. The simple and sparse vocals of disco recordings were as distinct as the beat of the music but were just another component of the sixteen-track productions.

In 1974, disco records designed primarily for dancing, not listening, became commonplace. That year, record manufacturers realized that dance clubs were the hottest spots in which to introduce their new product, and a number of disco records—including the Hues Corporation's "Rock the Boat" and George McCrae's "Rock Your Baby"—repeated "Soul Makossa"'s club-hit-to-radio-hit pattern. By the end of the year, the biggest dance revival since the advent of the twist was under way. While Gamble and Huff refused to utter the "D-word," they did have to contend with a host of recording studios, from Los Angeles to Detroit to New York, that began to appropriate Sigma's hallmark Philly sound. They "were bound to get imitations," said Gamble, who recalled how Philadelphia once copied the Motown sound. "What goes around, comes around I guess."[6]

BY EARLY 1975, WHEN VAN MCCOY'S DANCE-FLOOR CLASSIC "The Hustle" was released, disco was the dominant force in the pop music industry. Its popularity caused black music in general to become less soulful and more mechanical, and many veteran R&B performers had to struggle to adapt. Few suffered more than the Stylistics, who had yet to reach an even keel following Thom Bell's departure. Herb Murrell said that the Stylistics were "hurt by disco" because people did not associate "the dance thing" with the group's music.[7] On the other hand, disco's ascendency was embraced by Gamble and Huff's two leading groups, Harold Melvin and the Blue Notes and the O'Jays, as well as by the Thom Bell–produced Spinners. Early in 1975, the O'Jays' vigorous "Give the People What They Want" topped the R&B charts and propelled their latest album, *Survival*, to gold status. Harold Melvin and the Blue Notes were responsible for "Bad Luck," a socially conscious track on which Teddy Pendergrass preaches a sermon pointing to the recession era of Richard Nixon's presidency. "I cannot tell you the feeling of walkin' into that control room and hearin' 'Bad Luck' come back off the speakers," remembered guitarist T. J. Tindall, who played on the track. "Even without the vocals we knew it was a hit!" What they did not know was that "Bad Luck" would eventually come to be regarded as another milestone in the development of disco. Credit that to Thom Bell, who, although he had nothing to do with the record itself, was indirectly responsible for where (and thus how) "Bad Luck" was recorded. The landmark song emanated not from Sigma Sound's esteemed studio but from a subsidiary room tucked away in the Philadelphia International building.

After Philadelphia International moved into the former Cameo-Parkway headquarters, the building's main recording studio was converted into office space. But the smaller Studio B, which Tarsia described as "pretty state-of-the-art for its time," was left untouched. It also remained unused. With Sigma Sound just a few blocks away, who needed it? But as studio time in Philadelphia became harder to secure, Thom Bell thought the facility should be put to use. (Joe Tarsia recalled that it "was not unheard of" for an outside producer to have to wait three months to get into Sigma to record.) During the spring of 1974, Bell mentioned to Gamble that he wanted to do the Spinners' overdubs for "Then Came You" at Philadelphia International's idle studio. "That place is bad luck!" warned Gamble. "You're not gettin' any hits out of there!" Bell did not agree. "There's no such thing as bad luck, man," he said.

"You make the luck." And make it he did. After "Then Came You" sold over a million copies Bell decided to strut his stuff. "You still think [the studio] has bad luck?" he teased Gamble. "You're just lucky," Gamble tartly replied. "Well, okay," said Bell. "I hope I continue to be lucky then." Not long after that, Gamble and Huff announced their intention to record in the old Cameo-Parkway room. "They thought it was a jinx before, but I was getting hits out of that thing and all of a sudden they loved the idea of it," recalled Bell. (During the spring of 1974, Bell simultaneously recorded the Spinners' *New and Improved* and *Pick of the Litter* albums there.[8])

Gamble approached Joe Tarsia about refurbishing the tiny Philadelphia International studio as an adjunct of Sigma Sound. Sigma "was the house that Gamble built," recalled Tarsia, "so he didn't like to hear that he had to wait to get into the studio" to record. "You'll build a studio here, it'll be your studio," Gamble told Tarsia. "You'll rent space in my building, and we'll use it almost exclusively." (Ironically, Gamble and Huff's frequent use of the new studio caused Thom Bell to stop using the facility. He resumed recording at Sigma's original facility because, he recalled with a laugh, "I could get more studio time there."[9])

Thom Bell opened the door to the studio at 309 South Broad Street and Joe Tarsia updated the room. In doing so, each set the stage for the creation of one of disco's landmark sounds. Fittingly, the event centered around Earl Young, who, having developed his signature hi-hat disco groove the previous summer, was set to establish his up-tempo groove as a disco mainstay. Harold Melvin and the Blue Notes' latest album, *To Be True*, was one of the first to be recorded at the studio inside Philadelphia International. At that session, Young, who particularly enjoyed playing with the Blue Notes, "because I had a chance to play dance music, which is what I really like to play," was raring to go. Recording engineer Jim Gallagher, who had been hired as an assistant by Sigma Sound the previous year, recalled that this was "the first session we were really doing in the new room after rebuilding it . . . and we weren't accustomed to exactly the way things were going to sound. It was still pretty experimental." As a result, when the rhythm track to "Bad Luck," the album's first single, was laid down, Tarsia "accidentally recorded the hi-hat microphone, where just a little too much of it got into the other mikes. It came out a little bit too bright and a little bit too close. . . . And because Joe didn't have a lot of control over it, that hi-hat remained very loud in the mix. And that became part of the signature sound that helped bring disco about!" (Released at the beginning of 1975, "Bad Luck-Part 1" reached number five on *Billboard*'s Hot 100 and cemented the Blue Notes' reputation as a disco-friendly group.)

Whether it was a blistering dance track or a smoldering ballad produced by Kenny Gamble, Leon Huff, or Thom Bell, the predominant element in those records was the producers' assembly-line technique. (Although Bell began his production career by recording "live" in the studio, for expediency's sake, as Bell's career progressed, he generally adopted Gamble and Huff's method of operation.) First, the rhythm track was developed, then the lead vocals, backing vocals, and, finally, the "sweetening" were added in layers. Strip away the lead vocals on the majority of those records, and what remains exudes a kind of generic quality. One reason for this sameness is that the lineup of musicians who made the music rarely, if ever, varied. Another reason is that the background vocals on most of those records—for single artists and groups alike—were augmented by the same handful of anonymous studio vocalists.

BACKGROUND ENHANCEMENT OF THIS SORT had long been a common practice in the recording industry and, in and of itself, is hardly worth a mention. But the unspoken truth of the Philadelphia Soul production line is that on many of the group records recorded by Gamble, Huff, and Bell, only some—and sometimes none—of the background singers were actual group members. The practice began at least as early as 1968 for Gamble and Huff, when they and a few other studio vocalists became Archie Bell's "Drells." To many individuals involved in making the recordings for Kenny Gamble, Leon Huff, and Thom Bell, the topic of who did or did not sing on them is a sensitive one. Earl Young said that while it is true those studio vocalists were sometimes used in place of regular group members, he preferred not to address the subject, "because I don't like for people to know things like that. That's like a kick in the butt on the singers!" Evette Benton, who, with the other two Sweethearts of Sigma, sang anonymously on just about every record produced in Philadelphia during the mid to late 1970s, responded with a tentative "Yeeah" when asked whether certain lead vocalists at Philadelphia International had sometimes been backed by a group of anonymous studio singers. Citing concern about possible "legal stuff," Benton would not reveal any of the groups who were missing in action in the recording studio. But she did acknowledge that the practice did (and does) occur throughout the recording industry. Sigma engineer Joe Tarsia was privy to more Philadelphia Soul recording sessions than anyone else. The sound engineer made what he termed a "blanket statement" regarding Gamble, Huff, and Bell's (and other producers') use of anonymous background singers: "I don't care if it was the Stylistics or Harold Melvin and the Blue Notes, or whoever. All the backgrounds on all those songs were sung not by the groups, but by either Kenny Gamble, Leon Huff, Thom Bell, Carl Helm [or] Bunny Sigler." Tarsia's understudy, Jim Gallagher, agreed that "most groups" had their recordings enhanced by studio vocalists, and Bobby Eli, who produced a number of sessions on Blue Magic and other Philadelphia Soul groups, claimed that the use anonymous of background singers "was kind of the rule of thumb."

The demonstrative Bunny Sigler offered a more intimate glimpse into the practice. "Generally," he acknowledged, "the same three males and the same three females sang the background parts," giving the background vocals of groups such as Blue Magic and the Stylistics "the same texture." Kenny Gamble, Carl Helm, and he did "most" of the background singing on the Stylistics' hits. Sigler, Helm, "and either Kenny or some other person" sang the backing vocals for Blue Magic. That other person was often Ron Tyson (who eventually became a member of the Temptations) and Phil Hurtt. Hurtt said that "the guys who got the most work on the background [were] me, Bunny Sigler and Carl Helm. We were a lot of different groups. We were everybody that came in there!" Even the mighty Spinners received some assistance in the recording studio. "There was one [group member] who couldn't sing, so I just sang his part," revealed Bell, who also made ample use of the Sweethearts of Sigma on the Spinners' records. On some tracks, the female vocals are as prominent in the mix as are those of the group members.

Of the hit-making groups produced by Kenny Gamble, Leon Huff, and/or Thom Bell, the O'Jays were probably augmented least. Bell, who did his share of anonymous background singing, was quick to acknowledge that the O'Jays "can handle their singing, those boys *can* sing!" The only reason that background vocalists were added to the O'Jays' records, said Bell, was because "there was only two of 'em, so you needed a third and fourth voice." (Jim Gallagher recalled that "every once in a blue moon" Bunny Sigler would sing bass on an O'Jays track, and Phil Hurtt claimed that he and Sigler sang with the O'Jays on the *Back Stabbers* album.)

By far, the group that has generated the most controversy over how much they sang—or did not sing—on their own records is Harold Melvin and the Blue Notes. Thom Bell claimed that on most of the Blue Notes recordings, no Blue Note other than Teddy Pendergrass could be heard. The background singers were "usually me, Gambs, and Huff." Joe Tarsia recalled that "for the most part, the only people that sang on [the Blue Notes] records were Harold [and] Teddy," while Jim Gallagher said that "sometimes one or two of [the Blue Notes] were there, but not all of them. It depended on the song." The disregard Gamble and Huff apparently had for the Blue Notes' backing singers is evinced by the disparate recollections of group members Teddy Pendergrass and Bernard Wilson. Pendergrass claimed that the Blue Notes' input "was never discouraged," that group members were "always encouraged to contribute" their own ideas. Being the indispensable lead vocalist, perhaps that was the case for Pendergrass, but according to background singer Bernard Wilson, when it came time to record, the Notes "had no input." They went into the studio and were told, "Here's the music, record it [and then] get out!"[10]

The reasons for using studio background singers varied from group to group and situation to situation. Some group members simply did not sing all that well. "A lot of times they would record the groups singing the background, and the recordings were so awful!" exclaimed Sweetheart Carla Benson. "So they called the [studio] background singers in to help them out." Joe Tarsia pointed out how many of the groups were discovered "on the street corner" and, especially early in their careers, "sang a little off, out of tune, or so forth." Gamble, Huff, and Bell just "didn't have time in those days to teach guys [like that] to do backgrounds," he added. Instead, they relied on studio professionals to do the job.

There were also some groups capable of giving a dynamic stage performance but who "left a lot to be desired in the recording process," said Bobby Eli. When such groups were onstage, "it didn't matter, because they were dancin' around, whatever, and people didn't mind. But on the record, everything was so pristine, it had to be just so." Phil Hurtt agreed that singing onstage "is a different technique" than recording in the studio, where producers sought "a little smoother sound," which was sometimes difficult for street-corner singers to master. "You really have to have your skill honed to the point where you can just blend, and know how to enunciate and how to get the word out, and how to do those things so it's pleasing to the ear," added Hurtt. "There were very few groups who could do that. If you want[ed] a certain sound on a record you had to get professionals to do it. Bunny and I . . . could blend our voices and do those kinds of things. . . . And it worked out the way [the producers] wanted, especially during the time when there was an established hit sound, and everybody was tryin' to copy that sound."

On occasion, even a group that had mastered the studio blend ceded the recording microphones to studio singers, "not because they couldn't sing," said Earl Young, but because they were on the road touring, and a producer "would have to sit and rehearse with 'em." In addition to requiring rehearsal time, some singers needed to rest their voices before they recorded. Thom Bell explained how, with a lot of singers, "there is a creative voice in record and a voice for shows, and they're completely different kinds of voices. The voice you use on a show is not the voice you're gonna use on a recording, because one is more soft and sensitive and one is hollerin'." Bell tried to give singers coming off the road three weeks' rest before they went into the studio, "so their voices will heal before I start recording them. Because if you don't have a rested voice you're gonna have a problem. They're tired and they're raspy and they're hoarse. You're not gonna get them at their best."

For whatever reason they were used, the anonymous studio background singers employed by Gamble, Huff, and Bell closely approximated the sound of the group they mimicked or their vocals were mixed so unobtrusively with the vocals of the actual group that the average listener could not discern them. In retrospect, Bunny Sigler, for one, regretted being paid per session as one of those anonymous vocalists. "We shoulda got paid like percentages of the record because we had the sound!" he lamented. "But we weren't smart enough to know that." More likely, such singers simply did not care about future percentages. With the Philadelphia Soul sound in its entire splendor, the opportunities for singers such as Sigler to turn a fast buck from a workmanlike studio vocal session seemed endless.

ONLY THREE PHILADELPHIA INTERNATIONAL ALBUMS were released in 1974 (as opposed to seventeen in 1973), but a flurry of recording activity lay just over the horizon. The company's big guns—the O'Jays, Harold Melvin and the Blue Notes, Billy Paul, the Intruders, as well as some new acts—were in and out of Sigma Sound that fall to overdub their vocals onto MFSB's prerecorded rhythm tracks. As 1975 began, Philadelphia International not only released nine albums; the company made preparations to introduce a subsidiary label.

Since Gamble and Huff's company now had four acts with at least one gold record each, its goal subtly shifted from one of trying to break new artists onto the charts to that of trying to keep those artists there. At the start of the new year, Gamble and Huff succeeded in doing so with Harold Melvin and the Blue Notes and the O'Jays (their *To Be True* and *Ship Ahoy* albums, respectively, were eventually certified gold), but Gamble and Huff's success with other Philadelphia International artists was mixed, at best. MFSB's *Universal Love* album failed to equal the gold standard they established with their *Love Is the Message* collection a year earlier, and Billy Paul's *Got My Head on Straight* did not regenerate the brief crossover success he experienced two years earlier.[11] Perhaps the only act produced by Gamble and Huff that had more disappointing results than Billy Paul was the Intruders. Once the producers' flagship group, the Intruders had more recently been reduced to playing out the string as their contract with Gamble and Huff neared its end. The group scored an impressive hit the previous year with "I'll Always Love My Mama," but the album from which it was taken (*Save the Children*) was a commercial disappointment. The Intruders' latest album, *Energy of Love*, provided a bitter end to their long association with Gamble and Huff. (Its first single, "A Nice Girl Like You," stalled before it reached the R&B Top

20, and two subsequent singles fared progressively worse.) The under-achieving *Energy of Love* album not only marked the end of the Intruders' nine-year run with Gamble and Huff; it signified the end of their recording career. There were several reasons for the demise of such a talented group. For one, the Intruders had come of age during an era when single records dominated the pop music industry. Consequently, the group's albums, especially their early ones, were essentially a collection of singles and filler material. In 1974, with albums having long surpassed singles as the dominant force in pop music, the Intruders were still regarded as a singles group. On a more personal note, the Intruders' fortunes hinged on the fragile psyche of "Little Sonny" Brown, who, throughout his career, battled depression and a disinclination to sing. (Brown briefly left the group in 1971, ostensibly to get married, which forced the rest of the Intruders to hire a stand-in for their stage act and led to the single, "I'm Girl Scouting." (Little Sonny committed suicide in the 1990s, throwing himself into the Schuylkill River.)

On a more positive note, one of Philadelphia International's recently acquired acts turned into a hot item in 1974. The Three Degrees, a female trio consisting of Fayette Pinkney, Shirley Porter, and Linda Turner, was formed in Philadelphia in the early 1960s, and then taken under the wing of the streetwise, Svengali-like veteran producer, Richard Barrett.[12] Barrett became the group's manager and secured for the malleable young trio a recording contract with Swan Records, for whom he worked at the time. But Swan was on the brink of insolvency and could not properly promote the group. During this period of transition, Porter and Turner left, and Sheila Ferguson (formerly of the Royalettes) became the Three Degrees' new lead singer (several other women filled in as the third member). When Swan folded in 1966, Barrett took the Three Degrees, who had morphed into a sleek and sexy night club act, to Boston. After Valerie Holiday became the trio's permanent third member, the Three Degrees sang their way into Boston's best supper clubs, and then they graduated to the international stage. All the while, the crafty Barrett realized that a hit record would result in even more lucrative booking for his charges, but try as he did, he could not make that happen. Two major labels neglected the Three Degrees in the late 1960s, which prompted Barrett to try a local route to a hit record. Having known Kenny Gamble from the Three Degrees' days at Swan, when Gamble and Jerry Ross wrote for the Sapphires, he and Gamble agreed to a one-shot recording deal for the Three Degrees. A single was released on Neptune Records early in 1970, but did not sell. With Neptune's future in doubt, Barrett signed the group to former employer Morris Levy's Roulette Records. Later that year, the Three Degrees had a number five R&B hit and Top 40 pop hit with their remake of the Chantels' 1950s hit, "Maybe."

That chart success increased the Three Degrees' bookings, but the group was not able to develop a signature style. Although black, they sang in three-part harmony that set them apart from the pure "soul" acts. The trio sometimes performed soul songs, but they were just as likely to break into a Broadway show tune. One critic described them as "black Barbie Dolls." When the Three Degrees' contract with Roulette expired, Richard Barrett decided to give Philadelphia International a crack at his charges. In the summer of 1973, the Three Degrees signed with Gamble and Huff. Fayette Pinkney said the group was "very excited" about their new record company and found Gamble and Huff "very creative and easygoing." Gamble's smooth yet commanding persona was a welcome relief from Richard Barrett's overbearing brusqueness (Sheila Ferguson thought Gamble to be "wonderful in that he gave me the confidence to sing. He knew I was insecure, and he brought out Sheila"), but Gamble and Barrett, both strong-willed and determined individuals, soon clashed over who would guide the group's career. (Barrett, who declared that he had "nothing good to say about Kenny Gamble," declined to be interviewed for this book.[13])

If the relationship between Gamble and Barrett was cool, so was the Three Degrees' debut on Philadelphia International. That fall, their self-titled album went virtually unnoticed, due in large part to the first single chosen to promote it. Whose injudicious idea it was to issue "Dirty Old Man" is uncertain, but the decision to do so calls to mind the inadvisable release of Billy Paul's "Am I Black Enough for You?" The song's inciting title and subject matter resulted in limited airplay, and "Dirty Old Man" did not even make *Billboard*'s Top 50 R&B (it also failed to appear on the pop charts, but was inexplicably rereleased as a B-side single late in 1974.) By the end of 1973, when the Three Degrees' second single was released, radio programmers perceived the group to be old news, and that disc fared even worse than "Dirty Old Man." Then fate intervened to turn things around for the floundering group.

When the Three Degrees were at Sigma Sound putting their vocals on the rhythm tracks for their first album, they had been asked to sing some background vocals for an instrumental track being recorded by MFSB. The song turned out to be "TSOP (The Sound of Philadelphia)," which was included on MFSB's *Love Is the Message* album and also released as a single near the end of 1973. Already familiar as *Soul Train*'s theme, and an instant favorite among the growing dance-club crowd, "TSOP" raced straight to the top of *Billboard*'s R&B and Hot 100 charts. Suddenly, the Three Degrees were in great demand. This unexpected burst of popularity happened to coincide with the group's third single taken from their languishing album, the breathy "When Will I See You

Again." Released during the summer of 1974, "When Will I See You Again" quickly sold a million copies—a year after it first appeared (unnoticed) in album form.[14] This belated surge in popularity not only jump-started sales of the Three Degrees' first album, it dovetailed nicely with the release of the trio's second album, called *International*.

With the belated success of the Three Degrees, Gamble and Huff's label now had five acts that could lay claim to million-selling records, and, with much of the credit going to Philadelphia International, Clive Davis could boast that the first quarter of 1974 was Columbia Records' "biggest in history." "It's all been very satisfying the way the whole Philly sound has been accepted as an important movement in music," said Kenny Gamble. Philadelphia International Records' worldwide success (particularly with the Three Degrees, who were more popular around the globe than they were in the States) was "a great thrill to us all . . . [and] proof that the music from the City of Brotherly Love has the sound everyone wants to hear."[15]

Buoyed by this upbeat climate, Gamble and Huff made a bid to have even more of their sounds heard by the public. Since disc jockeys were historically opposed to programming too many records released by any one particular label—lest they be accused of favoritism or worse—record companies, in an effort to circumvent this practice, created subsidiary labels. With Philadelphia International's stable of hot recording acts on the rise, Gamble and Huff were ready for a new label of their own. TSOP (named for MFSB's hit recording) was also designed to showcase a decidedly funkier type of R&B music than the slick brand of Philadelphia Soul the public had come to expect from Gamble and Huff.

By 1974, FUNK (whose development was concomitant with the rise of disco) had begun to emerge as the preferred black music style. Self-contained urban bands—musically diverse groups of men, women, blacks, and whites—that would soon eclipse the traditional R&B/soul vocal groups appeared on the charts in greater numbers, and at higher positions, than ever before. That year, George Clinton, who was on the verge of becoming the preeminent funk bandleader of the decade, produced his first significant hits. The most prominent funk group of 1974, however, was B. T. Express, whose "Do It ('til You're Satisfied)" spent twenty-one weeks on *Billboard*'s R&B chart (where it reached number one). Not far behind were Kool and the Gang, whose down-home funk style kept them on the R&B charts throughout the year, and the California-based Rufus (with Chaka Khan). In addition, James Brown, who remained a motivating force in the black community despite having lost most of his white audience in 1969, had two big-selling albums in 1974. As the funk bands made their first dramatic moves, "hope was in the air, black pride was asserted and black power was held out as a real possibility," wrote R&B musicologist Robert Pruter.[16]

Gamble and Huff planned to enter the funk fray with timely music by the People's Choice, a well-seasoned group led by the booming baritone of Frankie Brunson. Brunson, who grew up in Buffalo, New York, was a preacher's son who became proficient on piano and organ as a child, but he did not begin working professionally in music until his mid-twenties. The five-feet-four-inch singer, initially billed as "Little Frankie Brunson," began recording in 1956, to little acclaim. With his career on a slow track to nowhere, Brunson left Buffalo in the early 1960s, "lookin' for fortune and glory." He landed in Philadelphia, where he joined Lynn Hope's Band (and became a band-mate of Bobby Martin). Over the next few years, Brunson made several additional recordings, but fortune and glory continued to pass him by. Then, in 1965, he formed the self-contained combo called the People's Choice. Recording success continued to elude Brunson, however, and, in order to survive, the group settled in as a local lounge act. In 1971, a record producer who first heard Brunson scatting over a funk groove laid down by his group took the People's Choice into Frank Virtue's studio to record a proto-funk opus called "I Likes to Do It." After fifteen years and some seventeen records, Frankie Brunson finally had his hit. That summer, the blustering dance number, replete with Brunson's grunting baritone and energetic keyboard work, reached number nine on *Billboard*'s R&B chart and number 38 on the Hot 100. Not long afterward, Kenny Gamble and Leon Huff attended a People's Choice performance, after which they told Brunson they wished the group had recorded "I Likes to Do It" for Philadelphia International. "So whenever y'all get free [from your contract], c'mon down and we'll sign you up."[17]

When the People's Choice signed with Gamble and Huff in 1974, they came under the auspices of Leon Huff.[18] Brunson described how he and Huff worked together. Huff carried "a boom box" as he paced Sigma Sound. "And then, *pop*, he got an idea!" said Brunson. "He'd have an idea, I'd have an idea." Huff and Brunson wrote two songs together in that manner. When recording them, Huff refrained from using any of the regular MFSB musicians along with the People's Choice, allowing Brunson's self-contained funk group to do everything. That summer, the two songs were released as TSOP's inaugural single. Neither side charted, so when the People's Choice returned to Sigma that fall to record an album's worth of material, Huff had Brunson adopt a singing style that was "a little less raw. . . . We had a sound!" he exclaimed.

That they did. The group's *Boogie Down USA* album, released near the end of the year, boded well for Philadelphia International's new funky side. The album's debut single was titled "Party Is a Groovy Thing." Although that song did not become a huge hit, the next single, "Do It

Anyway You Wanna," went through the roof. During the summer of 1975, it topped *Billboard*'s R&B chart, reached number nine on the Hot 100, and sold a million copies. Besides yielding those singles, *Boogie Down USA* contained a song called "Mickey D's," which, said Brunson, he and Huff recorded "sittin' at the same keyboard playin,' havin' fun!" But the fun at Philadelphia International was about to come to a screeching halt.

BY THE END OF 1974, KENNY GAMBLE, LEON HUFF, AND THOM BELL were the top three soul producers in the pop music industry. That year alone, they placed over twenty hits on the charts. After just two years, Philadelphia International was the second-largest black-owned record company in the country, just behind Motown.[19] But that lofty success came with a steep price tag. Gamble and Huff's current situation was a far cry from the early days, when the producers answered to nobody but themselves as they diligently cranked out modest hits for the Intruders. Now as Gamble and Huff worked, Columbia Records looked over their shoulders, anticipating another gold or platinum album. Ron Alexenburg recalled Gamble working simultaneously on five albums at one point. He "just pressured himself, and we put a lot of pressure on him, because every time we had a hit single we needed a hit album. And Kenny and Huff were just crankin' out the hits left and right."

It was a demanding situation, one in which the creative wheels never stopped turning. "Twenty hours a day, seven days a week is not an exaggeration," attested Joe Tarsia. "We were rehearsal fools," said Leon Huff. "I don't know if the average man can hold out from all those long hours. We rehearsed for hours and hours and hours, and stayed up half the night listening to the rehearsal on the tape. We didn't get to bed until three, four in the morning. . . . And then you've got to get up and be in the studio at 10:00. . . . I don't care how late you stayed out, how late you hung out, but you better be in the studio ready to perform the next day."[20] Thom Bell recalled how he, Gamble, and Huff were so busy that they did not have time to joke around. "You had too many things to do," said Bell, who claimed that he alone was doing the job of three or four men. "Most of the time we wouldn't even see each other, and we were in the same building, same floor, a few feet away. We were like worker bees." In addition, Kenny Gamble's quirky work habits added to the heavy work load. "We'd be in the studio and the session would be over and [Gamble would] want to listen to the song twenty times," recalled Tarsia. "And then he'd call Jimmy Bishop on the phone and play it for him."

In addition to this pressure-cooker work atmosphere, Kenny Gamble had other significant issues on his plate. One was Philadelphia International's heavily mortgaged Broad Street headquarters, whose monthly payments were underscored by the inherent vagaries of the record business. Gamble also had to contend with the ongoing federal investigation into payola, of which he, Huff, Bell, and several employees at Philadelphia International were now central targets. (Bell claimed that Gamble "was scared" during the payola investigation; Ron Alexenburg said the "most difficult time" for Gamble and Huff was after they became "a target" of that probe.) On top of everything else, Gamble's problems spilled over into his personal life, which had spiraled into chaos and contradiction as he toiled furiously in the recording studio.

Gamble's storybook marriage to Dee Dee Sharp, which had encountered fundamental differences from the start, was firmly on the rocks. From its inception, Gamble was opposed to Sharp's continuing her own singing career. As she sardonically pointed out, her husband was not the type of person "to be called 'Mr. Sharp'.... Kenneth wanted me to be a wife." No, she repeatedly told him, "You married a singer. It was [as] a singer that [I] helped you get into this business. So a singer I'll remain."[21]

As a compromise, Gamble suggested that Sharp become involved with some business aspect of his and Huff's budding music empire, where, presumably, Gamble would be able to exert some modicum of control over his wife's everyday routine. Sharp took Gamble at his word and became "so involved in the inner workings" of Philadelphia International's artist management and booking arm (Huga Management) that she neglected her own singing. "I was too busy trying to help him with the groups," she lamented. Meanwhile, the thirty-two-year-old Gamble was involved with another woman. If all of that was not enough for any one person to sort out, Gamble was also in the midst of a spiritual crisis.[22] Authoritative by nature, Kenny Gamble was thought by some to be unable to rectify his sacrosanct beliefs with the trappings of his worldly success. Even more distressing, Gamble seemed hard-pressed to decide on his own spiritual beliefs. Thom Bell thought Gamble's two main problems were "with his wife and his religion, actually two religions at the same time."[23] Gamble's mother was a Jehovah's Witness convert, and her son was apparently considering a similar conversion. But then Gamble began to be drawn to the teachings of the Black Muslims, which added more indecision to his life.

The enormity and complexity of Gamble's problems finally became too much to bear. "Kenny had a nervous breakdown and a lot of things changed after that," recalled Philadelphia International songwriter/singer Gene McFadden. "His personal life did that to him. Maybe the business was a little thing that turned the screw some more, but the screw had already been turned." Gamble's public unraveling began the day he implored Thom Bell to step into his office, telling him, "You're one of my disciples." Gamble then did the same with eleven others in the Philadelphia International building that day (including Bobby

Martin), then locked the door and fell into a ranting tirade. "We were in there for about eight hours straight," recalled Bell. Gamble was "hollerin' and screamin' and preachin' all kinds of things. That was the beginning of that breakdown, and it just escalated over a couple of days." Bell remained with his distressed friend for four days, "until he finally wore himself down." During that time he contacted WDAS vice president John (Fauntleroy) Bandy, who arranged for Gamble's medical treatment. Gamble was taken to Jefferson Memorial Hospital in a "very deep" depression, recalled Bell. He remained there "about a good three months, man. . . . It was a pitiful thing."[24]

With Gamble sidelined, Bell vowed he would not "see the label drop dead." But Philadelphia International's artists "were not my artists," he added. "I couldn't produce for those artists like Gambs could. He *heard* those artists. I couldn't hear those artists." Accordingly, Bell called on people who had been working with Gamble regularly "to step up to the plate." Earl Shelton, assisted by John Bandy, took hold of Philadelphia International's reins. As for the company's recording projects, "there were a lot of records that Huff actually went in and produced by himself," said Bobby Eli. "So there was a lot of stuff that, although it said 'Produced by Gamble & Huff,' Leon Huff was actually at the helm of those sessions." Just how much recording went on during that time is not clear, but only one new album emerged from Philadelphia International during the first nine months of 1975.[25]

Columbia Records could do nothing but wait for Gamble's return. Ron Alexenburg said that Gamble's absence "had an effect on the label," but that Columbia was "patient enough to want him healthy," so the company "backed off and waited until he was healthy enough to return. Nobody went in to finish" Gamble's work. "You're gonna have to wait" for his productions, Alexenburg told Columbia's marketing staff. "When he finished, he finished!'"

Kenny Gamble recuperated and returned to work at Philadelphia International. But when he did, it was no longer the company that was responsible for one platinum album, five gold albums, and eight million-selling singles over the past two and a half years. Philadelphia International continued to turn out gold and platinum recordings (for a time, anyway), but not much else within the company remained the same. Thanks to disco and funk, popular music, too, was experiencing its own consequential change. But this transformation was by no means Gamble and Huff's greatest concern. The producers' most pressing problem in 1975 was that much of their key personnel—including most of the vaunted MFSB rhythm section—had either left or were about to leave Philadelphia International's South Broad Street headquarters as if that building itself were a house on fire.

12

"Wake Up Everybody"

(1975)

THE MASS DEFECTIONS FROM PHILADELPHIA INTERNATIONAL by the talented group of musicians known collectively as MFSB were the first crack in the Gamble and Huff recording empire. (T. J. Tindall, who played guitar with both the old and the new rhythm sections, believes that neither Gamble and Huff nor Baker, Harris, and Young "were anywhere near as strong apart as they had been when we were all a unit.") Some thirty years later, those defectors claim that the producers exploited them. Initially, those musicians' studio session jobs for Philadelphia International were highly coveted. Besides affording the security of a steady gig, working for Gamble and Huff offered those musicians a chance to exercise their musical creativity. Gamble and Huff "just didn't have the knowledge and the know-how to do it without the rhythm section," claimed Earl Young. "I mean, Gamble doesn't play any instrument. He doesn't read any music. . . . [Huff] never really wrote music out. He just wrote the basic charts. So there was never a time that they called us in there and said, 'This is what I want you to play.' They really couldn't tell us what to play." The MFSB members "knew how to put songs together," he added, so Gamble and Huff "would bring the singers in the studio and let them sing in front of us. And we [would] learn the songs and go over the chord charts and come up with ideas and beats and grooves." Such was the case with Harold Melvin and the Blue Notes' "Bad Luck," which was created around a Ronnie Baker bass line. "Gamble and Huff just jumped all over that bass line and kind of wrote that song right around it," claimed former Sigma engineer Jim Gallagher. "It was one of those 'groove' sessions where Baker goes, 'Hey, check this out,' [plays a bass riff], and the next thing you know, Huff is arranging that and they've got a track! Baker just made the song happen."

Creative sessions with Gamble and Huff were a lot more interesting and challenging to the studio musicians than was the mere playing of notes written on sheets of paper. But as time went on, and only Gamble and Huff's names appeared as writers on many songs that the musicians helped to create (Baker, for example, received no writing credit for "Bad Luck"), dissatisfaction and resentment began to emerge. Asked to comment on this situation, Earl Young bristled. The drummer said he had experienced "a lot of bad things with Gamble and Huff" and preferred not to discuss them. Yet in his next breath, Young grew extremely vocal over how the MFSB rhythm section "got ripped off" by Philadelphia International. "We might be in there playin', and they might come up and say, 'Turn the tape on while y'all are playin' that.' And they'd turn the tape on and record it, and then come up next week with a song on it." Young claims that that is how the O'Jays' "For the Love of Money," a song he described as a MFSB "instrumental with words put to it," came about. "If you notice, there's no breaks" in the music, said the drummer. "It's not a song, it's just a groove! . . . They called us in there and we helped to create the sound, but we never got credit for it." Vince Montana conceded that if it had not been for Gamble, Huff, and Bell "getting the artists and putting the songwriters together to write the songs," nothing would have happened. He wholeheartedly agreed with Young that although MFSB created many songs "right there in the studio, we never got part writers' credit." Lenny Pakula, who put in more years with MFSB than did most of his fellow rhythm section musicians at Philadelphia International, also happens to be the most bitter of the lot. Pakula claimed that when he joined Philadelphia International, he was told by Gamble and Huff that he would "have a future" there, arranging and producing. "It didn't go that way," he ruefully remarked. "I was writing all their chord charts for 'em, and doin' a lot of fill-in arrangements and things. . . . They were very slick on how to take talent out of people. . . . They sucked my talent. I'm drained from that company!"

The few musicians in the MFSB rhythm section who chose to stay with Gamble and Huff have a more philosophical attitude about the treatment that they received from the producers. "I was kind of neutral," explained Bobby Eli. "I never wanted to cause a problem or raise a stink with anybody, so everybody hired me." Still, Eli agreed that the MFSB rhythm section "came up with a lot of the ideas—the licks and riffs and all that" for Philadelphia International. "A lot of the figures you hear were actually made up on the spot by the musicians." The guitarist recalled how he might come up with "some wild-ass guitar figure, and [Gamble and Huff] would say, 'Yeah man, that's it! Play that.' So in that sense, yeah, a lot of the stuff that you hear was definitely made up by us." T. J. Tindall, who, at the time, enjoyed a parallel career as a rock guitarist, said he "didn't care" that he received only a session fee, as opposed to future songwriting royalties, as a member of MFSB.

Although the MFSB musicians were "relatively well paid" for playing on sessions, Tindall added than he "made more money doin' *Wranglers'* commercials that I did on their stuff." The guitarist claimed he was "perfectly happy" with the situation as it was. "But on the other hand, we knew [Gamble and Huff] were makin' thirty-million a year!"

Earl Young decided to take matters into his own hands and began to develop an alternative career for himself and some of his studio cohorts. The drummer formed a singing group called the Trammps, who issued three singles for Buddah Records in 1972.[1] The Trammps recorded enough material for Buddah to fill an entire album, but after the group's singles garnered little airplay or interest, for the moment anyway, Buddah chose not to release any of it. Faced with the escalating disenchantment of Earl Young and his fellow studio musicians, Gamble and Huff sought to mollify them with public recognition. After Gamble and Huff copyrighted the name MFSB, each musician signed a recording contract as a member of the newly formed group (the contract allowed each member to also record on his own, for whomever he chose). If the musicians thought they would reap any writing, producing, or publishing opportunities from the MFSB venture, however, they were mistaken. When MFSB's self-titled album appeared early in 1973, the band's members were indeed extolled in the liner notes (as was "the creative genius" of Gamble, Huff, and Bell). But in regard to the two principal sources of revenue from the album's music—writing and publishing—companies owned by Gamble, Huff, and Bell published all six songs. In addition, the only writing credit awarded to a MFSB musician was a one-third share that Roland Chambers received (Gamble and Bell received the remaining two-thirds) for one of the album's six songs. Later that year, on MFSB's second album, titled *Love Is the Message*, none of the MFSB musicians received writing credit, while Gamble and Huff were listed as the writers of half of the album's songs. Lenny Pakula, who played organ on both of those albums, lamented over how the musicians "played their hearts out" and, for their efforts, received "minimum musician's scale and a lot of promises." Earl Young agreed that the MFSB musicians "never got paid" above and beyond their session fees. "We got ripped off on that." Bobby Martin thought that "that's how things break up when you've got a good thing going." Particularly after the success of the MFSB albums, "the musicians began to think they weren't being treated right."[2]

Ronnie Baker, Norman Harris, and Earl Young spearheaded the palace rebellion. Session work was pretty much all the three had to rely on for income at the time, said T. J. Tindall. "If they didn't get enough money out of it, then they were out of luck." It is uncertain which, if any, of the three musicians were the instigators of the revolt. "Back then,

I don't think there was one spokesman," said Bobby Eli, who thought that, early on, Baker "probably was the most outspoken" of the three, Harris "was more or less the passive one, [and] initially Earl was just glad to *be* there. Earl just kinda went along with the program." But as time went on and "things started movin'," Harris became "the main one" looking after the trio's business dealings.

Meanwhile, Baker, Harris, and Young became progressively distressed over Gamble and Huff's practice of relying on the band members to, as Young put it, "come up with a groove." Young said the working relationship between the trio and Gamble and Huff deteriorated to where some recording sessions were actually aborted. Reiterating that the band "didn't get paid" to create music, and that Gamble and Huff "were building their things off of our creativity," there were days on which they told Gamble and Huff: "We ain't gonna create this thing. We're just comin' in there to play. What do you want us to play?" Gamble and Huff "didn't like that," and, as a result, "sessions were canceled," claimed the MFSB drummer. "People don't know that, but that's really what it was all about." Shut out of any writing credit, music publishing, or production opportunities, Baker, Harris, and Young formed their own publishing and production companies, rented a tiny office (which they covered from top to bottom with fur) just blocks from Sigma Sound, and set up shop.[3]

One of their first clients was a local female trio called First Choice, which recorded for Stan Watson's Philly Groove label.[4] First Choice's debut album, *Armed and Extremely Dangerous*, which appeared on the heels of MFSB's first album, employed the original MFSB rhythm section as well as the same horn and string players used by Philadelphia International. Norman Harris and Watson produced the album for "Stan and Harris Productions." (According to Thom Bell's account of Watson's alleged production with the Delfonics, it is fairly safe to conclude that Norman Harris did most, if not all, of the production.) Of the ten songs contained on *Armed and Extremely Dangerous*, Harris had a share of writing six of them, and Baker, Harris, and Young's publishing company, Six Strings, merited a share of the publishing. Driven by the album's self-titled hit single, and two other funky proto-disco dance tracks, *Armed and Extremely Dangerous* fared well in the commercial marketplace and gave the nascent production team a boost in confidence. Baker, Harris, and Young, as part of MFSB, continued to record for Philadelphia International, but Gamble and Huff were no longer the only game in town.

Once again, Gamble and Huff sought to keep their restless musicians in tow. About the same time that Mighty Three Music and Great Philadelphia Trading were formed in the fall of 1973, a deal with Columbia Records was engineered by Kenny Gamble, whereby the Trammps received their own record label and publishing company (both called Golden Fleece). But Gamble and Huff kept their fingers in the pie. Publishing rights to the music released on Baker, Harris, and Young's new label was shared equally with Golden Fleece Publishing and Mighty Three Music. For the next two years, the Trammps and several other artists recorded for Golden Fleece, with Baker, Harris, and Young doing most of the writing, arranging, and producing. Reminiscent of Atlantic Records' contractual appropriation of the Stax master recordings in the 1960s, the deal with Baker, Harris, and Young was structured so that control of the Golden Fleece master recordings ultimately reverted to Columbia. (After the Trammps hit the big time in 1977 with "Disco Inferno," Gamble and Huff reissued many of the Golden Fleece tracks on their Philadelphia International label.[5])

The Golden Fleece experience served to exacerbate Baker, Harris, and Young's dissatisfaction with Gamble and Huff, who, nevertheless, endured the musicians' harangues until the summer of 1975. Vince Montana, who said that he wanted to stay at Philadelphia International because he "enjoyed working with everybody" there, claimed that all the musicians would have stayed had Gamble, Huff, and Bell "met [their] terms." Of course, those terms included "a hundred thousand apiece," to sign contracts, added Montana. "But nobody took us up on it. They just wanted us to sign contracts, and not pay [us] any money."

"You have to remember that Tommy and Kenny were out of the old school," said Jim Gallagher. "They started back in the days of Cameo-Parkway, when the deals that were struck were pretty 'skanky' [in terms of artists' benefits]. So they felt, 'Hey, this is the way this business is. Why are you trying to change it? You don't *get* to come in and tell us that we now have to give you" this and that. Carla Benson also thought that Gamble, Huff, and Bell operated the way they did "because that's what was done to them before they were in the positions of power. . . . That's how they learned the business." It was no surprise, then, that albums by the O'Jays (*Family Reunion*) and Harold Melvin and the Blue Notes (*Wake Up Everybody*), both recorded late in 1975, were the last Philadelphia International albums on which Baker, Harris, Young, and Montana played.

"Business is business, I gotta shove off," Montana told Gamble and Huff. At the time, Salsoul Records of New York City was wooing the percussionist. "Salsoul was offering money," explained Montana, "and I went there to produce my own music." On his first album produced for Salsoul, titled *The Salsoul Orchestra*, Montana used the original MFSB rhythm section as well as Philadelphia International's regular horn and string players, whom he augmented with additional horns and Latin percussion. The album's vocals, credited to "the Salsoul Hustlers," were actually sung by Barbara Ingram, Carla Benson, and Evette Benton. Of the six original songs on the album, Montana wrote four and Ronnie Baker wrote two. Released that fall, *The Salsoul Orchestra* album yielded three hit singles.

In addition to the production work of Baker, Harris, Young, and Montana, Gamble and Huff faced another challenge to the virtual monopoly that they heretofore enjoyed with Philadelphia's top R&B talent. This incursion was led not by a handful of disgruntled studio musicians but by Columbia Records' major rival, the giant Warner-Elektra-Atlantic combine. Atlantic Records first capitalized on the growing Philadelphia Sound by having Gamble and Huff produce albums for Dusty Springfield and Wilson Pickett. Then they landed Thom Bell to produce the Spinners. Now Atlantic attempted to grab a piece of Columbia Records' Philadelphia International action.

The late H. Lebaron Taylor, who, during the mid-'60s soul explosion, became a popular R&B disc jockey in Detroit, spearheaded the effort. (Taylor died in Philadelphia in 2000, at age sixty-five.) Taylor also owned a record label there, for which he produced records.[6] Taylor "did very well in Detroit, then left there," recalled Thom Bell, who eventually became a close friend of his. Taylor then "came down to Philadelphia and started working for DAS, and became big on that station, and he became program director." As a self-taught expert on Philadelphia Soul, Taylor was selected by Atlantic to spearhead the company's foray into Philadelphia. After being named vice president of A&R (artist and repertoire) at Atlantic in 1972, Taylor began to recruit some of Philadelphia's promising R&B writers and producers for his label. He called this group "the Young Professionals." Bobby Eli, who became one of Taylor's recruits, said that Taylor's goal was "to do sort of like what Berry Gordy did at Motown with the Corporation, that little conglomeration of producers that he had." Since Philadelphia International was now the creative font of the city's soul output, Lebaron Taylor wasted no time reaching as high into Gamble and Huff's company as possible to find a disgruntled employee ripe for the picking. He found one in Bunny Sigler, who was by far the most talented employee at Philadelphia International.

A BREATHTAKING STAGE PERFORMER with an ardent local following, Sigler was also a polished writer, arranger, and producer for Gamble and Huff's company. But as a recording artist, Sigler remained unfulfilled. Weldon McDougal thought that Gamble and Huff needed Sigler's behind-the-scenes talent "more than they needed an artist," and Sigler himself claimed that he was told by Gamble, "You don't want to be an artist 'cause they don't last. You need to be a writer!"[7] Sigler's initial writing success for Gamble and Huff came on Wilson Pickett's *In Philadelphia* album in 1970. But by the time Sigler's recording contract with Cameo-Parkway finally expired and he was free to record again, "Gamble saw more value in me as a writer," he recalled. "They cut some stuff on me, but they didn't really try to cut me like I [wanted them to]. They wanted me to just write." Sigler played the good soldier and did just that (for the Chambers Brothers and Joe Simon, among others). Meanwhile, his own first single for Philadelphia International became lost among the label's first batch of peculiar releases. Then, in the fall of 1971, Sigler recorded a duet with Gamble's wife (he had originally cut the tune with Cindy Scott, on the Neptune label). For that release, Gamble listed Sigler's first name as "David," because, said the singer, "he thought the name Bunny wasn't a musical name." It did not matter. As David or Bunny, Sigler's dearth of chart success continued into 1972 (despite the exquisite Thom Bell–arranged ballad "Regina," on which Phil Hurtt sang). Sigler finally broke through late that year, when his version of the old Bobby Lewis hit "Tossin' and Turnin'" (with a slowed-down version of "Love Train" on the flip) became his biggest hit since "Let the Good Times Roll." In 1973, Sigler finally got his wish to record an album's worth of material for Philadelphia International, but its release did not herald a willingness on the part of Gamble and Huff to promote Sigler's singing career. His follow-up album, *Keep Smilin'*, did not appear until early in 1975. Even after such a lengthy period, Sigler's latest song collection contained only three new tracks, with the remaining six songs inexplicably lifted from his previous album.

Bunny Sigler's other bone of contention with Philadelphia International was Gamble and Huff's preference that he use the MFSB rhythm section for his recordings. "At that time Sigma was usin' the one band and they had their sound, [and] like Motown had their own sound, they weren't ready to change," recalled Sigler. "But I have always been a maverick. I wanted to do somethin' different so I went in and tried to cut different, and they would tell me that it didn't sound right. So that's when I got the group Instant Funk, and I was able to cut them on a lot of different things."

Feeling unfulfilled under Gamble and Huff's yoke, Bunny Sigler saw in Lebaron Taylor's offer to join the Young Professionals a chance to obtain some breathing room and perhaps a firmer grip on his own performing career. Sigler was still under contract to Gamble and Huff as a writer, but it was not an exclusive contract. True, the publishing credit on anything Sigler wrote on his own would have to be shared with Gamble and Huff, but as things were, half of his publishing already went to the producers. With nothing to lose, Sigler joined Lebaron Taylor's Young Professionals.[8]

Taylor wanted yet another songwriter for his writing and producing crew, and he sought out Sigler's sometime writing partner, Phil Hurtt, as a likely candidate. Growing up in West Philadelphia, Philip Levi Hurtt attended the same church that two members of the legendary Flamingos vocal group attended whenever they were in town to perform. The congregation sang a capella, remembered Hurtt, "and that's where my musical interests came from." During the 1950s, Hurtt's older brother introduced him to the classic R&B harmony group sound and occasionally drafted the ten-year-old as a stand-in for a wayward group member. Barely into his teens, with a painted moustache on his face to make him look older, Hurtt sang professionally in the clubs of New York City, rubbing elbows with the likes of Frankie Lymon and Little Willie John. When Hurtt was not performing, he attended high school with Thom Bell and Bobby Eli. In 1963, following a stint in the Air Force, Hurtt and his brother joined a singing group called the Mohawks. He also began to do some production work around the city, and after Cameo-Parkway was sold, Hurtt and Bunny Sigler, whom he had known since they were kids, drifted into the offices of Gamble and Huff. "There was always something going on there and Bunny and I just sorta helped out," he recalled. "We found out that we had some chemistry goin' on as writers, so we started writin' together and some nice things started happening." Sigler and Hurtt hung a parachute from the ceiling of their office, "and we had a little desk, and dim lights and stuff," he said with a chuckle. They hung a sign outside their door that read "Madhouse" and they became part of Gamble and Huff's team of anonymous background singers.

Unlike Sigler, Phil Hurtt did not have any sort of contract with Gamble and Huff. Hurtt, who had been around the music business long enough to observe the onerous situations others had gotten themselves into by signing away their rights in a contract, chose to remain independent. Although deals were a necessary part of the business, Hurtt realized that he "didn't have to give it all away and [he] wasn't gonna give it all away." The only reason he was able to work at Philadelphia International without a contract was because Gamble and Huff had his writing partner, Sigler, under contract. Accordingly, Gamble and Huff owned the publishing on anything written by the pair and "didn't need to sign me," explained Hurtt. Likewise, sharing the rights to his work with Gamble and Huff did not bother Hurtt, who, not being under contract to them, could leave at any time "without having any problem." So when Lebaron Taylor, who "had seen [Hurtt] at work with Bunny and was impressed with some of the stuff [they] were doing," approached Hurtt about joining the Young Professionals, Hurtt agreed to do so.[9]

Contract or not, Hurtt's departure from Philadelphia International did not occur without repercussions. Gamble and Huff "told all of the other writers that I was crazy [to leave], that I made a big mistake," he recalled. In addition, the songwriter claimed that Gamble and Huff removed his name from the production credit he shared with Bunny Sigler on several O'Jays recordings. Hurtt also claimed that because he co-wrote the Spinners' "I'll Be Around" with Thom Bell, Gamble (unsuccessfully) "tried to take the publishing" on that song. (Hurtt may have been the last person to work at Philadelphia International without a contract. When he left to join the Young Professionals, Gamble and Huff "were signing everybody that was in there," he exclaimed. "They were signing janitors!")

Hurtt, who was not a musician, felt that, as one of the Young Professionals, he needed someone to write songs with who could play music. Thom Bell suggested his younger guitar-playing brother Tony, and it was Tony Bell who became the final member of Lebaron Taylor's musical cadre. The team then formed a collective production company called WMOT (We Men of Talent). The original MFSB rhythm section played on their sessions, and Baker, Harris, Young, and Eli did the majority of the producing and arranging. One of the first artists the Young Professionals worked with was Southern soul singer Jackie Moore. As Atlantic had done with Wilson Pickett two years earlier, the company sent Moore to Philadelphia's Sigma Sound in order to add a slicker feel to her upcoming *Sweet Charlie Babe* album. During the summer of 1973, Moore's pop-flavored single of the album's title song (written by Sigler and Hurtt) became a hit, and her follow-up single, the spirited "Both Ends against the Middle" (written by Hurtt and Tony Bell) also proved popular.

The Young Professionals' most significant success came with the Philadelphia soul group Blue Magic and its ethereal lead singer Ted "Wizard" Mills. Bobby Eli and female tunesmith Vinnie Barrett wrote one of Philadelphia's best sweet soul hits, called "Side Show" (on which Phil Hurtt sang anonymously) for the group. Produced by Bobby Eli and Norman Harris, "Side Show" became a million-seller in the spring of 1974. The same team followed "Side Show" with "Three Ring Circus," and that song also sold a million copies. With the decline of the Stylistics, Blue Magic emerged as Philadelphia's top falsetto-soft soul group.

Bobby Eli was also successful at producing and arranging for Major Harris (formerly with the Nat Turner Rebellion and the Delfonics), whose Grammy-nominated "Love Won't Let Me Wait" became a million-seller in 1975. Eli's writing and producing, particularly for Blue Magic, cast him as a pivotal member of the Philadelphia Soul scene.[10] It also resulted in an episode of levity, when a certain group sought to recognize his recent accomplishments. Eli preferred to remain out of the public spotlight, so not many people had ever seen him. This apparently included the contributing editors of *Who's Who of Black Americans*, who recommended that the white, Jewish guitar player have his biography published in the 1974–75 edition!

Despite the talent of the Young Professionals and Atlantic Records' deep pockets, Lebaron Taylor's crew was unable to sustain its initial burst of success. Blue Magic remained a viable soul act into the 1980s, although the group's popularity did embark on a slow decline. Other artists produced by the Young Professionals ("Man, there were never that many of 'em," lamented Bobby Eli) did not live up to their potential. Even so, as the Young Professionals faded as a creative force, its individual members were busy as ever. Bobby Eli continued to work for anyone who would hire him to play his guitar, produce, and/or arrange. Bunny Sigler, who divided his time between the Young Professionals and Philadelphia International, remained with Gamble and Huff until his contract with them expired in 1976. Sigler then signed with Salsoul Records' subsidiary, Gold Mind. Phil Hurtt and Tony Bell continued their respective work on an independent basis. Ironically, the biggest beneficiary of the Young Professionals concept turned out to be Columbia Records (and, indirectly, Philadelphia International), which, in 1975, lured the talented and well-liked Lebaron Taylor away from Atlantic and made him vice president in charge of the company's black music marketing division.

IN ADDITION TO FACING THE LOSS of key personnel and rising competition within the pop music industry, Gamble and Huff continued to be haunted by Project Sound, the federal government's two-year investigation into payola and the music business. On June 24, 1975, federal prosecutors in Newark, New Jersey, made public seven payola indictments in four cities. The charges included illegal payments to radio station personnel by record companies, income tax evasion, and mail fraud and interstate transport of stolen property. Among the six corporations indicted were the Gamble-Huff Record Company (the parent company of Philadelphia International Records) and Assorted Music, Inc. Among the ten individuals cited were Kenny Gamble and Leon Huff, as well as Harry Coombs, Ben Krass, Edward "Lord Gas" Richardson, and Earl Shelton. The indictments against the Gamble-Huff company and its principal employees stated that the defendants went to New York, Baltimore, Washington, Atlanta, Detroit, Cleveland, and other cities "in order to meet with and pay in excess of $25,000 in United States currency to disc jockeys, music directors, program directors, and other radio station employees." It was also alleged that the Gamble-Huff company arranged for disk jockeys, music directors, program directors, and other radio station employees to travel to Philadelphia, where they received (via Ben Krass) clothes worth more than $6,000. Still another part of the indictment alleged that the

Gamble-Huff defendants provided in excess of $2,300 in airline tickets "and other goods and services to disc jockeys, music directors, program directors and other radio station employees." When the indictments were handed down, Leon Huff, in a flash of bravado, opined that the government's allegations made him and Gamble "stronger musically. We felt that we hadn't done anything wrong. I think it was unfair what they were doing, but they got their reasons for doing whatever they were doing."[11]

Thom Bell's name was conspicuously absent from the list of those indicted. "That mess didn't bother me, 'cause I was never even involved in" Philadelphia International, he explained. That is not to say that Bell avoided being investigated. At times, the two-year, wide-ranging probe took on comedic overtones. The federal government "rounded up everybody," including himself, recalled Bell. Since he had nothing to hide, Bell went out of his way to befriend the investigators that were assigned to tail him. He effusively greeted the investigators who waited at his doorstep as he left for work each morning: "Hello gentlemen, how are you? Oh, it's so good to see you!" Bell then headed for the local bus stop (he did not drive an automobile) as the agents tagged along and climbed aboard with him. "It was so comical," he recalled almost thirty years later. "I used to fall down laughin', [wondering] what in the world they were following *me* for! . . . I thought, 'Boy, if you can find me doin' somethin' [wrong], I'll be happy to go to jail!'" Bell indignantly added that, "those fools had the nerve to give *me* a subpoena" to appear before the grand jury in Newark. "It was funny to me," he explained, "because I produce records. Producers don't promote records! But the words 'producer' and 'promoter' meant the same thing to them." Bell concluded his grand jury testimony by telling his inquisitors, "if you find something that's different than what I told you, please bring it back to me." The investigators "didn't like that," he remembered. "They didn't like that at all!

As part of the probe, investigators perused the album jackets of records produced by Gamble, Huff, and Bell. When they discovered a wealth of Italian names (Appolonia, DiStefano, Genovese, Montana, Renaldo, et al.) listed as musicians, the investigators surmised that the producers had been forced to deal with the black mob, and possibly the Mafia, in order to get their records made and distributed. "Now they thought that every name on there was an alternate name of some gangster," laughed Bell. "They couldn't understand that these were real people." Envisioning the favorable publicity to be gained from the exposure of Mafia connections, the government invited many of the musicians to testify about their knowledge of payola. "Oh, it was pitiful," exclaimed Bell, fighting to suppress his laughter. "What in the world did *we* (as musicians) know about paying anybody off? We were studio people. But they didn't understand. They thought that everybody was the same." Bell added that the investigators "had the nerve" to ask some of the violinists to play their instruments, "and all twenty, the women and the men, sat right up there and played those fiddles for 'em. And I mean played 'em! Oh man, they were singin'!" The government agents "almost passed out."

Despite those moments of unintentional levity, the federal investigation into payola was no laughing matter to Kenny Gamble, Leon Huff, and the others indicted. It was also a severe jolt to Columbia Records. Ron Alexenburg remembered the episode as "a very difficult time for all of us" at the record company. Alexenburg was not accused of any wrong-doing, and he was never a target of the grand jury, but as the former head of promotion at Columbia, as well as one of those responsible for overseeing Philadelphia International, he was asked to testify in Newark. The Epic Records president swore to the grand jury that he "had never seen or heard of or knew of any sorts of illegalities that were done in connection with any of the labels or any of the artists that [he] was involved with."

In calling people such as Alexenburg to testify, the investigators "were actually fishing," said Thom Bell. But in their fishing, the Newark investigators allegedly landed a big one. After months of delays, they had finally obtained subpoenaed material from Philadelphia International Records. On examining the documents, prosecutors said they were "astonished" at what they discovered. Despite the fact that bribery practices in the music business had grown more sophisticated since the direct payments of the 1950s were outlawed, the subpoenaed material resulted in what investigators described as "the most graphic paper trail of payola that one could imagine." The alleged payoff money stemmed from the quarterly checks that CBS gave to Gamble and Huff's company for promotional use. One government attorney who studied the evidence said that whenever Philadelphia International "got a check they cashed it, went out on the road, and gave the money to radio programmers in hotel rooms." The attorney insisted that prosecutors "had lists of the amount of money paid and who[m] it was paid to."[12] Apparently, the government also had canceled checks that Philadelphia International distributed by way of promo men Harry Coombs and "Lord Gas" Richardson. "Kenny and them always thought that nobody would play your record unless you paid 'em," claimed Weldon McDougal, who had been working in Philadelphia International's promotion department for about three months (after coming over from Motown) when the payola investigation began. "And Harry Coombs . . . continued to tell 'em they had to pay to get records played." Coombs also "did one of the dumbest things in the world," added McDougal. "He convinced Kenny to pay them by check."

McDougal, too, was called before the grand jury. When he arrived in Newark, he overheard the investigators talking about how the disc jockeys "down in North Carolina and Georgia all had Ben Krass suits, because that's how Kenny was payin' 'em off, with a suit!" (The first thing the investigators did was to check to see whether the suit he wore came from Krass. "Everybody had a Ben Krass suit!" he exclaimed. Everybody, that is, but McDougal. "I never wore that cheap shit!" he chortled.) McDougal was sworn in to testify, and "that's when they showed me those checks" from Philadelphia International. (His inquisitor held the checks in his hand, far enough away so that McDougal could not read them.) McDougal told the prosecutors that, having worked at Philadelphia International for only a few months, he "was in the dark" about the payola situation. He "didn't know what [the prosecutors] were talkin' about, or how deep [the probe] was."

MEANWHILE, GAMBLE AND HUFF tried to conduct business as usual. But before Philadelphia International was able to focus on its competition, a major business issue had to be addressed. Philadelphia International's original five-year production and distribution deal with CBS was set to expire at the end of 1975. During the life of that contract, CBS not only held the distribution rights for Philadelphia International's product, but they controlled the rights to the master recordings of that company and, through Blackwood Music, also administered Mighty Three music publishing. When the original Philadelphia International deal was struck, CBS, desperate to establish a foothold in the marketing of black music, went to great lengths to bring Gamble and Huff into the corporate fold. Now, however, CBS commanded a 17 percent share of the total pop and R&B music business and was no longer dependent on Philadelphia International for its sales of black music. In addition, the crossover sales of Philadelphia International product that Columbia foresaw when it cut the deal with Gamble and Huff had just about dried up. With CBS no longer having to cater to Kenny Gamble's whims, the negotiations over the control of Philadelphia International's future master recordings became protracted.

From Philadelphia International's inception, "there was no one inside the organization who was empowered to make a business decision without it being cleared by Gamble and Huff," said Bell's music business attorney David Steinbeg. Steinberg, who had considerable dealings with Gamble and with Philadelphia International, claimed that others who had some voice in running the company "were extremely afraid to challenge Gamble, so whatever Kenny wanted is what these people would eventually agree to do." Thus, said Steinberg, it was "difficult" for anybody to do business with Philadelphia International. Apparently, the situation grew more complicated when Gamble returned to work after about a four-month convalescence following his breakdown. Staff writer Joe Jefferson said that when Gamble returned to work, "nobody really talked about it in depth." The few times that Jefferson did see Gamble, he asked him how he was feeling, how things were going. "I'm great, man! I'm doin' great!" Gamble always replied. "That was his thing," remembered Jefferson. Sigma engineer Jim Gallagher, who worked extensively with Gamble before and after his illness, agreed that Gamble "seemed like he was perfectly fine" when he returned. But the assessments of Jefferson and Gallagher were based solely on Gamble's work in and around the recording studio. Thom Bell, who saw Gamble from several other perspectives, claimed that when his longtime friend returned to work, decision making became "the biggest thing" for Gamble. To this day, said Bell, "he'll take hours and hours, years and years" to reach a decision."[13]

At that time, most music business deals were consummated in a week or two. David Steinberg claimed that deals requiring Gamble's involvement took "six, eight, ten, twelve months, because there was no one on the business end who could negotiate the deal from 'A to Z.' Each time a different piece was brought to Kenny to decide what to do, and he didn't know. So he would sit on it for a while." (Allegedly, one of Gamble's demands of CBS during the negotiations was that he be named to the CBS board of directors.) Joe Tarsia thought that Gamble "slightly overvalued himself in looking for a new deal" with CBS. In the end, CBS refused to meet Gamble's demands for control of future recordings by Philadelphia International, although an agreement whereby CBS continued to market and distribute Philadelphia International's records was worked out. But beginning in 1976, the control of all future Philadelphia International master recordings, as well as the publishing rights to them, reverted to Gamble and Huff. Gamble then "went from company to company," attempting to cut a deal for those rights," said Tarsia, but he "couldn't sell the deal that he wanted" to anyone.[14] Mighty Three Music thus took on the administration of Philadelphia International's songs, "because [Gamble and Huff] didn't need a major company to do it," said David Steinberg. "They had so much going on they could afford to do it themselves and not turn over control copyrights to a third party."

Besides the alleged indecisiveness displayed by Kenny Gamble on his return to work, he became more public with his thoughts on society in general. Music critic Nelson George wrote in *The Death of Rhythm and Blues* that Gamble "no longer saw P.I.R. as merely a musical enterprise but also a platform from which to proselytize, espousing a world view that obliquely revealed his private belief in the tenets of Islam." This manifested itself in written mini-sermons that Gamble began to include in the record sleeves and covers of many Philadelphia International albums. "The message is in the music" became a company slogan, and Gamble wasted no time in extending his own personal message, laced with what George termed "a tough, male-dominant, antimaterialistic perspective." On the O'Jays' *Family Reunion,* Gamble's "comeback" album, released in the fall of 1975, Gamble talked of the "evil plan" to divide the family through the concept of the generation gap, "therefore creating a halt to the flow of wisdom from the wise to the young." With a sly nod to his shifting roster of house musicians, Gamble allowed how "we must recapture the family structure—Mother, Father, Sister, Brother—and give respect to everyone." Shortly after that, on Billy Paul's *When Love Is New* album, Gamble railed against the practice of abortion. "Be fruitful and multiply," he implored. "Let's keep on making babies so we can have a great, beautiful, wise, righteous, meek, but strong nation." Increasingly, Gamble spoke of "the Creator" or, simply, "God," as well as spiritually intangible concepts such as a "Universal Community of Truth" (where all people live together "with the Brotherhood of Man and the Fatherhood of Almighty God") and the "level of Universal Awareness, [where] . . . life can be beautiful." CBS did not care about such proselytizing as long as Philadelphia International continued to boost sales. And during the first half of the '70s, wrote Nelson George, "black families played albums by the O'Jays and the Blue Notes until the grooves were worn smooth."[15]

13

"Philadelphia Freedom"
(1976)

IN LATE 1975, PHILADELPHIA INTERNATIONAL was temporarily invigorated by the O'Jays' *Family Reunion* album and Harold Melvin and the Blue Notes' *Wake Up Everybody* album. The title of the O'Jays album could have been an oblique nod to Kenny Gamble's return to the Philadelphia International fold. The title of the Blue Notes album should have been heeded as a warning that, whatever the pending outcome of Project Sound, Philadelphia International could not survive indefinitely in its current depleted state. Former members of Lebaron Taylor's Young Professionals, as well as another local writer/arranger, Richard Rome, provided spirited competition in local R&B circles. Following Vince Montana's Salsoul Orchestra blueprint, Rome (who was occasionally employed by Philadelphia International), rounded up the same personnel Montana used, right down to vocalists Barbara Ingram, Carla Benson, and Evette Benton, and created and produced a studio disco group that, in self-homage, he dubbed the Ritchie Family. Rome's one-off lark resulted in a surprise hit album, *Brazil*. (When the Sigma Sweethearts refused to leave the recording studio to promote the album, lest they forfeit their now-multitudinous vocal backing sessions, Rome had to scurry to recruit three females to take their place on the road.)

By then, Philadelphia was also a magnet for a myriad of competing artists and producers, from both near and far. Most people in the music business "are followers," said Thom Bell. "So if there's a great sound coming from Jumpville, Georgia, they're gonna send their man to get that sound." In the mid-1970s, "Jumpville, Georgia" was Philadelphia, Pennsylvania. Those unwilling to pay Gamble and Huff's top-line production fee "would come to people like us," said Morris Bailey. "We knew how to get the Philadelphia sound, it's nothin' to get! That kept us busy. We were able to pay our rent, buy a couple [of] houses. Nothin' big like Kenny, but we were able to make a living." One would-be R&B

star answered a production company ad in a magazine, came to Philadelphia, and, for nine hundred dollars, recorded his own song. When put on the market, the song sold a million copies. Even the once uncontested Motown was ready to send some of its acts—including the Temptations and Eddie Kendricks—to Philadelphia to record under the aegis of Baker, Harris, and Young. In addition, the Trammps, who were finally in control of their own destiny, signed a contract with Atlantic Records that put them on the brink of stardom. (The Philadelphia fixation was not limited to R&B artists, either. Rockers David Bowie, Todd Rundgren, and the Rolling Stones each recorded tracks at Sigma Sound that year.) Perhaps the unkindest cut of all to Gamble and Huff occurred when *Soul Train* host and producer Don Cornelius returned to Sigma Sound to record a new theme for his popular televised dance show. This time Cornelius did not contact Gamble and Huff to produce the record for him, but instead sought out Ronnie Baker, Norman Harris, and Earl Young for the task. The original MFSB rhythm section was used to make the recording, and Bobby Martin was paid to arrange it. "Special thanks to the greatest musicians we've ever worked with," read the liner notes on the album that contained the new *Soul Train* theme (on which Cornelius was listed as a co-writer).[1]

To counter projects such as this latest Philadelphia foray by Cornelius, Gamble and Huff had to scramble to replace key personnel, including their requisite rhythm section. MFSB's revamped lineup was introduced on Dee Dee Sharp's *Happy 'bout the Whole Thing* album, released that fall. The band's new recruits centered around drummer Charles Collins, a black man who, after refining his technique while literally sitting at the right hand of Earl Young, was eminently qualified to fill the master's weighty shoes. Born in Mississippi and raised on Chicago's rough and tough South Side, Collins took to playing the drums at age sixteen as a means of survival. "Gangs and drugs and stuff were getting really strong in the ghettos," he recalled. "Music took me from that."[2] Collins played in various bands around Chicago and also partook in local recording sessions (including one for Gene "Duke of Earl" Chandler's first album). In 1969, Collins and the group he was with (the Constellations) moved to New York. After touring for a time as the opening act for Dionne Warwick and other name artists, the Constellations broke up.

In the early 1970s, Collins became a session drummer for Atlantic Records in New York, where he worked with many of the label's top artists. In the fall of 1973, Collins learned of a white rock band in Philadelphia, Duke Williams and the Extremes, that was in the market for an R&B drummer. He auditioned for the job and was hired. When the Extremes (whose lead guitarist was a skinny lad named T. J. Tindall) recorded an album at Sigma Sound, Collins got to meet Baker, Harris, and Young. Collins and the Extremes toured as the opening act for headliners such as Mountain, the Allman Brothers, and the J. Geils Band for several years. Then the band began to come apart at the very time that Baker, Harris, and Young were in the process of breaking away from Gamble and Huff. This afforded Collins the opportunity to do some session work at Sigma Sound. With Earl Young entrenched behind the drum kit, and Larry Washington set on congas and bongos, Collins turned to hand percussion instruments as a way to break into the lineup. Collins said he "started bringin' sorta like a more Island-like feel to what was happenin'" in the studio. But most of all, he continued to observe Earl Young in action. "Earl was the man!" he exclaimed. "Earl taught me, and he was very generous and really nice." As Young taught Collins to "really respect" Philadelphia Soul, more recording dates came his way. "If they couldn't get Earl, I would come in and play drums," he said. By 1975, Collins had played on several recording sessions with Blue Magic, the two Eddie Kendricks albums produced by Baker, Harris, and Young, and Dionne Warwick's *Track of the Cat* album (produced by Thom Bell).

Joe Tarsia, who engineered the Duke Williams and the Extremes album and had taken notice of the spirited Collins, was aware that Gamble and Huff were in the market for a new drummer. "Joe played my tracks for Gamble," said Collins, "and then I started getting calls from Philadelphia International. I started doing sessions with Bobby Martin, and I sort of eased in." Collins's first major Philadelphia International session was for Dee Dee Sharp's *Happy 'bout the Whole Thing* album.

ANOTHER DRUMMER SOMETIMES USED by Philadelphia International was Keith Benson, the brother of Carla Benson, who was brought to the company by songwriters Gene McFadden and John Whitehead. Benson was a "very good drummer and an integral part of the McFadden and Whitehead production team," recalled Bobby Eli. (Benson can be heard drumming on McFadden and Whitehead's mega-hit "Ain't No Stoppin' Us Now.") Musicians from Philadelphia whom Thom Bell had begun to use on a regular basis filled the two remaining slots in Gamble and Huff's rhythm section. Dennis Harris (no relation to Norman Harris) was brought in to play guitar, and Michael "Sugar Bear" Foreman became the new MFSB bass player. Foreman was "a great bass player," said drummer Charles Collins. "Sugarbear was very creative." When MFSB went on the road, Collins and Foreman often roomed together. "He was a fun guy," recalled the drummer, "a truly wild and crazy guy!" Dennis Harris "was definitely into the Sound of Philadelphia," said Collins. "If you couldn't get Norman [Harris] you got Dennis." Leon Huff continued to play piano on many of the MFSB sessions, and if vibes were required, Bobby Martin usually obliged.

The most significant addition to MFSB (and to Philadelphia International Records) came late in 1975, with the hiring of jazz-fusion musician Dexter Wansel. One of Philadelphia International's most pressing needs—especially with a disenchanted Bunny Sigler halfway out the door at 309 South Broad Street—was an additional producer. The changing state of the R&B and soul music scene was a contributing factor in the hiring of Wansel. In the past year or so, thanks largely to Stevie Wonder, the Moog synthesizer (a computerized device used for sound production and control) had begun to make its mark in pop music circles. Gamble and Huff's interest in the instrument was twofold. First, they realized that the newfangled instrument, then on the cutting edge of pop music, was a necessary addition if Philadelphia International hoped to keep abreast of the latest musical trends. Second, the synthesizer's ability to imitate other instruments meant that some studio musicians could be eliminated from the Philadelphia International payroll. Since Gamble and Huff were in the market for a new producer, it made perfect sense for them hire someone proficient on the synthesizer. As it was, they did not have to venture far to find that person. They did not even have to leave the Philadelphia International building.

Dexter Wansel, a black man born in Delaware, moved to Philadelphia at an early age. He developed an interest in R&B music and as a pre-teen landed a job as a gofer at the Uptown Theater, where he made certain that the performers always had plenty of food on hand and their stage uniforms were neatly laid out for them. Wansel began to study music in high school. After serving in the armed forces in Vietnam during the height of the U.S. buildup in the late 1960s, he and two other lifelong friends from his neighborhood were recruited by Roland and Karl Chambers to form a band called Yellow Sunshine. The music played by Yellow Sunshine was a fusion of white progressive rock and black elements, along the lines of Funkadelic and the Ohio Players. Early in 1973, Yellow Sunshine recorded an eponymous album for Philadelphia International Records. The record was "not really in the direction that P.I.R. was going . . . [and was] nothing to write home about," thought Bobby Eli, but Dexter Wansel's keyboard work so impressed Gamble and Huff that the producers began to employ him as a session musician. "Kenny really believed in Dexter, 'cause Dexter was *good*," said Cynthia Biggs, who eventually became Wansel's songwriting partner.[3] In 1975, Wansel was hired at Philadelphia International as a writer, arranger, and producer.

Working side by side with Gamble, Huff, and Bell in the studio "was a real eye-opener," recalled Wansel, who was a virtual wizard on the synthesizer. "If I wanted to compete as an arranger, guess who I was competing with?" When it came to songwriting, Wansel's competition included Thom Bell and Linda Creed, Bunny Sigler, Jefferson, Hawes and Simmons, as well as Gamble and Huff. "It was a great place to create," he remembered, "and a great time to be creative."[4] Wansel's first solo album, *Life on Mars*, yielded three singles, but none of them fared well commercially, partly because he was never a strong singer. But Wansel's adroitness and artistry on the keyboards fascinated audiences, and *Life on Mars* became a cult favorite at the dance clubs. "He was gettin' there," recalled Biggs. "He *was* gettin' there." Subsequent albums (including 1978's jazz-funk based *Voyager*) enhanced Wansel's reputation as a remarkable musician.

When Wansel wrote songs, he usually did so with Cynthia Biggs, the tall, talented, black lyricist whom Thom Bell affectionately dubbed "Biggsy." "Nice as pie and highly intelligent," he recalled. "She was the only person [at Philadelphia International] that almost had a Ph.D. degree. She worked as hard as anybody did down there. Everyone loved Biggsy 'cause she never bothered anybody and she always had a kind word for everybody. If you were mad at Biggsy, somethin' was wrong with you!" Biggs was born in North Carolina and moved to Philadelphia with her family when she was three years old. In high school, Biggs enrolled in an advanced program with a special concentration in music. (Meanwhile, her brother Tyrell developed into a heavyweight contender in boxing.) Biggs also became a member of her high school's renowned gospel octet. Employing original songs and arrangements and sounding, said Biggs, "like fifty" voices, that talented group consistently brought audiences to their feet. The departure of one of the group's student writers afforded Biggs the opportunity to write her first song. Biggs continued to write for them after she graduated, and some of her songs were incorporated into the group's repertoire.[5]

Hoping to land a recording contract with Philadelphia International, the high school gospel group auditioned for Jefferson, Simmons, and Hawes in 1975. Whenever the songwriting trio heard a number they particularly liked, they asked who the writer was. "And it would be a song that I wrote with somebody," said Biggs. As a result, Biggs was offered an exclusive songwriting contract with Philadelphia International. Joe Jefferson helped her to make the transition from gospel to secular music, but Biggs's initial songwriting output for Gamble and Huff remained almost nil.[6] "I needed to work with a musician, because I don't play piano well enough," she explained. "I needed somebody who was just as dynamic with the music as I was with the lyrics." One day she heard Dexter Wansel, whom she regarded as "a little bit of an oddball" because he "wasn't as rambunctious as some of the other guys" at Philadelphia International, playing the piano in his office. Biggs thought that because Wansel "was a gentle guy," he might be someone with whom she could share intimate thoughts. She knocked on Wansel's door and was invited in. He sat there, continuing to play the piano, and did not so much as glance up at her. Biggs told Wansel she was afraid that Gamble and Huff were about to fire her, that "if they want to trim their weight I'm probably the most likely candidate." Wansel continued to play the piano for a few moments, and then got up and left the room. When he returned, he sat down and began playing the piano again. Wansel then looked up at Biggs for the first time and told her she was right. "They were gonna let you go, but you don't have to worry about that. I just talked to Kenny and asked him to let you work with me on a trial basis. I could certainly use somebody to take the writing load off me." (At that point, Wansel was involved in producing, arranging, and recording.) From that point on, said Biggs, she worked "extra hard" to make sure Wansel would "never regret makin' that decision, because he stuck his neck out for me."

Teamed with Dexter Wansel, Cynthia Biggs had her first modicum of job security. "It was kinda like unspoken, a tacit understanding," that Philadelphia International "was a company built on teams," she explained. But songwriting partners were not formally assigned to one another. "A lot of times you'd just kind of try different things with different people and see where you fit the best," said Biggs. "Can you vibe with that person? Can you bounce from that person? It doesn't take long for you to learn if you're compatible with the person creatively." (There was one cardinal rule, however. "You don't write with people who are already committed to a team," emphasized Biggs. "That could get ugly!") Wansel was "the easiest person to work with in the studio," recalled Biggs with a sigh and a long pause (indicative of a time when their relationship extended beyond songwriting). "Dexter and I worked really well together."

Biggs said that Gamble and Huff had a production schedule, "and they told you who was comin' in first and who was comin' in second," for a quarter of the year. "They would write an artist's name on a black-board and tell the writers how many weeks they had. "They'd count down and they'd tell you, 'Get your songs ready! . . . You'd write your songs and you'd submit them to Kenny, like a week or two before the artist was scheduled to come in. Kenny listened to all the stuff that was submitted. Then he told you which ones he thought you should do. It usually got down to maybe two songs per team, or sometimes one. If he only heard one, then be glad you got that one, 'cause some people didn't even get one."

Other new faces at Philadelphia International included pianist Victor Leon Carstarphen, who also wrote songs and harbored ambitions to arrange and produce. Keith Benson befriended Carstarphen when the latter was fifteen years old. The black youth, whom Carla Benson described as a "very sensitive" person, spent his teenage years as an unofficial member of the Benson family. Living in Camden, New Jersey, Victor Carstarphen grew to idolize Leon Huff, and whenever Huff performed locally, Carstarphen was sure to be in the audience. Like Huff, Carstarphen became a keyboard player. In 1974, he asked Gamble and Huff for a job. "Baker, Harris and Young were gone, and they were looking for a new writing team, and Victor went in at the right time," recalled Carla. "He came home one day and said that he was a staff writer" at Philadelphia International.

Philadelphia International's revamped songwriting and producing corps was also bolstered by the increased input of Gene McFadden and John Whitehead. That duo, who had been with Gamble and Huff since 1971, worked closely with Victor Carstarphen. The three "were exquisite writers, very good writers," recalled Thom Bell. Employing a technique that Bell described as "a carbon copy" of Gamble and Huff's, McFadden and Whitehead began to produce music at Philadelphia International. The way Bell saw things, McFadden and Whitehead "experimented a little bit more" in their music than did Gamble and Huff and "were just as good . . . sometimes even better" than their employers.[7]

Also playing a greater role in Philadelphia International's musical affairs was songwriter/musician/arranger John R. (Jack) Faith (who was unavailable to be interviewed for this book). Faith, a white man who was born and raised in Philadelphia, had an older brother, Bill (deceased), and a younger brother, Russell. Both Bill and Russell played the guitar, and it was their hope, said the latter, that Jack would take up the bass so they would have "a nice little trio." But Jack confounded his brothers, choosing what Russell called "the woodwind route," becoming proficient on the saxophone and the clarinet. By the time Jack Faith became a studio musician in the mid-1960s, he was "a choice flute person when Burt Bacharach or any of those people like that would come in to record," said Russell. "He worked with a lot of big stars . . . [and] he had a good sound on the instruments."

Meanwhile, in the late 1950s, Russell Faith wrote, arranged, and produced for a local record company (Chancellor) and freelanced on the side. (The first hit he wrote was Frankie Avalon's "Bobby Sox to Stockings.") By 1964, Chancellor was out of business and Faith was on his own. The following year, at Frank Virtue's studio, Jimmy Bishop had Faith overdub strings onto Barbara Mason's landmark Philadelphia soul recording "Yes, I'm Ready." A young Kenny Gamble was visibly impressed by Russell Faith's handiwork and began to use him on various projects, including the string arrangements for the Romeos' recordings on Arctic. Faith said that Gamble would initially give him a track, "with the rhythm and everything pretty much finished," and tell him "to sweeten it up a little bit with strings." Eventually, Faith became so busy that he could no longer do everything he wanted, "plus what Kenny wanted [him] to do." He recommended his brother Jack (who played saxophone on Candy and the Kisses' "The 81" the previous year), who Gamble then "started to pursue." Jack Faith's initial tasks for Gamble and Huff were limited to copying music. "Kenny would have an arranger or somebody put down the tracks, and Jack would copy the parts out for the string players and for the horn players," explained his brother. "Then Kenny started to realize that Jack could play the woodwinds real good and he would use him on the sessions." Russell Faith also pointed out that because Gamble "was kind of not able to academically correspond" with many of the musicians, "it was a little easier if he had a Jack there, or if he had a Don Renaldo there, who could communicate [Gamble's] feelings to the musicians." In due time, Jack Faith began to arrange sessions at Philadelphia International. "Kenny was very good to my brother," said Russell. "He gave him a lot of experience."[8]

Another individual, who, like Jack Faith, saw his workload at Philadelphia International increase, was pianist/arranger Richard Rome, the architect of the Ritchie Family disco group. Richard DiCicco was born and raised in South Philadelphia. "Because of his Italian ancestry," said close friend Russell Faith, everybody began to call him Richard Rome. Rome made his debut as a recording artist in 1958, after which he developed an interest in songwriting and arranging. Beginning in the late 1960s, Kenny Gamble periodically employed Rome as an arranger. Rome also wrote arrangements for other parties, most notably the Tymes R&B group, whose 1974 hit, "You Little Trustmaker," Kenny Gamble had rejected for release on Philadelphia International. Rome also arranged a number of songs for Lebaron Taylor's Young Professionals, and in 1975, he became the arranger and conductor for the Ritchie Family, as well as the group's namesake. Rome was a "big talent, terrific arranger [and a] fabulous piano player," recalled John Madara. Joe Tarsia said that Rome was "most noted" for his string arrangements. Thom Bell had a more tempered opinion, describing Rome as one of Philadelphia's "second-line guys ... [who] didn't last very well with Gamble," because he "would always overdo" his arrangements and did not know "when to stop."

The addition of Dexter Wansel, Cynthia Biggs, and Victor Carstarphen at Philadelphia International, as well as the expanded roles of Gene McFadden, John Whitehead, Jack Faith, and Richard Rome, signaled a new musical direction for Gamble and Huff's company. It also provided a new model for how the company would henceforth be run. Before Gamble's breakdown, he had a hand in a majority of the productions emanating from Philadelphia International and also signed off on most every business deal. But, illness or not, wearing two hats did not prove conducive to the company's business transactions. David Steinberg, Thom Bell's business attorney who specializes in music, had professional dealings with Philadelphia International. Steinberg explained how a person relied on for his or her creativity "can't sit around with their lawyers or accountants . . . discussing different deals, and then step into the studio and turn a switch and be able to create. You think you can, but it really doesn't work that way." So when Gamble returned to work after his illness he continued to make the business decisions but began to delegate much of the in-house the production chores.[9] Although Gamble and Huff oversaw many of the sessions conducted by the company's new personnel, "they were there mostly just to shake your hand and everything, see how things was doin'," said Thom Bell. "Sometimes they would be there when the session started, and they would come back when it was just about finished. But everybody kinda had his or her own free will."

ON APRIL 8, 1976, ALMOST TEN MONTHS AFTER the payola indictments were issued, Kenny Gamble and the others indicted in the Project Sound investigation appeared in federal court to address the charges. By then, the outcome had been determined, with Gamble's culpability reduced to a relatively benign degree. It turned out that the Philadelphia International checks in the government's possession were useless to the Project Sound prosecutors. The reason for that was couched in the federal government's relatively toothless payola statute (passed in 1960), which did little to alter the "bribe-friendly" environment of the pop music business. The checks written by Philadelphia International Records to various radio programmers may have provided the physical evidence that prosecutors needed to prove their payola allegations. Nevertheless, any conviction on those charges remained problematical. According to the law at that time, both the givers and the recipients of the bribes were guilty of payola, but only one party could be prosecuted. To prove the payola charges in a court of law, corroboration of the evidence, in the form of one guilty party testifying against the other, was necessary. To induce such corroboration, immunity from prosecution was granted to one guilty party or the other—in this case, to the recipients of the alleged bribes. But the government was unable to get any of the recipients of the alleged bribes to confirm that the money and/or gifts bestowed on them had been given as an inducement to favor Philadelphia International's records.[10] Consequently, prosecutors were left with the dubious David Wynshaw as their chief witness. Not only was Wynshaw unable to corroborate the payola charges (he did not give or take any of the alleged bribes), what little, if any, credibility he had disappeared after it was disclosed that he was cooperating with prosecutors in order to mitigate his punishment for an unrelated drug charge. (Thom Bell claimed that it was obvious Wynshaw lied to save his own skin after the former CBS employee accused Bell, along with Gamble and Huff, of giving bribes, in the form of drugs, to disc jockeys. "Now that goes to show you the lie that was made up," he reasoned. "I didn't even have anything to do with Philadelphia International Records. But [Wynshaw] didn't know that. Hardly anybody knew that.") Unable to corroborate their allegation that Philadelphia International's checks were offered as bribes, when the frustrated prosecutors made their case they had no choice but to focus on the more mundane matter of the distribution of Ben Krass suits.

Charges that Leon Huff had offered inducements in exchange for airplay were dropped. (Huff "was a writer, he was a musician, that's it," said Joe Tarsia. "Gamble was the businessman.") Avoiding a jury trial, Assorted Music pleaded nolo contendere and was fined $45,000, and most of the charges against the publishing company were dismissed. After the Philadelphia International checks the government had in its possession became moot, Gamble's attorney's worked out a plea bargain with the prosecutors. As part of the agreement, Gamble read a statement "in which he admitted that he had made gifts of clothing, money, and airplane tickets to disk jockeys." He denied that the gifts carried a quid pro quo for favorable airplay but did admit that the intent of the gifts had been "to get more airplay for his releases." Gamble then pleaded guilty to a single count in the indictment, that of giving a suit of clothes to a disc jockey. "They nailed him on a suit!" exclaimed Thom Bell. "One funky suit!"[11]

In his overview of the pop music industry, *Pennies from Heaven*, Russell Sanjek observed, "Its sense of shock blunted by the Watergate disclosures and President Nixon's resignation, the American public showed little interest in the payola trials" and the fact that "they had dealt almost exclusively with soul music." But many blacks (and some whites), especially those involved in the music business, were keenly aware of what had transpired. All of the Project Sound defendants were black or dealt with black music, so "most blacks in the industry believed the investigation was racially motivated," wrote Nelson George in *The Death of Rhythm and Blues*. Their reasoning was that what they called "'white payola' went on unabated, with much higher stakes involved." The charge of racism had merit. Considering the tiny amount of the total output of recorded music that can possibly receive critical exposure, and factoring in human nature, it is logical to conclude that payola is endemic to the entire music business—black, white, and whatever else. (Disc jockey Alan Freed, payola's first victim, said in 1960 that the practices in the music business deemed to be "payola" by congressional investigators were considered "lobbying" in their own realm.)[12] So why, if not for reasons of race, did the government focus only on the black aspect of the practice?

Greg Hall, a black man who worked in the record business during the 1970s, said that Kenny Gamble, by making a success out of Philadelphia International, "alerted a race that they had value, telling blacks that their businesses could *survive*. He prospered, and that's something that bothered the white establishment. How did you get over that fence, the white guy wants to know. He can't figure it out because he knows how high he built that fence."[13] Thom Bell claims he sensed racist barbs. The first was when David Wynshaw, for self-serving reasons, decided to "put it all on the niggers" at Philadelphia International. The second was when federal prosecutors adopted the attitude that, because of Bell's blackness, he "didn't have the intelligence to do anything on [his] own" and thus had to resort to payola. Some whites also felt that racism was a factor in the government's prosecution. Ron Alexenburg thought the "urban only" investigation targeted black labels such as Philadelphia International "because of their success." Prosecutors believed that the black companies "had to be doing something illegal. God forbid it would be that the songs were so wonderful and the music was so great."

Racist practices no doubt fostered the development of black payola, but to claim that the federal government's case against the Newark defendants was motivated solely by racism is a tenuous assertion. More likely, black payola in the music business offered prosecutors an easy target. Beginning in the early 1950s, with the rise in popularity of rhythm and blues, payola became particularly rife among black deejays, who were paid considerably less than their white counterparts. "If any sector of the music business was subject to incentives it was black music," said Rick Swig, an executive with Columbia Records during the Project Sound investigation. "Black deejays and program directors traditionally were underpaid."[14] As long as such payola remained in black circles it was ignored by the white power structure. But during the Black Renaissance of the early 1970s, when black music flowed into the white mainstream, the worm turned. Also, around that time, the emergence of the "Black Mob" helped to create an interest in black payola. Organized crime had long been thought to infiltrate the entertainment business. Since Gamble and Huff dealt in black entertainment, some believed that Philadelphia International had been forced to pay the black syndicate in order to get its product aired. When the large amounts of cash that around that time began to emanate from Stax Records for causes unknown were added to the mix, law enforcement agents had what they believed was sufficient reason to focus their payola spotlight on black-oriented record companies.

Forever obfuscating the Project Sound investigation is the fact that the government's charges of guilt and the defendants' charges of racism both have some degree of merit. (Not to mention possible racist motives on the part of black recipients of the alleged payola, who refused to cooperate with the white government to convict a brother.) While a nominal conviction such as Kenny Gamble's could have been obtained against scores of white counterparts in the music business, it is also true that Gamble, and Philadelphia International, despite their denials of any illegal intent, engaged in dispensing gratuities to disc jockeys. Ultimately, the biggest casualty of Project Sound was not any of the defendants, but rather black music itself. Despite the embarrassingly insubstantial public results of the government probe, the aura of scandal caused major record companies such as Atlantic (whose "Young Professionals" program dissipated with CBS's hijacking of Lebaron Taylor) to back off from the marketing of black music and focus on the comparatively safer white pop field. As a result, black music entered a period of retrenchment that lasted into the early 1980s.

WHEN AMERICA COMMEMORATED ITS BICENTENNIAL IN 1976, nowhere were the festivities more fervent than in Philadelphia, where, that July, Queen Elizabeth presented the American people with a gift of a bell cast in the same foundry as was the Liberty Bell. To capitalize on the bicentennial, Gamble and Huff titled MFSB's latest album *Philadelphia Freedom* (after the Elton John hit, a version of which was contained on the album). Although the fortunes of Philadelphia International Records were never gauged by the popularity of MFSB albums, the release of *Philadelphia Freedom* held special significance for the company. This was Philadelphia International's fourth MFSB album, but it was the first outing for those rhythm section players hired to replace Ronnie Baker, Norman Harris, and Earl Young.[15] MFSB fans that placed *Philadelphia Freedom* on their turntables (or in their eight-track tape players) did not hear Philadelphia International's familiar heavy bass groove. Instead, they were introduced to Dexter Wansel's synthesized light jazz sound. Wansel's "discofied" style was emblematic of the stylistic shift in the music of most of Philadelphia International's recording artists, and the burning question at Gamble and Huff's company became: Would the public accept the change?

The transition was as smooth as Dexter Wansel's synthesized keyboard riffs. MFSB's *Philadelphia Freedom* not only reached number thirty-nine on *Billboard*'s album sales chart; it became the group's second-biggest album ever (after 1973's gold-certified *Love Is the Message*). Wansel's synthesizer and his coterie of new musicians were in the right place at the right time. His organizational skills and ability to compose suave melodies and vivid arrangements enabled him to seamlessly settle in as A&R and musical director for the reconstituted MFSB. Wansel was also destined to become a visionary, hit-making producer for other artists.[16]

The acceptance of the new MFSB provided relief and encouragement to Philadelphia International, whose roster of hit makers had fallen on hard times. The Three Degrees, who were never able to establish a domestic following equal to their international fan base, were no longer with the company. Their shrinking record sales, coupled with the enmity between Gamble and Huff and the group's Machiavellian manager Richard Barrett, led to a parting of the ways in 1975. Billy Paul, for whom there once seemed so much promise at Philadelphia International, had cooled to the point where his albums languished in the bottom quarter of *Billboard*'s Top 200 album chart. It was now obvious that Paul's "Me and Mrs. Jones" had been a fluke hit by a singer whose oft-dissonant voice would never win mass acceptance.[17] Even MFSB, despite Dexter Wansel's leadership, faltered later that year. The group's next album, *Summertime*, was largely the work of Philadelphia International's McFadden and Whitehead contingent. Record buyers literally did not buy this latest stylistic change, and *Summertime* stalled at number 106 on *Billboard*'s Top 200 album chart. It was the last MFSB album to reach the charts.

Another Philadelphia International act that failed to live up to its original potential was the People's Choice. In the spring of 1976, Frankie Brunson's funk group followed its hook-filled, down-and-dirty *Boogie Down U.S.A.* album with a disappointing watered-down second effort, hopefully titled *We Got the Rhythm*. Since the People's Choice was part of Leon Huff's bailiwick, Huff must shoulder much of the blame. When the People's Choice recorded their first album, Huff "would come up with some unique bass lines and rhythms," recalled Brunson. "That's what set him apart." Huff and Brunson coarranged most of the songs on that album, but on the second outing he collaborated with Brunson on just three arrangements. And, perhaps reacting to what he perceived as a creative challenge by Dexter Wansel, Huff gave the synthesizer a whirl. The result was a much smoother-sounding record than the first album. "I guess I would have liked to have had more say on the *funk* thing," lamented Brunson, "'cause we kinda lost somethin' [on the second album]. We lost our sound!" But Brunson was powerless to prevent the unwelcome change in musical style. The People's Choice went into the recording studio and "did what [we] had to do to get out of there," he recalled. The most successful single from the group's *We Got the Rhythm* album did not even make the pop charts and stalled at number fifty-two on the R&B charts—proof that blacks, as well as whites, did not go for the newly refined sound of the People's Choice. After that, thought Brunson, Huff "was startin' to back off of us a little bit." (Sure enough, the group's third album, *Turn Me Loose*, released in 1977, was produced and arranged by Roland Chambers.)[18]

Although MFSB, Billy Paul, and the People's Choice continued to record for Philadelphia International (albeit with diminishing returns), Bunny Sigler, after enduring years of what he perceived as neglect of his own recording career, finally left Philadelphia International. (In eight years of recording for Gamble and Huff, only three of Sigler's singles had appeared on *Billboard*'s Top 50 R&B chart.) Sigler claimed that he wanted to remain at Philadelphia International but that he wanted Thom Bell to produce his records. But Bell refused to do so, telling Sigler he "couldn't make the money [from Sigler that] he made from other people," because Sigler was signed to Philadelphia International.[19] Furthermore, Sigler claimed that he was being pressured by Gamble and Huff to sign a new contract. "But there was somethin' in it I didn't like, that was gonna hamper me from travelin' and stuff." Sigler said that Gamble and Huff "wanted me to just stay in Philly" and continue to work behind the scenes. But Sigler no longer wanted to make "other people big and neglect [his] own singing career, so [he] decided to leave." He prudently left on good terms, "'cause I still had songs that belonged to them." After forming his own production company, Sigler signed a recording contract with Norman Harris's Salsoul-affiliated Gold Mind label and, in a year's time, enjoyed the biggest hit of his singing career, "Let Me Party with You (Party, Party, Party)."

Even with the departure of Bunny Sigler, the biggest disappointment by far for Philadelphia International in 1976 and the one that threatened to hurt the company the most that year, was the loss of Harold Melvin and the Blue Notes. Over the past three years, the group had developed into a major force in R&B and were now Gamble and Huff's second biggest selling act. But most of the group's growing legion of fans had no idea that the lead singer of the Blue Notes was not Harold Melvin, but Teddy Pendergrass. Pendergrass maintained that he "didn't feel any resentment, at least at the time," toward Harold Melvin, "because I didn't sing all the lead vocals. All of us in the group were team players."[20]

Teddy Pendergrass's rosy recollections aside, his relationship with Harold Melvin was fraught with enmity. "Teddy was so upset [over

Melvin's receiving individual billing], 'cause Teddy was doin' all the singin'," exclaimed Blue Note Bernard Wilson. Pendergrass did give Melvin his due for being "a genius when it [came] to working on the stage," one who taught the inexperienced lead singer "a lot about . . . how to deal with people, how to bring people into what you're doing, how to work the audience." But he also said that Melvin was "the kind of person who thrived off making sure he had the authority. He was never a sharer, he never designated anything. . . . He always came first, no matter whether he had anything to do with a particular situation or not." To complicate matters, Melvin was also a contrary individual. "If someone said [something] was red, he said it was pink," added Pendergrass. "If the color was green, he had to make it blue." The fact that when Gamble and Huff first offered Melvin a recording contract, Melvin "negotiated it on our behalf without ever consulting any of us" also ate at the lead singer. Melvin "decided to let the world know this was *his* group," said Pendergrass, by taking the "unusual" step of having the Blue Notes signed to Philadelphia International not as a group, but as five individuals (which gave Melvin power to change personnel at his discretion).[21]

Pendergrass's relationship with the acerbic and dictatorial group leader continued to deteriorate over time. Bernard Wilson recalled how, when fans "started callin' Teddy 'Harold,' that freaked him. Oh, it ate him alive. Teddy was pissed! [He'd say], 'I'm the one that sings those songs!'" Pendergrass claimed that by 1974, he and Melvin "reached an understanding" that failed to last. Most likely, it ended in 1975, with the release of the Blue Notes' *To Be True* album, on which the group officially became "Harold Melvin and the Blue Notes featuring Teddy Pendergrass." Pendergrass maintained that "Harold and the other guys viewed Gamble and Huff's decision to put me out front on the records as a good career move for all of us." Melvin (who died in 1997) claimed that Pendergrass "never really wanted top billing. . . . Nobody wanted to put his name anywhere. That was my doing. I just believed that the brother deserved it. He had been with me for awhile and had proven himself." (Melvin also asserted that he and Pendergrass "never had any problems on stage, we never had any problems, period.")[22]

The oppositional recollections of Pendergrass and Melvin suggest that although the two sang in the same group, they lived in parallel worlds. Even though Pendergrass now received top billing, he claimed that "a constant underlying discontent was beginning to color [his] attitude" toward the Blue Notes. In addition to his struggle with Harold Melvin's imperiousness, Pendergrass was also dissatisfied with the size of his own paycheck and with what he described as "the other guys' ambivalence" to the Blue Notes.[23]

As 1975 drew to a close, Pendergrass was in California with the Blue Notes, "in the same rut." He claimed to have "no money, no nothing," at the time. It was then and there that he decided to quit the group. "I just didn't feel I was getting all I could out of everything around me," he explained. But as Pendergrass soon discovered, it was not that easy to walk away from Harold Melvin and the Blue Notes. When Philadelphia International learned of Pendergrass's decision he was told, "You can't do this, we have a business going on here." Pendergrass assured Philadelphia International that he had no intention of leaving the company, that he just needed "to make things better" for himself. "I can't stay where I am staying," he told Gamble and Huff. "I can't do what I am doing."[24]

Harold Melvin and the Blue Notes' contract with Philadelphia International was about to expire with their latest hit, "Wake Up Everybody," on its way to becoming certified gold. In the eyes of Philadelphia International (and Columbia Records), the sky was still the limit for the group, and their imminent breakup was viewed as a disaster in the making. Bernard Wilson remembered how "Kenny and a few people tried everything in the world to keep us together." "C'mon, man, think about this," pleaded Gamble to Pendergrass. "Go back to the group!" But Pendergrass had had enough. The way he saw things, because the singer was signed individually to Philadelphia International, Gamble and Huff "stood to benefit by my going solo if I was successful." That was a big "if." The music business was littered with the debris of over-inflated lead singers who thought they no longer needed the group with whom they had gained success. When Gamble recognized that Pendergrass was adamant about striking out on his own, he considered keeping him and Harold Melvin on Philadelphia International. But when he asked Pendergrass whether he would mind, the breakaway singer exclaimed, "Hell, yes," he would mind. "It's either him or me," he flatly told Gamble.[25]

When CBS heard that Pendergrass was determined to leave the Blue Notes, "none of us wanted that to happen," said Ron Alexenburg. So he, Gamble, and the attorneys for Pendergrass and for Philadelphia International "banged out a deal where Teddy would do a solo album." Gamble balked at the deal, "because it was more money than Kenny wanted to pay," claimed Alexenburg, and CBS contributed the additional money for Pendergrass's contract, "because the man was magic!" The deal was announced in the fall of 1975, at which time Gamble and Huff chose not to renew the contract of Harold Melvin. " We blew it," lamented Bernard Wilson in hindsight. "That breakup and all that other stuff, we did that. We broke up at the peak of our career. We were so hot, it was absolutely incredible!" Wilson called the breakup "the worst time" in his life and credited Gamble and Huff with being "the best thing in the world that ever happened" to the Blue Notes.[26]

In the spring of 1976, Pendergrass went into the recording studio, "acutely aware," he recalled, "that my future lay in the eight tracks Gamble and Huff were assembling for my solo debut album."[27] Skeptics abounded, including those at Philadelphia International, where it was hoped that Pendergrass's solo career would, at least, elicit consistent R&B sales. Almost no one thought that in a couple of years Pendergrass would be R&B's biggest male star.

FORTUNATELY FOR GAMBLE AND HUFF, while Harold Melvin and the Blue Notes were imploding, Philadelphia International still had the O'Jays to keep the company on the charts. With Gamble and Huff continuing to supply their leading act with consistently strong numbers, the O'Jays were in the midst of one of the most productive periods of their illustrious career. Of the group's four albums of new material and one live album released on Philadelphia International, two were certified platinum and the others gold. Even better, the O'Jays' unprecedented run showed no signs of abating. The group's electrifying *Message in the Music* album, released during the summer of 1976, featured another hefty dose of the trio's three-part "disco-gospel" harmonies.

Nevertheless, Philadelphia International was in need of new recording blood to pump some life back into the languid company. A singer who fit Gamble and Huff's most successful artist profile to a tee filled the bill. The soul/jazz fusion singer Lou Rawls was a three-time Grammy-winning recording artist. In addition, he had four Top 40 hits, five gold albums, and one platinum album to his credit. But he had not had a hit record in years.

Rawls was raised in poverty on Chicago's South Side by his grandmother and began singing in church choirs at age seven. As a teenager he developed an interest in jazz-influenced songs of the likes of Billy Eckstine and Joe Williams, whose resonant baritone voices were similar to his own voice. Rawls also embarked on a career as a gospel singer, first as a fifteen-year-old with the Holy Wonders and later with the Kings of Harmony quartet. After Rawls's grandmother died, he moved to Los Angeles in 1953 and joined the Chosen Gospel Singers. After two years as an army paratrooper, Rawls joined the Pilgrim Travelers gospel quartet in 1957. In November 1958, while on the road with the Pilgrim Travelers, Rawls and his close friend Sam Cooke were involved in a deadly car crash. (The driver was killed and Rawls was critically injured. Miraculously, Cooke sustained only minor injuries.) The accident contributed to the dissolution of the Pilgrim Travelers in 1959, after which Rawls, following the path taken by Cooke, cut his first secular records. Rawls sang anonymously with Cooke on Cooke's 1962 hit, "Bring It on Home to Me," and a producer at Capitol Records was so impressed with his four-octave range that he signed the unknown singer to a recording contract. Rawls did not begin to reach white audiences until 1966, when his *Lou Rawls Live* album (which contained the crossover hit "Love Is a Hurtin' Thing") became the first of his several gold albums. The following year, Rawls won a Grammy Award for his rendition of "Dead End Street," the first half of which contained a monologue (which helped to pave the way for a singing style that foreshadowed rap or hip-hop). During the late 1960s, Rawls appeared regularly on TV variety shows and became a show-room figure in the nightclubs of Las Vegas. But he had yet to achieve widespread white acceptance. Rawls switched to MGM Records in 1971, where he recorded the Grammy award-winning album *A Natural Man*. But then the hits stopped cold.[28]

It took a chance meeting with Weldon McDougal radically to alter Lou Rawls's stalled recording career. As Philadelphia International's director of special products, McDougal served, among other things, as Philadelphia International's representative at various music industry conventions. In 1974, McDougal was instrumental in signing jazz musician Monk Montgomery to Gamble and Huff's label. The following year, Montgomery invited McDougal to Las Vegas to take in the show he was playing for, which starred Lou Rawls. Montgomery introduced McDougal to Rawls, and the singer became animated when he learned that the publicity man worked for Gamble and Huff. Recalling that meeting, Rawls said that he envied the "music factory" that Philadelphia International had become, particularly because of its writers. "They had Dexter Wansel, Bunny Sigler, Cindy Biggs and McFadden and Whitehead. It just went on and on." Rawls was also being urged by the O'Jays' Eddie Levert to sign with Gamble and Huff. The singer told McDougal that he had wanted to talk to the producers about possibly signing a recording contract. McDougal called Gamble at his home, and then put Rawls on the line. "We always went after great voices, and [Rawls] had one of the great voices," recalled Gamble. "And it felt like it was time for him to get another hit." Rawls subsequently flew into Philadelphia and met with Gamble and Huff, and "we came up with the deal," he recalled.[29]

Rawls's image of Philadelphia International as a dynamic record company was bolstered on his arrival at 309 South Broad Street. "They had a blackboard up in the front and it said 'Project for the Week: Lou Rawls,'" recalled the singer. "That meant that all the writers would concentrate on writing stuff for me." Although Gamble and Huff's new modus operandi of involving company underlings in the production of Philadelphia International's music was now in effect, some venerable practices persisted. Gamble and Huff wrote (and later produced) what were deemed the prime tracks for Rawls's upcoming album, with the album's "filler" supplied by the likes of Bunny Sigler, Jack Faith, and Bobby Martin.[30] "They presented me with [the song] 'You'll Never Find Another Love Like Mine,' and that started it," said Rawls matter-of-factly. At the time, Rawls thought the song stood a chance of becoming a hit because of its title, which was an expression he heard constantly, in one form or another. "If people got in an argument or somethin', they'd say, 'that's all right. You ain't gonna find nobody else gonna put up with your [nonsense].'"

With the album's prospective songs in hand, Gamble and Huff went into Sigma Sound and, with their new rhythm section, laid down the requisite music tracks. Rawls said he "wasn't really aware of who was doin'" the music for his album, but Charles Collins, who played drums on it, certainly was. "When we got called to do that date, the movie *Jaws* had just been released and it seemed as if every musician at Sigma Sound that day had seen it," he recalled with a laugh. The movie "freaked everybody out. Everybody had a story about it. We spent about an hour talkin' about *Jaws*, and then we just grooved right into 'You'll Never Find Another Love Like Mine.'"[31]

Collins regarded Gamble and Huff's classic Sound of Philadelphia with reverence and was conscious of the size of the shoes he was being asked to fill as MFSB's drummer. Owing to his experience of "playing Caribbean-type and Cuban music in New York," he thought of giving the rhythm track to "You'll Never Find Another Love Like Mine" what he described as "an Island-like feel." Collins "played on the rims of the drums in the verses and then, in the choruses, I went into that thing on the high-hat we called 'T-Sop,' which stood for the Sound of Philadelphia."

The completed rhythm tracks were then given to Rawls, who said he "sat with the tracks for a week or two before [he'd] actually go in to record." As Rawls put his vocals over the music track to "You'll Never Find Another Love Like Mine," many of those in the studio that day sensed a particular quality to the song. "Certain sessions stick in your mind," recalled Joe Tarsia, who said that recording Rawls, whose voice was "among the best voices" he ever recorded, gave him "the most plea-sure" of all the artists he recorded over the years. With Rawls, "you always got more than you gave," exclaimed Tarsia. That certainly was the case with "You'll Never Find Another Love Like Mine," which Tarsia labeled "a piece of magic" in which Rawls's "fat voice ... the piano parts and everything else just fell in so perfectly."

"You'll Never Find Another Love Like Mine" emerged in the spring of 1976 in the form of a cultivated, buoyant disco number.[32] Bobby Martin, who arranged the song, said he strove to make it sound like "an Eddie

Duchin-type thing, very light with a soft melody building around the piano, ... [with] a touch of light strings." As the lead single from the presciently titled *All Things in Time* album, its release coincided with the peak popularity of the hustle dance craze. "You'll Never Find Another Love Like Mine" rocketed up the pop charts (to number two) and the R&B charts (to number one). It sold over a million copies and became Philadelphia International's biggest-selling single since MFSB's "TSOP." On the strength of that single, Rawls's *All Things in Time* album attained platinum status, at that time only the third Philadelphia International album to do so.[33] "You'll Never Find Another Love Like Mine" was also Lou Rawls's entry into the upper echelons of the pop market. The record won the TV-produced American Music Award, as well as a Grammy nomination for Best R&B Song of 1976. The *All Things in Time* album became the most successful album of Rawls's career. All of which, said the singer, "sort of" surprised him.

The select group of musicians who helped to bring back Lou Rawls from the recording netherworld was promptly dubbed the "Resurrection Rhythm Section," exclaimed the ebullient Charles Collins. "And Lou was always appreciative [of] the rhythm section guys, so it would be cool to see him." Gamble and Huff were also appreciative of their new musicians, whose names appeared on Rawls's next album *Unmistakably Lou*, officially confirming their status as Philadelphia International's new house rhythm section. Collins pointed out how, from that point on, whenever he and his fellow musicians got together to do a recording session, "everybody was just so comfortable and there was such a feeling of camaraderie and pride that [resulted from] recording in Philadelphia."

As a result of Rawls's blockbuster debut for Philadelphia International, his road bookings increased dramatically. The rejuvenated singer was so busy that Gamble and Huff had to summon him off the road late in the year to record a follow-up album. Rawls obligingly squeezed in the time, and the subsequent album, titled *Unmistakably Lou*, was released as 1977 began. If anything, Rawls's vocals improved over his previous album, his sweet baritone blending with a funky beat and eloquent strings that overshadowed the Gamble and Huff production team.[34] Even without a compelling single such as "You'll Never Find Another Love Like Mine," *Unmistakably Lou* was certified gold and won a Grammy Award, making Lou Rawls one of Philadelphia International's most important artists.

THE YEAR 1976 WAS ALSO THE ONE IN WHICH CBS exercised its seldom-used prerogative and had Gamble and Huff (who were paid as outside producers) produce one of the giant recording company's new acts. CBS scored a significant coup during the summer of 1976 when, following the Jackson 5's bitter departure from Motown, they signed the group to a recording contract. After Berry Gordy barred the Jackson 5 from continuing to use that name, at CBS's behest, the group became the Jacksons. Epic, like its parent company, Columbia, did not have many staff producers on hand, so when Columbia president Walter Yetnikoff asked Ron Alexenburg, who was instrumental in signing the Jacksons, whom he intended to have produce the group, Alexenburg told his boss he would consider "only two guys. I'm gonna go to Kenny Gamble and Leon Huff." Alexenburg went to Philadelphia and told Gamble and Huff, "We've been in business together for a long time. I need you to do something for me, I need you to produce the Jacksons." He claimed the producers were receptive to his plea because, first of all, it would be "prestigious" to be the first producers outside Motown to produce the Jacksons, and, second, Gamble and Huff "were looking to help me." The producers "wanted to do 'em," claimed Alexenburg, "but they wanted to do 'em on their turf! And I wasn't gonna argue with that."

Kenny Gamble had a different take on how and why he and Leon Huff came to produce the Jacksons. Gamble agreed that Alexenburg asked him and Huff to produce the group. But he added that, "in reality, we were trying to sign the Jacksons ourselves to our own label. No question we were trying to do that. But CBS had deeper pockets than ours." To secure the services of Gamble and Huff, a compromise was reached, whereby the Jacksons' album was released with a label that contained the logos of Epic and Philadelphia International. "That's the first time they ever did that," said Gamble.[35]

That summer, Michael Jackson said that he and his group "heard that Epic had Kenny Gamble and Leon Huff working on demos for us." The Jacksons, who, said Michael, "had great respect" for the records that Gamble and Huff had overseen, agreed to come to Philadelphia to record an album.[36] Extra efforts were taken to make the Jacksons feel welcome there, including a visit with Muhammad Ali at his mountain training camp in nearby Deer Lake, Pennsylvania. Besides meeting Ali, the Jacksons partook in a pickup basketball game with some of the boxer's contingent. Nevertheless, claimed Ron Alexenburg, there was "tension" present during the Jacksons' recording sessions, because, "Here they are, leaving Motown, the family that supported 'em." Kenny Gamble pointed out how the group was going through "trying times" because Jermaine had recently left the group to remain with Motown and his then father-in-law, Berry Gordy. "They were going through just a little bit of controversy there.... They came into our world, Philly International was a different environment for them." That it was. One of the reasons the Jacksons left Motown was to gain some artistic freedom.

Now, here they were, in Philadelphia for the first time, in an unfamiliar studio, with producers who were noted for their own dictatorial manner. Although Gamble maintained that the Jacksons "had a lot more freedom" at Philadelphia International than they had at Motown, and the group was "welcome to participate" in the production of their new album, the Jacksons remained wary.[37]

Michael said that the Jacksons hoped to include "a song or two" of their own on the upcoming album and had even cut two home demos. But they decided to wait for the right moment to introduce the songs to Gamble and Huff. "We felt there was no sense putting a gun to anyone's head," explained Michael. "We knew that Philly had a lot to offer us, so we'd save our surprise for them later." Michael also claimed that Gamble and Huff had been told about the Jacksons' demos and that the producers "promised to give [the songs] a fair hearing."[38] (They were included on the album.)

T. J. Tindall, who played guitar on the album, claimed that Michael occasionally dropped in during the cutting of the rhythm tracks and "was extremely quiet. Everything was, 'Mr. Gamble this, Mr. Huff that.' He was very, very timid." As Gamble and Huff, along with Dexter Wansel, Gene McFadden, and John Whitehead, worked on the lyrics of the songs, Michael said he watched them "like a hawk. . . . Just watching Huff play the piano while Gamble sang taught me more about the anatomy of a song than anything else. Kenny Gamble is a master melody man. He made me pay closer attention to the melody because of watching him create." The only members of the Jacksons to play instruments on the album were Tito (guitar) and Randy (congas), on the two tracks written by the Jacksons. Nevertheless, Tindall taught Tito how to play the guitar parts to all the songs, "because they were goin' on the road," where they would have to perform songs from their new album. The song "Enjoy Yourself," a spirited dance number destined to be the first single from the album, was constructed around a T. J. Tindall guitar riff. Tindall recalled how, after he came up with that riff, "I went into the studio one morning and I said to Huff, 'What do you think of this lick?' He said, 'Ah, that's really cool,' and he came back the next day and he had a song [written for it]. There was never any talk of [me receiving] any *credit* for it," said Tindall with a wry laugh. After MFSB laid down the rhythm tracks, Gamble and Huff came to the Jacksons' hotel "and play[ed] a whole album's worth of music for us," recalled Michael. "That's the way [we were] introduced to the songs they had chosen for our album—aside from the two songs we were writing ourselves."[39]

Michael claimed that Gamble and Huff assured the group that they "wouldn't mess with our singing," which, apparently, was the case. Once the rhythm tracks were completed, the group headed to Sigma Sound to add their vocals (to all of the tracks except the two original songs by Michael and Tito, whose vocals were later overdubbed in Chicago). Gamble said that he "enjoyed working with Michael, because he had his own ideas about how he wanted himself to sound." The group's lead singer "was very clever," which "made our job a little easier." Joe Tarsia likened his attempt to capture Michael's then-diminutive voice on tape to "recording a fog. I couldn't put my finger on it. You could put your hand right through the sound. [He had] this little, wispy-like voice. It was less mature than it is today."[40]

When the Jacksons' first album for Epic appeared, it was simply titled *The Jacksons* (and contained an unflattering cover photo of the Afro-coifed group that made them look like the Jackson quintuplets). A typical Gamble-Huff production, it contained ten tracks, half of them written and produced by Philadelphia International's owners. Dexter Wansel wrote and produced two others, while the McFadden, Whitehead, and Carstarphen team wrote and produced another. Bobby Martin arranged the two prospective Gamble and Huff–penned singles from the album, "Enjoy Yourself" and "Show You the Way to Go," and the "leftovers" were parceled out to Dexter Wansel and Jack Faith to arrange.

Released in September, "Enjoy Yourself," reached number two on the R&B charts and number six on the pop charts and was eventually certified platinum. Michael and Tito's song, "Style of Life," was put on the flip side, ensuring that the brothers would receive writers' (and a share of the producer's) royalties from sales of the single. "Enjoy Yourself" turned out to be the Jacksons' most successful single since "Dancing Machine," three years earlier. Largely on the single's strength, *The Jacksons*, which was long on danceable, if not innovative, material, was eventually certified platinum. If there was any disappointment, it stemmed from the follow-up single, "Show Me the Way to Go" (with Michael's song, "Blues Away," on the flip side). Michael was particularly fond of that tune, "because it showed what good regard the Epic people had for our singing. We were all over that record and it was the best one we did. I loved the high hat and strings fluttering alongside us like birds' wings." But the song did not live up to its expectations.[41]

The platinum status of *The Jacksons* ensured that Gamble and Huff would produce the group's next album. But for the producers who had once harbored thoughts of adding the Jacksons to their Philadelphia International roster of recording artists, this was a bittersweet moment. The album was a commercial success, but stylistically, it did not break new ground. "Certain companies stay in business by being innovators and some are great imitators," said Thom Bell. In the case of *The Jacksons*, Gamble and Huff's heavily "discofied" production showed them to be more imitators than innovators. This was just the latest example of how the rise of disco continued to undermine the freshness of Philadelphia soul.

14

"Kiss and Say Goodbye"

(1977–1978)

DUE LARGELY TO RISING OIL PRICES AND AN INCREASING trade deficit, America's economy had stagnated during the mid-1970s. Interest rates and inflation, both on the rise, ran in double digits, unemployment increased, and the stock market continued its prolonged slump. It was no surprise that, saleswise, 1977 was the worst year in the history of the recording industry. (Despite the abundance of economic factors, the principal bogeyman of the industry's woes was the home taping of music, which, since the introduction of the tape cassette, continued to rise.[1]) While most of the pop music business began to implode, black music, buoyed by disco's continuing popularity, seemed impervious to the slump.

BY THE SPRING OF 1977, PHILADELPHIA INTERNATIONAL's makeover was complete. Almost every person in a creative capacity originally hired by Gamble and Huff had been replaced.[2] Among the last to go were Linda Creed, Bobby Martin, and Thom Bell. Creed and Martin severed all relations with Gamble and Huff. Bell, who shifted his production activities to Seattle, Washington, continued as a partner in Great Philadelphia Trading and Mighty Three Music. Linda Creed's departure was particularly heartbreaking. Although Creed essentially wrote with Thom Bell, for whichever artists Bell chose to produce, she was originally signed as a writer to Assorted Music, and then Mighty Three Music. Since Gamble and Huff employed their own writers for their own artists, they were not interested in Linda Creed's songs. It became obvious that if and when Thom Bell's need for Linda Creed's songs diminished, Gamble and Huff would not take up the slack. Linda Creed's most creative period was the three years she wrote for the Stylistics, with Russell Thompkins Jr. the perfect vehicle to transport her romanticized lyrics. But, with rare exceptions, Creed's lyrics were not as suitable to the more animated style of the Spinners as were those of Joe Jefferson, Charlie Boy Simmons, and Bruce Hawes. Thus, each Spinners' album contained only one or two songs by the Creed/Bell team. Creed's hits with the Spinners "were good songs," said Eppy Epstein, but they were also "fluke songs" (such as "The Rubberband Man"). Creed saw the handwriting on the wall. Around 1974, she began work on a solo album of her own material. "Who knows what I'll do," she told writer Bruce Pollack, when asked at that time what her future held.[3]

One thing Linda Creed did do was to become pregnant. And when she gave birth to a daughter late in 1975, Gamble, Huff, and Bell went out of their way to accommodate her. They refitted the new mother's office at 309 South Broad Street so that it resembled a child's nursery. "Linda's office had a crib, a refrigerator, diapers, formula, so that she could go in there with the baby" and work, recalled Epstein. But despite Creed's modified facilities (and her biggest success for the Spinners, "The Rubberband Man," which sold a million copies during the summer of 1976), her days of writing for Mighty Three Music were numbered.[4]

As Creed sought to have her songs placed with the Spinners and other acts, tension mounted between her and Gamble, Huff, and Bell over her tenuous situation at Mighty Three Music.[5] Eppy Epstein's part in the process is uncertain, but he appears to have been a principal agitator. Epstein, a music business veteran, felt that his wife was being exploited by Mighty Three. "You should be getting [a share of the] publishing," he repeatedly told her. Even though his wife "wasn't the partner on paper and didn't share in the publishing, you never said Tommy Bell without saying Linda Creed," recalled Epstein. "They had a very special bond, they were like brother and sister." Epstein believed that Mighty Three Music "should have been Mighty Four Music."[6] Epstein was particularly angry with Thom Bell when he "didn't stick up" for Creed, "because Linda put as many bricks in that building as Kenny, Leon and Tommy. She didn't get what she was supposed to get, and that's what pissed me off."

Thom Bell laughed when he heard Epstein's recollection of why Linda Creed left Mighty Three Music. "No, that's not true," he said. "There was no way in the world she would have even wanted somethin' like [a share of Mighty Three]. For one thing, said Bell, Creed "didn't have the money to buy into [Mighty Three] . . . so that wouldn't work." In addition, Bell maintained that he had repeatedly informed his songwriting partner, "Creed, you gotta do more than just write lyrics. If you want to make more, you gotta do more. How can someone pay you more than they pay me? I play the piano, I rehearse these jokers, I write the arrangements, I get in the studio and I do it. And where are you? Nobody even sees you! Maybe you'll come to the studio; most of the time you won't. You don't even like the studio."

David Steinberg, Bell's music attorney, represented Linda Creed in her deals with Mighty Three. He flatly stated that talk about expanding Mighty Three to a Mighty Four "never took place." Steinberg was "sure" that Epstein wanted his wife to be part of a Mighty Four Music. But, explained Steinberg, Gamble, Huff, and Bell were involved, "not just in writing songs but also in producing records and playing on dates and doing all this other stuff. And I don't think . . . they ever looked at Linda as a, quote, 'equal partner.' And she wasn't. Linda was not a musician, she wasn't doing the same thing each of them were doing." Steinberg said that "the feeling was that she wasn't contributing, or she didn't have the ability to contribute, into a project the same way they all did."

When Creed's contract with Mighty Three ended, Steinberg claimed that "a new contract was formed where, instead of just getting the song-writer's share, she was given a substantially big bonus override . . . an extra percentage, which would be like a publisher." Epstein said that when Creed's contract with Mighty Three expired, "and they didn't offer her an equal share," he said to her, "C'mon Creed, we're getting' out of here!" The couple left Philadelphia and moved to California, home of the Latino funk-rock band War, whom Epstein was managing at the time.[7]

THOM BELL'S SONGWRITING PARTNERSHIP WITH LINDA CREED most likely would not have remained viable, no matter how her problems with Mighty Three were resolved. Bell's work template—by which he would take on a challenging project, develop it into a rousing success, and then move on to the next project—had been forged with the Delfonics and repeated with the Stylistics and the Spinners. Bell's involvement with the latter group was nearing the end of the line, and for the first time in his career, he was not focused on his next musical project. Bell's personal life, which had always taken precedence over his musical endeavors, now demanded a drastic change in his life-style. From 1968 until about 1975, Bell said he worked, "oh man, sometimes seventy-two hours straight. You know, that's what you had to do." During that time, Bell's wife was chronically ill and he never knew when a crisis would occur and he would have to "rush different places, to the hospital and stuff." In addition, Bell and his wife had three young children to care for. As the responsibilities of his personal life encroached on his work schedule, Bell devised a plan to allot more time to his family. First, he set a limit of just two albums a year for each artist he recorded, "in order to try to keep that home front together and be with the kids and help them with their schoolwork and get 'em off to school and stuff." Then, to create even more personal time, Bell began "doubling" his sessions, recording two albums' worth of material at one time (as he had first done with the Spinners' *New and Improved* and *Mighty Love* albums).

Being able to spend more time with his family helped when it came to everyday matters, but it did nothing for the aggravated state of his wife's health. Doctors finally diagnosed her as having an incurable case of arterial inflammation, a condition they believed was exacerbated by "tension, loud noises, and by living in the city and different things," said Bell. "The only cure for her is to take her out of the city, preferably the West Coast," Bell was advised. Bell had a brother who lived in Washington State, and in June 1976, the Bell family packed up and moved there. "It was totally quiet," recalled Bell, and his wife "loved it."[8] (The family has remained in Washington ever since.)

Bell's business ties to Gamble and Huff did not change when he moved to Washington. He remained an equal partner in Great Philadelphia Trading and Mighty Three Music. Bell planned to establish his own base of operations in Washington. He claimed that Gamble and Huff were originally "gonna finance part of the move." But Bell owned the majority of the stock in the new enterprise, so Gamble and Huff "didn't quite like the idea of putting that kind of money into something that they couldn't get involved in. . . . So they passed on it." Working both coasts, Bell continued his recording career, "trying to develop [in Washington], and at the same time trying to branch out." He used an existing studio in Seattle (and sometimes flew to Los Angeles) to lay down preliminary music tracks and then returned to Philadelphia to overdub the string and horn parts. Bell also had a "bunch of brand new writers that [he] was cultivating," including Casey James and his nephew, Leroy Bell.[9]

WHILE THOM BELL SET UP SHOP IN WASHINGTON STATE, Bobby Martin, the only remaining member of Philadelphia International's original principal players, prepared to leave the City of Brotherly Love. He, like so many others, had grown disillusioned with Philadelphia International. Over the past ten years, Martin had won two Grammy Awards and had to his credit fourteen gold and two platinum albums. In 1976, Martin's masterful work with Lou Rawls, the O'Jays, and the Jacksons made him an even more valued commodity by Gamble and Huff. Still, the adroit arranger-producer recognized that he could never be the "top guy" around Philadelphia International. Nevertheless, exclaimed Martin, he "was doin' all the work" there. It was not the work that Martin objected to, but his lack of production opportunities. Martin's former colleague and fellow songwriter Morris Bailey said that Gamble and Huff "wouldn't let Bobby produce anything . . . and we were producin' before they were twelve years old." To mollify Martin, Gamble and Huff, who remained interested in Martin for his arranging ability, gave him what he described as "the freedom of doing other things on the outside."

By far the most significant "other thing" Martin did was become producer-arranger for the Manhattans R&B group. After a string of insignificant singles dating from the early 1960s, the Manhattans experienced their first real hit in 1965, with "I Wanna Be Your Everything." Lacking affiliation with a major recording company, the group ground out records for eight years and became regular inhabitants (if not stars) of the country's R&B charts. Along the way, the Manhattans survived several personnel changes. Their big break came in 1972, when they signed with Columbia Records and were paired with Bobby Martin. Martin, using the original MFSB rhythm section, recorded them at Sigma Sound. Without sacrificing any of their distinctive soulfulness, the Manhattans recorded a series of harmony hits for Bobby Martin, beginning with 1973's "There's No Me Without You." At the height of the disco era, when just about every other black harmony group was driven off the charts, the Manhattans flourished under Martin's tutelage. The group reached its peak in 1976, with the hit "Kiss and Say Goodbye," an anachronistic tune that emerged from the oppressive disco din and dance-dominated R&B radio to top both the pop and the R&B charts.[10] "Kiss and Say Goodbye" was one of Columbia's biggest singles ever. "Platinum!" Martin proudly exclaimed. The Manhattans also chalked up two gold-certified albums (all of which helped CBS to get over its loss of control of Philadelphia International's master recordings). Martin's work with the Manhattans, in addition to his duties at Philadelphia International, made him so busy that he did not have time to "think about when [the hits] were gonna stop." In time, they would stop. But, unlike the cases of all the other individuals who already left Philadelphia International, they would stop for Bobby Martin only because he chose to have it that way.

Weldon McDougal, who left Philadelphia International in 1976, after a dispute with management, recalled the time during one of CBS's music conventions when he and Martin sat together. One of the corporation's executives announced that Columbia had just had "the biggest sales year ever, and Philadelphia International was number one," said McDougal. Martin turned to him and said, "Number one! Gamble and Huff must be makin' some big money!" The next time McDougal saw Martin, he noticed that Martin "was kinda upset." McDougal asked what was wrong. "Man, that ain't right!" exclaimed Martin. Gamble and Huff were paying him three hundred dollars per arrangement, "and he went in to see Kenny and said he thought he should now get six hundred dollars per arrangement. Kenny said no, and that kinda got him, so he got an attorney and they went back to talk to Kenny, and Kenny still said no.

So Bobby said, 'Man, I'm leavin!'" Morris Bailey agreed that Martin "got fed up" with his situation "and just went to California."

In Martin's 1977 A&M biography, he said that he had been "too long in one place" and had grown "stagnant" in Philadelphia. Referring to his employers there, Martin stated that "none of them lived up to what they'd promised, not a one." Martin said that he and his wife decided to "pull up stakes in Philadelphia altogether" and move to California, where they owned property.[11]

Martin also claimed in his A&M biography that he "stuck with Kenny for years as a team working together and I enjoyed it. The jobs, the sessions—that was a lot of gold, man—gold and platinum—a lot of success, a lot of work. The bread I was making was sufficient—how many steaks can you eat? It was enough to run you into bad health."[12] Two decades later, the urbane and unpretentious Martin insisted he "didn't have any regrets" about leaving Philadelphia International, that he "had a good time" while working there. "I didn't miss anything," he said. "If I'd missed something I woulda stayed there!" But Martin did take a backhanded swipe at Gamble and Huff in 1977. He stated that after working at Philadelphia International, he had gone "looking for the light in the darkness" and found it at A&M, where "even the top executives are down to earth" and treated him "like a human being."[13]

Also cast into the netherworld created by Thom Bell's departure was the songwriting team of Joe Jefferson, "Charlie Boy" Simmons, and Bruce Hawes. "It wasn't really a good time for us," recalled Jefferson. The ace songwriting trio was "real close to Thom." They had "never really done anything on the acts that were signed to Philadelphia International—the Gamble and Huff acts—unless Thom Bell was involved." Jefferson said that when Bell left for Washington, the songwriting trio felt "'caught in the middle [because they were] . . . really not in the Gamble and Huff clique." Gamble "never took our songs," added Jefferson. "I think he liked what we were doing, but our stuff was just a little more sophisticated and didn't quite have the harsh 'street edge' that Gamble had." The three songwriters realized that Bell "had to do what he had to do, but we always felt like he left us" in a difficult situation, said Jefferson. "And it kind of left a bad taste in our mouths." Adding to the frustration of Jefferson and most of the staff writers signed to Mighty Three Music, all of the publishing rights were assigned to Mighty Three. "That means they take fifty percent of the royalties off the top before the writers get to split anything," explained Gene McFadden. McFadden conceded that even though he and partner John Whitehead "didn't know a good deal from a bad one" when they signed on as songwriters with Mighty Three, "it's hard to have many regrets." What rankled McFadden was that he and Whitehead "started to meet more people in the business who did the same thing we did, and they were making *astronomical* money." It was then that they began to think they were not "getting our fair share. After all, we were writing the songs. Without the songs there's nothing!"[14]

DESPITE THE LOSS OF LINDA CREED, BOBBY MARTIN, and (to a large extent) Thom Bell, the burning question at Philadelphia International at the beginning of 1977 was whether Teddy Pendergrass was able to cut it as a solo act. There was no doubting his ability to put across a song without the backing of the Blue Notes. After all, Pendergrass's recordings with the group employed a varying number of other group members (ranging from minimal to none). But whether the Blue Notes fans would break the emotional bond they had with Pendergrass as a Blue Note and accept him as a solo act was yet to be seen.

The singer's debut album, straightforwardly titled *Teddy Pendergrass*, was recorded at 309 South Broad Street late in 1976. The first session was devoted to the album's crucial first single, "I Don't Love You Anymore." Pendergrass recalled how "Gamble would have me in there singing practically nonstop. There were times [he] made me sing until I literally could not talk. . . . Many an evening I walked into [the studio] and emerged to see the sun rising the next day."[15] Pendergrass knew from experience that Gamble was a producer who judged a performance "by its full effect. If given a choice between a technically perfect but dull take and a slightly flawed but riveting performance, he'd go with the latter every time." During Pendergrass's first solo session, Gamble lived up to his reputation. Jim Gallagher, who engineered the session (Joe Tarsia was in the hospital with appendicitis), recalled the session. The rhythm section, anchored by Charles Collins and Sugar Bear Foreman, was grooving, "and man, it's happenin'!" exclaimed Gallagher. "We got a great sound, and we're getting' ready to go, and Huff and the band have really got it locked. They're out there playin', Kenny's sittin' in there with me, and he says, 'Roll tape, let's go!'" About three and a half minutes into the song, just about where the single version was projected to end, Collins hit his snare drum and one of the wires across its underside broke, releasing the tension on the drumhead. "All of a sudden, the snare drum's 'crack, crack, crack' sound turned into almost a tom-tom sound," recalled Gallagher.

Often, when such a thing occurred, the musicians simply stop playing. Joe Tarsia would have made certain that things stopped right there, but Gallagher did not. It was his first day on the job as first engineer with Gamble, and Gallagher said he "was real nervous! I was doin' whatever Kenny was tellin' me to do." This occurred during disco's heyday, when many recordings contained a long vamp, or "outchorus."

With that in mind, Charles Collins continued to pound his drum kit. "They played another three minutes of Charles just beatin' on this snare drum, soundin' like a tom-tom," said Gallagher. When the band finished the song, they thought the take would be discarded. But Gamble ordered the tape rewound and, after listening to it, he shook his head. No, he told the musicians. That was exactly what he wanted. "I know the money take when I hear it," he told them. "That was the one that felt good!" Gallagher gently reminded Gamble of how the snare drum sound changed right in the middle of the take, which prompted Gamble to utter what Gallagher called the "classic" studio line: "Don't worry, we'll fix it in the mix!" "Yeah, right!" thought Gallagher, who was well aware of Joe Tarsia's philosophy of getting a track down "right on the tape in the first place," so it did not have to be fixed later. Gamble remained adamant about not redoing the track, "so we fixed the drum," said Gallagher, "and cut a couple more songs for the album."

By the time the rhythm tracks for Teddy Pendergrass's first solo album were completed, Joe Tarsia had returned to work. Listening to the completed tracks, he heard the drum break during "I Don't Love You Anymore." "What the hell is this?" he asked Gamble. "Don't worry, Joe. I know you'll figure out a way to fix it," replied Gamble. Tarsia became "all pissed off," recalled Gallagher. After pondering the situation for several moments, Tarsia offered a quintessential demonstration of his studio wizardry. First, he located the snare drum that Collins had played on the flawed take and, after setting up a speaker next to the drum, used a device called a varying oscillator to direct a loud tone at the drum. Tarsia then did "this amazing thing where he found the resident frequency of the drum by changing the tone of the oscillator until he got the drum to vibrate," explained Gallagher. Tarsia then placed two microphones, one out of phase with the other, over the drum, which canceled out the tone so the only sound was that of the vibrating snares. The Sigma engineer then recorded the rattling snares on an entire reel of tape. Tarsia fed that sound into the mixing board and, using some sort of triggering device, made the sound of the broken drum act as the trigger. That caused the triggering gate to open and close every time the sound of the broken drum occurred. That, in turn, allowed the sound of the newly recorded snares to come through and replace the broken drum sounds. It was a bit of "electronic magic," exclaimed Gallagher. To Joe Tarsia, it was just another day at the office. "And you, Gallagher," he angrily informed his understudy, "don't you ever, ever let them get away with anything like that again. If something breaks you make 'em do it over and do it right. Don't ever put me through this kind of thing again!"[16]

Pendergrass said that listening to the playbacks of his album "only deepened [his] faith in Gamble and Huff and the whole PIR operation. If the tracks they cut on me with Harold Melvin and the Blue Notes fit like a glove, these were like a second skin." Aided immeasurably by CBS Records' "Teddy Is Ready" campaign, which encompassed a plethora of interviews, radio station visits, and other promotional activities, *Teddy Pendergrass* reached number seventeen on *Billboard*'s album chart that spring. It remained there for thirty-five weeks. "I Don't Love You Anymore," which was among Pendergrass's best up-tempo songs ever, crossed over and became a pop hit and just missed making the Top 40. Pendergrass's sonic and emotional range was amply demonstrated when the second single off the album, a ballad called "The Whole Town's Laughing at Me," became a Top 20 R&B hit and ended any speculation that Pendergrass might return to the Blue Notes. Pendergrass lauded Gamble and Huff's ability "to tap into each artist's psyche and create for each a repertoire that was not just unique but uniquely suited to him. . . . The albums they wrote and produced for me didn't give me just songs to sing; they gave me a story about myself, told in music."[17]

As Teddy Pendergrass embarked on his solo career, Dee Dee Sharp Gamble was about to resume hers. She had not recorded since her ill-fated duet with Bunny Sigler in 1971, which was produced by her husband. For whatever reasons, Kenny Gamble had little success with producing female artists. "In my mind, women weren't his forte," thought Joe Tarsia. "Kenny didn't know how to cut women!" A chauvinist at heart, Gamble's beliefs were reinforced by his recent (1976) conversion to Islam. Jerry Butler recalled that when he worked with Gamble, Gamble's "focus was for the male ego. . . . It was kind of his personality that he was writing."

In 1976, Gamble insisted that one of his "disappointments" was not being able to "get a hit" from his wife. But he apparently did everything he could to hinder Dee Dee's singing career, steering her into running Huga Management. But Sharp's immersion in the back-room dealings of the music business only created further difficulties. (Joe Tarsia said that Sharp "was a very insecure woman with a very big ego, and the two were always conflicting.") Sharp noted that there were "a great number of songs, titles, lyric lines, choruses, or hooks that Kenny and I would do together and I never got credit." When she asked Gamble why her name was not on a song that she helped to write, he would reply, "I don't see what you're worried about. We're married. You're getting the money anyway."[18] Gamble and Sharp remained married, but by 1975, the union had ended in every aspect but in name. At that point, Sharp realized there was no point to abide Gamble any longer and resumed her recording career.

Dee Dee's new album, *Happy 'bout the Whole Thing*, was credited to "Dee Dee Sharp." Although her married name was conspicuously absent from the cover, her husband's written monograph to her, a two-sentence missive asking God to bless Sharp in all she did and counseling her to "Stay meek, righteous, be a wise woman," loomed large. Sharp's cover image was anything but meek, and deliberately so. A far cry from her "Mashed Potato Time" teen pop days at Cameo-Parkway, it featured a liberated, smiling singer, adorned with sparkling jewelry, clad in a sequined dress, and sporting a stylishly moderate Afro hairdo. In the album's grooves, Sharp was right at home with Bobby Martin's resonant arrangements and the production of Gamble, Huff, and her pianist/composer James Mendell. The album contained two outstanding proposed single releases (the title song and a cover of the hit "I'm Not in Love," by the rock group 10cc). But in the end, Sharp's *Happy 'bout the Whole Thing* album generated very little happiness. The title track failed to chart, and the second single stalled on the R&B charts at number sixty-two. The music was there for the taking, but Sharp did not believe that "Kenneth was that enthusiastic about promoting my product."[19] (Gamble did release his wife's album and its singles not on the prestigious Philadelphia International label, but on its TSOP subsidiary.)

Kenny Gamble may have been involved in producing the music tracks for Sharp's album, but, most likely, he did not offer any input into the recording of his wife's vocals. His and Sharp's presence together in the studio made those around them uncomfortable. Although the couple was still married, Sharp was "not with him [and] Kenny was with someone else," recalled Jim Gallagher, who was one of the engineers who worked on the album. "But they [were] back to workin' together." Gamble "didn't spend much time [in the studio] while she was there working," added Gallagher. Most of the time, he "just stayed in his office. But every once in a while he would walk in and she'd be there. And sometimes that felt weird!" There were times, added Gallagher, when it was obvious that "some kinds of residual issues were going on with Kenny and her."

Sharp's second Philadelphia International album, *What Color Is Love*, did not appear until the spring of 1977. By then, her hair had grown out to a shoulder-length coif and she appeared sultry instead of smiling in the cover photograph. Although she was billed on the front cover of her latest album as "Dee Dee Sharp *Gamble*," her husband's credits on *What Color Is Love* were sharply reduced from her previous effort. The nine tracks were the work of a potpourri of producers. Gamble was credited with co-production credit on the album's title song and on one other track. Sharp thought that "each album, as far as I'm concerned, got progressively better as I began to get involved." But the commercial response to *What Color Is Love* did not improve compared with her previous album. Over the next year, four singles (an unusually high number) were issued from *What Color Is Love*, but none of them, including a cover of England Dan and John Ford Coley's hit, "I'd Really Love to See You Tonight," charted. By then, Sharp and Gamble were locked in a bitterly contested divorce, and she was attending school part time in pursuit of a Ph.D. in psychology.

Except for his wife and the Three Degrees, the only other female singer Kenny Gamble had recorded was ex-Motown thrush Carolyn Crawford, whose records went unnoticed. In 1976, Gamble and Huff decided to give another female singer a try. They signed the classically trained Jean Carn, who was fresh off a Top 10 R&B duet, "Valentine Love," sung with bassist Michael Henderson.[20] Carn was born in Georgia as Sarah Jean Perkins. At age four, she began singing in a church choir and taking piano lessons. Perkins attended college on a musical scholarship, during which time she learned to play almost every instrument in the orchestra and sang everything from musical theater to opera. Perkins contemplated Juilliard, but instead she married jazz-fusion bandleader Doug Carn and became his vocalist. As Jean Carn, she made her first recordings in 1971. Carn also began singing studio-backing vocals for the R&B group Earth, Wind and Fire and other artists. When her marriage to Doug Carn ended, she became Duke Ellington's vocalist (Carn was the famed maestro's last singer). In the mid-1970s, drummer Norman Connors, who was putting together a stable of young talented vocalists, approached Carn. She signed with him, and four acclaimed albums ensued. Then, despite Kenny Gamble's sparse and dismal track record with female artists, Carn signed with Philadelphia International.

Because of Carn's most recent album successes, her signing by Philadelphia International was a coup for Gamble and Huff's label. Carn went into the studio in the fall of 1976 and recorded her first effort for her new record company. Bobby Eli, who eventually produced some tracks for the singer, described Carn as "the consummate professional [who would] . . . give you the shirt off her back. She was a trouper, one of the best as far as getting the job done. She would be out in the lobby at seven o'clock in the morning, sleeping. If you wanted her to do a quick 'punch-in' [vocal re-record] you'd just go out and wake her up and tell her what had to be done, and she'd get up from her sleep and go in and record."

Carn's self-titled album for Gamble and Huff was released near the end of the year (at the same time as Teddy Pendergrass's first solo album). The lead single, titled "Free Love," reached number twenty-three on *Billboard*'s R&B chart, but her second single failed miserably. Although Carn recorded three additional albums for Philadelphia International, Gamble's production bugaboo with female artists prevailed.

DESPITE THE RECORDING INDUSTRY DOWNTURN, Philadelphia International's bottom line for 1977 showed improvement over the previous year. Out of the seventeen albums released, one (by Teddy Pendergrass) was certified platinum and three (two by Lou Rawls and *Travelin' at the Speed of Thought* by the indefatigable O'Jays) reached gold status. But Kenny Gamble also passed on a future million-selling artist that year. Gamble "always thought only he had brains," recalled Thom Bell. "He always thought only he could create. If he didn't write it, that meant it was nothin'!" Evelyn King worked in the family janitorial business. One of the family's clients was Philadelphia International Records. "They would come in late at night and clean," recalled Bell. "No one knew she could sing." But one night, one of Gamble's third-line producers heard King sing. He approached Gamble and said he wanted to record her. "Gamble just laughed," said Bell. "He didn't want to be bothered with her." The producer then took Evelyn "Champagne" King to RCA Victor, where her debut single, "Shame, Shame, Shame," sold a million copies in 1978 and became the longest running disco hit in history. King went on to rack up three certified gold albums and two additional million-selling singles for RCA. Gamble lost Champagne King (and several other artists) "by thinkin' that only he could do something," said Bell.

Still, it seemed for the moment as if Gamble and Huff had managed to overcome most, if not all, of their mid-decade problems. In truth, however, 1977's improvement was merely a spike in the slow, downward spiral into which Philadelphia International had entered. Despite the gold and platinum brought home by the O'Jays, Teddy Pendergrass, and Lou Rawls, an indication of Philadelphia International's fortunes was evident that year with the release of a two-album collection of extended dance track versions of old material and of the Jacksons' second Gamble and Huff–produced album. The recycled dance material was intended to capitalize on the still-hot disco market. But the so-called marketing experts should have known that, historically, blacks do not buy back-catalog items. CBS's own Rick Swig recalled how the music industry could not sell to blacks a "best of" album, "for any reason, way, shape or form," and the dismal response to the Gamble and Huff reissue project bore him out.

MEANWHILE, THE JACKSONS RETURNED TO PHILADELPHIA early that summer to record their second album, *Goin' Places*, for Gamble and Huff. Despite the invigorating material and some new production ideas, plus arrangements that surpassed those the Jacksons had received in quite a while at Motown, the album proved to be a commercial disappointment when it was released later in the year. The fate of the album's first single, its title song, indicated that the Jacksons' second album would have a difficult time matching the crossover success of its predecessor. The single made the R&B Top 10, but it stalled at fifty-two on the pop charts. The second single, "Find Me a Girl," just edged into the R&B Top 40 and did not even make the pop charts. Unlike the Jacksons' first album for Gamble and Huff, *Goin' Places* was heavier on message songs, at the expense of the more-apt-to-please dance numbers. Michael Jackson thought their latest album was "more like the old O'Jays' 'Love Train' and not really our style." Michael claimed that he and the other group members felt they "were losing some of [their] identity" in subjugating themselves to Gamble and Huff's highly stylized production line.[21] After the release of the album, Michael and Joe Jackson, the group's father and manager, met over lunch with Ron Alexenburg "to convince him that we were ready now to take charge of our own music," said Michael. They told Alexenburg that the company "had done its best, and it wasn't good enough." We "felt we could do better, that our reputation was worth putting on the line," said Michael. With that, the Jacksons parted company with Gamble and Huff.[22]

The Jacksons' two Gamble and Huff–produced albums managed to keep the group in the limelight for almost two years, as they made the transition from Motown puppets to independent stars. But from the start, neither party needed to (or particularly wanted to) work with the other. The rather perfunctory results should not have been unexpected. It was the Jacksons' next album, *Destiny*, produced by Quincy Jones, on which the group had the freedom to write and begin to produce for themselves that propelled the Jacksons (and eventually Michael) toward their real destiny.

THE CARTER ADMINISTRATION HAD PROVEN TO BE INEFFECTIVE in solving America's economic problems, and by 1978, the country edged closer to recession. Nevertheless, the recording industry made a dramatic turnaround that year (due in no small part to a price increase for a third consecutive year), as monetary sales figures reached an all-time high of $4 billion, most of it from disco releases. The disco phenomenon seemed to run on perpetual motion, and nobody in the recording industry thought much about it, other than how to get the next disco record to the marketplace as quickly as possible. Nobody imagined (or wanted to imagine) that the disco phenomenon was about to crash. Of all things, the music's death rattle turned out to be the extravagantly successful disco film *Saturday Night Fever*, in which John Travolta played a sharply dressed, smooth-dancing ladies' man.[23]

Released during the summer of 1977, *Saturday Night Fever* served to make the disco lifestyle safe for middle America, as the Bee Gees put a white face on what was essentially black music. The film eventually made $85 million. The double-disc soundtrack album garnered a Grammy for Album of the Year and became the top-selling soundtrack album of all time (with 25 million copies sold). But because of the movie's widespread popularity, disco, which had been perceived by the country's heartland as an indistinct, predominantly black and gay occurrence safely removed from mainstream life-style, now became a threat to the insular (and macho) rock audiences. In 1978, a panicked, phobic "Disco Sucks!" backlash, aided and abetted by opportunistic rock deejays, began to take shape.[24]

But it was not disco alone that took the hit. Virtually all black music was tarred with the disco brush and became a pseudonym for any and all black music. Disco became "a dirty word," acknowledged Thom Bell. The labeling of all black music as "disco" helped to eliminate blacks from the mainstream competition and stigmatized black music to an even greater extent. "It was stupid. It was racist. It revealed how powerful a force semantics can be in the reception of music," wrote Nelson George in *The Death of Rhythm and Blues*. "Just as rock and roll came to mean white music, disco came to represent some ugly amalgam of black and gay music."[25]

The repercussions were felt at Philadelphia International, where, that year, apart from Teddy Pendergrass's second album, *Life Is a Song Worth Singing*, and the O'Jays' *So Full of Love* (both certified platinum), there was not much cause for optimism. Although the company's ratio of gold and platinum-certified albums to the number of albums released remained a favorable 25 percent, the year's total album output was cut almost in half, to eight. (There was a six-month gap during the middle of the year when no new Philadelphia International product was issued.) No longer the independent giant it once was, Philadelphia International was in danger of losing status within the industry.[26] Reduced to three viable acts, the label ceased to project its classically distinct sound and instead began to cater to the distinct styles of their high-profile lead vocalists: Eddie (Levert), Teddy, and Lou. Gamble and Huff went so far as to expand this latest concept. They signed Jerry Butler, with whom they enjoyed some of their earliest (and greatest) successes to a recording and production contract.

Butler left Mercury Records in 1974 and signed with Motown, hoping to rekindle the spark that was first ignited while working with Gamble and Huff. Motown's lure was a siren song, however, and by 1978, after a series of tasteful but lackluster albums for that company, Butler was disillusioned and without a recording contract. With Butler available, who better than the "Ice Man" himself to fulfill Gamble and Huff's quest for an additional strong, distinct male voice to record? The producers had once captured Butler's style better than anyone else had, to the degree that Butler said he was "spoiled" by working with them. Butler said he chose Philadelphia International because he was "trying to duplicate what we had been so successful with." He was eager and excited to work with "a bunch of young talent orchestrators who probably never would have gotten a chance" had it not been for Gamble and Huff. (Kenny Gamble may have had more than Butler's singing in mind when he was signed to Philadelphia International. Gamble turned over production of his female artists, including his wife, to him.)

Jerry Butler's initial album for Philadelphia International, *Nothing Says I Love You Like I Love You*, appeared in the fall of 1978. The recording was afforded an inordinate amount of attention by Gamble and Huff, who produced all but one of the seductive yet solid tracks. *Nothing Says I Love You Like I Love You* was Butler's best album since he recorded with Gamble and Huff in 1970. But in 1978, disco still prevailed (for the time being, anyway), and only one track from the album (the lead single, "Cooling Out," which featured one of Leon Huff's heated piano grooves) catered to the dance floor crowd. It became a Top 20 R&B hit, but the album's two follow-up singles generated little interest. Sales of Butler's album dropped accordingly, and Butler began to focus more on the production of other artists than on his singing.

While Gamble and Huff's endeavor to add another distinctive male voice to their recording roster foundered, even the durable Lou Rawls stumbled slightly. Live album releases were historically poor sellers (usually purchased only by the artist's hard-core fans), and Rawls's 1978 live double album was no exception. The only mark it managed to break was the singers' three-album string of gold and platinum recordings.[27]

THOM BELL HAD NOT EXACTLY SET THE WORLD ON FIRE since his move west in 1976. Late that year the Spinners released *Yesterday Today and Tomorrow*, their final album with their lead singer, Phillippe Wynne. In keeping with Bell's new strategy, the album was cut simultaneously with the group's *Happiness Is Being with the Spinners*, the previous spring. Wynne's departure from the group ended a long period of conflict between him and the other group members and also between Wynne and Bell. "What's wrong with you, man? Why do you want to do that?" asked Bell when he learned of Wynne's decision to leave the group. Like Teddy Pendergrass, Wynne was unhappy because the group's name was mentioned "more than they mention mine!" "When you go to the bank with a fifty-thousand dollar check, do you go in there and write the Spinners' names on the check or do you write Philipe Wynne's name on the check?" Bell wanted to know. "That Spinners nonsense don't mean a thing! Not when it comes to your paycheck. You're really making a mistake," cautioned Bell. "But would you believe," recalled the producer some twenty-five years later, "he left."[28]

John Edwards, who had filled in on the Spinners' live shows for years, replaced Wynne. During the late spring of 1977, Bell then took the group into the studio to record their first album, titled *Spinners/8*, with Edwards. Thom Bell collaborated with his nephew Leroy and/or Casey James on two of the tunes on the album, and the Leroy Bell–Casey James team, mentored by Thom Bell, wrote three others. It was apparent to Joe Jefferson and Charlie Boy Simmons (Bruce Hawes was not writing with them at the time), who were afforded just one song on the Spinners' latest album, that they were being squeezed out of the picture. "We didn't really feel the spark," recalled Jefferson, and "we just wanted to get out of there." Meanwhile, the unproven songwriting team of Leroy Bell and Casey James was not yet up to writing a substantial hit for the Spinners.[29] *Spinners/8* was the group's least successful album since signing with Atlantic.

After visiting Philadelphia to arrange two tracks on Teddy Pendergrass's *Life Is a Song Worth Singing* album, Bell returned to Seattle and began making plans for the Spinners' next album. [30] The first five of the group's seven studio albums produced by Bell had achieved gold status, but of late, his production with the Spinners had taken on a perfunctory quality. The group's effortless soul style, particularly on *Spinners/8*, began to sound dated. In the public's eye, Bell was now most associated with the Spinners, a group for whom he was no longer able to anticipate what he thought the group would sound like a year in advance. Bell no longer felt he could do "a good job" with the Spinners. "And if I couldn't do a good job, why do it? When it gets passe—'Ho-hum, the O'Jays are coming; ho-hum, the Spinners are coming'—that's no good. If you're not excited, then you picked the wrong thing to do." And Bell was no longer excited about working with the Spinners. "I felt I could not take them any further than where I took them," he recalled, adding that he was "really getting burnt out." Late in 1977, Bell told Atlantic, "The next album in hand will be my last album" for the Spinners.[31]

Around that time, Thom Bell began working with the flamboyant rock star Elton John. John wanted Bell to produce his next album, but the singer's ambitious touring schedule and animated stage performances had put him into a state of exhaustion. (In November, John would collapse during two of his shows; he subsequently announced his retirement from live performances.) Accordingly, for John's next recording, he wanted to cut a modest album, utilizing just piano and voice. He met with the Spinners, who were in London, and sent word with the group to Bell that he wanted to work with him. Unlike many rockers of that era, who had no business trifling with R&B, Elton John possessed a musical flexibility and a love of R&B that seemed as if it would mesh nicely with Thom Bell's style. John's record company flew Bell to England for his first meeting with the rock star. Bell claimed that when he asked John exactly what the singer wanted to do on the prospective album, John, most likely still recuperating from his stage exhaustion, "emphatically" replied that he did not want to do "anything." He did not want to write, produce, or even play the piano on it. "I want you to do everything," John reportedly told Bell. Bell did not think that was "a wise move," because John was such "a fantastically talented guy." He told the rock star, "I think that if we put our talents together we could come up with something even better." But John again said he was "tired of doing everything" and refused to collaborate with Bell. Undaunted, Bell approached John's lyricist, Bernie Taupin, and told Taupin that working together, the three of them could produce a great album. But Taupin, too, refused to become involved. "Okay, so all right then if that's what you want to do, I'll do it myself," said Bell.[32]

The sessions began that October, in Seattle. Bell flew his usual rhythm contingent west from Philadelphia to lay down the rhythm tracks. After fruitlessly "begging" John to play piano, Bell played the instrument himself. Before John put his vocals over the six rhythm tracks, Bell offered the singer a few vocal coaching tips about breathing and employing his lower register to a greater extent. From what has been written about the sessions, they apparently went well. In her biography of John, Ellen Rosenthal claimed that his singing "was firmly on a new trail, thanks to Thom Bell." After the session, John said that Bell was the first person who ever taught him anything about his voice and had been "right" in his coaching.[33]

Thom Bell had a different recollection of the Elton John sessions. He characterized them as "a disaster." There were problems from the start, said Bell, specifically with adhering to his swift, no-nonsense work ethic. John and his contingent "had never been used to anyone doing tracks and different things all in one day," he explained. Bell said they were used to being in the studio "for about two months" to record an album. "I don't work like that," said the producer. "So a day and a half later we had knocked out six songs. They couldn't *believe* it!" Bell also recalled the incessant partying, including drug and alcohol abuse, and an undercurrent of sexual tension that permeated the homosexual John and his musical coterie.

However the sessions went, when they were completed, Bell traveled to Sigma Sound and, apparently unbeknownst to Elton John, added overdubs by MFSB strings and horns, as well as backing vocals by Bell and James, the Spinners, and the Sigma Sweethearts—Barbara, Carla, and Evette—to the finished tracks. When Bell delivered the final mixes for the proposed album, Elton John heard the overdubs and decided the music was overproduced, that the orchestration was "too saccharine." He especially had misgivings about one particular song on which he had asked Bell to have the Spinners add backing vocals. "I only sang one verse and [the Spinners] did the whole lot," complained John. It was then, said the singer, he realized Thom Bell's finished product "didn't live up to his expectations." Plans for the prospective album were shelved, and a second session, slated for early the following year, was canceled.

Later that year Ron Alexenburg left Epic Records and joined MCA, the company that marketed and distributed Elton John's records in America. Alexenburg "wanted to hear all the stuff that was in the can," recalled Bell, and when he heard John's recording of "Mama Can't Buy You Love" his ears perked up. "Hey, what's this?" he asked. "What are you holdin' this up for?" he exclaimed to MCA. "Get this product out!" In 1979, three tracks from John's abandoned Thom Bell sessions were remixed in Philadelphia by Bell and released as a three-song twelve-inch extended play single. The EP bore the title: *The Thom Bell Sessions '77*, and "Mama Can't Buy You Love" was its plug song.[34] It is Bell's contention that the record was so titled "because they were scared of the product, that it wasn't really Elton. They decided, 'Well, we'll hedge our bet. We'll make it the 'Thom Bell Sessions.' And it came back to hit 'em in the face 'cause it was a hit!" he recalled with a laugh. "I took the bull by the horns, and gave the boy a top ten record." Bell also gave them a million-seller. "Mama Can't Buy You Love" became Elton John's biggest hit in almost three years.

15

"Ain't No Stoppin' Us Now"

(1979–1982)

A S 1979 BEGAN, THE BIG NEWS AROUND PHILADELPHIA INTERNATIONAL was the signing of a new vocal group—and a female group at that. That the Jones Girls—three sisters from Detroit—were veterans of the recording studio when they arrived at 309 South Broad Street was not unusual. What was surprising was that the trio had not been Kenny Gamble's first choice to add to Philadelphia International's roster. That distinction had gone to the masterful background singers Barbara Ingram, Evette Benton, and Carla Benson, a.k.a the Sweethearts of Sigma. Since 1971, the three young singers had developed into the consummate recording studio professionals and had sung on a majority of tracks recorded in Philadelphia during the decade. The Sweethearts were every producer's dream. Fastidiously talented, they took pride in their work and often refused to leave the studio until they obtained the exact sound they sought. Many producers insisted on recording a song on tape, line by line, but the Sweethearts preferred to learn a song "all the way down and [then record] the entire thing," said Evette. "That was better than 'stop, stop, stop.'" The Sweethearts reached a point where they did not even have to be told what to sing on a particular track. Producers would hire them for a session and simply tell them to put some background vocals on the song. "And then they would leave!" exclaimed Carla. The Sweethearts sometimes sang the background vocals to a track before the lead vocals were added. "And we could work fast," added Evette, which meant that a producer did not have to budget a lot of money for the Sweethearts' talents.

When the Sweethearts began singing, they decided to "ride the train until it [came] to a complete stop," said Evette. "But it didn't stop." The Sweethearts "never turned anything down," said Carla. "They called us, and we went anywhere." The trio also became a popular choice for radio and TV commercials, and the rise of disco, which was a bane to many, "was like a blessing" to the Sweethearts, said Evette. "There were so many anonymous background vocals to do," agreed Carla. "It was fast money." She added that it often "seemed like we never left the studio." There were times they would finish one session upstairs at Sigma and then "go downstairs and do another session," recalled Evette. "We were hot!"

Hot enough to cause the wheels in Kenny Gamble's head to begin to turn. Gamble approached them, "tryin' to find a group for a deal," said Evette. But there was a catch. To project a fuller group sound, Gamble wanted to add a fourth member to the Sweethearts. "We were determined it was just gonna be the three of us," said Evette. Gamble was "a little annoyed" by their reaction, and committed what she termed a "slip of the tongue." "The problem with you all is you're not *hungry* enough" any more, he allegedly told the trio. "You make too much money singin' background!" He was correct. The Sweetheart's reaction to him was a carefree "Whatever!"[1]

In hindsight, it appears likely that there were issues on the table to which Carla and Evette were not privy. Barbara Ingram, who conducted all of the trio's business, may have been pushing Gamble to sign her as a solo artist. Thom Bell confirmed that "all of a sudden" Barbara "wanted to be a lead singer [and] . . . a star." But Barbara "wasn't" a lead singer, added Bell. "I listened to her and I didn't hear it. Believe me, I would have been the first one to snatch her if I had heard a voice that great, 'cause I had 'em first." It is also likely that Ingram's proposal to Gamble was accompanied by an ultimatum: Accept her proposal or else the Sweethearts would stop singing background on Philadelphia International sessions. But Gamble "called Barbara's bluff," thought Carla. "What was supposed to happen was that we were supposed to come crawling to [Gamble, saying], 'Oh, sorry, sorry, sorry.'" But they did not. Whoever Philadelphia International signed as its new female singing group "was gonna be a choice between the Jones Girls, and us," said Evette. "And since we weren't interested and we didn't want to add another person, that's when [Gamble] . . . brought in the Jones Girls to replace us," added Carla.

The Jones Girls—Shirley, Brenda, and Valerie (who died in 2001)—were the daughters of a Detroit-based gospel singer and recording artist. As girls, they sang with their mother, but as teenagers during the 1960s, the daughters turned to secular music. Calling themselves the Jones Girls, the trio became an opening act for several Detroit headliners. They also made their first recordings, for a tiny local label. Toward the end of the decade the Jones Girls signed with Holland-Dozier-Holland's new record company, but they still could not get a hit. The trio began to rely on session background work and was soon in heavy demand in the recording studio. During the early 1970s, the Jones Girls continued to record (unsuccessfully) for other labels while they paid their bills by singing background in the studio. Halfway through the decade, the Jones Girls were recommended to Diana Ross as backing singers for an extended two-year tour. As part of Ross's act, she gave the Jones Girls a brief interlude in her performance, during which the trio sang a song as the headliner changed her costume.

One stop on the Ross tour was the Schubert Theater in Philadelphia. Cynthia Biggs and her boyfriend were in the audience that particular night, and, recalled Biggs: "We were listenin' to the background [singers] more than we were listenin' to Diana! That's how fascinated we were by their sound. . . . Those girls were exquisite!" Ross could not agree more. "Did you hear that?" she asked her audience when she returned to the stage after her break. "I hear Kenny Gamble and Leon Huff are in the audience!" Impressed by the Jones Girls, Gamble and Huff met them backstage after the show. But the young women had already left for their hotel room, so Gamble called them later that evening. "And the next day," exclaimed Biggs, as she laughed, "I saw those Jones Girls waltzin' into Philadelphia International, with their fur coats! I cracked up! Kenny jumped right on it! You gotta *move* in this business, yeah!"

Given the priority treatment normally reserved for Teddy Pendergrass or the O'Jays, the Jones Girls had an album recorded and on the market by early 1979. *The Jones Girls*, powered by the million-selling single, "You Gonna Make Me Love Somebody Else," did quite well. It became Philadelphia International's first gold record by an artist other than the company's Big Three since the Three Degrees'"When Will I See You Again," five years earlier. The Jones Girls also began doing studio backgrounds for Philadelphia International.

"Boom! All of a sudden we were shut out," exclaimed Carla Benson. "Suddenly, they weren't using us. We said, 'What the hell is goin' on here?'" Evette Benton thought that the trio continued to work for Philadelphia International, but that "we weren't doin' as much work as we were in the past." For a time, Philadelphia International used both groups of women indiscriminately on its recordings. Both groups, for instance, sang on Lou Rawls's *Let Me Be Good to You* album, with the Sweethearts heard on five tracks and the Jones Girls on three. Then, when the workload "died down," said Evette, the Sweethearts continued "working for about anybody who sang in Philadelphia."[2]

THE SUCCESS OF THE JONES GIRLS CAUSED A STIR at 309 South Broad Street, but the fuss was soon overshadowed by the buzz created by songwriters Gene McFadden and John Whitehead, who had maintained a bombastic presence at Philadelphia International for years. Had it not been for the deft production work and adroit songwriting of the duo, Kenny Gamble probably would have fired them years earlier. The song-writing team of Jefferson, Simmons, and Hawes originally viewed Gamble "like Papa Bear," said Joe Jefferson, and "everybody that ever worked for Philadelphia International always wanted to win his respect. . . . And I don't think that we were focused enough at the time to understand that this guy had a lot on his head. He was wearin' a lot of different hats and he really didn't have time, nor did he probably have the patience, to take each one of us under his wing individually." That apparently was the case with fellow songwriters McFadden and White-head. By the mid-1970s, they, along with Victor Carstarphen, had formed a writing and production team even more commercially viable than Dexter Wansel's. But for McFadden and Whitehead, each thirty years old, that was not enough. Like Bunny Sigler, they wanted to sing. Also like Sigler, McFadden and Whitehead were more valuable to Gamble and Huff working in the back room than out on the road promoting their latest record.

In "The Day the Soul Train Crashed," writer Stephen Fried said that by 1976, McFadden and Whitehead had become Philadelphia Interna-tional's "two biggest malcontents, who "long complained that they were being ripped off" by Gamble and Huff. McFadden and Whitehead "were pushing hard for more money," added Fried, "especially since Gamble and Huff had obviously been raking it in." Weldon McDougal, who worked at Philadelphia International at the same time as McFadden and Whitehead did, thought the two writer-producers had good reason for acting as they did. Apparently, McFadden and Whitehead did not know much about the machinations of the music business. McDougal told how the two entered his office one day, "all upset," wanting to know how to go about getting paid from BMI. (BMI, or Broadcast Music International, is one of several agencies that collects song royalties from airplay and, in turn, pays the artists.) McDougal expressed surprise that McFadden and Whitehead had written hit records yet "had no knowledge of BMI." McDougal suggested they call the agency, "and they didn't realize that they could do that." According to McDougal, McFadden and Whitehead borrowed money from Gamble against their forthcoming royalties, not realizing that Philadelphia International had already received the royal-ties from BMI. "But then they owed interest on the money they borrowed." After BMI supplied McFadden and Whitehead with a printout of how much money was in their performance royalty account, the duo allegedly confronted Gamble, who, said McDougal, became "really upset," because the company did not want McFadden and White-head "to have that much knowledge" about their BMI account. Meanwhile, McFadden walked around the Philadelphia International, complaining loudly, "I want my money from that fuckin' nigger."[3] Whether because of, or in spite of, this dance of distraction, Gamble and Huff finally allowed McFadden and Whitehead to record an album of their own.

Ain't No Stoppin' Us Now was released about the same time as was the Jones Girls album. It was Philadelphia International's most successful album in a year. What made McFadden and Whitehead's album a surprise was, of course, its self-titled lead single. Released in an abbreviated seven-inch 45 format and a twelve-inch extended disco version, "Ain't No Stoppin' Us Now" became a hit on the radio and in the dance clubs, selling over two million copies ("Disco's most assertive anthem," proclaimed critic Dave Marsh).[4]

Whether McFadden and Whitehead were on top of their BMI account by that time is uncertain, as was the meaning of their hit song. Long hailed by the civil rights movement as a black anthem of sorts, "Ain't No Stoppin' Us Now" actually came about "because after being kept away from singing for so long Gamble finally said we could make our own record," claimed John Whitehead. "If anything, the song was a declaration of our independence from Gamble." The song's lyrical reference to the "things that were keepin' us down" was not about society, he added. They referred to "Gamble's ideas about how we could best serve his company." Whatever the meaning of the song's lyrics, "Ain't No Stoppin' Us Now" contained "so much strength and conviction . . . especially in John Whitehead's preaching lead vocal—that nothing can deny it," opined Dave Marsh.[5] "Ain't No Stoppin' Us Now" made a lot of people believe that McFadden and Whitehead were ready to dominate the charts, but time would show that they were able to write a great song only every couple of years.

The fact that "Ain't No Stoppin' Us Now" was interpreted as an anthem of sorts in the black community was not surprising. As Kenny Gamble became more enthralled with the Muslim religion (he converted to Islam in 1976, taking the name Luqman Abdul-Haqq), more and more of the company's recordings reflected his views. Gamble's top priority became black unity through music, and "The Message Is in the Music," the title of the O'Jays' hit, became a company slogan (and was printed on its album covers). Increasingly, the message was that blacks should realize their own worth and join together to become a force in the community. As blacks proclaimed "Ain't No Stoppin' Us Now" their new black national anthem, white record buyers began to send their own "message," turning away from Gamble and Huff's product.

Gamble's plight was demonstrated by the reactions produced by an ambitious social project he devised in the spring of 1977. Gamble involved some of the Philadelphia International artists in a special neighborhood beautification project and recorded an album of songs by them.[6] The ensemble, known for the occasion as "The Philadelphia International All-Stars," recorded the centerpiece song, "Let's Clean Up the Ghetto." All profits from sales of the album were earmarked for a five-year urban cleanup project that included hiring a number of Philadelphia's inner-city youths to pick up trash, paint over graffiti, and sweep the streets in their neighborhood. Joe Tarsia told how Gamble arranged for "T-shirts and mops" to be distributed to the local black community, "tryin' to get the city involved." But Gamble's bid to get the entire city of Philadelphia involved in a cleanup was not unlike trying to get whites to buy his records. Gamble's project was endorsed nationally by the mayors of Atlanta, Chicago, Los Angeles, and Memphis (cities with large black ghettos of their own). But in Philadelphia, Mayor Frank Rizzo, who was a longtime antagonist of the city's black community, refused to partici-pate in the campaign.[7] In addition, the project's record sales indicated widespread white resistance (or disinterest). The album did not make *Billboard*'s Top 200 chart, and its single, despite being a Top 5 R&B hit, did no better than ninety-one on the pop charts.

In a way that was crucial, 1978 was too prosperous for the music industry's own good. Overly optimistic record manufacturers and retailers, buoyed by the year's resurgence in sales in what was otherwise a slumping economy, thought that 1979 would be even more profitable. Pushing the envelope, they raised prices a fourth time and stocked up on product. But the industry that smugly regarded itself as recession-proof was about to discover that it was not impervious to the American economy. Joe Tarsia recalled how, late in 1978, music sales peaked and "the blush was starting to fall off the rose." Ron Alexenburg was more direct. "If you remember, the bottom fell out of the music business. And it wasn't just Gamble and Huff. Everything caught up with us—the CD invention, the major retailers were in trouble, they weren't paying their bills." It was the beginning of an industry-wide sales decline in the recording business that persisted into the 1980s.

ONE WAY THAT KENNY GAMBLE reacted to the diminishment of Philadel-phia International's crossover hits (and to the fragmenting musical marketplace) was to co-found (with Ed Wright) the Black Music Associa-tion (BMA). By then, black radio had fallen prey to giant corporations that sought to appropriate community airwaves with the intent of launching their own new artists. Meanwhile, black mom-and-pop music retailers continued to disappear. The threat to black music and radio suggested by the recent payola investigations convinced Gamble and Wright to create some type of broad-based organization to bring all the elements of black music together. At the initial meeting, in La Costa, California, with "the air . . . ripe with rhetoric, much of it aimed toward the record industry and threatening to whites," wrote Nelson George in *The Death of Rhythm and Blues*, Gamble presented a report to the membership that was titled "The Final Call." His message sounded as though it might have been lifted from the back of one of his record albums. Steeped in Black Muslim ideology, Gamble's statement maintained that BMA members "have a responsibility to our community. The communities that you and I were born in, the communities that have been the birthplace for black music, the communities that are dying while the record industry flourishes. We no longer have time for mistrust or deceit. We have no time for jealousies or lies. We only have time for the business of survival, because otherwise, we will only have ourselves to blame." "Everybody thought [the BMA] was a good idea and it grew" quickly, stated David Steinberg, who became an original board member of the association.[8]

As the 1970s drew to a close, CBS Records Group president Walter Yetnikoff was on record as having declared that his company was "not interested in pursuing" an artist capable of selling only 100,000 records.[9] To CBS's way of thinking, as long as the O'Jays, Teddy Pendergrass, and Lou Rawls continued to deliver major crossover hits, everything was fine. But the crossover success of those artists only masked the fact that, overall, Philadelphia International was losing its white consumers. The team of McFadden and Whitehead, despite its blockbuster hit, was not the company's next great recording act. Jean Carn's debut on Philadelphia International drew a reaction as mellow as her polished and professional style. And the Jones Girls, for all their talent, would never gain the white acceptance of even the Three Degrees. Still, it was some comfort for Gamble and Huff to realize that in Teddy Pendergrass and the O'Jays, Philadelphia International still had two artists who could guarantee a gold or platinum album with each release.

Despite the loss of original member William Powell, in 1979, the O'Jays' popularity was still on the rise.[10] The focus of the group's sound remained on Eddie Levert's gravelly, shouting resonant tenor and Walter Williams's lighter, more resilient tenor, which was still able to drop down an octave or soar into a Philly falsetto. No one could fathom when, or even *whether*, the O'Jays' unyielding grasp on pop music's charts would ever loosen. The group's latest album, *Identify Yourself* and its predecessor, *So Full of Love*, were each certified platinum.

Besides having become Gamble and Huff's top-selling solo artist, Teddy Pendergrass was now America's reigning sex symbol and romantic balladeer. It was almost laughable to think that some people seriously doubted Pendergrass's decision to leave Harold Melvin and the Blue Notes. After two platinum albums and one gold album, Pendergrass's latest effort, the double-disc set titled *Live Coast to Coast*, was also headed for gold status. This recording came at a time when Pendergrass was at the peak of his popularity and sex appeal.[11] On stage, he made expert use of his swaggering come-on style, ample range, and adept timing to project provocatively his steamy love ballads. But the singer was equally adept with an up-tempo dance tune, as *Live Coast to Coast* demonstrated. Even so, there were hints that Pendergrass was not immune from the defection of Gamble and Huff's white audience. "It's You I Love," taken from Pendergrass's *Live* album, made the R&B charts in the fall of 1979, but it was his third single in succession not to have made the pop charts.

Lou Rawls remained a member of Philadelphia International's Big Three, but, following the release of his own live album, the singer's sales began to hint at listener fatigue. Rawls still sang in his composed, purposeful, and persuasive manner. *Sit Down and Talk to Me* (1978), as well as his latest album, *Let Me Be Good to You*, were commendable efforts (on the latter, Rawls abandoned his disco success and returned to the jazz-infused pop and soul that best displayed his talents). Although measures were taken to keep Rawls's voice up front in the song mixes and to provide him with minimal arrangements, the careless and indifferent production quality of his latest albums seemed to indicate a situation comparable to that of the Spinners under Thom Bell's guidance. On Rawls's first three albums for Philadelphia International, the Gamble and Huff team produced a preponderance of his material. But on *Let Me Be Good to You* they produced only three of the album's eight tracks, and on his latest album, only two. Rawls was increasingly pawned off on a pastiche of producers, and albums-by-committee resulted.

Archie Bell was no stranger to that scene. When he and the Drells signed on with Philadelphia International in 1975, visions of his late-1960s passionate and energetic production sessions with Gamble and Huff danced in his head. But the production of the group's first album for their new company, *Dance Your Troubles Away*, was assigned to Victor Carstarphen, John Whitehead, and Gene McFadden (Gamble and Huff did produce one track on the album, "Let's Go Disco"). *Where Will You Go When the Party's Over* (1976) was also produced by Carstarphen, Whitehead, and McFadden. By then, Bell had grown disillusioned with the disinterest in him shown by Gamble and Huff. "The way things were goin', we were just kind of neglected by the label," recalled Bell. Still, he tried to renew his contract with Philadelphia International when it expired, but "they just kinda dropped us," recalled the singer.[12]

THE FEATURE STORY IN THE DECEMBER 1979 ISSUE of *Black Enterprise* magazine was titled "Grooving to the Sound of Dollars" and continued, "Blacks are still making music as entertainers, but we are also cutting new grooves as executives and owners in the multi-billion dollar record industry." A photograph of Kenny Gamble and Leon Huff was prominently displayed on the magazine's front cover. "At a time when the record industry is experiencing an economic slump and two-thirds of all new releases are flops, records produced by blacks are proving to be the big moneymaker for record companies,"[13] wrote contributing editor DeWayne Wickham. The article went on to discuss the major record companies' newfound regard for black music, and how most of the majors now ran profitable black music groups. CBS's black music marketing division was cited as an example. Under the direction of former "Young Professionals" guru Lebaron Taylor, his department was credited with generating a quarter of CBS's record sales.

Black Enterprise called Philadelphia International one of the ten largest black-owned firms in the nation, with gross sales reported in excess of $30 million annually. Among black-owned record companies, Gamble and Huff's outfit was second only to Motown. They had arrived at that pinnacle, said Gamble, by becoming "trendsetters" in the recording industry. "One of the greatest compliments in this business is to have people follow your lead. Huff and I try to do what other companies are not doing." To the extent that other companies were not recording Teddy Pendergrass and the O'Jays, Gamble was correct. But to claim in 1979 that Philadelphia International was a "trendsetter" was grossly specious. Wickham apparently took the bait. Unlike Motown, he wrote, "Philadelphia International has shown no signs of decline. In fact, Gamble and Huff are busily signing new acts, are preparing to open oversees offices in England and Japan, and are contemplating moving into other communications areas such as television and motion pictures."[14]

In fact, 1979 was not a particularly good year for Philadelphia International and was an absolute disaster for the recording industry in general. Due in large part to disco's sudden meltdown, the bottom fell out of the pop music industry that year, bringing to an end a twenty-five-year run of expansion. The major recording companies, their warehouses brimming with an overabundance of newly minted product, suddenly stared disaster in the face. (At CBS, for instance, where music sales increased to one billion dollars in 1979, the company's operating profits actually fell 46 percent.[15])

As PHILADELPHIA INTERNATIONAL AND THE REST of the music industry limped into the 1980s, America's decade-long party of promiscuity screeched to a halt. Gamble and Huff's record company reached a point "where they weren't getting any promotion," said Thom Bell. "Gamble was hardly there, and the company was goin' downhill fast." Gamble and Huff's dwindling stable of artists was threatened by a new generation of black acts, most of them from the emerging funk genre.[16] Equally as damaging was an entirely new genre of music (there were legions that swore it was anything but music) that seemed to spring out of nowhere.

In this instance, "nowhere" meant the burned-out-tenement desolation of New York City's South Bronx. There, since around 1974, a new, youthful black music simmered under everybody's radar screen. This new sound was made by ghetto youths that spoke rhyming streetwise narratives over rhythm tracks that they purloined from the hottest R&B funk tunes of the day. The music industry (and most white record buyers) got their initial taste of this sound in the fall of 1979, when a group called the Sugar Hill Gang appeared on the R&B charts with an item called "Rapper's Delight." At the time, there was mild surprise that the peculiar track made it as high as number four on *Billboard*'s R&B charts, but it was shocking that "Rapper's Delight" also became a Top 40 pop hit.[17] The song, along with other bare-boned, straight-on, in-your-face recordings, were the product of what *Billboard* labeled "Disco Rappers." At first, the crude yet populist tracks were regarded more as novelty items than as groundbreaking sparks of a musical (and cultural) transformation. The hard-edged, minimal rap tracks were also the antithesis of Philadelphia International's smooth, lush orchestrations.

Black music was also reeling from the disco backlash. At Philadelphia International and throughout the recording industry, "record sales plummeted, concert revenues dried up, and the number of radio stations programming black music declined," recalled Teddy Pendergrass, who was about to record his next album that spring.[18] The production assignment for the album called *TP* hinted at significant internal problems at Philadelphia International. For Cynthia Biggs and Dexter Wansel, the telltale sign was when Gamble and Huff uncharacteristically bequeathed the production of Pendergrass's upcoming album to them.

Wansel claimed that he, believing Pendergrass needed "fresh new material" after having just completed a live album, told Kenny Gamble as much. "And Gamble was like 'okay, Huff's got to go out of town, and I'm going to be busy, so why don't you dig in there and see what you can do.'" Gamble and Huff were not in the habit of tossing off the production of their top artists to others, especially in such extemporaneous fashion, so being designated as the producer of Pendergrass's album "was like getting the keys to the car," added Wansel. (When Pendergrass learned that Wansel was going to co-produce his new album, the singer's reaction was a disbelieving "Why?"[19]) Cynthia Biggs had a good idea why. She said there was a "communication breakdown" between Gamble and Huff at that time, which made it "evident that they did not have the same interaction that they had earlier. The chemistry was gone!" Up to that point, added Biggs, Gamble and Huff had seemed "inseparable. They were tight! And somethin' got between that. There was a notable change in their interactions together. . . . I just know as an outsider lookin' in, watching them on a day-to-day basis, the closeness they once had had started to wane."[20]

The crux of the personal relationship between the pseudo-intellectual Kenny Gamble and the street-tough Leon Huff had remained enigmatic over the years that they worked together. Gamble, the high-minded sage, and Huff, the emotionally withdrawn silent facilitator, weathered their occasional differences and, over the years, managed to strike a functional equanimity. But unlike Gamble and Thom Bell, Gamble and Huff had not developed a relationship as friends. Whatever bond they then shared stemmed from their knack of being able to compose songs together. In this relationship, as opposed to a friendship, Gamble and Huff developed a codependence. This codependence of two highly successful individuals who had nothing in common but their work apparently ignited a latent spark of resentment between them. Music writer-critic Nelson George claimed that, despite Gamble and Huff's long relationship, "the pair had never been close, and success, instead of bringing them together, exacerbated their differences." There was talk that Huff, "the quiet piano player, hadn't received the recognition he deserved," observed writer Stephen Fried in 1983, while researching an article on Philadelphia International. "Huff had grown indignant, feeling that he was doing most of the musical work—and sharing all the credit."[21] Then, during Gamble's nervous breakdown, Huff was forced to emerge from his self-imposed cocoon, and the delicate balance that he and Gamble had attained was shattered. Jim Gallagher noticed that one of the "real significant changes" that occurred during Gamble's convalescence was that "suddenly Huff had to come out of his shell a little bit. And from that point on, he was a lot more personable. He was a lot more accessible and he was a lot more open to communication. It used to be that Kenny would get up and do all the talking, and Leon would just be standin' there. [Now] Leon was more of a force who would actually open his mouth and have things to say."[22]

The continuous pressure on Gamble and Huff to deliver hit songs heightened the tension between them. Over the years, Huff had developed a fierce pride in his and Gamble's collective songwriting ability. Staff writer Joe Jefferson recalled how Huff was always "very vocal about the strength of the *team* of Gamble and Huff. "Can't nobody do it like us!" he liked to sneer. "We're strong!" But as Gamble and Huff's hits decreased, their frustration with each other increased. Jefferson characterized Gamble and Huff's professional relationship as "rocky," but also "a typical writing relationship," saying he did not know any teams of writers "that at different times didn't want to bash each other's head in. . . . It's a lot like being married. It's tough, because you are in fact married to that person. They know everything you're feelin'. You've gotta spill your guts with them. You can't hide, because they're as sensitive as you are. . . . There's a lot of openness in those kinds of relationships, and you have a lot of fights . . . I think that's probably what made [Gamble and Huff's] relationship work." But now it no longer worked as it once did. "I'm sure that, being a musician, Huff wanted to do more," added Jefferson. "I picked that up. . . . I think that [Huff] wanted to prove to himself and to others that he was a viable source, even without Kenny."

Gamble constantly told his friend Joe Frazier, the former heavyweight boxing champion turned entertainer, "Don't just think your songs are good because they sound good in your basement. You gotta put 'em out there. You have to make songs that people can relate to, that everybody—even an infant—will like."[23] Bunny Sigler recalled the time he was assigned to write a song for the O'Jays' *Ship Ahoy* album. After writing one, Gamble asked him what he thought of it. "I think it's good," replied Sigler. "Well," snapped Gamble, "when you have one that you think is a hit, that's the one you can bring to me, not one you think is good!" Gamble once exclaimed to his staff of songwriters, "If you want to write a hit you got to spill your guts!"[24]

Brian Wilson, one of pop music's most renowned songwriters, has said that "writers actually do run out of material." That seemed to be the case with Gamble and Huff. By the latter half of the 1970s, the flow of classic hits such as "Love Train," "If You Don't Know Me by Now," "The Love I Lost," "When Will I See You Again," and "I Love Music" had slowed to a trickle. "They stopped writing the caliber of songs that they used to write," said Bobby Eli. In addition, the changing face of pop music appears to have confounded Gamble and Huff's songwriting. R&B music critic Nelson George observed that "songwriting went right down the toilet as the balance between riff and melody went awry. Fewer and fewer songs seemed written from an adult point of view. You might call it 'Chuck Berry revenge' as black music became as juvenile in attitude as rock and roll was." Furthermore, wrote George, musically R&B songs in general "weren't as good as in the sixties or early seventies. As dance records, the grooves were still inventive, but they were hampered by [the] disco backlash." Not only did Gamble and Huff's well of creativity begin to run dry, but the loss of the original MFSB rhythm section made songwriting more challenging for the songwriters. Thom Bell said that the original MFSB rhythm section had been "just as much part" of the creative process as were Gamble and Huff. During recording sessions, the musicians "would start taking a part and adding their own ideas. Gamble would say, 'Well, why don't we keep this, or keep that.'"[25]

That Gamble and Huff were both suffering through protracted divorce proceedings added tension to their strained relationship. Cynthia Biggs likened it to an already-taut rubber band, with "different tensions pullin' it and pullin' it and pullin' it, 'til it snapped." Tellingly, Biggs's rubber-band analogy stemmed from Kenny Gamble himself, who used it at one of his staff meetings. "You can take a rubber band and keep pullin' on it, and pullin' on it. When you're pullin' on it you're applying tension, and you're distressin' the band the further out you pull it. Eventually that rubber band is gonna pop," Gamble told his staff. "You could tie a knot in it, and that will temporarily fix the problem. It will function. [But] once you break that rubber band it's never gonna be the same. Eventually, the knot is not gonna withstand the stress." The solution, said Gamble, was not to stretch the repaired elastic, but to do everything "to keep it from separating . . . and just let the rubber band wear with time." Biggs laughed as she recalled the anecdote. When Gamble first offered the analogy, she thought "he was giving a little lecture on teamwork, and keepin' the stress off the band. But it was funny that that's exactly what happened to him and Huff." According to Nelson George, the rift between the two grew so wide that the two "even stopped talking to each other. . . . It wasn't an atmosphere conducive to creativity."[26]

"Whatever Gamble and Huff were goin' through, they couldn't resolve it, to get that album [*TP*] done," said Biggs. "Somewhere, whatever magic they had was startin' to go. . . . They were doin' their own separate thing. . . . So they handed the project to Dexter. That's when I knew it was serious, 'cause that just wasn't like them to do that." Gamble and Huff assigning the production of a Teddy Pendergrass album was "just like handin' over a million dollars!"

Pendergrass's Dexter Wansel/Cynthia Biggs–produced *TP* album was released during the summer of 1980. On it, claimed the singer, he came across as "more a devoted romantic than a seducer." Compared with his three earlier studio albums, his latest effort "glowed rather than burned."[27] (During the recording of "Can't We Try," the sensual singer self-deprecatingly and in an exaggerated deep voice told Bobby Eli that he was going to be the "next Barry Manilow!") Given an initial boost by the pre-album single "Can't We Try" (from the soundtrack of the film *Roadie*), *TP* moved quickly from the outset, stayed on *Billboard*'s album chart for thirty-four weeks, and was eventually certified platinum.

WITH THE RIFT BETWEEN GAMBLE AND HUFF apparently at its widest, Huff, who felt most comfortable and relaxed in the recording studio, retreated there in order to work on his own album, tellingly titled *Here to Create Music*. For his solo album, Huff called in the chips he was owed.

Guest artists who appeared on *Here to Create Music* included Stevie Wonder, Teddy Pendergrass, Eddie Levert and Walter Williams of the O'Jays, McFadden and Whitehead, the Jones Girls, and the Sweethearts of Sigma. In making his album of "proto-smooth-jazz," it was as if Huff went out of his way to distance himself from Philadelphia International's familiar sound. He can even be heard singing (albeit briefly) toward the end on the album's hit, "I Ain't Jivin', I'm Jammin'." Released at the same time as Teddy Pendergrass's *TP* album, *Here to Create Music* was a commercial flop. But Huff's solo project was not about selling records but about demonstrating his adroitness in composing a compelling musical groove.

Gamble and Huff's estrangement only added to a new tentativeness that began to percolate throughout 309 South Broad Street, where, recalled Carla Benson, "a definite darkness" began to descend. It was a stark contrast to Philadelphia International's early days, when the people who worked there "were just like a huge family," she explained. "We would have a session, say, from ten to three, and then hang around talking, socializing and playing. [Then] there came a point where everybody just seemed to become dissatisfied with the treatment they got at Philadelphia International." To Benson, the change began when the Sweethearts were sacked in favor of the Jones Girls. "People were suspicious, on the edge. Nobody felt safe" any longer, she recalled. "Everybody knew how much a part of Philadelphia International we were, and they figured, 'If [Gamble and Huff] could cut us off at the pass like that, they could do it to anybody.'"

Philadelphia International's staff writers "were the most disgruntled of all," said Evette Benton. They were each paid what Benton said was a "small fee," while everything they wrote belonged to the company (a common practice in the industry). There was also dissatisfaction among the writers about "having to give credit to somebody who actually didn't help to write the song, in order to get their song produced," added Benton. The staff writers were "pushin' out songs like crazy," then Gamble or Huff would come in and add a line or two to it. "And then they would get one-half of the percentage of the publishing." (Two of the most egregious cases involved McFadden and Whitehead with "Back Stabbers" and Hippie Gilbert with "Me and Mrs. Jones." Gamble and Huff shared equally in the writing of each song.) In addition, "Gamble and them automatically got a percentage of the publishing" for songs written by their staff writers, said Benton. "There were a lot of fights about that."

"In the beginning everybody was happy," agreed Carla Benson. Then the hits began to roll and Gamble and Huff "started feelin' like they were invincible." But the Philadelphia International writers, many who had "grown up" with Gamble and were friends with him, as Benson pointed out, did not share in the rewards of their creativity. "And then, a couple of million dollars later, [they were] just employees. It was very disheartening." It was "a *Philly* thing, man," said former Mighty Three Music staff writer Joe Jefferson with a rueful chuckle. "Once they got you involved, nobody would give you anything back! You would prove your worth and you still wouldn't get anything back. After three years of [writing] all those mega-hits, if [Gamble, Huff, and Bell] had just said, 'Look, from now on, everything you guys write, you get half,' we probably would still be there. And I think most of the other people would be there." Jefferson and his partners Charlie Simmons and Bruce Hawes grew so tired of making Gamble, Huff, and Bell rich that they wrote a song about it. The song became one of their biggest hits, which only made the owners of Mighty Three Music even richer! Jefferson told how he and his partners "always felt that [Gamble and Huff] were playing games with us." They began expressing their frustrations in words, and then in melody: "Games people play, night and day. It's just not stoppin', they just keep doin' the same stuff to us, over and over." ("Games People Play," sung by the Spinners, sold over a million copies in 1975.) "Nobody was willing to give anything back to the people who helped support" the company, thought Jefferson. "It was that kinda thing, a lot of resentful people, man."

The situation had even become disheartening to Thom Bell. Whenever he arranged a song for Gamble and Huff, they paid him his arranger's fee, but they also expected Bell to assist on the production, gratis. Bell claims he did so at first, but he became annoyed whenever one of those songs became a hit and he did not receive a production percentage.[28] "Because we were friends, they thought that they could do it on a friendly basis," he recalled. "Oh no," he finally told Gamble and Huff. "This is a business, man. We don't work like that. And until you decide to handle it and take care of it like a business, then I won't be doing any work with you."

Perhaps nobody was more saddened by the changes at Philadelphia International than Lenny Pakula. An early member of the classic MFSB rhythm section, Pakula recalled how, "toward the end, the company became cold." After leaving Philadelphia International, Pakula spent a few years in California before he returned to Philadelphia. Desperate for work, Pakula swallowed his pride and walked into 309 South Broad Street, where the receptionist asked him whether he had an appointment. "Do I have an appointment!" exclaimed Pakula some thirty years later. "My God, I helped build the company! If I thought it was gonna come to this I woulda never gave 'em all the talent that I [did]. I poured my heart out for those guys."[29]

The situation at Philadelphia International may have seemed cold or disheartening to the company's employees, but the goings-on were perfectly legal. The exploitation of blacks by white record company owners has been decried over the years, but it was not so much skin color as it was power that brought about such unilateral relationships. Berry Gordy amply proved that at Motown. Kenny Gamble, Leon Huff, and Thom Bell simply followed suit.[30] It was not purely by coincidence that the three worked in the very building where Bernie Lowe, Kal Mann, and Dave Appell once controlled the songwriting and publishing on almost every Cameo-Parkway hit record.

To further complicate matters at Philadelphia International, Kenny Gamble was losing interest in the day-to-day operation of the company. "It wasn't that Gamble had lost his marbles, as many Philly International employees believed," wrote Stephen Fried in 1983. "Gamble had just *found* his marbles." Indeed, success had been a double-edged sword for Gamble. It brought him fame and fortune, but it also created the everyday headaches encountered by the president of any large corporation. "He'd been doin' records for a long time," said Thom Bell. "The business is fallen out, the sales are goin' down, [and] Kenny's losin' interest. . . . He's getting more and more into just investing his money in real estate. . . . He got so into the business side of things that he got less and less into the studio." Gamble no longer needed the record business, and he began telling friends as much. He confided in Roland Chambers that "the music no longer motivated him [and] making records just wasn't fun anymore."[31]

Gamble began to focus on social issues linked to black causes. (Bobby Eli thought Gamble "actually could have been like another Malcolm X. He was always a good orator, a very, very good speaker.") With Gamble's deepening community interests came a significant domestic change. In 1980, his protracted divorce was finalized, and he married his current partner. The relationship between Gamble and his new family began to supplant the one he once shared with Leon Huff. [32]

THE YEAR 1980 WAS ANOTHER SAD ONE for the recording industry, one marked by the murder of John Lennon in New York City. Record companies began to show profits late that year, but only because they raised prices for a fifth consecutive year. Record sales dropped 30 percent as companies merged, laid off personnel, and/or cut back on their operations. Of the dozen albums issued by Philadelphia International, only those by Teddy Pendergrass and the O'Jays were of any consequence. Gamble and Huff became even more judicious with Philadelphia International's releases and began to mine the company's vaults for expense-free music to release. Even the once-invincible O'Jays succumbed to the dismal times. The group's stellar string of consecutive platinum and gold albums, dating back to *Back Stabbers* (and discounting their *In Philadelphia* reissue of 1973), came to an end with the release of *The Year 2000* that May.

The year 1980 also saw Jerry Butler's departure from Philadelphia International, a result of Gamble's increasing disinterest with the record business and Philadelphia International's mounting financial woes. Butler was no longer the focus of Gamble and Huff's attention. (His final Philadelphia International album, *The Best Love*, was assembled from four different sessions produced by Butler and several other producers. Gamble and Huff produced only two of the seven tracks.) Butler recalled how Gamble and Huff "had so much goin' on that for them to say, 'We're gonna drop everything and concentrate on Butler' would have been foolish." The parting was "amicable," insisted Butler. Things "just didn't happen. They said, 'Hey Butler, this ain't workin'. We want out of the contract.' I said, 'I agree with you. This ain't workin'. I'm outta here!'"

Lou Rawls also left Philadelphia International that year, following the release of his *Shades of Blue* album. "I don't know really what happened," said Rawls, "but the intensity was gone." Rawls pointed out that when he signed on with Gamble and Huff, the producers "would listen to me when I would say, 'I think this' or 'I think that,' or, 'I feel the people will accept this.'" But as time went on, Gamble and Huff "started passin' me around to other producers and stuff like that." Rawls felt like he "didn't quite have the same connection" with Gamble and Huff and "wasn't getting the input" that he once had.

One of the few bright spots for Gamble and Huff in 1980 was the return of a chagrined Bunny Sigler to the Philadelphia International fold. After Sigler left for Gold Mind Records and began working in New York, his recording career flourished. But the animated singer quickly grew weary of the miles he had to spend on the road, promoting his records, in addition to hearing others tell him "when to go [and] how long I could stay there." By then, thanks to his own recent hits (and the ones he created with Instant Funk for Salsoul Records), Sigler enjoyed the independence fostered by a sizable bankroll. What was most important to him now was a return to Philadelphia. "There's nothin' like workin' at home," recalled Sigler. "When I came back to Philly, Gamble put me in the office and said, 'Just write!' I was able to come out of my office and go home. I didn't have to drive a hundred miles from New York." Sigler relished newfound independence. "I was writing for Gamble, producing artists for Gamble, [and] producing other artists, and I had a lot of money comin' in from a lot of different areas."[33]

As 1980 came to a close, Gamble and Huff celebrated Teddy Pendergrass's latest platinum album with an elegant celebrity-studded party at a Philadelphia hotel (and a "Teddy Pendergrass Day" was declared in the city). At one point, Gamble stood before the audience, held up a platinum album, and said, "Teddy, the light you see shining from this album is the light of God. Don't ever forget that!" The audience, taken aback by Gamble's remark, grew silent. "Amen!" Pendergrass declared, and the audience followed suit. "For the next few seconds, all you heard was 'amen, amen, amen,'" recalled the singer. "Maybe not everyone fully understood what Kenny tried to put across, but I did. . . . I was truly blessed."[34]

The same could not be said of Philadelphia International's other artists. From the summer of 1980 to the summer of 1981, Gamble and Huff's cash-strapped company released no records. When production resumed, albums by the Stylistics, the flagging, temperamental Jones Girls, and the recently signed Patti Labelle further drained the coffers at 309 South Broad Street. Patsy Holt and Kenny Gamble had grown up together in the West Philadelphia ghetto. She had come a long way from those days in the early 1960s, when, as a teenager there, singing prospects were regarded with skepticism because she looked "too black."[35] She and her Blue Belles had two Top 40 hits (albeit one of them was actually sung by a different group) in the early 1960s, before her tenure with the trio Labelle resulted in the chart-topping, million-selling "Lady Marmalade." Patti went solo in 1977, and for almost three years she was responsible for a steady stream of solid R&B hits. After moving from Columbia's Epic subsidiary to Philadelphia International, she recorded enough material for three albums. The cream of those sessions was released that summer, on her *The Spirit's in It* album. But the album did not sell, and Kenny Gamble, never eager to throw good money after bad, chose not to release any other recordings by his longtime friend.

Teddy Pendergrass single-handedly kept Philadelphia International afloat with his *It's Time for Love* album, which was eventually certified gold. Many insiders believed that Philadelphia International, based on Pendergrass's continuous royalties, would ride out the bad times and that Gamble and Huff would be able to replace their other fallen stars, much as they had overhauled MFSB. (To augment the revenues from his records, Philadelphia International entered the fashion world, marketing a line of Teddy Bear designer jeans, with the singer's Teddy Bear logo on the back pocket.)

Despite the hard times, Gamble, Huff, and Bell did reach one milestone in 1981. That fall, Great Philadelphia Trading paid off its thirty-year mortgage on 309 South Broad Street. The trio managed to defy the bankers' original gloomy assessment of lending them the money in the first place, and paid it back (with interest) in just eight years. "The bank couldn't believe it!" exclaimed Bell as he broke into laughter. "It was comical. They could just not believe that these three black guys could pay off all this money in eight years!"

WHILE GAMBLE, HUFF, AND BELL BURNED THE MORTGAGE, Bell commenced to close down his base of operations in Seattle. The operation "was takin' too much of my time," he explained. Bell had recently resolved his differences with Gamble and Huff and was now being paid for his production services for them. He began to commute to Philadelphia on a more frequent basis. That summer he was reunited with the Stylistics, for whom, at Gamble and Huff's request, he produced four tracks on the group's *Closer Than Close* album. "But [the Stylistics] were on their way down then," he recalled, "and nothing came of the album."

Bell also began to produce Columbia recording artist Deniece Williams, who had been a member of Stevie Wonder's vocal backing group Wonderlove from 1972 to 1975. After Williams became widely known from her 1978 duets with Johnny Mathis, she worked with Bell on her *My Melody* album in 1981. (Some say that that record was the best Philadelphia Soul album released during the first half of the 1980s.) Later that year, Bell began to work with Williams on her next album, titled *Niecy*. Taken from that album, "It's Gonna Take a Miracle" became Williams's first solo number-one hit, and *Niecy* became the Gary, Indiana–born singer's biggest-selling solo album in over five years. Several years ago, Williams would more likely have been signed to Philadelphia International, and CBS would have been content to distribute her records. But CBS, like other major labels, now signed major black artists such as Williams directly. This change of policy left custom labels such as Gamble and Huff's out in the cold. Philadelphia International reaped no rewards from Williams's (or Thom Bell's) success.[36]

By 1982, although Gamble and Huff were barely speaking to each other, they attempted to get back to business. Teddy Pendergrass's next album was on the drawing boards, and now that Philadelphia International relied on the singer's recordings to keep them in business, no expense was spared for the project. Gamble and Huff maintained a Caribbean writing retreat in Jamaica, where they composed many of their songs. "By being away, me and Gamble were into ourselves," explained Huff. "We wouldn't do nothing but eat and sleep and wake up and write, go back, lay down." Early that year, they jetted to their distraction-free hideaway and began to work on songs for the last of their bankable recording stars. "No stress, no phone calls, no nothing," said Gamble. "Completely cut off." "That's when we heard about the car crash, on the news," recalled Huff.[37] The news was sickening. On March 18, Pendergrass, who had just returned home after a tour of England with Stephanie Mills, was involved in an automobile accident. He was driving home from a basketball game in Philadelphia when his Silver Spirit Rolls-Royce hit a guardrail, spun across to the other side of the road, and smashed against two trees. Pendergrass was pulled from the wreckage unconscious and paralyzed. "We came back the next day," said Gamble. "We flew back in, we went to the hospital and checked him out."

Thom Bell, who was in Philadelphia when he heard the grim news, rushed to the hospital. "Oh man! Oh boy!" he exclaimed as he recalled the traumatic moment. When Bell first saw Pendergrass, he was lying on his side, "all twisted like a pretzel," and attached to a respirator. "Oh-oh. This boy's in bad shape, bad shape," he thought. Bell returned to the hospital every day for about a week and talked to the stricken star, all the while thinking, "Aw man, what a drag! This boy's shot." Pendergrass's doctors determined that the discs in the stricken singer's spine "had been crushed, up to the second vertebra," recalled Bell. "Oh man, he was in bad shape!" he again exclaimed, thinking back to that tragic time. Joe Tarsia went to visit Pendergrass and came away "convinced he was never gonna be able to sing again. He had to take breaths between words."

The truth was, Philadelphia International's meal ticket had not been taking very good care of himself before the accident. Gamble said that while the news of Pendergrass's accident was "a shock" to him and Huff, "it was not totally unexpected—he had been having some reckless activity before then. At least two car crashes before then." Thom Bell also said it was "not surprising the way [Pendergrass] ended up, because every time you'd look around he was doing something to create problems for himself, man. He's a nice cat, nice as pie, but he would always do something detrimental to his health. If it wasn't one thing it was somethin' else."[38]

The overriding concern of Gamble, Huff, and Bell, then, was for Teddy Pendergrass's physical well-being, but almost as important to Gamble and Huff was what the singer's accident meant to Philadelphia International Records. Huff called the accident "a wake-up call for all of us [that] . . . changed everything." Thom Bell claimed that the accident "really took the heart out of it for Gamble." The loss of Philadelphia International's biggest artist—their *only* artist, really—"created a new perception," said Gamble. The "uncertainty that was happening" forced him and Huff to "readjust."[39]

Teddy Pendergrass was desperately in need of cash. He had his manager scour his residence for tapes of unreleased recordings, after which he appealed to Kenny Gamble to release the songs as an album, "for which I'd be paid my customary advance." The album, *This One's for You*, was released later that summer. Although it consisted entirely of material originally deemed too inferior to release, *This One's for You* did spin off a couple of minor hits. Sales of the album were boosted by the singer's legion of emotionally distraught fans (and consumers with a morbid curiosity), but Pendergrass claimed that "the money it earned didn't even begin to cover my expenses."[40]

Pendergrass's prognosis for recovery was as dim as the business relationship between Philadelphia International and CBS. The odds were good that Pendergrass would never sing again. Even if he did, he could never again have the impact he once had. But in the cold corporate boardroom of CBS's Black Rock headquarters in Manhattan, there was little concern about the loss of Pendergrass's niche in the record-buying market. Columbia Records now had former session background singer Luther Vandross (a year Teddy's junior) under contract, and Vandross's debut album for the corporation had just been certified gold. CBS decided to play hardball with Philadelphia International. The business relationship between that corporation and Philadelphia International had been in decline for some time. When Philadelphia International's sales began to falter, CBS reportedly amended the deal so that it was obligated only to distribute the recordings of Pendergrass and four or five other Philadelphia International artists of CBS's choosing.[41]

Gamble and Huff expressed interest in ending the amended deal, but CBS held fast to the agreement. Gamble and Huff would have to deliver four more albums to the mighty corporation. Why, at this point, CBS opted to hold a gun to the head of Philadelphia International is debatable. Perhaps CBS did not wish to see the stockpile of unreleased tracks by Teddy Pendergrass put on the market by a competitor. Perhaps it was the result of the corporate "a deal is a deal" mentality, whereby the contract remained sacrosanct. Or maybe it was payback time for Kenny Gamble, who, during the time the deal with CBS was in effect, had grown pontifical and inconstant in his dealings with the corporate brass.

Had Gamble "been nicer when things were [going] well for him, if he had been a more decent guy and given [CBS] a little bit more room to play, he could have had that deal a lot longer than he did," thought Thom Bell. "But he made so many demands when he was doing well, totally ridiculous demands, like a movie star." When Philadelphia International was doing well, "every week" Gamble proposed "ridiculous, crazy deals, impossible deals." Then, after considerable wrangling between both sides, Gamble would change his mind and want to alter the deal. Bell told Gamble, "Right now you're feeling terrific, like you're top dog in the pound, because [CBS] is even givin' you the time of day. . . . When you're making money [for CBS] they'll take a whole lotta crap from you that they wouldn't necessarily take. Right now they have to do it, simply because it's business. They're listening to all that nonsense that you're talking and all that crazy crap that you do—get 'em on the telephone all hours of the night and start talking about putting deals together—simply because you're makin' them money. They don't have to take all that crazy stuff you're doin'. When you stop makin' them money, they're gonna stop listenin' [and] start tellin' you to kiss their backside.' And sure enough. . . ."[42]

In the end, said Pendergrass, Gamble "was no match for the suits in New York." By the end of the summer, Philadelphia International laid off half of its staff. The few artists that remained signed with Gamble and Huff began to search elsewhere for new recording deals. (The Jones Girls, for example, signed with RCA.)

IN NOVEMBER, CBS OFFICIALLY TERMINATED its eleven-year distribution deal with Philadelphia International. After a characteristic delay, Gamble accepted the inevitable and, except for attorney Phil Asbury, terminated what was left of the Philadelphia International staff. Roland Chambers said it was "more of a relief than anything when Kenny finally had to fire everyone."[43] Sigma engineer Jim Gallagher solemnly recalled the closing of the company's 309 South Broad Street facility. Joe Tarsia "literally pulled the plug. He pulled the speakers out, he pulled the tape recorders out, and he pulled the board out. It was an empty shell of a studio. There was nothin' but wiring in the walls."

As bad as things were for Philadelphia International, they were worse for Teddy Pendergrass. "Given my long and lucrative association with Gamble and Huff, you might assume I could have turned to PIR for some help," Pendergrass wrote in his autobiography. That was not the case. When Gamble and Huff dismantled Philadelphia International, they unexpectedly terminated Pendergrass's recording contract. Pendergrass, Gamble, and Huff had been friends as well as business associates. Coming when it did, Gamble and Huff's decision to cut loose the artist at the time of his greatest need, particularly after he had single-handedly kept Philadelphia International in business the last few of years, seemed particularly heartless. Joe Tarsia was perplexed. Citing the numerous "mixed stories and feelings about [how] Kenny dropped Teddy" that have continued to circulate, Tarsia speculated that perhaps "there was a big renewal due" to Pendergrass if Gamble and Huff renewed the singer's contract. Whatever the case, thought Tarsia, "it was sorta strange that Kenny dropped Teddy at that time." (Sources who wish to remain anonymous have stated that Pendergrass remains upset over money he claims he is owed by Philadelphia International and that he will not discuss Gamble until that money has been paid. Efforts to reach Pendergrass for an interview for this book were unsuccessful.[44])

Pendergrass wrote in his autobiography that considering his "phenomenal record sales and the millions of dollars [he'd] made for CBS," he felt "strongly" that he "should have at least had the option of signing to CBS directly." Indeed, the stricken singer's manager made overtures to CBS about doing so but was turned down. "It hurt me deeply to realize that they simply assumed that I would no longer be a creative force in the music business," said Pendergrass.[45]

Meanwhile, Gamble and Huff still owed CBS four completed albums as part of their distribution deal. They completed the O'Jays' *When Will I See You Again* album in 1982, and the following year they waded into the tape vaults to piece together three more albums acceptable to the corporation. Gamble and Huff literally struck gold with their first effort. After recording a trove of tracks for Philadelphia International in 1981, Patti Labelle left the company. She and fellow Philadelphian Grover Washington Jr. then had a big R&B hit with "The Best Is Yet to Come." It was the biggest hit of Patti Labelle's solo career and thrust her back in the spotlight. Gamble and Huff promptly pieced together an album from the couple of dozen unreleased tracks they had in their vaults. The album was called *I'm in Love Again*. Its first single, "If Only You Knew," caught on with the public and rose to the top of the R&B charts. It crossed over to become a Top 20 hit as well. Another track off the album, "Love, Need and Want You," did almost as well. To everyone's surprise, Patti Labelle not only had a hit album, but one that became certified gold, as well. Furthermore, Kenny Gamble had his first hit album by a female artist—despite the fact that its songs had been lying dormant for a couple of years.

Gamble and Huff tried the same tack with the Jones Girls, who, thanks to their debut album for their new record company, were once again on the charts. Their *Keep It Comin'* album on Philadelphia International comprised twelve previously rejected tracks. But lightning did not strike twice, and nobody bought the Jones Girls record. Still, Gamble and Huff were one album away from fulfilling their obligation to CBS. The album appeared in the form of another Teddy Pendergrass collection, called *Heaven Only Knows*. With the quality of music and the emotional reaction of the singer's fans both on the wane, *Heaven Only Knows* did not make *Billboard*'s Top 100 albums. But after a dozen years, Gamble and Huff and CBS were free of one another.

16

"Love, Need and Want You"

(1983–2001)

PHILADELPHIA INTERNATIONAL RECORDS, after being cut loose by CBS in 1983, was only a shell of what it once had been. The company's stable of recording artists was depleted and its offices at 309 South Broad Street were shuttered. Philadelphia International was able to keep its profile in the music marketplace by releasing several "best of" albums (by the O'Jays, Teddy Pendergrass, and Lou Rawls) and a handful of compilation albums (*Dance Classics*, *Philly Ballads*, et al.). While Gamble and Huff viewed Philadelphia International's near-dormant state as temporary, some fundamental roadblocks stood in the way of any comeback.

Riding the crest of a neo-conservative political coalition wave that swept him into office in 1980, Ronald Reagan (loosely) presided over a federal government intent on gutting America's Great Society antipoverty programs, which disproportionately affected the nation's blacks. Reagan also sharply reduced income taxes for the rich, which hardly affected blacks at all. "Reaganomics," as the administration's new economic philosophy was dubbed, was based on the "trickle-down" theory, whereby government benevolence to those at the top of the economic ladder theoretically worked its way through them to those less fortunate. In reality, the 1980s became the decade of greed, where the pursuit of wealth, status, and a good time took precedence. Once again, being black in America took on an added burden. If blacks were involved in the pop music business, as were Kenny Gamble and Leon Huff, they had an additional problem. As black music in general continued to suffer from the disco backlash, a new nemesis in the form of the all-music cable channel called the Music Television Network (MTV) appeared.

MTV debuted during the summer of 1981, providing a twenty-four-hour diet of promotional video clips of artists singing their latest recordings. MTV's concept was not original (it dated back at least to the early 1950s), but it seemed revolutionary to the music channel's target audience of pre-teens to thirty-four-year-olds. MTV was originally a money loser, but as America quickly became wired for cable the fledgling music channel began to turn a profit. By 1983, MTV reached 17 million American homes and music videos became the fastest growing record-business product. *Billboard* determined that new acts airing on the music channel enjoyed an immediate 10 to 15 percent increase in sales.[1]

MTV afforded record companies a way to reverse their recent decline, but the all-music channel did not initially program black music, other than established hits. Therein lay the problem for any comeback by Gamble and Huff: MTV's target audience was precisely the age group the owners of Philadelphia International needed to appeal to, lest their music lapse into the netherworld of "middle-of-the-road" pop or (even worse) "oldies." To compound matters, this dearth of black music not only occurred on MTV, but on "almost all AOR [album-oriented rock] radio stations," wrote Russell and David Sanjek in *American Popular Music Business in the 20th Century*. This policy of exclusivity "was regarded by many as 'rock racism.'"[2] In some ways, the situation was akin to the pre–rock and roll era, when black music was barred from white radio. The color barrier was lowered somewhat in 1983, by Michael Jackson's blockbuster *Thriller* album. *Thriller*, which sold over twenty million units, was laden with potential singles so compelling that MTV could not ignore them without losing its credibility as America's top hit purveyor.

Even so, black music suffered from its disco hangover. Dance music continued to flourish, but in the form of what the recording industry called "new wave" music. White artists, as exemplified by 1983's slick and sexy film *Flashdance*, performed most of this genre. The popular film (it grossed $50 million in a matter of several weeks) spawned number-one dance hits in Irene Cara's movie title song and Michael Sembello's "Maniac." As *Flashdance* and other music-oriented films (including 1984's *Footloose*) saturated the airwaves with white dance music, black artists, unless they were mega-stars such as Michael Jackson, Prince, and Diana Ross, were reintroduced to the back of the broadcasting bus. Black-oriented record companies, including Philadelphia International, suffered accordingly.

THE CONTINUING SURGE IN POPULARITY of rap music and break dancing pointed to another obstacle Gamble and Huff faced in attempting a comeback with Philadelphia International Records: Their core audience was aging along with them. The only significant new black dance of the early 1980s was known as "break dancing," itself an offshoot of rap

music. Break dancing's intricate and acrobatic moves (and male domi-
nance) ensured that it would remain a dance of the young. Furthermore,
the baby boomers who helped to fuel Philadelphia International's spec-
tacular crossover success of the early 1970s now had mortgages and
other family expenses to contend with and had little, if any, money to
spend on music. [3]

Gamble and Huff were tired at the time, recalled Joe Tarsia, and
"looking for a payoff-type deal" with a major label. (The pair was apparently prodded by Philadelphia International's attorney and its accountant,
who, recalled Tarsia, sought to "get Kenny back in the studio [because] . . .
their meal ticket, like mine for a large part, had expired.") But Gamble and
Huff's attempt to sell a distribution deal for Philadelphia International to
a major recording company was conducted in a buyer's market. Independent record labels now controlled as little as 5 to 10 percent of the
recording industry's sales. Rather than foot the bill to establish a minority
recording artist, the major companies could afford to wait until an artist
on an independent label showed promise, and then offer that artist a
lucrative contract. With CBS out of the picture, there were only a few
viable prospects for Gamble and Huff to consider. As it was, their best
hope was Capitol-EMI. Although Capitol-EMI was then the third largest
in the recording industry (behind CBS and WEA), it lacked a strong presence in black popular music. David Steinberg surmised that Capitol-EMI's
interest in Philadelphia International came about because the company
was "looking to expand, to try to challenge CBS." In 1985, Gamble and
Huff struck a distribution deal with Capitol-EMI.

To some, the signing appeared to be a coup of sorts for Capitol-EMI.
"But the record heads are not stupid!" exclaimed Joe Tarsia. "They know
that people have their run! It had been almost fifteen, twenty years" for
Gamble and Huff, who were now depending more on their reputation
than on their creativity. Following the loss of Teddy Pendergrass, Philadelphia International had the O'Jays and not much else. Shirley Jones, the
oldest of the Jones Girls, and the Whitehead Brothers (John and Kenny)
were also signed to Gamble and Huff's company, but their most
promising artist was singer, actress, and fashion model Phyllis Hyman.
(Hyman also fit the profile of most of Gamble and Huff's signees—a well-
traveled recording veteran with several labels under her belt.)

The Philadelphia-born Hyman had grown up in Pittsburgh. After
singing in the All-City Choir as a teenager, she opted to pursue a career
in music. Hyman sang with several touring choruses and made her first
recordings, which consisted of typical disco fare, in the mid-1970s. In
1978, she signed with Clive Davis's Arista label. Davis envisioned the
beautiful, statuesque Hyman as a female Barry Manilow, but she soon
became disenchanted with the pop fare foisted on her there. In the early

1980s, Hyman starred in the Broadway musical *Sophisticated Ladies* (for which she received a Tony award nomination) and also appeared in *Dreamgirls*. Kenny Gamble said he was captured by Hyman's "unique · voice resonating, as she sang from her soul," and signed her to Philadelphia International.[4]

Hyman's first album for Gamble and Huff, called *Living All Alone*, was released in 1986. Hyman worked with a variety of producers on *Living All Alone* (including Kenny Gamble and Thom Bell, who co-produced four tracks), but she maintained that the finished product "reflects Phyllis Hyman—not what producers think I am or should be musically."[5] Many, including Hyman herself, thought *Living All Alone* was one of her best, if not *the* best, albums. But not all of Phyllis Hyman was reflected in that exquisite album. The singer led a troubled personal life characterized by bouts of heavy drinking and occasional public outbursts of offensive language. Nobody could foresee it, but Phyllis Hyman's career—indeed, her very life—were headed for a premature end (as was Philadelphia International's distribution deal with Capitol-EMI).

Besides the album by Phyllis Hyman, Philadelphia International issued only four others: two by the O'Jays and one each by the Whitehead Brothers and Shirley Jones. The O'Jays' *Let Me Touch You*, which was released in March 1987 (the same month that Norman Harris died from a heart attack), was even more successful than Hyman's *Living All Alone*. The O'Jays, too, had lost a considerable portion of their crossover audience by then, but *Let Me Touch You* did result in two Top 10 R&B hits, including a number-one single, the superb ballad "Lovin' You." But that fall, during what has become known as the crash of 1987 (when the Dow-Jones average fell almost 23 percent in a single day, the worst single-day percentage decline since its creation), Philadelphia International Records neared the end of the line.

Leon Huff recalled that by the time Philadelphia International's distribution deal with Capitol-EMI ran out, "the industry changed so much, the music changed, rap music was in, and sampling, and we basically were just trying to adjust."[6] They never could. "Every celebrated local [music] scene has a half-life," observed pop music critic Jon Pareles. "To survive beyond the initial buzz, the music has to point someplace new."[7] Thom Bell thought that Gamble and Huff's "inability to hear new things" was a "big factor" in Philadelphia International's downfall. Gamble "doesn't have the ability to hear outside of his own creation, he just can't do it." Bell asserted that most creative people "cannot hear past themselves," but the successful ones have "sense enough to know" that, and allow somebody else do it. Gamble "won't do that, either," added Bell. "I would venture to say if [Gamble and Huff] were to go in the

studio now they would come out with stuff soundin' like the 1970s." Joe
Tarsia agreed that Gamble and Huff were not "capable of growing with
the music" and were "victim[s] of time, not of anything else." The head
of Sigma Sound remarked in 2001 how Gamble and Huff "are still over
there foolin' around with music as more or less a hobby. To my mind,
they're in a time warp of where they were thirty years ago. . . . Their
talent is unquestioned!" he exclaimed. "Their taste becomes questioned,
because it hasn't moved with the trends."

Phil Hurtt cited Gamble and Huff's insularity as having contributed
to their failure to stay current musically. "What would have happened
if they had allowed guys to come in and create and bring other people in
to create?" he wondered. "If they had allowed people other than [them-
selves] to be more involved they would have drawn in some younger
people. That's the way you keep it growing." Philadelphia International
could have combined "the influence of [its] older musicians and older
writers" with new writers and musicians to "create a whole new *type* of
music, with rappers, who could really write. "You look at the scene in
Philadelphia now, there's so much talent around." How much more
opportunity would they have had, wondered Hurtt, "if Gamble and
Huff had evolved to their fullest potential? What they would have done
in the industry would be incredible!"

Attorney David Steinberg thought that when the Capitol-EMI deal
ended in 1987, Gamble and Huff "started drifting downhill." "The wind
had gone out of the sails of the big ten-year Sound of Philadelphia thing
and it was winding down," said Thom Bell. "Just like the Motown sound,
the Memphis sound, just like anybody's sound, anywhere, it starts
from nothing, it becomes something, it gets big, it lasts for a while, it
fades, and it goes away." Archie Bell, too, who was cut loose by Philadelphia International in 1977, thought that "time just ran out" on that
company.

That summer, Gamble and Huff returned to their former independent
status. They formed Gamble and Huff Records Inc., as a division of
Philadelphia International Records. "I want you to put the room [at 309
South Broad Street] back in running order," Gamble told Joe Tarsia.[8] Jim
Gallagher said that Tarsia reconstructed the room into "a decent and
running studio. It wasn't the state of the art that Sigma had always been.
It had an older board, but it was a working studio and it was fine."
(Gamble and Huff, not Sigma Sound, owned the refurbished studio.)

Gallagher, who quit Sigma Sound in 1982 to attend film school,
returned to Philadelphia in 1987. Forty years old and still a "starving
student," Gallagher had grown weary of his impoverished life-style.
When he called on Kenny Gamble to renew old acquaintances, he
mentioned that he was interested in doing some freelance engineering.

"Funny thing you should walk through my door right now," replied Gamble. "I need someone to run this room." Jim Gallagher became the manager and chief engineer of Gamble and Huff's recording studio.

That fall, Gamble and Huff Records released its debut album, Lou Rawls's *Family Reunion*. Rawls's reunion with Gamble and Huff had been a "sort of a mutual consensus," he recalled. During a music convention in California that the three happened to attend, "Kenny and Leon showed interest that they wanted to do something," recalled the singer. "We talked about it and I gave 'em some ideas about some songs. And so they wrote 'em and then I came in and recorded 'em." (Gamble and Huff Records may have been formed specifically for this project, as it was the only album released on the label. On the album cover, Rawls gave "Special thanks to Gamble and Huff for putting the family back together again ... where it's supposed to be.") The album's first single (and the debut single for Gamble and Huff Records) was called "I Wish You Belonged to Me." It reached number twenty-eight on *Billboard*'s R&B chart late in 1987.[9]

Gamble and Huff did not issue any new music on the Philadelphia International label until Phyllis Hyman's *Prime of My Life* album in 1991. Co-produced by Gamble and Hyman's personal producer Nick Martinelli (Leon Huff was not involved with the project), the jazz-tinged album, which consisted of ten tracks of passionate soul backed by the familiar swell of strings, was Hyman's first recording in almost five years. The single "Don't Wanna Change the World" became a number-one R&B song as well as the biggest hit of Phyllis Hyman's long career. After two subsequent singles from Hyman's *Prime of My Life* became Top 10 R&B hits, it appeared as though Hyman was living up to the album's title and that Gamble and Huff had an artist around whom they could build a viable—albeit small—recording company.

The revived Philadelphia International Records also released an album by the legendary Chicago vocal group the Dells, who remained one of Kenny Gamble's favorite harmony groups. In 1992, Gamble (along with Leon Huff, Bunny Sigler, and others) produced the group's *I Salute You* album. Gamble and Huff "spent a lot of time and effort" on the Dells' album, recalled Joe Tarsia. *I Salute You*, which, said the sound engineer, sounded "almost like the old school" when it was finished, generated two minor R&B hits for the Dells (the last chart appearances of their lengthy career).

ALTHOUGH GAMBLE AND HUFF were no longer writing and producing for the mainstream, their albums with Phyllis Hyman and the Dells demonstrated that the producers were capable of addressing the musical interests of smaller, niche-type audiences. Once again, however, circumstance and fate bedeviled Gamble and Huff. First, the Dells' project was only a one-shot deal. Then, in 1994, the troubled Phyllis Hyman was found dead by her own hand. With her died any comeback Gamble and Huff hoped to engineer for Philadelphia International. The pair experienced even greater difficulty in getting their recordings distributed. "That's when we did Dexter Wansel's *Universe* album," recalled Jim Gallagher. "And Huff did an amazing song for Little Richard that was never released. I did work with Harold Melvin's last album in there [but] it never came out. We did all kinds of stuff in there those couple of years, a lot of cool sessions. They're still sittin' on the shelf somewhere." Gallagher then left the Philadelphia International studio, but it "kept on functioning," he said.

As new recordings by Philadelphia International Records were relegated to the company's tape vault, its vaunted 1970s back catalog was also neglected. Despite the introduction of the compact disc during the mid-1980s and the subsequent bonanza most labels reaped from reissuing their back catalog on that new medium, Gamble and Huff's legendary recordings remained overlooked. This was not from any lack of demand for the music but for the want of a cohesive effort on Gamble and Huff's part to reintroduce its rich music legacy to the marketplace. It took Kenny Gamble's mentor, Jerry Ross, to remedy the situation. Ross had recently returned to Philadelphia after years of living in California and was trying to "direct" himself "into licensing . . . as a music supervisor." "What the hell's goin' on here!" he exclaimed to his old songwriting partner. "You can't buy a CD on Teddy Pendergrass or Lou Rawls. There's nothing out there!" Ross pointed out to Gamble how "he was getting no attention from CBS." The giant company was "not marketing the Philadelphia International catalog into compilations, they were not getting 'em into the movies and television shows, they were not doing any licensing." Convinced that he and Huff were losing a significant amount of potential revenue from their back catalog of music, Gamble hired Ross as an independent and exclusive consultant to Philadelphia International Records, in charge of special products and product licensing.[10]

Two rival companies controlled the reissue rights to the Philadelphia International catalog. Recordings up to 1976 were controlled by CBS, which was now owned by the Japanese-based Sony Corporation, which had purchased the company in 1988. Recordings from 1976 and later were under the control of Capitol-EMI. In 1992, Capitol-EMI, through its CEMA Special Products division, began reissuing some of its Philadelphia International recordings. Sony planned to issue a four-compact-disc comprehensive overlook of Philadelphia International's entire history the following year. But Sony's project became bogged down during negotiations for the cross licensing of Philadelphia International tracks controlled by Capitol-EMI. Kenny Gamble, who was in the midst of an unsuccessful bid to regain the rights to the Philadelphia International catalog, "was sorta against" the project, recalled Joe Tarsia, and was "sorta resistive" to Sony's proposal. Jerry Ross said the project was shelved indefinitely after Gamble and Huff initiated a "lot of legalese and bullshit" and acted as though they "didn't want to do business" with Sony. Sony then began reissuing its classic 1971–75 Philadelphia International tracks, via a "best of" artist series on their Epic/Associated logo. In 1994, after Capitol-EMI began releasing complete Philadelphia International albums on its new Right Stuff reissue label, Sony decided to go ahead with a scaled-down Philadelphia International overview, consisting solely of the tracks they controlled. Sony's attitude became, "The hell with all the politics, let's put this album out and get it done!" claimed Jerry Ross.

In 1997, the long-awaited *The Philly Sound: Kenny Gamble, Leon Huff and the Story of Brotherly Love* three-compact-disc retrospective was released. The boxed set, a collection of forty-eight tracks beginning with 1966's "Expressway to Your Heart" and boasting fourteen million-selling hits (plus the Jacksons' two-million gem "Enjoy Yourself"), was accompanied by a photo-jammed sixty-five-page hard-cover booklet printed on slick paper. (The set and its producer, Leo Sacks, were both nominated for Grammy awards.) For all of that, Sony's retrospective also provided a stark reminder of what could (and should) have been. The package's foldout cover was designed to hold four discs, but the fourth one, which was to contain the best of the EMI-controlled tracks, commencing with Lou Rawls's "You'll Never Find Another Love like Mine," was conspicuously absent. Leo Sacks was with Gamble when Gamble first saw the completed package. Sacks recalled how Gamble opened it up and "pointed to the blank space in the box where [the] fourth CD should have been. In retrospect, I think Kenny really wished he had cooperated."[11]

IN CONJUNCTION WITH PHILADELPHIA INTERNATIONAL's resurrection of its back catalog, a large green and white sign denoting "Philadelphia International Records" was prominently placed on the facade of 309 South Broad Street. Jim Gallagher, who was working there at the time, chuckled at the thought. "When they put the sign up, I was like, 'Now you do this? When you're not doin' anything!'"

Jerry Ross claimed that as the "exclusive worldwide consultant" for licensing the Philadelphia International catalog, he "was able to generate millions of dollars of new revenue," money that Gamble otherwise "never would have seen." But things did not end well between the verbose, slick-talking mentor and his paternalistic and venerable former understudy. Ross said it was in 1998 that he "closed the most recent deal [with Capitol] and then I closed their European deal. . . . [But] instead of a celebration it became a confrontation. . . . [Gamble] was never happy or satisfied with anything that anybody did, including me. All I heard was, 'We don't like the deal; it's not a good deal; we could have done better!'" The dispute became acrimonious, and attorneys had to sort things out. In 2003, Ross, who would not discuss the particulars of the dispute, emphasized that his relationship with Gamble had always been "loyal and positive." Ross also said the dispute with Gamble "was like the ending of a marriage." If so, Ross was fortunate in that he had a prenuptial agreement of sorts. "Everything I ever did with [Gamble], I always had it in writing," he claimed. "That's why I was able to settle this whole thing. I came out whole; that's where I'd like to leave it."

While the licensing dispute between Philadelphia International and Jerry Ross played itself out, there was a flurry of activity at 309 South Broad Street, where some of Philadelphia International's old guard, including Dexter Wansel, Bunny Sigler, and Harry Coombs, still worked. In 1998, the company signed a new distribution deal with EMI Distribution. Gamble and Huff were reportedly in the studio (together), working on a posthumous Phyllis Hyman collection, as well as greatest hit packages on Philadelphia International's former stars. Also in the works was the release of some contemporary music, including a hip-hop compilation, and compact discs by a street harmony quartet known as No Question and a young artist by the name of Damon. "Damon's my man, we've been working close," said Kenny Gamble in 1998. "He's going to be an artist that can compete in the marketplace."[12]

This new phase in the history of Philadelphia International Records was part of an ambitious plan to pass the company torch to the next generation, which included Gamble's sons, Caliph "Poppa Chief" and Salahdeen, and Leon Huff's son, Leon A. "Pops" II. The spokesperson for this new generation was Chuck Gamble, Kenny's nephew. But if the four-foot portrait of Kenny Gamble and Leon Huff, their eyes fixed on Chuck Gamble as he sat in his recently renovated office, was not reminder enough of who really ran Philadelphia International, the regular appearance of Kenny Gamble, there to solicit his counsel, was. Chuck Gamble acknowledged that it was up to his generation to keep Philadelphia International "moving or to let it die. And the only way I feel that we can keep it moving is to come up with new and brighter sounds."[13] Accordingly, during the summer of 1999, Philadelphia International released No Question's self-titled compact disc. It was a solid, soulful collection of harmonic ballads that echoed the earlier Philly Soul sound of the Delfonics, the Stylistics, and the O'Jays blended with the day's modern soul group sounds. That fall, Damon's self-titled debut, a combination of gospel-influenced, romantic, and passionate soul ballads reminiscent of the best work by Teddy Pendergrass and Barry White, was released. But Philadelphia International's latest distribution deal with EMI, unlike the company's previous distribution agreements, stipulated that Gamble and Huff's company was responsible for every aspect of marketing, sales, and promotion of its product. Philadelphia International was clearly not up to such tasks, which doomed the valiant efforts of the company's heirs-apparent.

BY THE TIME OF PHILADELPHIA INTERNATIONAL's final distribution agreement, Kenny Gamble's preoccupation with community rehabilitation and urban renewal reached new heights. The practice of acquiring blighted urban property had begun during the flush times of the mid-1970s, when Gamble, Huff, and Thom Bell had money to burn. Rather than put that money into distant, intangible investments, the three opted to invest in real estate (by way of the Great Philadelphia Trading holding company, which still exists in 2003). Only Kenny Gamble chose to carry this practice to a higher level. Whereby Philadelphia International Records once defined Gamble's essence, that role was assumed by Universal Community Homes, a nonprofit community development corporation that he founded in 1990. Universal Community Homes evolved into Universal Companies ("Promoting opportunities for positive community change"), which became one of the largest concentrated community development programs in Philadelphia's history. Universal Companies embarked on an ambitious plan to purchase and redevelop an area of South Philadelphia that contained some of the city's worst public housing, including the neighborhood (and actual row house) in which Gamble was born and lived during his early years. "Our intention," said Gamble, "is to try to make a model out of this area."[14]

In August 2000, at the Republican National Nominating Convention held in Philadelphia, following performances by the Delfonics and Harold Melvin's Blue Notes, Kenny Gamble addressed the delegates. Dressed in a conservative dark green suit, wearing a necktie and a *topi* (Islamic cap), Gamble outlined his beliefs about economic self-reliance and urban revitalization. He told the delegates how, "after much soul-searching and deliberation," he and his family moved from their opulent suburban home back to his old blighted South Philadelphia neighborhood in 1990, because "you can't revitalize the inner cities of America, our communities, without being there—hands-on management." Gamble felt obligated to return to his urban roots because his "consciousness has been lifted. I started thinking, 'What is the best thing you can do with your life?'" he told Associated Press reporter David Caruso in 2003.

"There has to be some kind of commitment from people in the community. It can't be your goal just to leave."[15]

Kenny Gamble is "out to help people," thought Georgie Woods, longtime community activist in North Philadelphia. Gamble not only "rehabilitated about 100 row houses, [he] even built a mosque for Muslims," said Woods. "You gotta give him credit! He's taken a whole neighborhood that was addicted with crack and cocaine and crap like that and turned it around."

Even so, controversy continues to dog Gamble. Just as he ruffled more than a few feathers during his stewardship of Philadelphia International, Gamble has done likewise in his urban development endeavors. One area of contention stems from the fact that Gamble, himself a product of one of the nation's numerous impoverished black communities, has chosen to work outside the system to remedy the situation by eschewing integration as a policy of failure. Claims have been made that Gamble intends to sell his redeveloped properties to blacks only. The biggest practical complaint seems to be that Gamble's original goal to make his housing available to low-income people is, to some extent, being ignored. Gamble, whose efforts appear to be sincere, has a point. The conventional methods of previous urban redevelopment have been spotty, at best. Why not try something new? It would have been easy for him to take the money he made in the music business and run with it. But he did not. "I hope I haven't made any fatal mistakes," he told *Philadelphia Inquirer* staff writer Annette John-Hall in 2003. "I just have to get moving and keep praying. My intention has always been to do good."[16]

The prospect of Gamble's returning to music production grows dimmer with each urban rebuilding block that is put in place. "If you ask [Kenny], he's gonna make music again, *tomorrow*," said Joe Tarsia in 1999. "But it's [only] a toy in his mind." (In the early 2000s, Gamble was rumored to have turned down an opportunity to produce an album for Aretha Franklin.) The chances are far greater that Leon Huff or Thom Bell will be heard from again. Huff "never wanted to stop" recording, claimed Jim Gallagher. "He was still doin' it in the '90s, when I was there. He had his own little studio set up [at Philadelphia International], all the keyboards and stuff, where he could sit and write." He was there "almost every day . . . fiddlin' and figurin,' and tryin' to write new stuff. He loves it." As for Thom Bell, despite a long stretch of inactivity, he, too, has an itch to return to the recording studio. Bell became semi-reclusive in the 1980s, during which time he underwent a divorce and a second marriage. Bell's new bride is from Hawaii, where he and his family spent four years (on the island of Maui) in the 1990s, before returning to the Seattle area. In 2002, Bell described himself as "a very lucky guy; I've done very well. I made decent money in this business. Music was always fun for me. I could do music forever!" When Bell spoke those words he had not been in a recording studio in seven years. He confessed that he was "starting to feel the pull" to record again. "I can feel it comin', the juices are startin' to flow. It's going to be hard work because I'm starting all over again, but that's fun. Who wants to start at the top? There's no place to go!"

GAMBLE, HUFF, AND BELL CONTINUE TO COMMAND local status as the majordomos of Philadelphia soul. In 1993, all three were installed onto the Walk of Fame presided over by the Philadelphia Music Foundation (of which Gamble and Huff were among its founders). Bronze plaques honoring the three were embedded in the sidewalk on Broad Street, just across the street from 309 South Broad Street. (Baker, Harris, and Young were similarly enshrined there in 1995.) Two years later, Gamble and Huff were inducted into the National Songwriters Hall of Fame. In 2001, a musical revue titled *Me and Mrs. Jones*, featuring forty-five hit songs from the 1970s written by Gamble, Huff, Bell, and others, opened in Philadelphia. The production's headliner, Lou Rawls, came up with the idea to do such a show after guest-starring in the highly popular *Smokey Joe's Café* the previous year. Rawls said he discussed the idea with Gamble, who told him, "Well, hey man, it sounds good. If you want to try it, go ahead."[17]

Sigma Sound remains in business at the same Philadelphia location, with Joe Tarsia at the helm. ("Creating hits since 1968" is the company slogan, with Tarsia's son Michael now the chief hands-on guy at the fabled studio.) At its peak, Sigma had ten functioning "rooms," including five in New York City that Tarsia sold in 1992. In 2002, it was rumored that Sigma's founder was looking to sell his venerable enterprise—provided he got his price. Philadelphia International Records, which closed its doors early in 2001, continues to exist on the marketing of its back catalog. Over the past decade, museums to commemorate Motown and Stax have been established, and recently, there was talk of converting Philadelphia International's empty headquarters, located in the heart of the city's redeveloped Avenue of the Arts area, into a museum to honor that company in a similar manner.

Epilogue

(2002–2003)

As Philadelphia International's golden era fades further into history, two things about the famous recording company stand out. The memorable music produced by that company has guaranteed it a rich and entertaining legacy. At the same time, a pervasive feeling of disappointment among those who worked for Philadelphia International persists. Phil Hurtt recalled that "there was something special that happened [at Philadelphia International] between 1970 and 1974. It was a nice flow." But by and by, thought Hurtt, "power [and] money got in the way. It was basically Kenny [who] sowed the seeds" of dissension by the way he "started treating people. . . . You sow that discontent and you show that you don't respect people's talent and their abilities, and eventually it'll come back to get you." T. J. Tindall also cited what he termed as "Gamble's nature to keep everything for himself," as a reason for the widespread resentment among former employees of Philadelphia International. Not that Tindall was one of them. The guitarist said that he had no complaints about working for Gamble and Huff, who "were always extremely good to me. I never had a problem; I always got paid." But Tindall did feel "kind of bad for what happened to some of the other guys. They deserved more than they got in the long run; that was their whole life! I always thought that was a little bit fucked up. If [Gamble] had been a little more giving, everybody would have come out better."

The truth is, the employees of Philadelphia International were not treated much differently (if at all) from those at other record companies. Gamble and Huff were the owners and they reaped the profits. Their situation differed in that Gamble and Huff hired a preponderance of friends and acquaintances, many of whom they had grown up with. Consequently, Gamble and Huff's employees mistakenly regarded Gamble as a "brother" and not as their boss. Bobby Martin told how, during Philadelphia International's early years, there was a feeling among the company's employees that everybody was working together. Martin described that feeling as a "oneness. Everybody [was] clicking and everybody [was] working hard together to make the thing a success." But as time went on and disillusionment set in, added Martin, "the 'oneness' of the whole thing started falling apart."

Some black critics have taken pot shots at Gamble for being an opportunist. They say Gamble's participation in the Republican Nominating Convention in 2000 cast him as just another prop in the Republicans' dog-and-pony show of minority peoples backing them. But what these critics fail to recognize is that, first and foremost, Kenny Gamble is a capitalist. "I support people, not [political] parties," said Gamble, a registered Independent, in 2003. "It's all business with me."

If Gamble is guilty of anything, it is that he hired too many of his so-called friends and acquaintances to work for him. Don Renaldo, Gamble's longtime string and horn contractor, thought that Gamble "was too loyal . . . to guys who didn't deserve his loyalty, guys he picked up off the street and gave jobs to because he thought they had something. Guys who would curse him behind his back."[1] Jerry Ross agreed that Gamble "always had a lot of hangers-on with him, people that couldn't do—and shouldn't have been doing—what they were doing." Ross claimed that he used to tell Gamble: "You don't surround yourself with the people that you should. You don't have the best accountants; you don't have the best product managers; you don't have the best secretaries. You don't even have a good elevator operator!"

Perhaps the most damning charge leveled at Kenny Gamble is the matter of Philadelphia International's contested artists' royalties. Artists' claims of being shortchanged on royalties paid by their record companies are nothing new. But in the case of Philadelphia International, the dissatisfaction not only remains loud and consistent; it is bolstered from an unexpected quarter. Speaking of royalty payments, Thom Bell claimed he recently told Gamble that he "never thought I'd see the day that you would do the same thing to people that they did to us, man. . . . All the money you've made, you now want to make yours and theirs, too?" Bell also said he would not be surprised if certain Philadelphia International artists began to "sue the crap out of" Gamble and Huff. In the case of Billy Paul, at least, Bell's prophecy has borne itself out. In 2003, Paul was awarded $500,000 by a Los Angeles jury for unpaid royalties on "Me and Mrs. Jones," from between 1994 and 2002.[2]

In May 2002, Roland Chambers, his body ravaged by a chronic stomach ailment and a lifelong drug dependency, died at age fifty-eight (just three months after his brother Karl died). Chambers, laid to rest in Philadelphia on a chilly wet and windy morning, left this world penniless, but not forgotten. Kenny Gamble spoke at the funeral service, and Bunny Sigler, accompanied by Dexter Wansel on the organ, sang "Psalm 23." After the funeral, more than a hundred mourners gathered in the empty Philadelphia International offices to pay tribute to their departed comrade. "Havin' such a sad occasion, it was good to be there and sit down and talk to your friends," recalled Weldon McDougal. Kenny Gamble footed the bill for day's sad proceedings, including the funeral.

In January 2003, there was reason for a much happier get-together. After an absence of almost two decades, Thom Bell returned to Philadelphia, ostensibly for an intimate family celebration in honor of his upcoming sixtieth birthday. In reality, Bell walked into a surprise birthday party attended by over a hundred of his friends and former business associates. The ruse was carried out to perfection. This was evinced by the dazed expression of disbelief on the maestro's face as he entered the celebration and was greeted by the time-honored cry of "Surprise!"

The night was one of emotion and joyful reunion. Joe Tarsia, Jack Faith, Joe Jefferson, Charlie Boy Simmons, Phil Hurtt, Carl Helm and Weldon McDougal were there, as well as a number of the great studio musicians he worked with, including Bob Babbitt, Charles Collins, Bobby Eli, Richie Genovese, and Fred Joiner. The pre-party's buzz focused on Kenny Gamble. Had he been invited? (Yes.) If so, would the enigmatic legend attend? Nobody knew for certain. (Leon Huff, who was never particularly close to Bell, was not expected to attend, and he did not.) The festivities were reminiscent of a high school or college reunion. Warm memories and cheerful thoughts abounded as a hundred scenarios from years gone by were played and replayed. A band performed on a stage set up at one end of the room, as vocalists James Ingram and Russell Thompkins Jr., the voice of the Stylistics (and he still has it), provided the entertainment.

By and by, Kenny Gamble unobtrusively appeared and joined the celebration. Whatever those in attendance that evening thought about Gamble, one by one, as they noticed his presence, they made it a point to establish contact and literally to touch the hem of his garment. After all of the obligatory formal tributes were uttered, Thom Bell mounted the stage and spoke to the gathered crowd. The honored guest then summoned Gamble to join him, and the pair, grinning widely, locked arm-in-arm, bantered on about their lengthy friendship as only those who have known each other for almost fifty years could. In perhaps the closest thing to a time warp as humanly possible, Kenny and Tommy were once again idealistic teenagers in a recording studio, preparing to cut their first record. Then a voice in the audience called out for the two to sing something. Although Bell and Gamble declined, for at least one wintry night in Philadelphia, the Love Train was back on its track.

Appendix I

Song List

Note: All chart figures are from *Billboard*.

"Ain't No Stoppin' Us Now": McFadden and Whitehead (PIR 3681), February 1979. #13 Hot 100, #1 R&B. Two-million-seller.

"Am I Black Enough for You?": Billy Paul (PIR 3526), January 1973. #79 Hot 100,#29 R&B.

"Are You Happy": Jerry Butler (Mercury 72876), November 1968. #39 Hot 100, #9 R&B.

"Are You Ready for Love?": Elton John (MCA 12"), April 1979.

"Arkansas Life": Gideon Smith (PIR 3501), March 1971.

"Armed and Extremely Dangerous": First Choice (Philly Groove 175), early 1973. #28 Hot 100, #11 R&B.

"A Baby's Born": Johnny Mathis (Columbia LP 32435), August 1973.

"Back Stabbers": O'Jays (PIR 3517), May 1972. #3 Hot 100, #1 R&B. Million-seller.

"Bad Luck—Pt. 1": Harold Melvin and the Blue Notes (PIR 3562), January 1975. #15 Hot 100, #4 R&B.

"Be Thankful for What You've Got": William DeVaughn (Roxbury 0236), January 1974. #4 Hot 100, #1 R&B. Million-seller.

"The Best Is Yet to Come": Patti Labelle and Grover Washington Jr. (Elektra 69877), October 1982. #14 R&B.

"Betcha by Golly, Wow": Stylistics (Avco 4591), January 1972. #3 Hot 100, #2 R&B.

"Blues Away": Jacksons (Epic/PIR 50350), February 1977.

"Body and Soul": Coleman Hawkins (Bluebird 10523), 1939; (Bluebird 30–0825), re-released in 1944. #4 Harlem Hit Parade.

"Boogaloo Down Broadway": Fantastic Johnny C (Phil-L.A. of Soul 505), August 1967. #7 Hot 100, #5 R&B.

"Both Ends against the Middle": Jackie Moore (Atlantic 2956), September 1973. #28 R&B.

"A Brand New Me": Jerry Butler (Mercury LP 61234), August 1969.

"A Brand New Me": Dusty Springfield (Atlantic 2685), September 1969. #24 Hot 100.

"Branded Bad": O'Jays (Neptune 18), September 1969. #41 R&B.

"Break Up to Make Up": Stylistics (Avco 4603), December 1972. #5 Hot 100, #5 R&B. Million-seller.

"Break Your Promise": Delfonics (Philly Groove 152), July 1968. #35 Hot 100, #12 R&B.

"Bring It on Home to Me": Sam Cooke (RCA Victor 8036), April 1962. #13 Hot 100, #2 R&B.

"Can I Get a Witness": Marvin Gaye (Tamla 54087), September 1963. #22 Hot 100, #15 R&B.

"Can't We Try": Teddy Pendergrass (PIR 3107), June 1980. #52 Hot 100, #3 R&B.

"Christmas Ain't Christmas (New Years Ain't New Years)": O'Jays (Neptune 33), November 1970.

"Close the Door": Teddy Pendergrass (PIR 3648), March 1978. #25 Hot 100, #1 R&B. Million-seller.

"Could It Be I'm Falling in Love": Spinners (Atlantic 2927), October 1972. #4 Hot 100, #1 R&B. Million-seller.

"Cowboys to Girls": Intruders (Gamble 214), January 1968. #6 Hot 100, #1 R&B. Million-seller.

"Cry Baby": Garnet Mimms and the Enchanters (United Artists 629), July 1963. #4 Hot 100, #1 R&B.

"Dancing Machine": Jacksons (Motown 1286), January 1974. #2 Hot 100, #1 R&B.

"Days Go By": Wilson Pickett (Atlantic LP 8270), July 1970.

"Dead End Street": Lou Rawls (Capitol 5869), January 1967. #29 Hot 100, #3 R&B.

"Deeper (in Love with You)": O'Jays (Neptune 22), January 1970. #21 R&B.

"Didn't I (Blow Your Mind This Time)": Delfonics (Philly Groove 161), December 1969. #10 Hot 100, #3 R&B.

"Dirty Old Man": Three Degrees (PIR 3534), August 1973. #58 R&B.

"Disco Inferno": Trammps (Atlantic 3389), early 1977. #11 Hot 100, #9 R&B.

"Do It Any Way You Wanna": People's Choice (TSOP 4769), April 1975. #11 Hot 100, #1 R&B. Million-seller.

"Do It 'til You're Satisfied)": B.T. Express (Roadshow 12395), June 1974. #2 Hot 100, #1 R&B. Million-seller.

"Do the Choo Choo": Archie Bell and the Drells (Atlantic 2559), August 1968. #44 Hot 100, #17 R&B.

"Don't Let the Green Grass Fool You": Wilson Pickett (Atlantic 2781), December 1970. #17 Hot 100, #2 R&B. Million-seller.

"Don't Stop Loving Me": Kenny Gamble (and the Romeos) (Arctic 123-B), summer 1966.

"Don't Wanna Change the World": Phyllis Hyman (PIR 14005), May 1991.

"Drowning in the Sea of Love": Joe Simon (Spring 120), September 1971. #11 Hot 100, #3 R&B. Million-seller.

"The 81": Candy and the Kisses (Cameo 336), September 1964. #51 Hot 100. No R&B chart published.

"Engine Number 9 (Get Me Back on Time)": Wilson Pickett (Atlantic 2765), July 1970. #14 Hot 100, #3 R&B.

"Enjoy Yourself": Jacksons (Epic/PIR 50289), August 1976. #6 Hot 100, #2 R&B. Two-million-seller.

"Everybody Can't Be Pretty": Casinos (Del-Val 1002-B), summer 1965.

"Everybody Monkey": Freddy Cannon (Swan 4149), June 1963. #52 Hot 100.

"Expressway to Your Heart": Soul Survivors (Crimson 1010), August 1967. #4 Hot 100, #3 R&B.

"Find Me a Girl": Jacksons (Epic/PIR 50496), December 1977. #38 R&B.

"Flashdance ... What a Feeling": Irene Cara (Casablanca 811440), February 1983. #1 Hot 100, #2 R&B. Million-seller.

"For the Love of Money": O'Jays (PIR 3544), February 1974. #9 Hot 100, #3 R&B. Million-seller.

"Forgive Me Girl/Working My Way Back to You": Spinners (Atlantic 3637), October 1979. #2 Hot 100, #6 R&B. Million-seller.

"Free Love": Jean Carn (PIR 3614), December 1976. #23 R&B.

"Funny Feeling": Delfonics (Philly Groove 156), April 1969. #94 Hot 100, #48 R&B.

"Gee I'm Sorry Baby": Sapphires (ABC-Paramount 10639-B), spring 1965.

"Get Out (and Let Me Cry)": Harold Melvin and the Blue Notes (Landa 703), October 1964. #38 R&B.

"Give the People What They Want": O'Jays (PIR 3565), February 1974. #45 Hot 100, #1 R&B.

"God Only Knows": Capris (Gotham 304), August 1954.

"Goin' Places": Jacksons (Epic/PIR 50454), August 1977. #52 Hot 100, #8 R&B.

"Gonna Be Strong": Intruders (Excel 101), summer 1965.

"Gossip": Tiffanys (MRS/Atlantic 2240), June 1964.

"Gravy (for My Mashed Potatoes)": Dee Dee Sharp (Cameo 219), May 1962. #9 Hot 100, #11 R&B.

"Greatest Love of All": Whitney Houston (Arista 9466), January 1986. #1 Hot 100, #3 R&B. Million-seller.

"Green Power": Archie Bell and the Drells (Atlantic LP 8226), summer 1969.

"Groovy People": Lou Rawls (PIR 3604), July 1976. #64 Hot 100, #19 R&B.

"Happy 'Bout the Whole Thing": Dee Dee Sharp (TSOP 4776), November 1976.

"He Don't Really Love You": Delfonics (Moonshot 6703), early 1967; re-released spring 1968. #92 Hot 100, #33 R&B.

"Help a Lonely Guy": Companions (General American 002), early 1965.

"Help the Needy": Wilson Pickett (Atlantic LP 8270), July 1970.

"Hey, Western Union Man": Jerry Butler (Mercury 72850), July 1968. #16 Hot 100, #1 R&B.

"Hold Me": Teddy Pendergrass and Whitney Houston (Asylum 69720), April 1984. #46 Hot 100, #5 R&B.

"The Horse": Cliff Nobles and Co. (Phil-L.A. of Soul 313-B), March 1968.
#2 Hot 100, #2 R&B. Million-seller.

"How Could I Let You Get Away": Spinners (Atlantic 2904), June 1972.
#77 Hot 100, #14 R&B.

"Hurry Up This Way Again": Stylistics (TSOP 4789), May 1980. #18
R&B.

"The Hustle": Van McCoy (Avco 4653), February 1974. #1 Hot 100, #1
R&B.

"I Ain't Jivin', I'm Jammin'": Leon Huff (PIR 3122), September 1980. #57
R&B.

"I Can't Stop Dancing": Archie Bell and the Drells (Atlantic 2534), June
1968. #9 Hot 100, #5 R&B.

"I Didn't Know": Three Degrees (PIR 3561), December 1974. #18 R&B.

"I Don't Love You Anymore": Teddy Pendergrass (PIR 3622), January
1977. #41 Hot 100, #5 R&B.

"I Likes to Do It": Peoples' Choice (Phil-L.A. of Soul 349), May 1971.
#38 Hot 100, #9 R&B.

"I Love Music—Pt. 1": O'Jays (PIR 3577), September 1975. #5 Hot 100, #1
R&B. Million-seller.

"I Miss You—Pt. 1": Harold Melvin and the Blue Notes (PIR 3516),
March 1972. #58 Hot 100, #7 R&B.

"I Really Love You": Dee Dee Sharp (Cameo 375), fall 1965. #78 Hot 100,
#37 R&B.

"(I Wanna Be a) Free Girl": Dusty Springfield (Atlantic 2719), March
1970.

"I Wanna Be (Your Everything)": Manhattans (Carnival 507), November
1964. #68 Hot 100, #12 R&B.

"I Wish It Were Yesterday": Billy Paul (PIR 3515), March 1972.

"I Wish You Belonged to Me": Lou Rawls (Gamble and Huff 310),
September 1987. #28 R&B.

"I'd Really Love to See You Tonight": Dee Dee Sharp Gamble (PIR 3636),
October 1977.

"If Only You Knew": Patti Labelle (PIR 04248), September 1983. #46 Hot
100, #1 R&B.

"If You Don't Know Me by Now": Harold Melvin and the Blue Notes
(PIR 3520), August 1972. #3 Hot 100, #1 R&B. Million-seller.

"I'll Always Love My Mama": Intruders (Gamble 2506), March 1973.
#36 Hot 100, #6 R&B.

"I'll Be Around": Spinners (Atlantic 2904), June 1972. #3 Hot 100, #1
R&B. Million-seller.

"I'll Be Sweeter Tomorrow (Than I Was Today)": O'Jays (Bell 691),
September 1967. #66 Hot 100, #8 R&B.

"I'll Get By": Kenny and Tommy (Heritage 108), spring 1962.

"I'm a Fool to Care": Castelles (Grand 114), October 1954.

"I'm Coming Home": Johnny Mathis (Columbia 45908), July 1973. #75
Hot 100.

"I'm Coming Home": Spinners (Avco 3027), March 1974. #18 Hot 100, #3
R&B.

"I'm Doin' Fine Now": New York City (Chelsea 0113), January 1973. #17
Hot 100, #14 R&B.

"(I'm Just Thinking about) Cooling Out": Jerry Butler (PIR 3656), August 1978. #14 R&B.

"I'm Not in Love": Dee Dee Sharp Gamble (TSOP 4778), January 1976.

"I'm Sorry": Delfonics (Philly Groove 151), March 1968. #42 Hot 100, #15 R&B.

"I'm Stone in Love with You": Stylistics (Avco 4603), August 1972. #10 Hot 100, #4 R&B. Million-seller.

"I'm Weak for You": Harold Melvin and the Blue Notes (PIR 3543), January 1974. #87 R&B.

"In a Moment": Intrigues (Yew 1001), June 1969. #31 Hot 100, #10 R&B.

"It Happens Every Day": Persianettes (Or 1256), 1964. Did not chart. No R&B chart published.

"It's Gonna Take a Miracle": Deniece Williams (ARC 02812), February 1982. #10 Hot 100, #1 R&B.

"It's Too Soon to Know": Orioles (It's a Natural 5000), July 1948. #13 pop seller, #1 Best-selling race records.

"It's Unbelievable": Larks (Sheryl 334), February 1961. #69 Hot 100.

"It's You I Love": Teddy Pendergrass (PIR 3742), November 1979. #44 R&B.

"The Joke's on You": Kenny Gamble (and the Romeos) (Arctic 123-A), summer 1966.

"Just Can't Get Enough": O'Jays (Neptune 33), November 1970.

"Just Don't Want to Be Lonely": Ronnie Dyson (Columbia 45867), May 1973. #60 Hot 100, #29 R&B.

"Just Don't Want to Be Lonely": Main Ingredient (RCA Victor 0205), December 1973. #10 Hot 100, #8 R&B.

"Just Out of Reach (of My Empty Arms)": Solomon Burke (Atlantic 2114), August 1961. #24 Hot 100, #7 R&B.

"Just You and Me Baby": Spinners (Atlantic LP 7256), January 1973.

"K-Jee": MFSB (PIR LP 33158), January 1975.

"King Love": Allures (Melron 5009), ca. mid-1964. No R&B chart published.

"King Tim (Personality Jock)": Fatback Band (spring 199), August 1979. #26 R&B.

"Kiss and Say Goodbye": Manhattans (Columbia 10310), February 1976. #1 Hot 100, #26 R&B. Two million-seller.

"Lady Marmalade": Labelle (Epic 50048), October 1974. #1 Hot 100, #1 R&B. Million-seller.

"La-La Means I Love You": Delfonics (Philly Groove 150), January 1968. #4 Hot 100, #2 R&B.

"Let Me Party with You (Party, Party, Party)": Bunny Sigler (Gold Mind 4008), November 1977. #43 Hot 100, #8 R&B.

"Let the Good Times Roll and Feel So Good": Bunny Sigler (Parkway 153), May 1967. #22 Hot 100, #20 R&B.

"Let's Break Up for Awhile": Sapphires (ABC-Paramount 10559), April 1964. No chart. No R&B chart published.

"Let's Clean Up the Ghetto": Philadelphia All Stars (PIR 3627), April 1977. #91 Hot 100, #4 R&B.

"Let's Go Disco": Archie Bell and the Drells (TSOP LP 33844), November 1975.

"Life Is a Song Worth Singing": Johnny Mathis (Columbia 45975),
   October 1973. #54 Hot 100.
"Life Is a Song Worth Singing": Teddy Pendergrass (PIR LP 35095),
   March 1978.
"Limbo Rock": Chubby Checker (Parkway 849), August 1962. #2 Hot
   100, #3 R&B. Million-seller.
"Livin' It Up (Friday Night)": Bell and James (A&M 2069), September
   1978. #15 Hot 100, #7 R&B. Million-seller.
"Living a Little, Laughing a Little": Spinners (Atlantic 3252), January
   1975. #37 Hot 100, #7 R&B.
"Long Lonely Nights": Lee Andrews and the Hearts (Main Line 102,
   Chess 1665), July 1957. #45 Top 100, #11 R&B.
"Looky Looky (Look at Me Girl)": O'Jays (Neptune 31), June 1970. #17
   R&B.
"Lost (but Found in the Nick of Time)": Jerry Butler (Mercury 72764),
   November 1967. #62 Hot 100, #15 R&B.
"Love Don't Love Nobody": Spinners (Atlantic 3206), July 1974. #15 Hot
   100, #4 R&B.
"Love Has No Time or Place": MFSB (PIR 3576), June 1975
"The Love I Lost—Pt. 1": Harold Melvin and the Blue Notes (PIR 3533),
   August 1973. #7 Hot 100, #1 R&B. Million-seller.
"Love in Them There Hills": Vibrations (Okeh 7311), February 1968. #93
   Hot 100, #38 R&B.
"Love Is a Hurtin' Thing": Lou Rawls (Capitol 5709), July 1966. #13 Hot
   100, #1 R&B.
"Love Is Alright": Cliff Nobles and Co. (Phil-L.A. of Soul 313-A), March
   1968.
"(Love Is Like a) Baseball Game": Intruders (Gamble 217), May 1968.
   #26 Hot 100, #4 R&B.
"Love Is So Wonderful": Moniques (Benn-X 58), 1964. Did not chart. No
   R&B chart published.
"Love, Need and Want You": Patti Labelle (PIR 04399), November 1983.
   #10 R&B.
"A Love That's Real": Intruders (Gamble 209-B), summer 1967. #82 Hot
   100, #35 R&B.
"Love Train": O'Jays (PIR 3524), November 1972. #1 Hot 100, #1 R&B.
   Million-seller.
"Love Won't Let Me Wait": Major Harris (Atlantic 3248), January 1975.
   #5 Hot 100, #1 R&B. Million-seller.
"Love's Theme": Love Unlimited Orchestra (20th Century 2069),
   October 1973. #1 Hot 100, #10 R&B.
"Lovin' You": O'Jays (PIR 50084), June 1987. #1 R&B.
"Make Your Move": Volcanos (Arctic 103-B), December 1964.
"Mama Can't Buy You Love": Elton John (MCA 41402), April 1979. #9
   Hot 100, #36 R&B.
"Maniac": Michael Sembello (Casablanca 812516), April 1983. #1 Hot
   100.
"Mashed Potato Time": Dee Dee Sharp (Cameo 212), February 1962. #2
   Hot 100, #1 R&B. Million-seller.

"Maybe": Three Degrees (Roulette 7079), April 1970. #29 Hot 100, #4 R&B.

"Me and Mrs. Jones": Billy Paul (PIR 3521), September 1972. #1 Hot 100, #1 R&B. Million-seller.

"Mickey D's": People's Choice (TSOP 4781), April 1976.

"Mighty Love—Pt. 1": Spinners (Atlantic 3006), December 1973. #20 Hot 100, #1 R&B.

"Mr. Dream Merchant": Jerry Butler (Mercury 72721), September 1967. #38 Hot 100, #23 R&B.

"Mixed-Up Shook-Up Girl": Patty and the Emblems (Herald 590), May 1964. #37 Hot 100. No R&B chart published.

"Music Please Music": Landslides (MFSB) (Huff Puff 1001-B), summer 1968. Did not chart.

"My Hero": Blue Notes (Val-ue 213), July 1960. #78 Hot 100, #19 R&B.

"Never Can Say Goodbye": Gloria Gaynor (MGM 14748), September 1974. #9 Hot 100, #34 R&B.

"Never Give You Up": Jerry Butler (Mercury 72798), April 1968. #20 Hot 100, #4 R&B.

"A Nice Girl Like You": Intruders (TSOP 4758), August 1974.

"992 Arguments": O'Jays (PIR 3522), October 1972. #57 Hot 100, #13 R&B.

"No Mail on Monday": Kenny Gamble (Epic 9636), Late 1963.

"One Man Band (Play All Alone)": Ronnie Dyson (Columbia 45776), December 1972. #28 Hot 100, #15 R&B.

"One Mint Julep": Ray Charles (Impulse 200), February 1961. #8 Hot 100, #1 R&B.

"One Night Affair": O'Jays (Neptune 12), May 1969. #68 Hot 100, #15 R&B.

"One of a Kind (Love Affair)": Spinners (Atlantic 2962), February 1973. #11 Hot 100, #1 R&B. Million-seller.

"Only the Strong Survive": Jerry Butler (Mercury 72898), January 1969 #4 Hot 100, #1 R&B. Million-seller.

"Ooh Child": Dee Dee Sharp Gamble (TSOP LP 33839), November 1975.

"Party Is a Groovy Thing": People's Choice (TSOP 4759), November 1974. #45 R&B.

"Peanuts": Little Joe and the Thrillers (Okeh 7088), January 1957. #22 Top 100.

"People Make the World Go Round": Stylistics (Avco 4595), April 1972. #25 Hot 100, #6 R&B.

"Philadelphia Freedom": MFSB (PIR3589), February 1976.

"Popeye (the Hitchhiker)": Chubby Checker (Parkway 849), August 1962. #10 Hot 100, #13 R&B. Million-seller.

"The Power of Love": Joe Simon (Spring 128), May 1972. #11 Hot 100, #1 R&B. Millionseller.

"Pretty One": The Masters or Rockmasters with Phil Hurtt (unissued B&L), Recorded early 1964.

"Put Your Hands Together": O'Jays (PIR 3535), September 1973. #10 Hot 100, #2 R&B.

"Rapper's Delight": Sugarhill Gang (Sugar Hill 542), August 1979. #36 Hot 100, #4 R&B.

"Ready or Not Here I Come (Can't Hide from Love)": Delfonics (Philly Groove 154), November 1968. #35 Hot 100, #14 R&B.

"Regina": Bunny Sigler (PIR 3519), mid-1972.

"Rhythm Talk": Jocko Henderson (3739), November 1979.

"Rock the Boat": Hues Corporation (RCA Victor 0232), March 1974. #1 Hot 100, #2 R&B. Million-seller.

"Rock Your Baby": George McCrae (T.K. 1004), March 1974. #1 Hot 100, #1 R&B.

"Rockin' Roll Baby": Stylistics (Avco 4625), August 1973. #14 Hot 100, #3 R&B.

"The Rubberband Man": Spinners (Atlantic 3355), July 1976. #2 Hot 100, #1 R&B. Million-seller.

"Run Jesse Run": Lou Rawls, Phyllis Hyman, and Rev. James Cleveland. (Gamble and Huff 312), early 1988.

"Sadie": Spinners (Atlantic 3268), March 1975. #54 Hot 100, #7 R&B.

"Shiftless Shady Jealous Kind of People": O'Jays (PIR LP 31712), March 1972.

"Ship Ahoy": O'Jays (PIR LP 32408), September 1973.

"Show You the Way to Go": Jacksons (Epic/PIR 50350), February 1977. #28 Hot 100, #6 R&B.

"Side Show": Blue Magic (Atco 6961), February 1974. #8 Hot 100, #1 R&B. Million-seller.

"The Slide": Lavenders (CR 1008), spring 1962.

"Slow Twistin'": Chubby Checker and Dee Dee Sharp (Parkway 835), February 1962. #3 Hot 100, #3 R&B.

"Soul Makossa": Manu Dibango (Atlantic 2971), April 1973. #35 Hot 100, #21 R&B.

"Soul Train '75'": Soul Train Gang (Soul Train 10400), August 1975. #9 R&B.

"Standing in the Shadows": Kenny Gamble (Epic 9636), Late 1963.

"Stop, Look, and Listen (to Your Heart)": Stylistics (Avco Embassy 4572), March 1971. #39 Hot 100, #6 R&B.

"Storm Warning": Volcanos (Arctic 106-B), May 1965. #33 R&B.

"Style of Life": Jacksons (Epic/PIR 50289), August 1976.

"Sweet Charlie Babe": Jackie Moore (Atlantic 2956), April 1973. #42 Hot 100, #15 R&B.

"Teardrops": Lee Andrews and the Hearts (Chess 1675), November 1957. #20 Top 100, #4 R&B.

"Tell the World How I Feel about Cha Baby": Harold Melvin and the Blue Notes (PIR 3588), January 1976. #94 Hot 100, #7 R&B.

"That's the Way Girls Are": Freddy Cannon (Swan 4155), July 1963.

"That's What Girls Are Made For": Spinners (Tri-Phi 1001), April 1961. #27 Hot 100, #5 R&B.

"Then Came You": Dionne Warwick and the Spinners (Atlantic 3202), May 1974. #1 Hot 100, #2 R&B. Million-seller.

"There Ain't Nothin' I Wouldn't Do for You": Dee Dee Sharp (Cameo 382-B), late 1965.

"There's Gonna Be a Showdown": Archie Bell and the Drells (Atlantic 2583), November 1968. #21 Hot 100, #6 R&B.

"There's No Me without You": Manhattans (Columbia 45838), April 1973. #43 Hot 100, #3 R&B.

"There's Someone Waiting (Back Home)": O'Jays (Neptune 20), November 1969.

"These Will Be the Good Old Days": Dreamlovers (Cameo 326), spring 1964. Did not chart. No R&B chart published.

"'They Just Can't Stop It' (The Games People Play)," Spinners (Atlantic 3284), June 1975. #5 Hot 100, #1 R&B. Million-seller.

"Three Ring Circus": Sideshow (Atco 7004), August 1974. #36 Hot 100, #5 R&B.

"This Can't Be True (Girl)": Eddie Holman (Parkway 960), fall 1965. #57 Hot 100, #17 R&B.

"This Is Magic": Ballads (Tina 102), late 1964. No R&B chart published.

"This Is Your Life": Billy Paul (PIR 3515), March 1972.

"Three-Way Love Affair": Elton John (MCA 41402), April 1979.

"Tighten Up:" Archie Bell and the Drells (Atlantic 2478), February 1968. #1 Hot 100, #1 R&B. Million-seller.

"Together": Intruders (Gamble 205), February 1967. #48 Hot 100, #9 R&B.

"Tossin' and Turnin'": Bunny Sigler (PIR 3523), Late 1972.

"TSOP (The Sound of Philadelphia)": MFSB (PIR 3540), December 1973. #1 Hot 100, #1 R&B. Million-seller.

"Use ta Be My Girl": O'Jays (PIR 3642), November 1977. #4 Hot 100, #1 R&B. Million-seller.

"Valentine Love": Norman Connors with Jean Carn and Michael Henderson (Buddah 499), September 1975. #97 Hot 100, #10 R&B.

"Wake Up Everybody": Harold Melvin and the Blue Notes (PIR 3579), September 1975. #12 Hot 100, #1 R&B.

"We Don't Need No Music": Landslides (MFSB) (Huff Puff 1001-A), summer 1968.

"Wedding Bells (Are Ringing in My Ears)": Angels (Grand 115), October 1954.

"(We'll Be) United": Intruders (Gamble 201), May 1966. #78 Hot 100, #14 R&B.

"(We'll Be) United": Music Makers (Gamble 210), fall 1967. Did not chart.

"What Am I Gonna Tell My Baby": Kenny Gamble (unissued B&L), recorded ca. spring 1964.

"What Are You Doin' to Me": Cindy Scott and the Cousins (unissued B&L), Recorded ca. 1964.

"What Kind of Lady": Dee Dee Sharp Gamble (Gamble 219), summer 1968.

"What'd I Say": Ray Charles (Atlantic 2031), June 1959. #6 Hot 100, #1R&B.

"What's the Use of Breaking Up": Jerry Butler (Mercury 72960), July 1969. #20 Hot 100, #4 R&B.

"What's Your Name": Don and Juan (Big Top 3079), January 1962. #7 Hot 100.

"When the World's at Peace": O'Jays (PIR LP 31712), March 1972.

"When We Get Married": Dreamlovers (Heritage 102), May 1961. #10
      Hot 100.
"When Will I See You Again": Three Degrees (PIR 3550), July 1974. #2
      Hot 100, #4 R&B. Two-million-seller.
"When You Dance": Turbans (Herald 458), July 1955. #33 Top 100, #3
      R&B.
"Where Are All My Friends": Harold Melvin and the Blue Notes (PIR
      3552), September 1974. #80 Hot 100, #8 R&B.
"Who Do You Love": Sapphires (Swan 4162), August 1963. #25 Hot 100,
      #25 R&B.
"The Whole Town's Talkin' about Me": Teddy Pendergrass (PIR 3633),
      July 1977. #16 R&B.
"Yes, I'm Ready": Barbara Mason (Arctic 105), March 1965. #5 Hot 100,
      #2 R&B.
"You Are Everything": Stylistics (Avco 4581), August 1971. #9 Hot 100,
      #10 R&B. Million-seller.
"You Better Be a Good Girl Now": Swans (Swan 4151), June 1963.
"You Don't Know What You've Got until You Lose It": Kenny Gamble
      (Columbia 43132), ca. August 1964. R&B chart not published.
"You Got Yours and I'll Get Mine": Delfonics (Philly Groove 157), June
      1969. #40 Hot 100, #6 R&B.
"You Little Trustmaker": Tymes (RCA Victor 10022), June 1974. #12 Hot
      100, #20 R&B.
"You Make Me Feel Brand New": Stylistics (Avco 4634), January 1974. #2
      Hot 100, #5 R&B. Million-seller.
"You'll Never Find Another Love like Mine": Lou Rawls (PIR 3592),
      March 1976. #2 Hot 100, #3 R&B. Million-seller.
"You'll Never Stop Me from Loving You": Sapphires (ABC-Paramount
      10753), summer 1965.
"You're a Big Girl Now": Stylistics (Avco Embassy 4555), November
      1970. #73 Hot 100, #7 R&B.
"You're Gonna Make Me Love Somebody Else": Jones Girls (PIR 3680),
      February 1979. #38 Hot 100, #5 R&B. Million-seller.
"You're the Greatest": Billy Scott (Cameo 121), December 1957. #73 Top
      100.
"You're the Reason": Ebonys (PIR 3503), March 1971. #51 Hot 100, #10
      R&B.
"You've Been Untrue": Delfonics (Cameo 472) spring 1967.

Appendix II

Gold and Platinum Records of Gamble, Huff, and Bell

Gamble and Huff's Gold and Platinum Singles

"Cowboys to Girls," Intruders, 1968
"Only the Strong Survive," Jerry Butler, 1969
"Don't Let the Green Grass Fool You," Wilson Pickett, 1970
"Drowning in the Sea of Love," Joe Simon, 1971
"Power of Love" Joe Simon, 1971
"Back Stabbers," O'Jays, 1972
"If You Don't Know Me by Now," Harold Melvin and the Blue Notes, 1972
"Me and Mrs. Jones," Billy Paul, 1972
"Love Train," O'Jays, 1972
"The Love I Lost—Part 1," Harold Melvin and the Blue Notes, 1973
"TSOP (The Sound of Philadelphia)," MFSB, 1974
"When Will I See You Again," Three Degrees, 1974
"Do It Anyway You Wanna," People's Choice, 1975
"I Love Music—Pt. 1," O'Jays, 1975
"You'll Never Find Another Love like Mine," Lou Rawls, 1976
"Use Ta Be My Girl," O'Jays, 1978
"Close the Door," Teddy Pendergrass, 1978
"Ain't No Stoppin' Us Now," McFadden and Whitehead, 1979 (platinum)
"You're Gonna Make Me Love Somebody Else," Jones Girls, 1979

Thom Bell's Gold Singles

"Didn't I (Blow Your Mind This Time)," Delfonics, 1969
"You Are Everything," Stylistics, 1971
"Betcha by Golly, Wow," Stylistics, 1972
"I'll Be Around," Spinners, 1972
"I'm Stone in Love with You," Stylistics, 1972
"Could It Be I'm Falling in Love," Spinners, 1972
"Break Up to Make Up," Stylistics, 1973

"One of a Kind (Love Affair)," Spinners, 1973
"You Make Me Feel Brand New," Stylistics, 1974
"Then Came You," Dionne Warwick/Spinners, 1974
"'They Just Can't Stop It' (The Games People Play)," Spinners, 1975
"The Rubberband Man," Spinners, 1976

Gamble and Huff's Gold and Platinum Albums

Back Stabbers, O'Jays, 1972
360 Degrees of Billy Paul, Billy Paul, 1972
Ship Ahoy, O'Jays, 1973 (platinum)
Love Is the Message, MFSB, 1973
Live in London, O'Jays, 1974
To Be True, Harold Melvin and the Blue Notes, 1975
Survival, O'Jays, 1975
Family Reunion, O'Jays, 1975 (platinum)
Wake Up Everybody, Harold Melvin and the Blue Notes, 1975
All Things in Time, Lou Rawls, 1976 (platinum)
Message in the Music, O'Jays, 1976
Teddy Pendergrass, Teddy Pendergrass, 1977 (platinum)
Unmistakably Lou, Lou Rawls, 1977
Travelin' at the Speed of Thought, O'Jays, 1977
When You Hear Lou You've Heard It All, Lou Rawls, 1977
Life Is a Song Worth Singing, Teddy Pendergrass, 1978 (platinum)
So Full of Love, O'Jays, 1978 (platinum)
McFadden and Whitehead, McFadden and Whitehead, 1979
Teddy, Teddy Pendergrass, 1979 (platinum)
Identify Yourself, Teddy Pendergrass, 1979 (platinum)
Live Coast to Coast, Teddy Pendergrass, 1979
TP, Teddy Pendergrass, 1980 (platinum)
It's Time For Love, Teddy Pendergrass, 1981
I'm in Love Again, Patti Labelle, 1983

Thom Bell's Gold Albums

The Stylistics, Stylistics, 1971
Round 2: The Stylistics, Stylistics, 1972
Spinners, Spinners, 1973
Mighty Love, Spinners, 1974
New and Improved, Spinners, 1974
Pick of the Litter, Spinners, 1975
Happiness Is Being with the Detroit Spinners, Spinners, 1976

Notes

Preface

1 In 1958, the Recording Industry Association of America (RIAA) began certifying gold albums for sales of 500,000 units or more. In 1976, the RIAA began certifying platinum albums for sales of a million units or more. From 1958 through 1988, the RIAA required sales of a million units or more for a gold single and (beginning in 1976) two million units for a platinum single. Beginning in 1989, the RIAA lowered the requirements for gold singles to sales of 500,000 units or more and platinum singles to a million or more. Some record labels have never requested RIAA certification for recordings that would have qualified for these awards.

2 This and the other quotes by Sigler in this book are from his interview with the author.

3 Butler, *Only the Strong Survive*, 155.

4 This and the other quotes by Bell in this book are from his interviews with the author, unless otherwise noted.

5 Gamble's quote is from Miller, "Gamble and Huff: The Hit Men," 173.

6 This and the other quotes by Bailey in this book are from his interview with the author.

1. "I'll Get By"

1 All quotes by Woods in this book are from his interview with the author.

2 Weigley, *Philadelphia: A 300-year History*, 4.

3 The city's first blacks, 150 slaves, arrived in 1684. By the 1890s, Philadelphia's black population was the largest of any northern city. Around this time, the first black ghettos began to appear just south of Center City (ibid., 531).

4 Southern, *Music of Black Americans*, 110.

5 The Dixie Hummingbirds were actually a quintet who sang four-part harmony supporting the lead vocalist.

6 Zolten, *Great God A'Mighty*, 31.

7 Ibid., 80.
8 The Capris' "God Only Knows," the Angels' "Wedding Bells Are Ringing in My Ears," and the Castelles' "I'm a Fool to Care" appeared on Philadelphia's R&B charts, which originated earlier in the decade, in 1954.
9 The catchy "When You Dance" did not represent the Philly Sound in its strictest sense. A true Philly Sound vocal group record never did crack the national best-seller charts, most likely because the complicated sound was too top-heavy and busy-sounding to appeal to the masses.
10 All quotes by Andrews in this book are from his interview with the author. All quotes by McDougal in this book are from his interview with the author, unless specified otherwise.
11 Gamble's junior high classmate was Greg Hall. His quote is from Fried, "The Day the Soul Train Crashed," 119. All quotes by Martin in this book are from his interviews with the author, unless specified otherwise.
12 The original *Bandstand*, hosted by local disc jockey Bob Horn, became Philadelphia's most popular TV program. In 1956, the irreproachable Clark replaced Horn, who was bedeviled by charges of statutory rape and drunken driving. A year later, Clark convinced ABC to broadcast the show nationally.
13 In 1957, Philadelphia contained the nation's third-largest black population. The city's interracial difficulties were partly a result of the city's schizophrenic regard of its black population. Historically an abolitionist stronghold, Philadelphia was also the most southern of northern cities in the United States. Historian Russell F. Weigley noted that during the eighteenth century there had been little racial friction in Philadelphia, and "great hopes were held for the future" of the city's black population. Over the ensuing years, however, a tide of racism began to rise in the City of Brotherly Love. Such sentiment led to the establishment of segregated bars, restaurants, and hotels (Weigley, *Philadelphia: A 300-Year History*, 255, 353, 531, 669).

American Bandstand was born in this racist climate, amid the specter of institutionalized racism in national broadcasting. It was no accident that performers (black or white) on *American Bandstand* did not dance or mingle with the teenagers in the show's audience. Instead, they were quickly marshaled to the show's autograph table, which served as a barrier against any direct interracial contact. Just weeks before Clark's show made its network debut, disc jockey Alan Freed's nationally televised rock and roll show was canceled by ABC after guest artist Frankie Lymon, a black, was shown dancing with a white girl, to which ABC's southern affiliates objected vehemently.

One method used to exclude blacks from *American Bandstand* was to issue membership cards. But even if a black teen managed to obtain such a card, it was not unusual for him or her to be turned away. One such instance occurred in 1957, when a local black singing star appeared on Clark's show. A number of the singer's black fans arrived with reservations for the show, only to be told the "guest list was closed because of the great number of advance reservations" (reported in "The Lowdown" entertainment column, *The Call* (Philadelphia), October 11, 1957, 8). For a detailed account of the history of *American Bandstand*, including its policy toward blacks, see Jackson, *American Bandstand*. Gamble's "they wouldn't let too many black kids" quote is from Smith, *Off the Record*, 323.

14 All quotes by Kelly in this book are from his interview with the author.

15 Labelle's quote is from Labelle, *Don't Block the Blessings*, 64.

16 Early, *One Nation under a Groove*, 65.

17 All quotes by Ross in this book are from his interviews with the author. Ross was characteristically unrestrained as he assessed his own role in Gamble's development: "Even though his mother gave birth to Kenny Gamble, I discovered him! I was the first one to give him any opportunity to really express what he wanted to do."

18 Gamble's conversation was recalled by McDougal in his interviews with the author; "It's Unbelievable," with Jackie Marshall on lead and McDougal singing bass, became Jerry Ross's first national chart hit.

19 In the song, a forlorn lover who has just broken up with his sweetheart vows to survive the emotional ordeal. Ross thought perhaps the song was recorded in the spring of 1962, at the end of a Dreamlovers session, but it may have been recorded at a later date.

20 Huff's quote is from Cummings, *Sound of Philadelphia*, 76. For Huff's comments to Olsen, see Olsen, "Billy Paul Wins . . ."

21 Huff's quotes are from Cummings, *Sound of Philadelphia*, 76; Johnson's quote is from his interview with the author.

22 Johnson's quote is from his interview with the author.

23 Huff also reportedly fronted a studio group called the Locomotions, named for Little Eva's recent million-selling dance novelty, as well as a group called the Dynaflows.

2. "Who Do You Love"

1 Bernie Lowe's company began as Cameo Records. The Parkway label, on which Checker's records were released, was added in 1959. Clark and Lowe were old friends, having met while working on a locally televised teenage show during the early 1950s. All quotes by Jackson in this book are from his interview with the author.

2 Cameo-Parkway's inner circle consisted of Lowe, his songwriting partner Kal Mann, and bandleader-writer Dave Appell. Lowe was the major stockholder in Cameo-Parkway. Mann has often been mistakenly credited as having been Lowe's partner in Cameo-Parkway. In fact, Lowe, Mann, and Appell, in conjunction with Cameo-Parkway, each had their own music publishing companies and each received songwriting credit where applicable.

3 After first recording with a gospel group, Mimms formed a secular rhythm and blues group called the Gainers, who had two Cameo releases in 1958. But Cameo chose to concentrate on the teen idol phenomenon and let the Gainers go. Mimms and one other group member formed the Enchanters (although on "Cry Baby," the Sweet Inspirations, not the Enchanters, backed Mimms. See Dahl, "Garnet Mimms' Melismatic Voice," 26.

4 The first mention of the word "soul" in popular music may have been in the song "Body and Soul," which originated in 1930 as a pop song.

"Body and Soul" was transformed into a jazz classic a decade later by tenor saxophonist Coleman Hawkins. The word "soul" subsequently appeared in the titles of several 1950s jazz albums by artists who had come of age during the era when Hawkins's song was immortalized.

5   Charles's "little bit o' soul" was heard on the instrumental "One Mint Julep" in the spring of 1961. That July, "soul" unofficially became a music genre when, in a trade paper review, pianist Les McCann was dubbed a "soul pianist" (*The Cash Box*, July 8, 1961, 22).

6   The recording company, which began as Satellite Records, became Stax in 1961. Two of Stax's early Top 40 hits, one by the all-white Mar-Keys and the other by a biracial outfit called Booker T and the MG's, were instrumentals. The members of these two groups became session players for Stax, and were largely responsible for the label's vaunted "black" sound.

Stax's owners were under the impression their national distribution agreement with Atlantic applied only to the releases of the father-daughter team of Rufus and Carla Thomas. To their dismay, they discovered that the onerous deal actually awarded the distribution rights of *all* Stax releases to Atlantic, for five years.

7   The Ross/Gamble composition "You Better Be a Good Girl Now," sung by the Swans, from Camden, New Jersey, was released about the same time as was "Everybody Monkey." Cannon's follow-up to "Everybody Monkey" was the Ross/Gamble–penned "That's the Way Girls Are."

8   Bernie Lowe originally acquired the American distribution rights for "She Loves You" for Cameo-Parkway. After weighing the cost of acquiring the master recording against the long odds of its success, Lowe got cold feet and sold it to Swan. Beginning with "Who Do You Love" and ending with "You'll Never Stop Me from Loving You," the Sapphires released at least ten songs composed by Ross-Gamble.

9   All quotes by Madara and White in this book are from their interviews with the author.

10   All quotes by Eli in this book are from his interviews with the author. Gamble's single release, "Standing in the Shadows" and "No Mail on Monday," was most likely recorded during the late summer of 1963 and released later that year; Thom Bell questioned Ross's interest in Gamble as a recording artist. Bell believes that Ross, having sized up Gamble as a promising writer, felt the best way to woo him was "to pacify him as an artist."

3. "Mixed-Up Shook-Up Girl"

1   As late as 1963, Motown ran hot and cold on the charts. While Berry Gordy had developed genuine stars in the Miracles, the Marvelettes, and Mary Wells by then, two of his other groups—the Supremes and the Temptations—could not buy a hit. In addition, the Marvelettes were unable to match the chart strength of their early hits; the moody and difficult Marvin Gaye had yet to achieve a significant breakthrough; and even the Miracles' releases continued to be unpredictable.

2   George, *Where Did Our Love Go*, 53. H-D-H not only broke the Four Tops, one of Motown's super groups, onto the charts, they started the Supremes on a string of five successive number-one records.

3 Lowe's quote was recalled by Lit in his interview with the author.

4 Lead sheet writers copied songs from demo recordings onto paper.

5 When Roland Chambers was about fourteen, he and Karl formed a singing duet called the Rialtos.

6 All quotes in this book by Wilford are from his interview with the author. The handsome Wilford gave up music in the late 1960s to become an actor. In 1974, he joined CBS Records' department of press information and artist affairs, where he worked his way up to vice president. Wilford left CBS in 1982. For a time, he was married to dancer-choreographer Debbie Allen, the sister of Phylicia Rashad, who starred on television's *The Cosby Show*. Wilford continues to work as a talent manager.

7 Bell recalled this exchange in his interviews with the author.

8 Gamble's "basically a show band" quote is from Smith, *Off the Record*, 23; his "sharkskin suits" quote is from John-Hall, "His Music Is the Blueprint."

9 Gamble's "Now those guys are singers" quote is from Miller, "Gamble and Huff," 23. Huff's "control . . . Decision-making on all creative levels" quotes are from Riley, "Philly Sound," 34.

10 During this session, the Dreamlovers recorded the retro-ballad "These Will Be the Good Old Days."

11 Tarsia's first notable engineering session at Cameo-Parkway was for the two-sided Chubby Checker hit, "Limbo Rock" and "Popeye (the Hitch-Hiker)." All of the quotes by Tarsia in this book are from his interviews with the author, unless otherwise noted.

12 Renzetti soon arranged numerous Jerry Ross–produced hits for Spanky and Our Gang, Jay and the Techniques, and others. Renzetti later moved to Hollywood where he wrote film scores. In 1962, Wisner, a jazz pianist, used the sobriquet "Kokomo" and recorded a pop instrumental piano hit. He later wrote, arranged, and produced for Ross and for Cameo-Parkway.

13 Gamble's quote is from Miller, "Gamble and Huff," 23.

14 Huff later said that the sessions he did with Spector's renowned Ronettes were "one of the real highlights" of his career (Cummings, *Sound of Philadelphia*, 76).

15 All quotes in this book by Bendinelli are from his interview with the author. Bendinelli, who became proficient on the trumpet while playing in his high school band, spent World War II playing the instrument in the army. After the war, Bendinelli attended music school in Philadelphia. He then began to write songs and gig on weekends with a vocal group that he formed. During the early 1950s, Bendinelli added club dates to his musical activities.

Lovett was born in the Germantown section of North Philadelphia in 1910. He led his own band before going on the road in the 1940s, with the likes of Noble Sissle and Lucky Millinder. After spending part of the 1950s in California, Lovett returned to Philadelphia in the early 1960s to write musical arrangements and to produce, just as soul music began to make its mark. Lovett and Bendinelli met in 1962. That year they formed B&L Productions, Ben-Lee Music, and a couple of record labels; it was through B&L that Huff met renowned producers Jerry Lieber and Mike

Stoller. They subsequently used the pianist on a regular basis, "and we just developed a good relationship," recalled Huff. He also said that Lieber and Stoller helped him "get the knack of the studios" (Huff's quotes are from Cummings, *Sound of Philadelphia*, 76). For a detailed account of the recording of "Mixed-Up Shook-Up Girl," as well as a history of Patty and the Emblems, see Robert Bosco, "Straight Outta Camden."

16 Huff's principal songwriting partner at B&L was Cindy Scott (born Sandra Kay Tucker, the daughter of Ira Tucker of the Dixie Humming-birds). The Huff/Scott-penned "What Are You Doin' to Me," recorded by Cindy Scott and the Cousins, was a terrific record that inexplicably went unreleased. Exactly when Huff stopped writing for B&L is unclear. The Huff-Scott composition "Help a Lonely Guy," produced by B&L and released as the B side of the Companions' "Be Yourself," was probably released near the beginning of 1965. In all likelihood, Huff had stopped writing for B&L by then. Although Huff credited Leroy Lovett with teaching him "quite a bit" about producing (Cummings, *Sound of Philadelphia*, 84), Bendinelli said that when Huff teamed up with Gamble, he and Lovett "never heard from Huff again." Bendinelli lamented over how the sharing of B&L publishing with Madara and White "screwed us up bad!"

17 Gamble's high-quality demo, on which Patty and the Emblems and Cindy Scott reportedly sang background, can be heard on the CD *The Intruders and Friends* (Collectables COL-5771).

18 Those gains were met with new levels of violence and disorder, typified by the death of four young girls in a Birmingham Sunday School church bombing and the murder of three civil rights workers in Mississippi.

19 The black disturbances in Philadelphia, which were sparked by a routine stop by the police that escalated into an angry rock- and bottle-tossing exercise, were not the first to occur in America in 1964. Ten days earlier, similar uprisings began in Harlem, New York.

20 Ross, in his interview with the author, said that Gamble's Jimmy Wisner–arranged album contained "some great sides." The backup singers were Melba Moore and Ashford and Simpson; Ross also blamed the album's lack of success on Columbia's studio engineers, who, he said, were "more intent on watching dials than really getting into the music." Of course, part of the problem was with the music itself. Who knows what would have happened had Gamble (as he had done on his demo for B&L) used the Romeos instead of white-bread studio musicians on those recordings.

21 Gamble's plight was similar to that of Aretha Franklin, who had been recording for Columbia for four years when Gamble cut his album. During that time, Franklin meandered through a string of producers and several unessential albums that kept her in search of a distinct style. Shortly after moving to Atlantic Records, Franklin established herself as the First Lady of Soul.

22 Some sources erroneously credit "The 81" as being Gamble and Huff's first production, despite the fact that Jerry Ross is listed as the producer on the record label. Ross, in his interviews with the author of this book, insisted that he was indeed the sole producer of the record. Wisner, who

arranged "The 81," did not think it was accurate to classify the song as a Motown copy. In his interview with the author, Wisner claimed that "the nature of the business is that you're influenced by what's happening" elsewhere (i.e., Motown). (Such as with Dee Dee Sharp's "Mashed Potato Time," which was so close in style to the Marvelettes' "Please Mr. Postman" that, to avoid a lawsuit, Bernie Lowe split the publishing rights with Motown.) Wisner did concede that "The 81" was "certainly the genre of the period ... [but] it really wasn't Motown. ... It was just kind of Philadelphia R&B at that point."

23 In Miller, "Gamble and Huff," 23, Gamble claimed that he and Huff wrote "The 81." Gamble's "grinding out songs ... It didn't take either of us too long ... So I got together with Huff" quote is from Riley, "Philly Sound," 34; Huff's quote is from Olsen, "Billy Paul Wins." It may be true that Gamble and Huff decided to write together while riding in the Schubert Building elevator. It is unlikely, however, that the two met in that elevator. Jerry Ross recorded such acts as the Dreamlovers and the Sapphires, beginning in 1961. "Kenny was working with me and Huff was playing keyboards," recalled Ross in his interviews with the author. The liner notes to Ross's *Yo! Philadelphia: Look What I Found* (Heritage HYP 002), a compilation of Ross's early Philadelphia productions, credits Huff as the piano player on Gamble and Bell's Kenny and Tommy session, recorded in 1962 or early 1963. "Whenever we did a session, Huff was there," added Ross. "I *wanted* him; I *needed* him; I *hired* him. He was gifted. He brought life to the session. And that's where Kenny met him and heard his musical contributions. Kenny didn't hear Huff's musical contributions on the elevator!"

24 Huff's "started talking about collaborating" quote was made to Vaughn Harper, in Nooger, "Philadelphia," 96.

25 The makeshift studio group that sang "Pretty One" was dubbed the Rock Masters, or simply the Masters, when the song was released many years later. "Pretty One," with Phil Hurtt singing lead and backed by a sweet-sounding chorus and silky strings, was highly derivative of the Impressions' style. Len Stark owned Melron Records, on which the somewhat less soulful "King of Love" was recorded. Another rhythm and blues ballad portending Philadelphia soul to emerge out of Sound Plus studio around that time was the Moniques' "Love So Wonderful."

26 All quotes in this book by Gaber are from his interview with the author. Gaber's most well-known artist was Philadelphia's Ronnie Walker, whose soaring falsetto became quite popular there in the 1960s and 1970s.

27 Bosco's quote is from his interview with the author.

28 In 1959, the Virtues achieved "one hit wonder" status when they cracked the Top 10 with their version of Arthur Smith's "Guitar Boogie Shuffle."

29 McDougal, Randolph, and Stiles called their new label MRS, combining their initials.

30 Bishop's quote is from Cummings, *Sound of Philadelphia*, 78.

31 The Atlantic release was the Tiffanys' "Gossip," originally released on MRS.

32 The first southern soul record to reach the pop Top 10 was Joe Tex's "Hold What You've Got," recorded at Rick Hall's Fame studio in Muscle

Shoals, Alabama. Like Stax, Fame recorded black artists who were backed by a group of predominantly white musicians. In 1966, Atlantic began utilizing Fame in order to obtain for many of its black artists, including Wilson Pickett and Aretha Franklin, the renowned "Muscle Shoals Sound."

4. "Expressway to Your Heart"

1 George, *Death of Rhythm and Blues*, 87.
2 Huff's "seven or eight songs" quote was made to Vaughn Harper, and appeared in Nooger, "Philadelphia," 96.
3 Pendergrass's quotes about Gamble are from Pendergrass and Roma-nowski, *Truly Blessed*, 116, 117.
4 Huff's "So you got your own Cadillac" quote is from ibid., 116. All quotes in this book by Gallagher are from his interview with the author.
5 Gamble's "just had the feeling quote" is from Cummings, *Sound of Philadelphia*, 83; the conversation between Gamble and Huff was recalled by Bailey in his interview with the author; Bell's "was the engine" quote is from Sacks and Prescott, "The Philly Sound," 12.
6 Huff told Eric Olsen that the first song he and Gamble wrote together was the Sapphires' "Gee I'm Sorry Baby," which was released in the spring of 1965 (Olsen, "Billy Paul Wins"). Gamble's "We had to take the initiative ... we had to produce together" quote is from Cummings, *Sound of Philadelphia*, 83.
7 McDougal's quote is from Cummings, *Sound of Philadelphia*, 85. The Volcanos were formed in West Philadelphia in 1963 by Steven Kelly and the Wade brothers, Harold and Stanley. The trio subsequently added John Hart Jr. and the powerful lead voice of Gene Faith (Eugene Jones).
8 Gamble also wrote Sharp's follow-up record, "There Ain't Nothin' I Wouldn't Do for You," which was her final release for Cameo-Parkway.
9 The split between Dynodynamics and Bishop came about after the release of Barbara Mason's "Yes, I'm Ready." It was then that McDougal, Randolph, and Stiles, who were allegedly led by Bishop to believe that they owned an equal share of Arctic Records, discovered that Bishop and Universal Distributors' Harold Lipsius actually owned the label.
10 Gamble's "scuffled around trying to raise some capital" quote is from Cummings, *Sound of Philadelphia*, 83; Rudman touted himself as "the wildest child on the radio dial" and "the round mound of sound." He had a deep commitment to the civil rights movement and "was a great guy to have in your corner," said Georgie Woods in his interview with the author. "He was very helpful to Kenny Gamble."
11 Terry's "sounds flat" quote is from Cummings, *Sound of Philadelphia*, 86.
12 Daughtry's "we crashed the party" quote is from Taylor, *Classic Soul*, 118; Gamble's "so we pursued them" quote is from Miller, "Gamble and Huff," 30.
13 Daughtry's quote is from Taylor, *Classic Soul*, 119.
14 Joe Tarsia stated in his interview with the author that Bishop helped Gamble "a great deal." Huff's "it was no big thing" quote is from Cummings, *Sound of Philadelphia*, 84.
15 During that time, Martin Luther King confidentially told President

Johnson that he feared a "full-scale race war" ("King Warned of a Race War," *New York Times*, April 14, 2002).

16 Martha Reeves, the lead vocalist on "Dancing in the Street," told author Gerri Hirshey that although some people called the song "a call to riot.... My Lord, it was a party song" (Hirshey, *Nowhere to Run*, 145).

17 George, *Death of Rhythm and Blues*, 143. Huff's "hanging out a lot" quote was told to Vaughn, in Nooger, "Philadelphia," 96.

18 After Lowe sold his interest in Cameo-Parkway, Kal Mann and Dave Appell left; one of Bell's Cameo-Parkway productions was an early recording by future teen heartthrob Bobby Sherman, made during the summer of 1966.

19 Bell, in his interview with the author, recalled the conversation by Watson.

20 The genesis of the Delfonics involved two groups, the Veltones and the Orphonics. In 1959, Poogie Hart formed the Veltones. Randy Cain was also a member. Later, Hart became an original member of the Orphonics, along with Ritchie Daniels, Reggie Hart, and Bootsy Gainer. It is uncertain whether Daniels, Gainer, or Reggie Hart took part in Bell's audition of the group; in his interview with the author, Poogie Hart unknowingly supported Bell's claim of being unsatisfied with the overall quality of the Orphonics. Hart said that Cain "never was really a good singer. He looked the part, and I figured I could carry the group." Hart's quotes in this book are from his interview with the author unless otherwise noted; Watson's "all you motherfuckers" quote was recalled by Bell in his interview with the author. Watson, who had an inexplicable interest in the 1950s vocal group the Del-Vikings, instituted the group's name change to Delfonics. Although Watson claimed he had briefly been a member of the Del-Vikings, there is no evidence to support his contention.

21 Tarsia's "man, if you do this one more time" quote was recalled by Bell in his interview with the author. "He Don't Really Love You" was issued on the Moonshot label, which was owned by the hulking, brutish Nate McCalla, a reputed enforcer for New York music mogul Morris Levy. At the time Moonshot was formed, McCalla worked for Cameo-Parkway. In his interview with the author, Bell said McCalla "loved" the Delfonics' record, but "didn't have the money to really branch out nationally."

22 "You've Been Untrue" was released just as Cameo-Parkway reported a yearly fiscal loss of a million and a half dollars. Not long after that, Allen Klein, who was the business adviser to the Rolling Stones, purchased a controlling interest in the company. Klein's company was then absorbed by Cameo-Parkway, and its name was changed to Abkco (Allen B. Klein Company).

23 Gamble's "right blend ... more sophisticated" quotes are from Cummings, *Sound of Philadelphia*, 86. His "about how we hoped ... and we dreamed" quote is from Smith, *Off the Record*, 323.

24 Although Gamble hired a full-time clerk to run his record shop, he did spend time there. In addition, he kept his pulse on the local music scene by picking up each day's order from a local record distributor.

25 Shively, in his interview with the author, recalled Gamble's conversation. Gamble Records had other recording artists at the time—namely, the Cruisers, the Baby Dolls, and the Mad Men. In his interview, Shively

described their records as a "whole bunch of junk that [Gamble and Huff] just let go, and just went on to the next [Intruders release]."

26 Shively, who is a lifelong friend of the Crimson owner to whom Gamble allegedly made his production offer, recalled Gamble's quote in his interview with the author.

27 Blavat's quotes are from Sacks and Prescott, "The Philly Sound," 57. Gamble's alleged offer to produce for Crimson, and his "put me on the payroll" quote, were noted by Shively, a lifelong friend of the Crimson owner to whom the offer was allegedly made.

28 Gamble's "people couldn't understand" and "that brought our attention" quotes are from Miller, "Gamble and Huff," 23. Gamble's "soul-influenced pop" quote is from Cummings, *Sound of Philadelphia*, 89.

29 Gamble's "in the whole industry" quote is from Cummings, *Sound of Philadelphia*, 89.

30 In his interview with the author, White waxed philosophical about Huff's departure. Gamble and Huff "were just attracted to each other," he said. "It was just meant to be that they would finally get together. We were just a stepping stone to that."

31 In the buyout of Huff's contract, Madara reportedly received a cash payment and half of the publishing rights to everything written by Huff up to that point. "It cost Gamble and Huff a lot of bread, an arm and a leg!" said Bell in his interview with the author.

32 Funk is improvisational, polyrhythmic dance music driven by a powerful bass line and augmented by a staccato brass section. Its melody is secondary to the heavily syncopated rhythm.

33 All quotes by Butler are from his interview with the author, unless otherwise noted.

34 In Bell's interview with the author, he said that spelling Thom with an "H" was a West Indian custom.

5. "Cowboys to Girls"

1 Following the devastating riots in the summer of 1967, President Lyndon B. Johnson created the National Advisory Commission on Civil Disorders (a.k.a. the Kerner Commission). The committee's findings were released in March 1968. One of the conclusions was that the United States was "moving toward two societies, one black, one white—separate and unequal" (National Advisory Commission on Civil Disorders report).

2 Huff's quote is from Miller, "Gamble and Huff," 30.

3 Martin, in his interview with the author, recalled Gamble's telephone conversation.

4 Martin's account of how his relationship with Gamble developed was recalled in his interview with the author.

5 Cummings's "eccentrically meandering lead" quote is from Cummings, *Sound of Philadelphia*, 92; the late Rick Sklar, who was WABC's program director when "Cowboys to Girls" became a hit, made the assertion about WABC's effect on nationwide sales (Sklar, *Rocking America*, 94).

6 Rudman's "almost $100,000" take from "Cowboys to Girls" is from Sklar, *Rocking America*, 94; Gamble's "Now they accepted" quote is from

Cummings, *Sound of Philadelphia*, 92; Dave Marsh included "Cowboys to Girls" in his *The Heart of Rock and Soul: 1001 Greatest Singles Ever Made*. He noted that the song exhibited "the template of the Philly International sound ... [and was] perhaps the most charming song" Gamble and Huff ever wrote (Marsh, *Heart of Rock and Soul*, 582, 583).

7 Gamble's quote is from Cummings, *Sound of Philadelphia*, 86.

8 James and Martin had already teamed up on another Philadelphia rhythm and blues classic, the Fantastic Johnny C's (Johnny Corley) lively rhythm and blues dance number called "Boogaloo Down Broadway." James's "I don't give a shit" quote is from ibid., 88.

9 All quotes by Montana in this book are from his interview with the author.

10 Martin's "made a bad mistake" quote is from Cummings, *Sound of Philadelphia*, 88.

11 Stiles's quote is from ibid., 96.

12 Eli has been credited with playing on the Kenny and Tommy session, but he does not recall having done so. His first sessions for Gamble and Huff were done with the Intruders. Although Eli also played on "Expressway to Your Heart," "Boogaloo Down Broadway," and "The Horse," a steady association with Gamble and Huff did not begin until the "Cowboys to Girls" session. Eli's first work for Thom Bell came on "Didn't I (Blow Your Mind This Time)."

13 It has been widely written and accepted that Young was originally a member of the Volcanos. Steven Kelly, during his interview with the author, agreed. Young, in his interview with the author, begged to differ. The drummer, who was a member of the Exceptions vocal group in 1963, insisted he "wasn't actually in" the Volcanos. Young claimed that he had played drums for the group "because I was in the studio" at the time. All of Young's quotes in this book are from his interview with the author; Tarsia's quote is from Sacks and Prescott, "The Philly Sound," 61.

14 Ashford went on to make a name for himself as part of Motowns "Funk Brothers" rhythm section.

15 Gamble's quotes are from Riley, "Philly Sound," 34.

16 Gamble's quote and Butler's "Huff and Kenny" quote are from Butler, *Only the Strong Survive*, 153. Butler's "something fierce" and "brought out my best" quotes are from Sacks and Prescott, "The Philly Sound," 53.

17 Gamble's quote is from Butler, *Only the Strong Survive*, 153.

18 All quotes in this book by Archie Bell are from his interview with the author.

19 Huff's quotes are from Miller, "Gamble and Huff," 30.

20 Judging from Hart's interview with the author, he harbors many issues with Thom Bell. In it, he claimed to have had a hand in writing the melodies of the Delfonics songs composed with Bell. Hart, like Bell, claimed that the two sat "side by side" at the piano when they wrote. But Hart insisted that, along with the fact that he "wrote all the lyrics," he also "hummed the melodies" and that Bell "wrote them down. . . . I really wrote the songs," said Hart. Bell "arranged the songs." All of Poogie Hart's quotes in this book are from his interview with the author, unless otherwise specified.

21 The French horn, rarely, if ever, heard on a soul or R&B recording, became one of the most identifiable instruments on the Delfonics' subsequent records. Bell, in his interview with the author, said that he discovered the instrument while listening to opera. Hart, in his interview with the author, claimed it was Hart's idea to use the French horn.

22 Sigma Sound is fully explored in Cogan and Clark, *Temples of Sound*, 150–63.

23 Tarsia first discovered Reco-Art early in his career, when he performed some repair work at the studio; Morris Bailey, who cut some of Patti Labelle and the Blue Belles' tracks at Reco-Art, said that the studio "probably had the best sound going." Jimmy Wisner thought Reco-Art's rooms "had magic in them." From the 1940s until 1958, Reco-Art was located on Market Street. During that time, the venerable room turned out dozens of pop and rock and roll hits, including Charlie Gracie's "Butterfly" and Danny and the Juniors' "At the Hop."

24 Gamble's "tremendous part of our team" quote is from Butler, *Only the Strong Survive*, 153; Gamble and Huff's "give it a try" quote was recalled by Eli in his interview with the author. Part of the sound check conducted that day can be heard as "We Don't Need No Music" (a reference to Sly and the Family Stone's recent hit, "Dance to the Music") and "Music Please Music," which were both released that year on Gamble and Huff's short-lived Huff Puff label. The songs, attributed to the Land-slides, were little more than an extended studio vamp by the rhythm section, along with some vocalizing, presumably by Gamble and some of the musicians.

25 The recording tapes made at Sigma were mastered at Tom Steele and Wayne Wilfong's Frankford-Wayne Mastering, which originally operated out of Steele's basement. After Tarsia signed the lease for the building in which Sigma was housed, Steele and Wilfong subleased space there for their business.

26 Werner, *A Change Is Gonna Come*, 167.

27 Ibid., 104.

28 Georgie Woods bestowed Butler's "Ice Man" sobriquet on him. Woods, in his interview with the author, said he was inspired to do so because Butler was "so cool" onstage.

6. "Only the Strong Survive"

1 Butler's quote is from Butler, *Only the Strong Survive*, 155.

2 Perhaps "Only the Strong Survive" was thought to be a bit too political. As was the case with Aretha Franklin's "Respect," the advice preached in Gamble and Butler's lyric was code for the black pride and power movement. Gamble remained ambiguous about the song's lyrical intent, calling it a "message song … with a lot of meanings to it" (ibid., 156).

3 Werner's quote is from Werner, *A Change Is Gonna Come*, 118.

4 Gamble's "really need a staff" quote is from Cummings, *Sound of Philadelphia*, 97. The year 1969 was the first one in the history of the recording business that album sales equaled that of singles. The problem of racism in the music business was daunting to blacks. During the early years of Motown's existence, the wily Berry Gordy hired a white man to

head the company's marketing and distribution. Motown also kept the black faces of its artists off their own album covers so as not to inhibit retail display, particularly in the South.

5 Gamble and Huff had known the Chess brothers for some time, which helped to close the Neptune deal; Chess Records, which also sold records on its Checker and Cadet subsidiaries, was owned and operated by the Polish immigrant brothers Leonard and Phil Chess (Chez). During the first half of the 1950s, operating as a rhythm and blues label, Chess turned a steady profit. Beginning in 1955, the company scaled new heights when Chuck Berry began turning out guitar-powered teenage anthems aimed at the white rock and roll market. During the 1960s, Chess successfully cross-marketed black albums by the Dells, Ramsey Lewis, Etta James, Billy Stewart, and others.

6 Other accounts, including Petrie's, claim that Eddie O'Jay, who died in 1998, suggested the group take his name.

7 The O'Jays were no longer a neo-Drifters rhythm and blues harmony group. They had completely revamped their stage act, replacing Walter Williams's smooth tenor lead with that of the rougher-voiced Eddie Levert. In addition, the group's arrangements became gospel-infused, with the vocal line split between Levert, Williams, and Bobby Massey.

8 Levert's quote is from Cummings, *Sound of Philadelphia*, 99.

9 Marshall Chess's quote is from Cohodas, *Spinning Blues into Gold*, 289.

10 Gamble's quote is from Cummings, *Sound of Philadelphia*, 103.

11 AM radio's early prowar hits included Johnny Sea's "Day for Decision" and Sgt. Barry Sadler's "Ballad of the Green Berets" (both 1966). The more hip FM outlets broadcast music that opposed the war. But public opinion against the war began to build after the 1968 Tet Offensive. AM radio then began to program antiwar songs; Edwin Starr's "War," which became a number-one pop hit in 1970, was soul music's dominant response to the war. "There Is Someone Waiting" was rereleased in November 1969; its reappearance happened to coincide with a massive antiwar mobilization in Washington, D.C. Gamble averted any personal involvement in Vietnam when he failed his army induction physical. At the time Gamble wrote "There Is Someone Waiting Back Home," he was classified 4-F.

12 Tarsia also hired Cameo-Parkway's former general manager, the dapper Harry Chipetz, to run the emerging studio.

13 All quotes in this book by Wexler are from his interview with the author.

14 "A Brand New Me" first appeared on Butler's *Ice on Ice* album. The cover of Springfield's *Brand New Me* album indicated that it was produced by Roland Chambers and Ugene Dozier, "for Gamble-Huff Productions, Inc."

15 The *Billboard* quote is by Ed Ochs (*Billboard*, November 22, 1969); R&B and soul music accounted for only about 20 percent of total pop music sales. Because those genres continued to lag behind rock in adopting the record album as its main carrier, Gamble and Huff faced long odds with their own record company.

16 Ward's quote is from Ward, "Just My Soul Responding," 388, 389.

17 Among Neptune's releases in 1970 were the O'Jays' "Deeper in Love with You" and "Looky Looky (Look at Me Girl)." The former was one of

the best soul records of the year, while the latter, powered by Leon Huff's piano, is arguably one of the best records of the O'Jays' entire career; George's quote is from George, *Death of Rhythm and Blues*, 143.

18 Gamble's quote is from Miller, "Gamble and Huff," 30; Huff's quote is from Cummings, *Sound of Philadelphia*, 103; Neptune's final release of new material (by the Indigos) was ca. July 1970. The label's final release included the previously released O'Jays tracks "Christmas Ain't Christmas" and "Just Can't Get Enough." It was released in November 1970. Bobby Massey left the O'Jays in September 1971 to concentrate on music production.

19 Butler's quotes are from his interview with the author.

20 Bill Yale was Butler's manager at that time. Yale's "Mercury agreed to the first raise" quote originally appeared in *Blues and Soul* magazine, April 25, 1971. It was subsequently cited in Cummings, *Sound of Philadelphia*, 103. Yale's account sounds quite plausible. Gamble has been accused of periodically displaying a vexing tendency to attempt to change the terms of an agreement after its details have been finalized. Gamble's "for precisely the reason . . . never been as successful" quotes are from Riley, "Philly Sound," 34. During his interview with the author, Butler denied that there were ever any hard feelings between him and Gamble. Gamble, in his 1974 statement, left the door ajar to rapprochement with Butler, stating: "I think we could burn right now if we could get right down on something with him again. But, hey" (Riley, "Philly Sound," 34.) The split between Butler and Gamble and Huff apparently occurred during the recording of Butler's *You and Me* album. Released in 1970, the record contained only a handful of tracks produced by Gamble and Huff. Queried further about Gamble's 1974 comments, Butler laughed, then replied, somewhat cryptically, that his most recent comment on the matter was "just the truth, and history bears it out."

21 Tarsia, in his interview with the author, recalled the conversation between Pickett and Huff. Pickett's "sat in the booth" quote is from the *Pickett in Philadelphia* album jacket (Atlantic SD 8270).

22 Gamble and Huff wrote all or part of the ten songs on Springfield's album. They wrote just three of the nine tracks on Pickett's album. The songwriting team of Jerry Akines, Johnnie Bellmon, Victor Drayton, and Reginald Turner (formerly Neptune Records' R&B group known as the Corner Boys), had three of their songs (one written with Bunny Sigler) placed on Pickett's album. Sigler and Ugene Dozier had a hand in writing two of the others. The liner notes for the album state: "Produced by the staff (for Gamble-Huff Productions, Inc.)."

23 Thom Bell described Pickett as a "whirlwind" in the studio, who could not keep still and was "always up all over the place."

24 In his interview with the author, Eli recalled with a musician's pride how, right in the middle of his "real crazy fuzz-guitar solo," Pickett yelled out, "Play that guitar, son!"

25 Joe Tarsia, who presented the bill to Atlantic, said the record company was "pretty concerned" when they found out what it cost to make the album.

26 Huff's quote is from Cummings, *Sound of Philadelphia*, 109.

7. "Betcha by Golly, Wow"

1 The Delfonics' misleadingly titled *Super Hits* album was released in 1969. Aside from the group's current hit, five of the eleven tracks were either the B sides of old singles, or album tracks.

2 In his interview with the author, William Hart disputed Bell's claim about Hart's wanting to receive individual billing on the group's records. Hart claimed the idea was Stan Watson's. "I was determined that the group was called the Delfonics," insisted Hart; all of the Delfonics records on which Bell was involved bore the designation: "Produced by Stan and Bell." Only on the group's second single release ("I'm Sorry" and "You're Gone") was Bellboy Music acknowledged. William Hart's account to Marc Taylor of Bell's departure from the Delfonics was somewhat conflicted. Hart credited Bell with being "a great part of what happened. I don't think what happened would've happened if he wasn't there." In that same interview, Hart played down Bell's importance, stating that if and when Bell moved on, "all I had to do was get somebody to put the music under my songs the way I'd like it and it should carry on." However, Wilbert Hart claimed that Bell's departure "did have a big effect on us. . . . It hurt" (Taylor, *Classic Soul*, 36, 40). In William Hart's interview with the author he also claimed that he *and* Bell were responsible for producing the early Delfonics songs. Hart asserted that he "did production on each and every song we did." Yet Bell "got all the production credit." The Delfonics "didn't know anything about the music business," claimed William Hart. All they knew was that their songs "were being played on the radio. We didn't know how the pay thing went. . . . I did not know I was supposed to get production credit for sittin' all those hours with Thom Bell."

   Apparently, the Delfonics received the same treatment from Watson that Bell experienced. Wilbert Hart told Marc Taylor that although the group's hit "'Ready or Not Here I Come" crossed over . . . "big time," the Delfonics "didn't get the proper accounting for it. . . . They didn't want to tell us it was a million seller because they didn't want to pay us on a million" (ibid., 38). While undergoing several changes in group personnel, the Delfonics had a string of R&B hits during the early 1970s. But their recordings never again engendered the broad crossover appeal they had when Thom Bell called the shots for the group.

3 Warner-Seven Arts acquired Atlantic Records in 1967. The Kinney Corporation purchased Warner-Seven Arts the following year. Stax became a wholly owned subsidiary of Gulf and Western that year. The percentage figures for money-losing records are taken from Sanjek, *American Popular Music and Its Business*, 216. As the music industry came to depend more and more on the sale of black albums, independent black-oriented recording companies such as Gamble Records found it increasingly difficult to reach white consumers. Gamble Records albums were readily available in the mom-and-pop stores that traditionally serviced inner-city neighborhoods, but they were not found in the major department stores and other large white-oriented retail outlets that were serviced by rack jobbers.

4 The functions of popular culture were stated in Dwight Macdonald's landmark essay, "A Theory of Mass Culture," written in 1953. This essay was cited in Rothstein, "Damning (Yet Desiring) Mickey."

5 Cosby was the first black to gain a starring role in a network dramatic series (*I Spy*, 1965). While Wilson was castigated for his racial stereotyping, and for not being controversial enough, *The Flip Wilson Show*, in its first season, became the second-highest-rated TV program in America.

6 Gamble's quote is from Cummings, *Sound of Philadelphia*, 107.

7 The Columbia Phonograph Company was founded in 1889. The post–World War II big four included (in size order) Columbia, Decca, RCA Victor, and Capitol. Collectively, those companies accounted for almost 90 percent of the records released in 1946. In 1951, Columbia activated its long dormant rhythm and blues subsidiary, OKeh, but most black artists and their management still preferred to deal with independent black labels, who were more familiar with (and more adept at) marketing black music.

8 The expanding Warner-Seven Arts complex challenged Columbia's preeminence in the pop music business. In 1970, Elektra became part of Warner-Seven Arts, and the resulting Warner-Elektra-Atlantic complex (WEA) soon displaced Columbia as the industry's sales leader.

9 In his interview with the author, Atlantic producer Jerry Wexler said that Columbia "didn't know whether they wanted [Franklin] to be Judy Garland or Barbra Streisand. . . . I just heard this glorious voice . . . and I couldn't wait to sign her up and take her home, back to church." Franklin's stunning success on Atlantic "was most embarrassing," recalled Clive Davis (Davis, *Clive*, 169). "The explosive crossover potential of black music" quote by Davis is from ibid., 164. The "create a black marketing staff" quote is by Westbrook, as repeated in Bowman, *Soulsville*, 280. The six-month *Harvard Report* was submitted to Columbia on May 11, 1972. It found that Columbia was "perceived as an ultra-rich, ultra-white giant which has for the most part chosen to snub Blacks in the business." Clive Davis was mistakenly credited with having commissioned the *Harvard Report*. It was actually commissioned by another CBS executive. Whether Davis even saw the results of the *Harvard Report* is uncertain. He makes no reference to it in his autobiography. But judging from the date the report was received by CBS, it was not a factor in the (already completed) Philadelphia International deal. (The *Harvard Report* quotes are from Bowman, *Soulsville*, 281; for a detailed history of the report, see 279–81.)

10 The Vibrations recordings were released on Columbia's R&B subsidiary, OKeh. With the group in need of a hit, Gamble and Huff responded by writing and producing the infectious "Love in Them There Hills." Propelled by Leon Huff's classic up-tempo piano groove and Bobby Eli's guitar work, the song was one of the best dance records of the era. Hampered, perhaps, by Columbia's inept R&B promotion, the song was also a commercial disappointment. In 1969, Gamble and Huff signed the Vibrations to their own Neptune label.

Alexenburg was raised on Chicago's South Side. In 1962, he went to work for one of that city's major record distributors, where he gained valuable experience in the sales, marketing, and promotion of rhythm and blues records. In 1965, Alexenburg became Columbia's Midwest regional promotion man for the company's new Date Records subsidiary. In 1968, he moved to New York to become head of promotion for Date. Alexenburg then became assistant head of promotion, and then head of promotion, for Columbia Records itself. In May 1971, Alexenburg was made vice president of Epic Records. He and Kenny Gamble developed a close relationship that continued into the 1990s. For a brief time, Alexenburg was a consultant for Philadelphia International Records. All of the quotes by Alexenburg in this book are from his interview with the author.

11 Gamble's "was more excited" quote is from Miller, "Gamble and Huff," 30, 32.

12 Gamble's quote is from Cummings, *Sound of Philadelphia*, 107.

13 Connie Haigler, who previously worked for local R&B impresario Irv Nahan, assisted Shelton at PIR. Haigler "knew the ropes," recalled Thom Bell. "She knew the publishing inside and out." When Shelton died, Haigler assumed his duties at PIR.

14 Simon's quote is from Dahl, "Soul Serenader," 147.

15 Gamble and Huff did write and produce a follow-up single, which was not included on the Soul Survivors' *Expressway* album. But that song is so derivative of its predecessor that most people who purchased *Expressway* were not compelled to do likewise with its follow-up.

16 The *Oh My God* album was released in Europe in 1972. The quotes of Willie and Joe Chambers are from Roeser, "Chambers Brothers," 52.

17 The Stylistics group was formed in 1968 from the remnants of two other Philadelphia vocal groups, the Monarchs and the Percussions. Besides Russell Thompkins Jr., the group consisted of Airrion Love (first and second tenor), James Smith (bass), Herbie Murrell (baritone and sometimes lead), and James Dunn (baritone).

18 Airrion Love's quote is from Petrie, *Black Music*, 99.

19 Billy Jackson claims that Creed first met Bell at Jackson's house, around 1968. Creed became a staff writer for Gamble and Huff's Assorted Music. Assorted thus received one-half of the publishing royalties for any songs that she wrote. Quotes by Creed are from Pollack, *In Their Own Words*, 228. All quotes by Epstein in this book are from his interview with the author.

20 Herb Murrell's quotes are from Taylor, *Classic Soul*, 264; Airrion Love's quote is from Petrie, *Black Music*, 99; Cummings's quote is from Cummings, *Sound of Philadelphia*, 105.

21 "Betcha by Golly, Wow" reached number two on *Billboard*'s R&B chart and number three on the Hot 100 chart. Among the eight tracks contained on *The Stylistics* (Avco 33023) were the group's first five hits; Wynne's quote is from Erlewine, *All Music Guide to Rock*, 741.

22 The fifteenth Philadelphia International single release was Billy Paul's "I Wish It Were Yesterday" and "This Is Your Life" (PIR 3515), both taken from the singer's *Going East* album; Columbia's quote to Jackson was

recalled by Jackson in his interview with the author. Jackson said that Clive Davis and Ron Alexenburg gave him the instructions to go to Philadelphia.

23 Masco Young's quote is from Fried, "Day the Soul Train Crashed," 136; Kronfeld's quote is from Dannen, *Hit Men*, 88. Kronfeld later became Clive Davis's personal attorney.

24 Before going to work for Philadelphia International Records, Richardson emceed R&B shows in a small Broad Street club next to the Uptown Theater. Large in stature, Richardson was fond of wearing "Superfly" garb, right down to the ostentatious gold medallions and fur coats. Guitarist T. J. Tindall, in his interview with the author, called Richardson "Gamble's super-promo man, an amazing character who was able to get things on the radio." It would later be alleged that Richardson used more than his quirky personality to induce radio stations to play Philadelphia International's records.

8. "Love Train"

1 All of the quotes by Joiner in this book are from his interview with the author.

2 Tindall, in his interview with the author, recalled Gamble's quote. All of the quotes by Tindall in this book are from his interview with the author.

3 Pakula, in his interview with the author, recalled Huff's quote. All of Pakula's quotes are from his interview with the author.

4 Tindall, in his interview with the author, recalled Gamble and Huff's response.

5 Throughout his career, Tindall kept one foot in R&B and the other in the rock idiom from which he stemmed. He played and recorded with rock luminaries such as Bonnie Raitt.

6 Gamble and Huff used Reed's horns at least as early as the 1968 Archie Bell sessions. Reed also contracted the horns for Gamble and Huff's sessions with Jerry Butler and Wilson Pickett, among others. All of the quotes in this book by Reed are from his interview with the author.

7 One of the first sessions on which Reed used Joiner was for Cliff Nobles's "The Horse," in 1968.

8 In 1968, Genovese played on Cliff Nobles's "The Horse." He also began playing on Thom Bell's Delfonics sessions around that time. All quotes by Genovese in this book are from his interview with the author.

9 Later in his career, DeAngelis toured with Frank Sinatra and other notable singers.

10 In his interview with the author, Reed claimed that his final contracting session for Gamble and Huff involved Billy Paul's *360 Degrees* album. However, the album's liner notes credit Don Renaldo as being the horn and string contractor. In 1978, Reed returned to Philadelphia, having become the musical director for old friend Teddy Pendergrass (they're both from the same town in South Carolina) the previous year. Reed worked for Pendergrass in that capacity until 1982.

11 Renaldo was also expert on the mandolin and the lute.

12 The year 1968 seems to be about when Renaldo entered the local

recording scene. One of his earliest contracting credits for strings was for Archie Bell's sessions with Gamble and Huff that year. Reed contracted the horns those sessions. It was also in 1968 that Thom Bell asked Renaldo whether the violinist could round up some string players for one of Bell's early sessions with the Delfonics. All of the quotes in this book by Russell Faith are from his interview with the author.

13 Apparently, these highly regarded, well-paid musicians had to fight for their esteemed status. Fred Joiner, in his interview with the author, said that until the end of the 1960s, studio musicians in Philadelphia did not receive union scale, but instead were paid per song (twenty-five dollars per song, he thought). Around 1970, during a session for Gamble and Huff, one of the musicians was severely chastised for playing a wrong note. This did not sit right with Joiner, the self-described "militant" of the group, who was having "a bad day" to begin with. Joiner protested that the musician's fee of twenty-five dollars per song, "when you guys are making a million dollars, is out of the question!" He then instigated a work stoppage among the musicians, which "shut things down" for about two hours. Bobby Martin huddled with Gamble and Huff, Don Renaldo, and Joe Tarsia, who then told the musicians that, from then on, they would be paid union scale.

Considering that it sometimes took an entire day to record just one song, being paid union scale was more lucrative to the musicians than being paid for each song they recorded. Furthermore, if a musician played two instruments, according to union regulations, he or she would now receive double pay. Joiner also claimed that once Philadelphia International began to turn out the hits, "every year the rhythm section got a very big bonus—five, ten, fifteen thousand dollars."

14 Tindall, in his interview with the author, recalled this exchange.

15 The concept of recording the studio musicians as a designated "group" extended back at least to 1967–68, when two records by the "Music Makers," who were actually studio musicians, were released on Gamble Records. Gamble and Huff had also billed their rhythm section as "Family" on several records released an the Gamble and North Bay labels, ca. 1970.

16 The venerable R&B quintet the Dells had been turning out classic recordings since 1955. By 1971, the year the Dells were allegedly courted by Gamble, the group had successfully made the stylistic change from rhythm and blues to soul.

17 Melvin's quote was recalled by Wilson in his interview with the author.

18 Wilson, in his interview with the author, recalled this conversation. All of Bernard Wilson's quotes in this book are from his interview with the author.

19 Brown's "It wasn't easy" quote is from Petrie, *Black Music*, 83. Only the Blue Notes' 1964 rendering of "Get Out (and Let Me Cry)" charted.

20 It has been widely written that as senior members of the Blue Notes left the group, Harold Melvin was given the rights to the name "Blue Notes." Bernard Wilson, who eventually underwent an acrimonious split with Melvin, vehemently took exception. "Harold wasn't given shit!" exclaimed Wilson. Thom Bell agreed, maintaining that when the original Blue Notes broke up, "Harold left with nothing, so he decided

to take the name Blue Notes and still work." Ultimately, Melvin emerged as the leader of the Blue Notes and, as such, began to give himself individual billing.

21 Melvin's quotes in this paragraph are from Taylor, *Classic Soul*, 173; Thom Bell pointed out the similarities in the Dells' Marvin Junior's gruff, booming baritone and that of Pendergrass. "Now if you listen to Pendergrass, he sounds exactly like Marvin. A lot of times you can't tell the difference between the two! That's not an accident either. No, no, that's not an accident."

22 The quote by Huff is from Miller, "Gamble and Huff," 32. According to Lawrence Brown, around 1966 or 1967, Gamble approached the Blue Notes about signing with Gamble Records. Brown said the group "hadn't been very keen" on the idea because they "didn't have a very serious attitude towards recording" at the time. Since club work sustained the Blue Notes, "working with Kenny and Leon would mean a month with no pay so to speak!" (Brown's quote is from Petrie, *Black Music*, 85, 86.) But Thom Bell insisted that Gamble had tried to sign "the original guys now," members of the pre–Harold Melvin group. But "those cats just couldn't get along between themselves to save their lives," added Bell, "and they didn't want to be bothered."

23 Melvin's "decided what we were going to do" quote is from Taylor, *Classic Soul*, 173; Melvin's "We did it! We got a deal!" quote is from Pendergrass and Romanowski, *Truly Blessed*, 115; Gamble's quote was recalled by Harold Melvin in Taylor, *Classic Soul*, 173.

24 Brown's quote is from Petrie, *Black Music*, 85, 86.

25 Melvin's quotes are from Taylor, *Classic Soul*, 173.

26 The splitting of a lengthy album track such as "I Miss You" into two parts for single release became a common practice of Gamble and Huff.

27 In 2002, "If You Don't Know Me by Now" was listed as number sixty-two in *Billboard's* "Top 100 Songs of the Century."

28 Williams's "kept in touch with Gamble and Huff. . . . Those people make all the groups sound alike" quotes are from Cummings, *Sound of Philadelphia*, 112, 113; Williams's "no follow-up" quote is from Taylor, *Classic Soul*, 215, 216. The allegation that Gamble and Huff wanted to sign Levert as a solo artist appeared in ibid., 215.

29 Levert's "always felt that Kenny . . . just wanted to be the O'Jays . . . accomplish that better" quotes are from Petrie, *Black Music*, 31; Levert's "had good vibes. . . . . We knew we could go into the studio" quotes are from Dahl, "The O'Jays," 40.

30 The Epsilons backed up Arthur Conley on his 1967 hit, "Sweet Soul Music." The lyrical theme of "Back Stabbers" bore a considerable resemblance to "Smilin' Faces Sometimes," which Norman Whitfield composed for the label's R&B group, Undisputed Truth, after failing to woo the O'Jays to Motown.

31 Gamble's quote is from Miller, "Gamble and Huff"; Levert's quote is from Dahl, "The O'Jays," 40.

32 Martin and Bell "did all the major music arrangements" for Gamble and Huff, said Joe Tarsia. "It was not uncommon for Gamble to do a production where Tommy did all the string charts and Bobby Martin did all the horn charts." Bell, who arranged tracks for the Blue Notes and the

O'Jays in 1972, said that, in doing so, he never considered the lengthy, disappointing recording careers that both groups brought with them to Philadelphia International. "I approached them as brand-new groups, the same as I did with the Stylistics," he explained. "And when you get that kind of energy, when a mind hears something brand new, boy, now you've got a feasible program of working with that artist." Bell said he "looked to their strong suits and to the song. The song is the beginning, the essence, and the embryonic part. I go wherever the song takes me."

Arranging for such disparate groups as the Blue Notes and the O'Jays summoned all of Bell's considerable talents. "The O'Jays, their stuff is really totally different than the Blue Notes," he pointed out. "Instrumentally, you've got to augment certain things, add on to what Walter and William are singing" in the background. "With Pendergrass and the Blue Notes, they need a lot more air; a lot of silence back there because Pendergrass is gonna do a lot of preaching. You can't do a whole lot of preaching if you have a whole lot of music on top of it. [Not until] the time comes [do] you start bringing in other instruments to add onto what you're doing. Because if you do it too soon you'll take away from what he's doing and it's gonna sound like three minutes of yelling. So you have to study him and study the effect of what he's trying to do."

33   All of the quotes by Phil Hurtt in this book are from his interview with the author.

34   George's quote is from George, *Death of Rhythm and Blues*, 144; Gamble's quote was recalled by Eli in his interview with the author.

35   Levert's quote is from Cummings, *Sound of Philadelphia*, 114.

36   Light's quote is from Light, "Soul of the Seventies," 52.

37   Tyrell's quote is from Bowman, *Soulsville*, 311.

38   Huff's quote is a combination of his recollections from Miller, "Gamble and Huff," 32, and from Waller, "Kenny Gamble and Leon Huff," *Billboard*. Gamble's "stick basically . . . anyone could feel . . . identify with" quote is from "Gamble and Huff: The Men behind the Record Stars," 60. His "about the world as we saw it . . . we were trying to relate" quote is from Butler, *Only the Strong Survive*, 155, 156.

39   With little or no mention of Gilbert, Gamble and Huff have fostered the notion that "Me and Mrs. Jones" was written after the pair observed an affair in progress. Gilbert (now deceased) received one-third of the writer's credit for "Mrs. Jones," but various sources have contended that it was Gilbert who originally brought the core of the lyric to Gamble and Huff. It is reasonable to assume that Gamble and Huff created much, if not all, of the song's music. How much they contributed to—or altered—Gilbert's lyrics remains uncertain. Reportedly, Gilbert died an unhappy man, claiming to anyone and everyone who would listen that it was he who wrote "Me and Mrs. Jones." Carla Benson, one of Philadelphia International's backing vocalists, said in her interview for this book that Gilbert "constantly told" that to her and the other Sweethearts. Benson thought that when Gilbert died, "those probably were the last words on his lips."

40   Paul's quote is from Taylor, *Classic Soul*, 233. Over the years, Paul has espoused conflicting opinions of "Me and Mrs. Jones." In 1996, he told author Marc Taylor that when he first heard the song, he "knew it was

a hit" (ibid., 233). In 1997, Paul claimed that he initially "despised" the
song (Leo Sacks and Virginia Prescott, eds., "The Philly Sound," 9).

41 All of the quotes by Swig in this book are from his interview with the
author.

42 Gamble's "Now that we have gotten . . . sort of an outmoded concept"
quote, and the other quotes from *Jet*, are from "Gamble and Huff: The
Men behind the Record Stars," 60, 61; Gamble's "we work mainly with
black artists . . . working with pop acts" is from Cummings, *Sound of
Philadelphia*, 108.

9. "Am I Black Enough for You?"

1 The words to "Am I Black Enough for You?" begin with blacks moving
up "one by one." Then, the number increases incrementally, concluding
with "eight by eight." Gamble's "great" quote was recalled by Bell in
his interview with the author; Paul's "turn off a lot of people" quote is
from Fried, "Day the Soul Train Crashed," 138. His "was CBS's and
Kenny Gamble's" quotes are from Taylor, *Classic Soul*, 234.

2 Paul's quote is from Fried, "Day the Soul Train Crashed," 138. For all his
talk of living in peace and harmony, Gamble now strives to create
communities for blacks only. He believes that the pursuit of integration
"has cost [blacks] too much," that the integration movement "was not
well thought out, because you devastated the black community." As an
urban developer in 2003, Gamble's goal is to create a black community
whose residents are empowered to control their neighborhood's
economy and restore the mix of incomes that existed before integration.
(Gamble's quotes are from "Doing It the Old Fashioned Way.")

3 Paul's quote is from Taylor, *Classic Soul*, 234.

4 Just after the release of MFSB's first album early in 1973, Gamble and
Huff reissued Billy Paul's first two albums (with updated covers), the
O'Jays' three-year-old Neptune album, and a "Super Hits" collection of
old Intruders tracks.

5 At the time of his dismissal, Clive Davis had been wearing two hats: as
president of Columbia Records and as head of CBS Records Group,
including Columbia, Epic, and all the other labels marketed and distributed by CBS. CBS TV executive Irwin Segelstein was named to head
Columbia Records, while Goddard Lieberson became president of CBS
Records Group. After Davis was fired, CBS instituted a civil suit against
him, seeking the return of $94,000 in company money that Davis
allegedly used for private purposes. In *Hit Men*, Fredric Dannen's book
about the inner workings of the pop music business, Dannen described
Wynshaw as Davis's "personal aide and gofer par excellence."
Wynshaw, wrote Dannen, was known around the CBS offices as "Clive's
pimp," the "royal procurer," and "Dr. Feelgood." Traylor's "meticulous
records of wrongdoing" quote is from Dannen, *Hit Men*, 95.

6 That past February, the FBI linked Wynshaw to Pasquale (Patsy)
Falcone, an associate of the Genovese crime family, alleging that the two
had conspired to bilk CBS out of at least $75,000. Wynshaw then became
a cooperating witness in the FBI's heroin smuggling case against
Falcone; Rudman was alleged to have received $7,000 a week from

Columbia, to distribute among black disc jockeys and other radio station personnel in key cities to encourage airplay of the company's records.

Columbia Records' alleged involvement in payola was a topic of investigators even before Wynshaw's allegations. In October 1972, one month after Stax joined Philadelphia International in Columbia's Custom Label Department, Stax associate and alleged black Mafia member Johnny Baylor flew from Memphis to Birmingham, Alabama. Acting on a tip, FBI agents apprehended Baylor, who had in his possession $130,000 in cash. The FBI subsequently alleged that Baylor and his cohorts used cash payments, drugs, force, and intimidation to get airplay for Stax records (Bowman, *Soulsville*, 252). It was no great surprise to federal investigators, then, that Wynshaw, after completing grand jury testimony in the Falcone heroin case, implicated CBS in the practice of payola through Clive Davis's promotional agreements with Philadelphia International.

Federal investigators alerted CBS brass of Wynshaw's ties to Patsy Falcone, and in April, CBS initiated the internal audit that ultimately uncovered Wynshaw's illegal use of company funds. CBS fired Wynshaw shortly before they dismissed Davis (who claimed he was unaware of any misappropriation of company funds).

Besides payola, the FBI was then investigating other possible criminal charges against Philadelphia International. During the 1970s, what was referred to as "the black mob" controlled Philadelphia's cocaine market, a market frequented by many musicians and other entertainers. Since Philadelphia International's artists occasionally performed at functions allegedly associated with the "black mob," law-enforcement officials sought to establish whether or not a link existed between Gamble and Huff's company and drug activity (Fried, "Day the Soul Train Crashed," 134).

If there was drug use at Philadelphia International Records, it was no more prevalent than at any other record company. Weldon McDougal, who worked for Motown at that time, later claimed that drug dealers became involved in the music business "to the point where it was more important to hire a guy with a drug-related 'in' than to hire a guy with good business sense. People in the record business weren't dealin' in records; they were dealin' in drugs. So many guys were into cocaine. Kenny himself always stayed away from it. But a lot of guys around Kenny were into drugs" (McDougal's quotes are from ibid., 138). One Philadelphia International artist alleged to be struggling with a heavy drug habit at that time was singer Billy Paul (see ibid., 138).

7 In 1960, several disc jockeys in New York were convicted of taking payola. They were convicted under an untested commercial bribery statute that had been on the books since the 1930s and had not been written with broadcasting payola in mind. The most famous casualty of that episode was rock and roll pioneer Alan Freed, whose career was ruined by his conviction. For a more thorough look at the payola scandal of 1959–60, see Jackson, *Big Beat Heat*, 243–65, 268–77, and Jackson, *American Bandstand*, 171–73, 176, 177, 179, 183, 185, 188–92.

In the 1973 case, Goldstein had to choose to prosecute one party or the other. Both parties could not be prosecuted, because, in payola-related cases, the "corroboration" of one party against the other is necessary. In New York, immunity had been given to the record companies and distributors in order for them to testify against the disc jockeys. Armed (weakly) with the federal payola statute, Goldstein had the power to grant immunity from prosecution to either party for testimony against the other.

8 Bedraggled as it looked, the downtown structure was on the Philadelphia Historical Society's list of protected buildings. While the inside of the building could be renovated, the outside had to remain unchanged. Since the grimy red building blocks could not be replaced, they had to be cleaned, "so we had to steam clean a whole bunch of stuff," recalled Bell.

9 Over the years, the misconception that Thom Bell owned a piece of Philadelphia International has persisted. The misconception may have begun when Great Philadelphia Trading purchased 309 South Broad Street, after which Earl Shelton made a misleading public announcement about "the new partnership" of Gamble, Huff, and Bell that "will cover a wider spectrum of contemporary music. Not only will we record so-called soul records, but we'll go into practically all categories of contemporary music" (Shelton's statement is from Salvo and Salvo, "The Philadelphia Men (and Women) of Music," 71, 72). The "GHB" logo that appeared on the door handles at 309 South Broad Street no doubt added to the erroneous assumption that Bell owned a piece of Philadelphia International.

At the time, Gamble and Huff had four song publishing companies: Razor Sharp Music (originally Sharpe Music Company), Assorted Music, Downstairs Music, and World War 3 Music. Bell's publishing company was Bellboy Music. Gamble and Huff already derived income from Bellboy because of Linda Creed, whom the pair had under contract as a staff writer for Assorted Music. Whenever Creed and Bell wrote together, "Assorted owned half of the song and Bellboy owned half of the song," explained Bell's attorney David Steinberg in his interview with the author.

10 Huff's quote is from Cummings, *Sound of Philadelphia*, 115.

11 Pendergrass's quote is from Pendergrass and Romanowski, *Truly Blessed*, 131.

12 Pendergrass's quote is from ibid., 129. Earl Young claimed that when "The Love I Lost" was being recorded, the MFSB drummer told Gamble and Huff that he did not care for the song as a ballad, and then proceeded to increase the song's tempo himself.

13 Teddy Pendergrass, in his autobiography, claims to have written some of the lyrics to "Satisfaction Guaranteed" ("the first lyrics I ever wrote"), but Gamble and Huff took all the writing credit because Pendergrass "wasn't savvy about claiming credit or the intricacies of music publishing" (ibid., 131).

14 Gamble continued to proclaim his social consciousness, both through his songs and through his writings contained on Philadelphia International's album covers. "Kenny, aware of the black man's plight, was always looking to express his moral values in his music," said Joe Tarsia " ... [and] always tried to put a message" on his albums. Tarsia said

Gamble's messages were "absolutely" coming from the heart. Gamble's penchant for delivering such messages began early in 1973, with the Intruders' *Save the Children* album. There, Gamble urged the current generation of mankind ("the strongest and wisest") to "protect, educate and love" its children, lest it become the last generation.

15 *Ship Ahoy*'s eight tracks dealt with the social ills of greed, envy, and racism; Levert's quote is from Sacks and Prescott, eds., "The Philly Sound," 32.

16 Wynne's quote is from Erlewine, et al., *All Music Guide to Rock*, 574.

17 Bell's, Gamble's, and Huff's quotes are from Riley, "Philly Sound," 34.

18 The genesis of "TSOP" is a story in itself. *Soul Train* host and creator Don Cornelius needed a theme song for his up-and-coming dance show. Sometime in 1972, he contacted Kenny Gamble about producing it. Gamble then told Thom Bell, Leon Huff, and some of the MFSB rhythm section about Cornelius's song quest. "So the next day we all came in and wrote about four or five songs right on the spot!" said Bell. Bobby Eli's recollection was that "everyone in the rhythm section submitted songs to be used that we thought were pretty good. And the one that was chosen was the one that Gamble and Huff wrote." Bell and Bobby Martin added strings and horns, and "Gambs put the Three Degrees on it," said Bell.

     Gamble and Cornelius agreed that the song chosen to be the *Soul Train* theme was to be used exclusively for that purpose. Beginning in November 1973, *Soul Train*'s new theme was heard by the show's national audience at the beginning and at the end of each episode of the show. After the tune took on a life of its own, Gamble told Cornelius it was silly to hold back the release of a surefire hit record. Cornelius agreed, but told Gamble that he could not use the name *Soul Train* in its title. It was then that Gamble decided to call the song "TSOP" and hastily added it to MFSB's forthcoming album.

19 Gamble's quote is from Cummings, *Sound of Philadelphia*, 137.

20 Gamble's quote is from ibid., 127.

10. "I'll Be Around"

1 Female background singers had already been employed on many of the early tracks that Gamble, Huff, and Bell cut at Sigma Sound, including those of Archie Bell, Jerry Butler, Wilson Pickett, and Dusty Springfield. Although not certain, Thom Bell thought perhaps it was the Sweet Inspirations (Cissy Houston, who left the group in 1970, Estelle Brown, Sylvia Shemwell, and Myrna Smith) who sang on some of those recordings. Bobby Eli said the female voices heard on Jerry Butler's two albums recorded in Philadelphia for Mercury Records, and on other early Gamble and Huff productions, belonged to Mikki Farrow and Jean and Tina Thomas, a trio whom Leon Huff knew from Camden.

2 Bell, in his interviews with the author, recalled Ingram's reply.

3 All quotes in this book by Benson and Benton are from their interviews with the author.

4 Benson and Benton, in their interviews with the author, recalled Huff's quotes.

5 "I'm Stone in Love with You" reached number four on *Billboard*'s R&B chart and number ten on the Hot 100.

6 Bell's quote is from Petrie, *Black Music*, 44.

7 At the time the group took the name "Spinners," Smith's Cadillac had giant chrome hubcaps called "spinners."

8 "It's a Shame," written and produced by Stevie Wonder, reached *Billboard*'s R&B Top 5 and the top 20 of the Hot 100.

9 Those four tracks can be heard on the 1995 compact disc reissue of the Spinners' *Mighty Love* album (Atlantic/Rhino R2 71586).

10 "That's What Girls Are Made For" contained what Bell called a "strictly jazz-bebop chord, which is very strange for a group to sing. It was one you just didn't hear in rock and roll."

11 Bell's quote is from Sacks, "A Mighty Love" (liner notes).

12 The other two Spinners songs recorded by Bell during his first session with the group were "Could It Be I'm Falling in Love" and "Just You and Me Baby." "I'll Be Around" had a thudding mid-tempo rhythm, which, noted Tony Cummings, the industry dubbed "the Thom Bell beat." This rhythm became one of 1970s soul's most influential sounds (Cummings, *Sound of Philadelphia*, 115); "How Could I Let You Get Away" was such a quality song that it is still regarded as one of the Spinners' hits.

13 Bell's account of his experience with New York City does not jibe with that of the group's lead singer, Tim McQueen, who claimed that when the group went into Sigma Sound to overdub their vocals, "the session was so easy, so relaxed, everyone just mellowed out down there" (ibid., 124).

14 Bell's "He has a fantastic voice, man" quote is from Petrie, *Black Music*, 44. Bell's remaining quotes in this paragraph are from his interview with the author.

15 Mathis's quote is from Carpenter, "How Johnny Mathis Keeps," 24.

16 A second single from the *I'm Coming Home* album, "A Baby's Born," did even worse, failing to make *Billboard*'s Top 100 late in the year.

17 One song of particular interest on the Mathis album was "Life Is a Song Worth Singing." Released as a single that fall, it was a modest hit, but in 1978, Teddy Pendergrass recorded the song for his album of the same title. That album became one of Philadelphia International's all-time best sellers; Mathis's "one of the best albums" and "the person who instigated the record" quotes are from Carpenter, "How Johnny Mathis Keeps," 24. Mathis and Bell teamed up again for the singer's 1977 *Mathis Is* album.

18 All quotes by Jefferson in this book are from his interview with the author.

19 Like Linda Creed, Jefferson was signed to Assorted Music, which meant that Gamble and Huff received half of the publishing on anything he wrote for that company.

20 Love's quote is from Cummings, *Sound of Philadelphia*, 123.

21 Creed's quote is from Pollack, *In Their Own Words*, 230. Creed said that her writing "changed completely" after she got married. "For some reason it made me very creative." Creed added that she had always been

"basically a happy person, but before I got married I was writing sad tunes" (ibid., 230).

22 Bell, in his interview with the author, recalled Creed's quote.

23 When Bell recalled this particular incident, he revealed how Creed "used to do that nonsense all the time to try to get those lyrics over" on him.

24 Bell said that he first had the idea to move Love to the forefront of the group during the time that "You Are Everything" was recorded. The record label for "Let's Put It All together" stated: "The Stylistics, Featuring Airrion Love and Russell Thompkins, Jr."

25 "You Make Me Feel Brand New" was hastily added to the group's forth-coming album, which was produced by Hugo and Luigi. This created the misconception that Bell produced the entire album.

26 Love's quote is from Petrie, *Black Music*, 96. The Stylistics did not miss the songs and productions of Thom Bell very much at first; the group's initial post-Bell album was the biggest of their entire career. But that album, and future Stylistics albums (which were all recorded in New York City), educed a pattern of aloof, overproduced triviality. The public seemed to accept this insipid sentimentality for a time, and the Stylistics enjoyed several big hits. But the group soon disappeared permanently from the charts.

27 During the time that Bell wrote with Creed, only one or two of their songs appeared on each of the five Spinners albums produced by Bell. Of that total of seven songs, only four of them charted. The most successful of them all was "The Rubberband Man," from the group's *Happiness Is Being with the Spinners* album (1975).

28 Joe Jefferson, in his interview with the author, recalled Gamble's quote.

29 Jefferson, in his interview with the author, recalled his conversation with Simmons.

30 Gallagher, in his interview with the author, recalled Bell's "Never have a hit record" quote. Bell's new rhythm section consisted of his younger brother Tony, Don Murray, and Bobby Eli on guitar; Andrew Smith on drums; and Bob Babbitt, formerly with Motown's renowned Funk Brothers, on bass. "Then Came You" was written with the second song-writing team under contract to Bell, Sherman Marshall and Philip Pugh.

31 Bell's "made a face ... she didn't like it much ... there was an apology on it" quotes are from Rees and Crampton, *Encyclopedia of Rock Stars*, 808. Although a duet album by Warwick and the Spinners was discussed, it never materialized.

32 Gallagher, in his interview with the author, recalled all of Bell's quotes pertaining to the recording of "Sadie."

11. "TSOP (The Sound of Philadelphia)"

1 In France, during World War II, the French words *disque* (record) and *bibliothèque* (library) were joined to describe the "record libraries" of wartime Paris. One of the first American discotheques, Le Club, opened in Manhattan on New Year's Eve, 1963 (see Andriote, *Hot Stuff*, 15). The fervent dance activity of the early 1970s was firmly entrenched well before the media and entertainment moguls got around to codifying it as "disco." By 1972, to pull people onto the dance floor, club deejays sought

out up-tempo dance records, as well as records with extended instrumental improvisations. Pioneering club disc jockey Francis Grasso has been credited with first mixing records together, in 1968, at a Manhattan club. Later on, Grasso developed the technique of matching the beats of different records in order to keep two songs playing simultaneously for as long as possible.

2 Huff's quotes are from Palmer, *Rock and Roll*, 25

3 Huff's "giving people a beat they like" quote is from Wickham, "Blacks in the Record Industry," 39; his complete "house on fire" quote is: "Yeah, there's a house on fire in those records" (Palmer, *Rock and Roll*, 257); Gamble's "heading the discotheque boom" quote is from Cummings, *Sound of Philadelphia*, 137; his "funky dance records . . . dictated the beat" quote is from Palmer, *Rock and Roll*, 257. Unlike Gamble and Huff, Thom Bell was quite comfortable with disco. "It helped to create something brand new," he recalled. "One of a Kind Love Affair" was one example of how the disco phenomenon influenced Bell's music. Club disc jockeys "would take those drums and overdub them four or five times and go in and start dancing to the stuff," said Bell. As a result, Bell became "subconsciously involved" in the disco movement, "not purposely doing it as such, but doing it because you love doing what you do. Now, if you want to give it a [disco] label, that won't hurt my feelings."

4 Pendergrass's "perhaps the first disco hit" quote is from Pendergrass and Romanowski, *Truly Blessed*, 130.

5 Marsh, *Heart of Rock and Soul*, 264.

6 In 1974, record companies began to release twelve-inch vinyl singles specifically designed for deejays to play in clubs. These discs included extra verses and longer instrumental breaks for maximum effect on the dance floor. In some cases they also included a regular mix and a disco mix of a particular song.

   The first hit song that was specifically recorded for the disco market is uncertain. One contender is the elaborately orchestrated, Barry White–produced "Love's Theme," which was recorded by the Love Unlimited Orchestra. "Love's Theme" became a million-selling number-one hit early in 1974. Besides Gamble, Huff, and Bell, it was White who perfected the stirring synthesis of soulful R&B grooves accompanied by the sounds of an entire orchestra (see Andriote, *Hot Stuff*, 11). Others cite Gloria Gaynor's "Never Can Say Goodbye" as the first record produced expressly for the new disco market (see Haskins and Stifle, *Donna Summer*). Gamble's "were bound to get . . . what goes around" quote is from Cummings, *Sound of Philadelphia*, 138.

7 Murrell's quote is from Taylor, *Classic Soul*, 269.

8 *Pick of the Litter*, the most successful of the four Bell-produced Spinners albums, was made available to eager consumers in the spring of 1975. The album's showcase was the lead single, the bouncy Simmons, Jefferson, and Hawes–penned "They Just Can't Stop It (the Games People Play)." On this song, which became the group's fifth million-seller, all five Spinners got a chance to sing lead.

9 The conversation between Gamble and Tarsia was recalled by Jim Gallagher in his interview. The anecdote concerning the old Cameo-Parkway studio, and Gamble and Huff's words were recalled by Bell.

Tarsia installed the latest equipment in Philadelphia International's tiny recording facility, which became Sigma Studio 4. (Sigma 1 was the original Reco-Art room at 212 North Twelfth Street; Sigma 2 was the downstairs room in that same building; and Sigma 3 was a tiny music editing and voice-over room in the same building. In 1976, Tarsia opened a Sigma branch in New York City.)

10 Gallagher claimed that the Blue Notes studio lineup often consisted of Pendergrass, Gamble, Carl Helm, "and sometimes, one of the Blue Notes." Sigler claimed the background singers on "If You Don't Know Me by Now" and some other Blue Notes songs were he, Kenny, and Huff; Pendergrass's quote is from Pendergrass and Romanowski, *Truly Blessed*, 131.

11 MFSB's *Universal Love* album did contain a noteworthy track, "K-Jee," which was largely an extemporaneous jam by Leon Huff. As MFSB got set to record the album, "the organ was sitting there, on and miked, and not being played," recalled Jim Gallagher, the assistant engineer for the session. Suddenly, Huff appeared, "literally as we hit the red button and the track began." Huff had not heard the song before. He listened for about a minute, and then walked into the studio and sat down at the organ, "right in the middle of the take," continued Gallagher. When the song reached a certain point, Huff joined in and played off the cuff for the rest of the tune. It was "a killer track!" exclaimed Gallagher. In 1978, "K-Jee" was included in the movie soundtrack to *Saturday Night Fever*, the only Philadelphia International track to have that distinction.

12 Barrett began his career as the leader of a 1950s teenage rhythm and blues vocal group. He is also said to have discovered the legendary R&B group Frankie Lymon and the Teenagers. In the late '50s and early '60s, Barrett recorded on his own for several labels. He also became a record producer.

13 The "black Barbie Dolls" phrase was mentioned in Cummings, *Sound of Philadelphia*, 125; Sheila Ferguson agreed with that characterization. The Three Degrees were "as soulful as white people could handle at the time," she explained. "That was the way the white world perceived blackness—glitzy, slick, feminine and smooth" (O'Brien, *She Bop*, 284). Ferguson's quote about Gamble is from ibid., 285; Pinkney's "very excited" quote is from Cummings, *Sound of Philadelphia*, 125; her "very creative" quote is from Taylor, *Classic Soul*, 279; Bobby Eli, who, for a time, was the Three Degrees' road guitar player and conductor, said that the relationship between Gamble and Barrett was so inimical that it was "hard to really figure out who did what, if anybody did anything" to the other.

14 "TSOP" won a Grammy Award for Best R&B Instrumental Performance of the Year. The artist credit for the song stated: "MFSB (featuring the Three Degrees)." Despite their recording success, the Three Degrees apparently never saw much money from Philadelphia International. Sheila Ferguson remarked that the group would take the bows "and the record company would take the money" (O'Brien, *She Bop*, 285).

15 Davis's quote is from Davis, *Clive*, 335. Gamble's quote is from Cummings, *Sound of Philadelphia*, 131.

16 Pruter's quote is from Pruter, "When Soul Music Lost Its Soul," 170.

17   Gamble and Huff's quote was recalled by Brunson in his interview with the author. All of the quotes by Brunson in this book are from his interview with the author.

18   The original People's Choice lineup consisted of Brunson, Roger Andrews (bass), Dave Thompson (drums), Stanley Burton (guitar), and Leon Lee (congas). Guy Fiske eventually replaced Burton, and by the time the group signed with Philadelphia International, Lee had been replaced by Darnell Jordan and Daniel Ford was added to the group.

19   By the mid-'70s, Philadelphia International employed about 150 persons and grossed about $25 to $30 million a year (Fried, "Day the Soul Train Crashed," 116, 117).

20   Huff's quote is from Miller, "Gamble and Huff," 34.

21   Sharp's quotes are from Russi, "Dee Dee Sharp," 27. In retrospect, Thom Bell's reluctance to introduce Gamble and Sharp appears prescient. Joe Tarsia claimed that Sharp was "a person who needed constant attention." She "used to call [the studio] constantly, and Gamble used to pick up the phone and say, 'I'll see you when I get there!'" (That expression became so popular that Lou Rawls recorded a song with that title, written by Gamble and Huff.)

22   Sharp's quotes are from ibid., 27. The "other woman" in Gamble's life was Harlem-born and -raised Dyana Williams, who, while in college, decided to become a disc jockey. Williams subsequently built strong radio followings, first in Washington, D.C., then in New York, and, finally, in Philadelphia. At various stages in her career, Williams also worked as a journalist, a media coach, a television producer, and a business executive. She is the co-founder (and former president) of the International Association of African-American Music (IAAAM), an organization dedicated to the preservation and promotion of black music worldwide. It was during Williams's tenure as a disc jockey that she met Gamble. "They were together for the longest while," said Thom Bell. (The couple had three children together.) But Gamble "wasn't really lookin' for a woman who was a worker." And, he exclaimed, Williams was "a hustlin' mama, boy!"

23   Tarsia said Gamble "really struggled, really searched, for a long time about what [religion] he was." Bobby Martin, who became a Jehovah's Witness in 1976, after learning about the religion from Gamble's mother, recalled that Gamble, prior to his breakdown, was "studying the Bible" (a copy of which he kept on the mantelpiece in his office). Instead, Gamble "became a Moslem," added Martin. But not before the intellectual-minded Gamble formulated what Joe Tarsia described as the producer's own "universal concept" religion. According to Tarsia, Gamble even had a ring made that bore a crucifix and a Jewish star, and when the Pope visited Philadelphia in the late 1980s, Gamble flew a flag with markings similar to those on his ring from the Philadelphia International building. Gamble "doesn't take [Islam] lightly," said Tarsia. "It's a deep part of his life."

24   McFadden's quote is from Fried, "Day the Soul Train Crashed," 144; Gamble's "disciple" quote was recalled by Bell, in his interview with the author; John Bandy died in the late 1990s.

25   Bell claimed that he sought to keep Philadelphia International func-

tioning, because "Huff couldn't do it. Huff is a real nice guy [but] he didn't have the personality." Philadelphia International's lone album release during that period was by Bunny Sigler, a collection that contained only three new tracks, all produced by Sigler.

12. "Wake Up Everybody"

1 Members of the Trammps included Jimmy Ellis, who had sung lead in the Exceptions, of which Young had been a member, along with members of the now-defunct Volcanoes. Young said that he wanted a group name that "people would always remember." Thinking that people would remember a name with a negative connotation "more than [a] good" one Young came up with Tramps, to which he added another "m" "and went on from there." (On the group's first record, they were listed as "the Tramps.")

2 "The creative genius" quote appeared on MFSB's self-titled debut album (Philadelphia International 32046) early in 1973. The studio musicians who recorded under the MFSB name received a session fee and artist's royalties on any MFSB's record sales. In his interview with the author of this book, Lenny Pakula claimed that he was misled (by Earl Shelton, not Gamble or Huff) into thinking that if he signed a contract to record as a member of MFSB, doing so would preclude him from recording for anybody else. Pakula also claimed that because of that misunderstanding, he did not sign such a contract and never received any money for his recordings with MFSB. Martin's "the musicians began to think" quote is from McClosky, "Bobby Martin."

3 Baker, Harris, and Young's office was located at 12th and Arch Streets, in what Weldon McDougal described as a "little rinky-dink building."

4 First Choice, originally known as the Debronettes, consisted of Rochelle Fleming, Annette Guest, and Joyce Jones.

5 Most of the tracks contained on *Disco Champs* (Philadelphia International 34728) originally appeared on the Trammps Golden Fleece album (33163) released early in 1975. That album itself was a collection of previously released singles.

6 Taylor owned Ric-Tic Records, for which Edwin Starr recorded. Ric-Tic's artists went to Motown when Taylor sold the label to Berry Gordy.

7 Gamble and Huff's "Hey man, you don't want to be an artist" quote was recalled by McDougal in his interview with the author.

8 In 1974, Sigler also teamed up with Norman Harris to produce a series of recordings for the Whispers R&B vocal group. The following year, Sigler produced some tracks on Carl Carlton, who was backed up by Instant Funk.

9 As a "Young Professional," Hurtt discovered the female R&B group Sister Sledge and recommended that Atlantic sign them.

10 Among Eli's biggest commercial successes was "Just Don't Want to Be Lonely," which was originally recorded in 1973 by Ronnie Dyson. Later that year, the Main Ingredient recorded a million-selling version of the song.

11 *United States v. Kenneth Gamble et al.*, Case No. 373 (1975), U.S. District Court, Eastern District of Pennsylvania. Project Sound indictments

unrelated to Gamble and Huff included those of Clive Davis, then president of Arista Records (for income-tax evasion), and David Wynshaw and Pasquale Falconio (for defrauding CBS). Also named were Brunswick Record Corp. and its president, Nat Tarnopol (alleged payola involvement), and WAOK-AM programming director Paul Burke Johnson (for alleged perjury after he denied receiving payola from Gamble). The "in order to meet with and pay" quote is from Schumach, "Payola Indictment"; Huff's quote is from Miller, "Gamble and Huff," 34.

12 The "astonished . . . most graphic paper trail . . . got a check, they cashed it . . . had lists" quotes are from Dannen, *Hit Men*, 103, 104.

13 All of the quotes in this book by David Steinberg are from his interview with the author. Jefferson recalled Gamble's quote in his interview with the author.

14 "Kenny looked to be on the board of directors," maintained Tarsia, in his interview with the author. When Gamble and Huff struck a distribution deal with Capitol-EMI in 1980, they also leased the marketing rights to the post-1975 Philadelphia International masters to them. Thus, the legendary Philadelphia International catalog, up to 1976, is presently controlled by Sony (who purchased CBS Records), while the post-1975 catalog is controlled by Capitol-EMI. During the 1980s, said Steinberg, Gamble and Huff "took [the publishing] over themselves and kept it that way until the sale of the whole ball of wax to Warner-Chappell" Music in the 1990s.

15 George's quotes are from George, *Death of Rhythm and Blues*, 145. Gamble first exhibited the practice of including written messages on his albums with the release of the Intruders' *Save the Children* album in 1973, at which time he railed against child abuse: "Animals, lower forms of life, treat their children better than man" (Gamble LP 31991). Gamble's "evil plan" quote is from the liner notes to PIR LP 33807) which was released about the time that Gamble converted to Islam. His "be fruitful and multiply" quote is from the liner notes to PIR LP 33843. His "Universal Community of Truth" quote is from Billy Paul's *Let 'Em In* album (PIR 34389); his "level of Universal Awareness" quote is from Teddy Pendergrass's *Life Is a Song Worth Singing* album (PIR 35095).

13. "Philadelphia Freedom"

1 The do-it-yourselfer was William DeVaughn, whose "Be Thankful for What You Got" reached number four on *Billboard*'s Hot 100 during the early summer of 1974. Chicago studio musicians and singers (dubbed the Soul Train Gang) recorded a new theme called "Soul Train '75," which replaced MFSB's theme for Cornelius's TV program. In 1976, the second Soul Train Gang album (Soul Train LP BVL1–1844), from which the quote in the text was taken, contained an updated version of the *Soul Train* theme.

2 All the quotes by Collins in this book are from his interview with the author.

3 All of the quotes by Biggs in this book are from her interview with the author.

4 Wansel's quote is from Miller, "Gamble and Huff," 34. One of his earliest efforts on the Moog synthesizer was for Major Harris's 1975 *Jealousy* album, produced by Baker, Harris, and Young.

5 Biggs sometimes co-wrote for the gospel group with another former member, Bruce Hawes. Ted Wortham and the original members of the female trio First Choice were also members of the group.

6 The gospel group, pared down to six workable voices, recorded an album called *City Limits* for Philadelphia International. At Philadelphia International, Biggs did some writing with Bruce Hawes. The two wrote "Love Has No Time or Place," which, in 1975, became her first song to be recorded (by MFSB).

7 McFadden and Whitehead, in addition to their other tasks at Philadelphia International, continued to record as part of the quartet Talk of the Town until 1975. One of the biggest hits they wrote was the Intruders' "I'll Always Love My Mama." McFadden, Whitehead, and Carstarphen had their greatest success with Harold Melvin and the Blue Notes, for whom the trio wrote "Bad Luck," "Where Are All My Friends," and "Wake Up Everybody." With Bobby Martin, they wrote the Blue Notes' "Tell the World How I Feel about 'Cha Baby."

8 Thom Bell, too, recognized Jack Faith's musical proficiency. Faith played alto saxophone and flute on the Stylistics' albums.

9 Rawls's initial album for Philadelphia International was recorded early in 1976. Gamble produced four tracks on it. From the time of Gamble's absence until that album was released—almost a year—Gamble had produced only four albums. They were the O'Jays' *Family Reunion* (released September '75), the Blue Notes' *Wake Up Everybody* (September '75), Billy Paul's *When Love Is New* (November '75), five tracks co-produced with Jack Faith on MFSB's *Philadelphia Freedom* (November '75), and Lou Rawls's *All Things in Time* (March '76).

10 During the first payola scandal, in 1960, the New York City district attorney granted immunity to the record manufacturers and distributors who tendered the bribes, in order for them to testify against the disc jockeys who took the bribes.

　　The federal government's case against influential black disc jockey Frankie Crocker (then program director for the powerful WBLS-FM in New York) demonstrates the difficulty prosecutors had in corroborating bribery charges against Philadelphia International. The government alleged that, in December 1973, Harry Coombs gave Crocker $400 in payola, so as to have Philadelphia International records played on WBLS. Crocker, under oath, denied that the money was a form of payola. The government subsequently indicted Crocker for giving false testimony. He was convicted of that charge, but the conviction was ultimately overturned in appeals court.

11 The "in which he admitted that he had made gifts" and "to get more airplay for his releases" quotes are from Sanjek, *Pennies from Heaven*, 557. According to Bell, the suit transaction to which Gamble pleaded guilty occurred when the mother of a Texas disc jockey whom Gamble had befriended died. The jock did not have a suit to wear to the funeral. Bell claimed that when Gamble learned of the situation he went to Ben Krass and bought a suit and sent it to the bereaved disc jockey. The

government then "traced the receipt" for the suit back to Krass and connected it to Gamble.

Just days after Gamble's plea, five record company executives of the Brunswick and Dakar Record Corporation were convicted on conspiracy and fraud charges and were fined and sentenced to jail. All of those verdicts were eventually overturned by a court of appeals. Those reversals did not necessarily indicate that payola did not change hands, only that proving in a court of law that it did occur was difficult, if not impossible. Clive Davis was charged with six counts of income tax evasion and was found guilty on one of those counts. His conviction, too, was overturned on appeal. Davis was never charged in any payola matters.

12 For a brief history of payola in the pop music business see Jackson, *Big Beat Heat*, 244, 245. George's quote is from George, *Death of Rhythm and Blues*, 165; Sanjek's quote is from Sanjek, *Pennies from Heaven*, 558; Freed's quote is from Wilson, "Alan Freed's Story."

13 Hall's quote is from Fried, "Day the Soul Train Crashed," 119, 134.

14 Swig's quote is from his interview with the author. In that interview, Swig said he left the music business in 1978, because it was "totally out of control. . . . Success contaminated the whole process. You went from selling a million black singles to a million black albums, [which] changed the whole dynamic" and brought a "corporate greed factor" into the mix.

15 Gamble and Huff were able to retain the original MFSB string and horn sections, as well as the perennial background singers, the Sigma Sweethearts. But only Bobby Eli, Roland Chambers, Larry Washington, and (on a part-time basis) T. J. Tindall remained from the original rhythm section.

16 Wansel's name can be found, in one capacity or another, on approximately thirty gold and platinum albums.

17 After Paul's 1979 album *First Class* failed to chart, he left Philadelphia International.

18 The People's Choice left Philadelphia International in 1978. In 1980, the group had a minor R&B hit on Casablanca.

19 Sigler, in his interview with the author, recalled Bell's "couldn't make the money" quote.

20 Pendergrass's quote is from Pendergrass and Romanowski, *Truly Blessed*, 132.

21 Pendergrass's quotes in this paragraph are from ibid., 115, 116, and Smith, *Off the Record*, 321, 322.

22 Pendergrass's quotes are from Pendergrass and Romanowski, *Truly Blessed*, 132, 140; Melvin's quotes are from Taylor, *Classic Soul*, 177, 178.

23 Pendergrass's quotes in this paragraph are from Pendergrass and Romanowski, *Truly Blessed*, 133, and Smith, *Off the Record*, 322.

24 Pendergrass's quotes in this paragraph are from Smith, *Off the Record*, 322. Pendergrass claimed that Melvin had been cheating the Blue Notes out of money, "thousands of dollars that Gamble and Huff had given to Harold in a check with the understanding that he would cash it and split it equally among the group" (Pendergrass and Romanowki, *Truly Blessed*, 145). More than one source, each wishing to remain anonymous, told the author of this book that Melvin had, indeed, been stealing

money from the Blue Notes for many years. "We had an issue with money, and we let Harold go," Bernard Wilson said in his interview with author. "We fired his ass!" One aspect of Pendergrass's departure from the Blue Notes remains murky. He wrote in his autobiography that the decision to leave the group was not his alone, that "the people [he] was involved with convinced [him] it was time to go" (Smith, *Off the Record*, 322). Pendergrass currently will not discuss anything pertaining to Gamble and Huff, claiming that he is owed millions of dollars in royalties by Philadelphia International.

25 Gamble's "C'mon, man" quote and Pendergrass's quote are from Pendergrass and Romanowski, *Truly Blessed*, 147, 154.

26 Harold Melvin claimed that it was his decision to leave Philadelphia International, that he did not "want any arguments between Gamble and Teddy, and Gamble and me.... I walked out on a lot of money but I'm happy" (Melvin's quotes are from Taylor, *Classic Soul*, 179). Wilson and Lawrence Brown reunited with Lloyd Parkes and former lead singer John Atkins as the Blue Notes and recorded a little-noticed album called *Truth Has Come to Light* for the Florida-based Glades label. Harold Melvin, employing lead singer David Ebo, whom he had discovered at a South Philadelphia bar, formed his own set of Blue Notes. "We went to court for a while on [who owned the Blue Notes' name], but the judge said you both can use it,'" Bernard Wilson told the author of this book. Neither group of Blue Notes ever had another significant hit record

27 Pendergrass's quote is from Pendergrass and Romanowski, *Truly Blessed*, 159.

28 After *A Natural Man*, Rawls released three additional albums on MGM, one on Bell in 1974, and one on Polydor in 1976, none of which charted.

29 Gamble's quote is from Miller, "Gamble and Huff," 36. McDougal, in his interview with the author, recalled the conversation between him and Rawls. All of the quotes by Rawls are from his interview with the author.

30 Rawls recalled "workin' mainly with Leon and Kenny" on the album. Of the album's nine tracks, four were produced by Gamble and Huff, two by Bunny Sigler, and one each by Jack Faith, Dexter Wansel, and Bobby Martin. Still Gamble and Huff's premier arranger, Martin arranged five of the album's songs, Richard Rome arranged two, and Faith and Wansel each arranged one. Both of the singles released from the album, "You'll Never Find" and "Groovy People," were written and produced by Gamble and Huff and arranged by Martin.

31 Collins's quotes are from his interview with the author.

32 Martin's quote is from McCloskey, "Bobby Martin."

33 The other two platinum albums were the O'Jays' *Ship Ahoy* and *Family Reunion*.

34 Structurally, *Unmistakably Lou* bore a sharp similarity to *All Things in Time*. Using the same musicians, Gamble and Huff wrote and produced six of the album's nine tracks. The "filler" was written by Jack Faith, Phil Terry, and Dexter Wansel, and produced by Faith, Wansel, and Bobby Martin. Arrangements were split between Martin and Faith.

35 Gamble's quotes are from Miller, "Gamble and Huff," 36.

36 Jackson's quotes are from Jackson, *Moonwalk*, 122.

37 Gamble's quotes are from Miller, "Gamble and Huff," 36.

38 Jackson's quotes are from Jackson, *Moonwalk*, 123, 126. The two demos were for "Blues Away," one of the first songs written by Michael, and "Style of Life," written by Michael and Tito.

39 Jackson's quotes are from Jackson, *Moonwalk*, 123, 126.

40 Gamble's quote is from Miller, "Gamble and Huff," 36.

41 Jackson's quotes are from Jackson, *Moonwalk*, 127.

14. "Kiss and Say Goodbye"

1 In 1977, the pop music industry had estimated pretax losses of over $208 million. That same year, sales of black music represented approximately two-thirds of the industry's $3.5 billion retail gross (Sanjek, *American Popular Music and Its Business*, 238). There were other problems, some caused by the music industry itself. Chief among them was a 100 percent album return by the manufacturers, which meant that distributors (and retailers) could order merchandise in quantity and return at no cost to them whatever did not sell. By the late 1970s, the industry-wide return rate was about 40 percent (ibid., 237). In addition, hit albums were heavily bootlegged.

2 One of Philadelphia International's most important creative links to the past was guitarist Bobby Eli, who, despite his own production activities, continued to play on sessions for Gamble and Huff. Roland Chambers also continued to play guitar on sessions for Gamble and Huff. After an opportunistic start as a producer with Gamble and Huff, Chambers, as did his brother, Karl, succumbed to a life of drug abuse and eschewed most positions of responsibility, drifting into the periphery of Philadelphia International. Roland and Karl "were always doin' them drugs," said Thom Bell in his interview with the author. Charles Collins remembered Roland Chambers as "flighty" and said that "everybody always waited" for him. One time after Roland appeared late, he was asked why. Charles Collins recalled with a laugh how, "in front of everybody, Roland said, 'I was dealin' with time and with a lot of crazy people!'" Needless to say, Kenny Gamble cut his old neighborhood pal quite a bit of slack. Bobby Eli said that despite Roland's "tendency to show up late a lot," he remained with Gamble and Huff "the whole time." Another creative link to Philadelphia International's past was former Intruder Phil Terry, who worked there as a songwriter and producer.

3 Creed's quote is from Pollack, *In Their Own Words*, 230. All of the quotes by Epstein in this book are from his interview with the author.

4 Bell claimed that Creed "hated" "The Rubberband Man" so much that she did not want her name to appear on it as a writer. When the song became a huge hit, "she started liking it then," he laughed. "But it never really became one of her favorites."

5 Creed and Bell also wrote for Johnny Mathis, Dionne Warwick, and Ronnie Dyson, among others.

6 Initially, half of the songwriting royalties of any Creed-Bell songs went to Gamble and Huff's Assorted Music, to which Creed was signed as a writer, and the other half went to Bell's company, Bellboy Music.

Gamble, Huff, and Bell eventually formed the three-way partnership called Mighty Three Music, which absorbed Assorted and Bellboy.

7 In California, Creed started her own publishing company. She continued to write songs and dabbled in production. In 1977, Creed learned she had breast cancer. She returned to Philadelphia in 1979 to be closer to her family as she struggled with her disease. She continued to write and composed the lyrics to the Teddy Pendergrass–Whitney Houston duet "Hold Me" and to Houston's "Greatest Love of All." In April 1986, as "Greatest Love of All" reached number five on its way to the top of the pop charts, Creed succumbed to her cancer.

8 Bell first moved to Lakewood, Washington. In 1979, he moved to Seattle.

9 Bell did his Seattle recording at the Kaye-Smith studio, which had been owned by actor Danny Kaye and singer Kate Smith. In 1979, Leroy Bell and Casey James would write and perform the million-selling hit, "Livin' It Up (Friday Night)."

10 Not everybody saw the hit coming. Bobby Eli, who introduced a country-flavored guitar figure at the very beginning of "Kiss and Say Goodbye," told how bassist Ronnie Baker "got up and laughed and took his music paper and made believe it was toilet paper. Ronnie said, 'Man, you can take this and wipe your butt with it! That's country stuff; that'll never make it!'"

11 When Martin got to Los Angeles he signed on as a producer-arranger with A&M Records, where he began producing the R&B group LTD. In 1980, as Martin had vowed, he quit his job. "I haven't been in the record business since then," he said in his interview with the author. Martin learned the Chinese language and "started working with the Chinese congregations of Jehovah's Witnesses." He and his wife eventually moved to Washington State, where they continued their missionary work.

12 Martin's "stuck with Kenny for years . . . enough to run you into bad health" quote is from McCloskey, "Bobby Martin."

13 Martin's "too long in one place . . . stagnant . . . none of them lived up to . . . looking for the light . . . like a human being" quotes are from ibid.

14 McFadden's quotes are from Fried, "Day the Soul Train Crashed," 143.

15 Pendergrass's quotes are from Pendergrass, and Romanowski, *Truly Blessed*, 119, 120.

16 This anecdote, and Tarsia's words, was recalled by Gallagher. Sigma Sound got a lot of mileage out of Tarsia's reconstructed tape. "We all used it in a lot of mixes from that day on," said Gallagher. "We did a lot of creative things with it and no one could figure out how we were doin' it. We used it until synthesizers became a lot more sophisticated and we didn't need it anymore."

17 Pendergrass's quote is from Pendergrass and Romanowski, *Truly Blessed*, 159.

18 Gamble's quote is from Cummings, *Sound of Philadelphia*, 95; Sharp's "a great number of songs . . . I never got credit" quote is from Russi, "Dee Dee Sharp," 27. Gamble's "I don't see" quote was made by Sharp, in ibid., 27.

19 Gamble's "bless . . . Stay meek . . . be a wise woman" quote is from the

album cover of *Happy 'bout the Whole Thing* (TSOP 33839). Sharp's "I don't feel ... promoting my product ... each album ... as I began to get involved" quotes are from Russi, "Dee Dee Sharp," 25, 27.

Although they were not credited for singing on Sharp's album (most likely to avoid royalty payments and/or lawsuits), Sharp claimed that the Tymes did backing vocals on "Ooh Child" and "I'm Not in Love" (Russi, "Dee Dee Sharp," 27).

20 Philadelphia International never attempted an album by Crawford. By late 1975, the three singles she made for the company had gone unnoticed. Bandleader-drummer Norman Connors was listed as the artist on "Valentine Love."

21 *Goin' Places* spent a mere eleven weeks on *Billboard*'s album chart, where it stalled at number sixty-three, whereas the certified-gold album *The Jacksons* spent almost seven months on the same chart. Jackson's "more like the old O'Jays ... were losing some of [their] identity" quote is from Jackson, *Moonwalk*, 128.

22 Jackson's "to convince him ... had done its best ... felt we could do better ... on the line" quote is from ibid. 129, 130.

23 The $4 billion in sales figure is from Wickham, "Blacks in the Record Industry," 37, 38. Gamble and Huff managed to have one of MFSB's songs, "Kay-Gee," included in the movie (and on the soundtrack recording).

24 The apogee of this movement occurred during the summer of 1979 in Chicago, where a local disc jockey organized a "Disco Demolition" between games of a baseball double-header. An estimated 10,000 disco records were burned, touching off a disturbance and forcing the second game to be canceled.

25 George's quote is from George, *Death of Rhythm and Blues*, 181.

26 For anyone anticipating a "sophomore jinx" for Pendergrass, the release of his *Life Is a Song Worth Singing* album convinced all but the most severe doubters that his decision to leave Harold Melvin and the Blue Notes was the correct one. Although the album generated only one R&B hit, its mix of strong ballads and up-tempo tunes demonstrated that Pendergrass had the sound, personality, and style to make it on his own. His million-selling single "Close the Door" "took the audience response and adulation to a whole new level," recalled the singer. Pendergrass added that he was "embarrassed [by] ... the screaming and swooning ... the ladies ... tossing flowers, notes with phone numbers, house keys, and teddy bears ... [and the] silky panties [that would] sail over the crowd and land at my feet" (Pendergrass and Romanowski, *Truly Blessed*, 178). The O'Jays' *So Full of Love* album was the biggest of their career (number 6, platinum), even if it was no artistic match for, say, *Ship Ahoy*. The million-selling single "Use ta Be My Girl" guaranteed its success.

27 Rawls's live album originated after he was booked to do a show on Broadway. "Kenny and them decided this would be the place to do a live album," recalled the singer in his interview with the author.

28 Bell, in his interviews with the author, recalled Wynne's quotes. Wynne was no Teddy Pendergrass. Like numerous lead singers before and since, Wynne discovered that the public related to the Spinners, not to

him. After leaving the Spinners, Wynne had one Top 20 R&B hit, and then bounced around the lower levels of the R&B charts. In 1984, forty-three-year-old Wynne, as part of his act, jumped off the stage into the audience. As he did, he suffered a massive heart attack and died.

29 For whatever reason, Bell did not record any additional material for a second album when he recorded *Spinners/8* in Seattle and in Philadelphia. Perhaps he did so because Atlantic was planning a "best of" collection for 1978 and two new albums were unnecessary. The following year, Leroy Bell and Casey James wrote and recorded their million-selling "Livin' It Up (Friday Night)." Jefferson and Hawes had one song placed on the final Spinners album produced by Bell (1979's *From Here to Eternally*). Around 1981, they finally left Mighty Three Music. Jefferson said that, over the years, he, Simmons, and Hawes, who "were sorta like a team off and on . . . decided to take a little time off." The three "never lost contact," added Jefferson, but they never wrote together again.

30 The title track for Pendergrass's album was a Bell-Creed composition. That summer, working in Seattle, Bell continued to produce (albeit sporadically) for Gamble and Huff.

31 Bell's final album with the Spinners, *From Here to Eternally*, was recorded during the late spring of 1978. Belying the producer's growing indifference to the group, the album did not sound much different from their previous effort. After Bell's departure, the Spinners hooked up with disco producer Michael Zager. Zager brought the group back to the top during the fall of 1979, with a medley of "Forgive Me Girl" and the Four Seasons' "Working My Way Back to You." That song became the Spinners' seventh and final gold single.

32 The "couldn't wait" quote is from Rosenthal, *His Song*, 152. Bell, in his interviews with the author, recalled the conversation among himself, John, and Taupin.

33 Rosenthal's "firmly on a new trail" quote and John's "right" quote are from ibid., 154.

34 John's "too saccharine . . . I only sang one verse . . . didn't live up to his expectations" quotes are from ibid., 154. Alexenburg's quotes were recalled by Bell. The other songs on the EP were "Are You Ready for Love" (with the Spinners) and "Three Way Love Affair." Bell believes they all "sound decent," but he conceded that "Mama Can't Buy You Love" was "the best one." In 2003, John's "Are You Ready for Love" was rereleased in England. The singer's emotive plea and Bell's smooth groove caught on, and that summer the song became a hit there.

15. "Ain't No Stoppin' Us Now"

1 Benton, in her interview with the author, recalled Gamble's "The problem with you all" and the Sweethearts' "Whatever" quote.

2 But the salad days were over for the Sweethearts. Their studio work "dwindled," said Benton. Unable to agree on one direction to follow, the group broke up around 1981. Barbara then sang in her brothers' band, the Ingrams. The Sweethearts reunited in 1984, to tour with Patti Labelle. During that time, Barbara Ingram's young daughter died, which

sent her into a downward spiral from which she never recovered. Ingram developed lupus, then cancer, but refused to stop singing. When the gig with Patti Labelle ended in 1989, the Sweethearts split up again. Benson eventually returned to school to become a paralegal, while she continued to sing. Benton, who earned her degree in education, left the music business altogether. The Sweethearts temporarily reunited in order to sing on a Bobby Rydell album shortly before Barbara died in 1994. Today, Benton is a director in the Head Start program and Benson teaches high school music.

3 The "two biggest malcontents . . . pushing hard . . . been raking it in . . . being ripped off" quotes are from Fried, "Day the Soul Train Crashed,"142; McFadden's "I want my money" quote was recalled by Don Renaldo, in ibid., 142.

4 Marsh's quote is from Marsh, *Heart of Rock and Soul*, 519.

5 Marsh's quote is from ibid., 519; Whitehead's quotes are from Fried, "Day the Soul Train Crashed," 144.

6 The artists included Archie Bell, the O'Jays, Billy Paul, Teddy Pendergrass, Lou Rawls, and Dee Dee Sharp. Gamble said in his address to the Republican National Nominating Convention in 2000 that the project had been inspired "because every day on my route to my downtown office I would ride through my old neighborhood in South Philadelphia, the place where I was born and raised. My neighborhood had become so devastated, just like many other African American communities all around America."

7 Rizzo reportedly took offense to the song's lyric, "You can no longer depend on the man downtown," as well as the word "ghetto" to describe the inner city.

8 George's quote and Gamble's "have a responsibility to our community" quote are from George, *Death of Rhythm and Blues*, 166. Wright was a former head of the National Association of Television and Radio Announcers. The BMA was a brilliant idea, but ultimately it proved to be a disappointment. A preponderance of the BMA's financial support stemmed from white record companies, entities that traditionally did not have the well-being of black music as a top priority. The BMA quickly swept aside its affiliations with radio-related personnel (including Ed Wright) and came under the direction of black record-industry executives (Gamble became its first president). The BMA was also hobbled by flare-ups of internal bickering and racial discord. When Gamble hired a white man (Jules Malamud, formerly with National Association of Record Merchandisers) to be the executive director of the organization, "he got a little flack . . . [for] hiring old white Jewish guys," said Joe Tarsia in his interview with the author. The BMA, severely curtailed by the late 1970s recording industry slump, remained an ineffective organization, preoccupied with internal problems, especially financing and leadership.

9 Yetnikoff's quote is from Sanjek, *American Popular Music and Its Business*, 233.

10 In 1976, Sammy Strain, formerly of Little Anthony and the Imperials, replaced Powell, who was suffering from heart disease. Powell died a year later. In 1993, Nathaniel Best replaced Strain in the O'Jays.

11 Pendergrass said that he "certainly didn't consciously work on being viewed as a sex symbol . . . it just came naturally, like sitting on the front steps, rappin' to the neighborhood girls. Only now the neighborhood was bigger, and I had a better rap" (Pendergrass and Romanowski, *Truly Blessed*, 169).

12 Archie Bell said that after the group signed with Philadelphia International, unlike their Atlantic recordings, "it was mostly me and the Drells" who sang on the records. Bell said he "hated to break up" with Philadelphia International. "Kenny was always a gentleman, a helluva writer. And if it hadn't have been for Gamble and Huff, I might have been one of those artists who had one record and that was it."

13 Wickham's quote is from Wickham, "Blacks in the Record Industry," 37.

14 All of Wickham's quotes in this paragraph are from ibid., 38; Gamble's quotes are from ibid., 39.

15 Sanjek, *American Popular Music and Its Business*, 240.

16 These acts included Cameo, Chic, Con-Funk-Shun, the Gap Band, Rick James, and Prince, among others.

17 "Rapper's Delight" became the first rap hit but it was not the first rap record. That distinction goes to the Fatback Band, whose "King Tim III (Personality Jock)" was released one week earlier. Not long after that, Philadelphia International issued its own rap record, by Philadelphia's legendary rhyming R&B disc jockey, Douglas "Jocko" Henderson. Spoken over the instrumental track to McFadden and Whitehead's "Ain't No Stoppin' Us Now," "Rhythm Talk" charted in the United Kingdom early in 1980. "Rhythm Talk" and "King Tim" were both delivered in an old school, black radio style and are more transitional than historic, while "Rapper's Delight" is a seminal recording.

18 Pendergrass's quote is from Pendergrass and Romanowski, *Truly Blessed*, 205, 206.

19 Wansel's quotes are from Miller, "Gamble and Huff," 38, 166, as is Pendergrass's "Why" quote, which was recalled by Wansel in that article.

20 Carla Benson also thought there was "some kind of a major tiff" between Gamble and Huff, "a big fight, a big somethin,' and one of them [she thought Huff] had threatened to quit, or to leave. . . . And that's how Cynthia and Dexter got that particular project." Stephen Fried wrote that "McFadden and Whitehead confirmed the rumor [he] had been hearing on the street for weeks: that Gamble and Huff had had a serious falling out. Once close friends, the two were now barely on speaking terms" (Fried, "Day the Soul Train Crashed," 143).

21 Fried's quotes are from ibid., 143, 146.

22 George's quotes are from George, *Death of Rhythm and Blues* 179, 180.

23 Huff's "Can't nobody do it like us" quote was recalled by Jefferson in his interview with the author; Gamble's "Don't just think . . . even an infant—will like" quote was recalled by Frazier, in Whitaker, "Cool at Last."

24 Gamble's "spill your guts" quote was recalled by Biggs in her interview with the author.

25 Wilson's quote is from his interview in *Rolling Stone*, November 4, 1976. It was reprinted in *Rolling Stone* of October 15, 1992, 81. George's quote

is from George, *Death of Rhythm and Blues*, 180, 181. The new MFSB rhythm section did help to create its share of songs with Gamble and Huff. Cynthia Biggs recalled how the Stylistics' 1980 hit "Hurry Up This Way Again" "came about because the musicians were jammin' as they were learnin' the song. Somebody struck up a groove and all the other musicians jumped in. Dexter [Wansel] heard it and said, 'Let's do that!' . . . It wasn't like he had that written out."

26 George, *Death of Rhythm and Blues*, 180.

27 Pendergrass's quotes are from Pendergrass and Romanowski, *Truly Blessed*, 206.

28 Bell claimed that one such song was the O'Jays' million-selling "Use ta Be My Girl."

29 Pakula eventually was rehired at Philadelphia International. He worked there sporadically after that.

30 Gamble claimed that "Motown was our inspiration. They were a blueprint for us. We used the Motown formula—a competitive environment for songwriters and producers—and expanded on it with our own ideas" (Hunter,"Soundman of Philadelphia").

31 Fried's quote is from Fried, "Day the Soul Train Crashed," 146; Gamble's "making records just wasn't fun" quote was recalled by Chambers in the same article.

32 Gamble's community interest first manifested itself in a desire to invest his music business profits in ghetto real estate. Gamble "would buy old houses and rehab 'em," said Bobby Eli in his interview with the author.

33 In his interview with the author, Sigler said he "shoulda stayed" at Philadelphia International in the first place. Sigler then cited songs he wrote and/or produced for Philadelphia International during his first tenure there, for which he still collects royalties. Had he listened to Gamble and not left Philadelphia International, he "mighta had a better life."

34 The quotes by Gamble and Pendergrass are from Pendergrass and Romanowski, *Truly Blessed*, 210.

35 Morris Bailey, who discovered Holt while he produced records for Harold B. Robinson's Newtown Records, made the "too black" assertion.

36 Other major black artists signed directly to Columbia (or Epic) at that time included Michael Jackson, the Isley Brothers, and Earth, Wind and Fire.

37 Gamble and Huff's quotes are from Miller, "Gamble and Huff," 166.

38 Gamble's quotes are from ibid., 166.

39 Gamble and Huff's quotes are from ibid., 166.

40 Pendergrass's quotes are from Pendergrass and Romanowski, *Truly Blessed*, 248, 249.

41 After an arduous two-year rehabilitation, Pendergrass recovered partial movement and actually performed and recorded again. Thom Bell claimed that in 1974, Gamble and Huff passed on the opportunity to sign Vandross, then a background singer in David Bowie's road band, "because they had Teddy, they didn't need Luther." Pendergrass claimed that Gamble told him about CBS's amendment of the agreement with

Philadelphia International (Pendergrass and Romanowski, *Truly Blessed*, 249).

42 Gamble's demands to CBS included "his own satellite and his own satellite station, like Black Entertainment Network," claimed Thom Bell.

43 Pendergrass's quote is from Pendergrass and Romanowski, *Truly Blessed*, 249; Chambers's quote is from Fried, "Day the Soul Train Crashed," 146.

44 Pendergrass's quote is from Pendergrass and Romanowski, *Truly Blessed*, 249. In his autobiography, Pendergrass wrote, "it was widely reported that PIR awarded me an unusually generous royalty rate on my records, when in fact the deal was way below what other multi-platinum artists commanded from other labels. Out of loyalty to Gamble, Huff, and PIR, I'd let that slide for many years, but before the accident, I had been planning to renegotiate a more equitable deal and make other major changes in how I ran my business and my career" (ibid., 248).

45 Pendergrass's quotes are from ibid., 249, 250.

16. "Love, Need and Want You"

1 Sanjek, *American Popular Music and Its Business*, 251.

2 The quote by the Sanjeks is from Sanjek, ibid., 251. In response to the dearth of black music on MTV, ABC-TV introduced a black-oriented, after prime-time music video show called *New York Hot Tracks*, and NBC-TV instituted its own integrated *Friday Night Videos*. Cable TV's Black Entertainment Channel increased its "Video Soul" segment from two to fifteen hours a week. On the other hand, an attempt by New York's powerhouse black radio station WBLS-FM to adapt its programs, featuring only black performers, to cable TV was unsuccessful.

3 The rise in the popularity of video games also hurt the record business. Between 1979 and 1982, the manufacture of arcade and home video games became a $1 billion industry. Sales edged close to $2 billion in 1982, and that figure almost doubled in 1983 (Sanjek, *American Popular Music and Its Business*, 255).

4 Gamble's quote is from Miller, "Gamble and Huff," 166.

5 Hyman's quote is from Nathan, *Soulful Divas*, 308.

6 Huff's quote is from Miller, "Gamble and Huff," 166.

7 Pareles, "New York Rock's."

8 Jim Gallagher, in his interview with the author, recalled Gamble's quote.

9 Rawls's "thank you" quote is from "Family Reunion" (Gamble and Huff LP 100). Early in 1988, "Run Jesse Run," an overtly political single sung by Lou Rawls, Phyllis Hyman, and the Reverend James Cleveland, which encouraged black activist Jesse Jackson's presidential campaign, was released on Gamble and Huff Records.

10 Although Gamble and Huff remained business partners, Huff was never a factor in the decision to market Philadelphia International's back catalog. Ross said he "acted purely as a consultant to Kenny, not Leon. Although Leon was privy to any and all of our meetings, he never even bothered to attend. He just wasn't there! He was Leon Hush instead of Leon Huff."

11 In 1993, the Mighty Three Music catalog, which contained the publishing

rights to the majority of songs written by Gamble, Huff, and Bell, was sold to Warner-Chappell publishing. David Steinberg, who served as an adviser in that sale, explained how Gamble, Huff, and Bell "still receive royalties as songwriters . . . [but] they don't receive anything from the publishing on the songs and they have no legal control over how the songs are used." In addition, Gamble, Huff, and Bell retained control of the few songs they wrote that were never part of Mighty Three Music, as well as any songs they wrote after the 1993 deal. Sacks's quote is from his interview with the author.

12 Gamble's quote is from Miller, "Gamble and Huff," 166.

13 Chuck Gamble's quote is from ibid.

14 Gamble's quote is from Caruso, "Kenny Gamble." Gamble also serves as chairman of the board of Universal Companies. In 1999, Universal Community Homes established a charter school in Gamble's old South Philadelphia neighborhood. In 2002, as part of the largest experiment in privatization attempted by an American school district, a state panel voted to transfer control of forty-two of Philadelphia's failing schools to seven outside managers. Universal Companies was assigned to run two of them.

15 Gamble's quote about "after much soul-searching . . . hands-on management" is from the transcript of the 2000 Republican Convention. Gamble's quote about "consciousness has been lifted . . . just to leave" is from Caruso, "Kenny Gamble."

16 Gamble's quote is from John-Hall, "His Music"; Woods's "wasn't him . . . He moved back to the city . . . built a mosque for Muslims" quote is from Sacks, Leo, and Virginia Prescott, eds., "The Philly Sound," 56. Other quotes by Woods in this paragraph are from his interview with the author. See "Doing It the Old-Fashioned Way," *Issues and Views* for a discussion on Gamble's intention to sell his properties to blacks only.

17 Rawls, in his interview with the author, recalled Gamble's quote.

Epilogue

1 Gamble's quote is from John-Hall, "His Music"; Renaldo's quote is from Fried, "Day the Soul Train Crashed," 141.

2 At the time of publication of this book Gamble and Huff were expected to appeal the Billy Paul decision (Olsen, "Billy Paul Wins").

Bibliography

Books

Andriote, John-Manuel. *Hot Stuff: A Brief History of Disco*. New York: HarperCollins, 2001.

Belz, Carl. *The Story of Rock*. New York: Harper Colophon, 1972.

Booth, Stanley. *Rhythm Oil: A Journey through the Music of the American South*. London: Vintage, 1993.

Bowman, Rob. *Soulsville, U.S.A.: The Story of Stax Records*. New York: Schirmer, 1997.

Breithaupt, Don, and Jeff Breithaupt. *Precious and Few: Pop Music in the Early '70s*. New York: St. Martin's Griffin, 1996.

Busnar, Gene. *The Rhythm and Blues Story*. New York: Julian Messner, 1985.

Butler, Jerry, with Earl Smith. *Only the Strong Survive*. Bloomington: Indiana University Press, 2000.

Christgau, Robert. *Rock Albums of the '70s: A Critical Guide*. New York: Da Capo, 1981.

Clarke, Donald, ed. *The Penguin Encyclopedia of Popular Music*. New York: Penguin, 1990.

Cogan, Jim, and William Clark. *Temples of Sound: Inside the Great Recording Studios*. San Francisco: Chronicle, 2003.

Cohodas, Nadine. *Spinning Blues into Gold: The Chess Brothers and the Legendary Chess Records*. New York: St. Martin's Griffin, 2000.

Cummings, Tony. *The Sound of Philadelphia*. London: Methuen, 1975.

Dannen, Frederic. *Hit Men: Power Brokers and Fast Money Inside the Music Business*. New York: Vintage Paperback, 1991.

Davis, Clive, with James Willwerth. *Clive: Inside the Record Business*. New York: Ballantine Paperback, 1976.

DeCurtis, Anthony, and James Henke, with Holly George-Warren. *Rolling Stone Album Guide*. New York: Random House, 1992.

Early, Gerald. *One Nation under a Groove: Motown and American Culture*. Hopewell, N.J.: Ecco Press, 1995.

Erlewine, Michael, Vladimir Boqnadov, and Chris Woodstra, eds., *All Music Guide to Rock*. San Francisco: Miller Freeman Books, 1995.

Franklin, Aretha, and David Ritz. *Aretha: From These Roots*. New York: Villard, 1999.

Friedlander, Paul. *Rock and Roll: A Social History*. Boulder, Colo.: Westview Press/Div. of HarperCollins, 1996.

George, Nelson. *The Death of Rhythm and Blues*. New York: Plume/Penguin, 1988.

———. *Hip Hop America*. New York: Penguin, 1998.

———. *Where Did Our Love Go?: The Rise and Fall of the Motown Sound*. New York: St. Martin's Press, 1985.

Gonzalez, Fernando L. *Disco-File: The Discographical Catalog of American Rock and Roll and Rhythm and Blues*. Flushing, N.Y.: Fernando L. Gonzalez, 1976.

Gordy, Berry. *To Be Loved: The Music, the Magic, the Memories of Motown*. New York: Warner Books, 1994.

Griben, Anthony J., and Matthew M. Schiff. *The Complete Book of Doo-Wop*. Iola, Wis.: Krause Publications, 2000.

Haskins, Jim, and J. M. Stifle. *Donna Summer: An Unauthorized Biography*. Boston: Little, Brown, 1983.

Hildebrand, Lee. *Stars of Soul and Rhythm and Blues*. New York: Billboard, 1994.

Hirshey, Gerri. *Nowhere to Run: The Story of Soul Music*. New York: Times Books, 1984.

Jackson, John A. *American Bandstand: Dick Clark and the Making of a Rock 'n' Roll Empire*. New York: Oxford University Press, 1997.

———. *Big Beat Heat: Alan Freed and the Early Years of Rock and Roll*. New York: Schirmer Books, 1991.

Jackson, Michael. *Moonwalk*. New York: Doubleday, 1988.

Jacobs, Dick, and Harriet Jacobs. *Who Wrote That Song?* Cincinnati: Writers Digest Books, 1994.

LaBelle, Patti, with Laura B. Randolph. *Don't Block the Blessings: Revelations of a Lifetime*. New York: Riverhead Books, 1996.

Lacomme, Jean. *Philadelphia International Records: A Discography*. Paris, France: Self-published by the author, 1998.

Larkin, Colin, ed. *Guinness Encyclopedia of Popular Music*, Vols. 1–5. New York: Stockton Press, 1992.

Lydon, Michael. *Ray Charles: A Man and His Music*. New York: Riverhead Books, 1998.

Marsh, Dave. *The Heart of Rock and Soul: The 1001 Greatest Singles Ever Made*. New York: New American Library, 1989.

Miller, James. *Flowers in the Dustbin: The Rise of Rock and Roll, 1947–1977*. New York: Simon and Schuster, 1999.

Nathan, David. *The Soulful Divas*. New York: Billboard Books, 1999.

Norman, Philip. *Sir Elton: The Definitive Biography*. New York: Carroll and Graf, 1991.

O'Brien, Lucy. *She Bop: The Definitive History of Women in Rock, Pop and Soul*. London: Continuum, 1995.

Olsen, Eric, Paul Verna, and Carlo Wolff, eds. *The Encyclopedia of Record Producers*. New York: Billboard Books, 1999.

Palmer, Robert. *Rock and Roll: An Unruly History*. New York: Harmony Books, 1995.

Pareles, Jon, and Patricia Romanowski. *The Rolling Stone Encyclopedia of Rock and Roll.* New York: Rolling Stone Press, 1983.

Pendergrass, Teddy, and Patricia Romanowski. *Truly Blessed.* New York: G. P. Putnam's Sons, 1998.

Petrie, Gavin, ed. *Black Music.* London: Hamlyn Publishing, 1974.

Pollack, Bruce. *In Their Own Words: Twenty Successful Song Writers Tell How They Write Their Songs.* New York: Macmillan, 1975.

Pruter, Robert, ed. *Blackwell Guide to Soul Recordings.* United Kingdom: Basil Blackwell, 1993.

Redd, Lawrence N. *Rock Is Rhythm and Blues [The Impact of Mass Media].* East Lansing: Michigan State University Press, 1974.

Rees, Dafydd, and Luke Crampton. *Encyclopedia of Rock Stars.* New York: DK Publishing, 1996.

Romanowski, Patricia, and Holly George-Warren, eds. *[The New] Rolling Stone Encyclopedia of Rock and Roll.* New York: Rolling Stone Press/Fireside, 1995.

Rosenthal, Elizabeth J. *His Song: The Musical Journey of Elton John.* New York: Billboard Books, 2001.

Sanjek, Russell. *American Popular Music and Its Business: The First Four Hundred Years; Vol.3: From 1900 to 1984.* New York: Oxford University Press, 1988.

———. *Pennies from Heaven: The American Popular Music Business in the Twentieth Century.* Updated by David Sanjek. New York: DaCapo, 1996.

Shaw, Arnold. *Black Popular Music in America.* New York: Schirmer Books, 1986.

Shipler, David K. *A Country of Strangers: Blacks and Whites in America.* New York: Alfred A. Knopf, 1997.

Sklar, Rick. *Rocking America.* New York: St. Martin's Press, 1984.

Smith, Joe. *Off the Record: An Oral History of Popular Music.* New York: Warner Books, 1988.

Southern, Eileen. *The Music of Black Americans: A History.* New York: W. W. Norton, 1997.

Stambler, Irwin. *Encyclopedia of Pop, Rock and Soul.* New York: St. Martin's Press, 1977.

Szatmary, David P. *Rockin' in Time: A Social History of Rock and Roll.* Englewood Cliffs, N.J.: Prentice-Hall, 1987.

Taraborrelli, J. Randy. *Michael Jackson: The Magic and the Madness.* New York: Birch Lane Press/Carol Publishing, 1991.

Taylor, Marc. *Classic Soul: Soul Singers of the Early 1970s.* Jamaica, N.Y.: Aloiv, 1996.

Thernstrom, Stephan, and Abigail Thernstrom. *America in Black and White: One Nation, Indivisible.* New York: Simon and Schuster, 1997.

Tobler, John, and Stuart Grundy. *The Record Producers.* London: British Broadcasting Corporation, 1982.

Vincent, Rickey. *Funk: The Music, the People, and the Rhythms of the One.* New York: St. Martin's Press, 1996.

Wade, Dorothy, and Justine Picardie. *Music Man: Ahmet Ertegun, Atlantic Records, and the Triumph of Rock 'n' Roll.* New York: W. W. Norton, 1990.

Ward, Brian. *Just My Soul Responding: Rhythm and Blues, Black Consciousness, and Race Relations.* Los Angeles: University of California Press, 1998.

Ward, Ed, Geoffrey Stokes, and Ken Tucker. *Rock of Ages: The Rolling Stone History of Rock and Roll.* New York: Rolling Stone Press, 1986.

Warner, Jay. *American Singing Groups: A History 1940–1990.* New York: Billboard Books, 1992.

Weigley, Russell F., ed. *Philadelphia: A 300-Year History.* New York: W. W. Norton, 1982.

Werner, Craig. *A Change Is Gonna Come: Music, Race and the Soul of America.* New York: Plume, 1998.

Whitburn, Joel. *Top Pop Albums 1955–1992.* Menomonee Falls, Wis.: Record Research, 1993.

———. *Top R&B Singles 1942–1988.* Menomonee Falls, Wis.: Record Research,1988.

———. *Top Pop Singles 1955–1993.* Menomonee Falls, Wis.: Record Research, 1994.

Wolff, Daniel, with S. R. Crain, Clifton White, and David Tenenbaum. *You Send Me: The Life and Times of Sam Cooke.* New York: William Morrow, 1995.

Zolten, J. Jerome. *Great God A'mighty: The Dixie Hummingbirds and the Rise of Soul Gospel Music.* New York: Oxford University Press, 2002.

Articles and Documents

"Blue Notes' Harold Melvin; Bandleader a Major Force in Philly Sound." *Newsday*, March 26, 1997.

Bosco, Bob. "Billy and the Essentials: The Dance Ain't Over!" *DISCoveries*, June 1997.

———. "Bongo Stompin'." *DISCoveries*, September 1994.

———. "The Joker's Wild: The Daytons." *Echoes of the Past*, spring 2001.

———. "Straight Outta Camden." *Echoes of the Past*, no. 41.

Bundy, June, and Bob Rolontz. "R.&B. Disk Jockeys in Hit-Making Role; Break Singles and Spawn Fresh Issues." *Billboard*, July 3, 1961.

"Buses Stoned Carrying City Negroes Home." *Philadelphia Journal*, August 29, 1963.

Carpenter, Bill. "How Johnny Mathis Keeps the Music Playing." *Goldmine*, May 28, 1993.

Carter, Kevin L. "Where Did Walk of Fame Walk Off To?" *Philadelphia Inquirer*, March 28, 1995.

Charles, Don. "Donna Summer: The First Ten Years." *Goldmine*, May 1, 1992.

Christgau, Robert. "Innocence in Records and Its Inevitable Flip Side, Greed." *Newsday*, June 24, 1973.

———. "So Payola Isn't Good, but It Isn't Such a Bad Thing Either." *Newsday*, June 1973.

Clark, Joe. "Ex-DJ Remembers a Man and His Guitar." *Philadelphia Daily News*, August 18, 1977.

Dahl, Bill. "Garnet Mimms' Melismatic Voice." *Goldmine*, December 3, 1999.

———. "Soul Serenader: Once a Top R&B Star, Joe Simon Gave It All Up to Join the Ministry." *Goldmine*, October 23, 1998.

———. "The O'Jays: Thirty Years on the Love Train." *Goldmine*, December 28, 1990.

Davis, Steve. "Payola 1970." *Rock*, 1, no. 17.

Dawson, Sandra. "Making the Most of Black Music." *Black Enterprise*, February 1979.

"Deejay King of Rock 'n Roll." *Our World*, November 1955.

DeLuca, Dan. "Honorees Announced; Walk of Fame to Grow." *Philadelphia Inquirer*, April 26, 1996.

———. "The World Finds a Home at Sigma." *Pulse*, September 1992.

Devich, Michael. "CBS's One-Sided Singles: Half as Much Music and Zero Consumer Interest." *Goldmine*, September 9, 1988.

Ditlea, Steve. "The Dawn of the 'Disco Disk'." *New York Times*, June 10, 1979.

Edmonds, Ben. "Final Frontier: The Temptations' Road to Cloud Nine." *Mojo*, August 2001.

Ferretti, Fred. "C.B.S. Ousts an Executive and Sues Him for $94,000." *New York Times*, May 30, 1973.

"Four Record Company Officers Given Prison Terms for Payola." *New York Times*, April 13, 1976.

Freeland, Bill. "Golden Boy: Georgie Woods." *Philadelphia Magazine*, April 1967.

Fried, Stephen. "The Day the Soul Train Crashed." *Philadelphia Magazine*, June 1983.

"Gamble and Huff: The Men behind the Record Stars." *Jet*, December 28, 1972.

Gersten, Russell. "Polishing the O'Jays: An R&B Group Gets Respectability." *Village Voice* (New York), October 18, 1976.

Gibbs, Vernon. "Chambers Brothers: Love, Peace, Happiness, Etc." *Rock*, April 26, 1971.

———. "The Delfonics Love You." *Rock*, June 7, 1971.

Goldberg, Marv. "The Castelles." *DISCoveries*, January 1997.

———. "The Dreams." *DISCoveries*, December 1997.

———. "The Turbans." *DISCoveries*, January 1996.

Gordon, Harmon Y. "4 Fined in 'Soul' Payola." *Philadelphia Bulletin*, April 9, 1976.

———. "Payola Cases Reversed." *Philadelphia Bulletin*, August 11, 1977.

"Harold Melvin, 57; Led the Blue Notes to Success in the 70s." *New York Times*, March 26, 1997.

Hershey, Gerri. "Learning to Fly" (Michael Jackson). *Mojo*, December 2001.

Hochman, Steve. "Pouring Heart into Soul: Teddy Pendergrass." *New York Daily News*, June 23, 1991.

Holden, Stephen. "Lou Rawls: Back in Club, Back to Blues." *New York Times*, July 7, 1989.

Horner, Charlie. "The Birth of the Philly Sound." *Harmony Times United in Group Harmony Association*, no. 1, autumn 1980.

Hoskyns, Barney. "The Chambers Brothers: Their Time Has Come." *Mojo Collections*, winter 2001.

Huff, Claire. "Radio Hiring Bias Charged." *Philadelphia Inquirer*, May 9, 1965.

"Intruders' Singer Dies." *St. Petersburg Times*, January 2, 1995.

Johnson, Herschel. "Motown: The Sound of Success." *Black Enterprise*, June 1974.

"King Warned of a Race War in Conversation with Johnson." *New York Times*, April 14, 2002.

Kooper, Al. "Jerry Ragavoy: From Ragavoy to Riches; Philly Boy Makes Good." *Goldmine*, March 29, 1996.

Kwitney, Jonathan. "Is It Just Business as Usual in Record Industry, or Do New Probes Reveal Crime at High Levels?" *Wall Street Journal*, June 19, 1973.

Lichtenstein, Grace. "Columbia Payola Put at $250,000." *New York Times*, June 6, 1973.

Light, Alan. "The Soul of the Seventies." *Rolling Stone*, May 2, 1991.

Lubasch, Arnold H. "Recording Executive Is Fined in Tax Case." *New York Times*, September 24, 1976.

McGarvey, Brendan. "Allah behind Bars: Even La Cosa Nostra Members Fear the Nation of Islam in Jail." *Philadelphia City Paper*, November 7–14, 2002.

Miller, Chuck. "Gamble and Huff: The Hit Men." *Goldmine*, October 23, 1998.

"Music News." *Downbeat*, December 24, 1959.

"NAACP Honors 3 Entertainers." *Philadelphia Journal*, September 4, 1963.

Naulty, William P., and John J. Gaffney. "Rioting in N. Phila." *Philadelphia Bulletin*, August 29, 1964.

Niepold, Mary Martin. "Food for the Mind and Music for the Soul." *Philadelphia Inquirer*, March 26, 1979.

Nooger, Dan. "Philadelphia." *In The Blackwell Guide to Soul Recording*, ed. Robert Pruter. Oxford: Basil Blackwell, 1993.

Page, Clarence. "TV's Racial Divide Reflects Society." *St. Petersburg Times*, December 31, 1998.

Pareles, Jon. "New York Rock's Latest Hangover." *New York Times*, October 19, 2003.

———. "There's a New Sound in Pop Music: Bigotry." *New York Times*, September 10, 1989.

Peters, Art. "N. Phila. Is Loser as Georgie Woods Kisses It Good-Bye." *Philadelphia Inquirer*, May 1, 1972.

Pruter, Robert. "The Jerry Butler Story: Only the Strong Survive." *Goldmine*, March 1, 1996.

———. "Johnny Williams: They Loved Him in Chicago." *Goldmine*, April 24, 1987.

———. "When Soul Music Lost Its Soul." *Goldmine*, October 14, 1994.

Raines, Jenyne. "TP: Teddy Pendergrass Refined and Better with Time." *Beats*, May 1991.

Rainey, J. "What Makes Georgie Tick?" *Philadelphia Tribune*, November 21, 1959.

Riley, Clayton. "The Philly Sound of Brotherly Love." *New York Times*, March 31, 1974.

Ritz, David. "State of Luxe: Luther Vandross." *Rolling Stone*, September 6, 1990.

Robinson, Richard. "The Recording Studio—Pt. II." *Rock*, April 26, 1971.

Roeser, Steve. "The Chambers Brothers: Love, Peace and Happiness." *Goldmine*, May 13, 1994.

Rothstein, Edward. "Damning (Yet Desiring) Mickey and the Big Mac." *New York Times*, March 2, 2002.

Russi, Randy. "Dee Dee Sharp: First Lady of the Philly Sound." *DISCoveries*, March 1993.

Salvo, Patrick, and Barbara Salvo. "The Motown Empire." *Sepia*, September 1974.

——. "The Philadelphia Men (and Women) of Music." *Sepia*, April 1975.

Saunders, Jack. "Jack Saunders Says" (column). *Philadelphia Tribune*, July 12, 1975.

——. "The Passing Parade." *Philadelphia Independent*, February 3, 1962.

Schumach, Murray. "Payola Indictments Name 19, Including 3 Company Heads." *New York Times*, June 25, 1975.

Selvin, Joel. "Lucifer Rising: Sly Stone." *Mojo*, August 2001.

Sharp, Ken. "Hall and Oates: Life, Liberty and the Pursuit of Soul." *Goldmine*, April 10, 1998.

Sutherland, Sam. "Bobby Martin: Reaching a New Level of Creative Control." *Record World*, September 3, 1977.

Takiff, Jonathan. "Music Hall of Fame Puts Wings on Its Feet." *Philadelphia Daily News*, April 26, 1995.

Taylor, Dottie. "Lou Rawls: The Philadelphia Years." *Goldmine*, December 28, 1990.

Torres, Richard. "A Hit Parade of '70s R&B." *Newsday*, December 7, 1997.

Tortelli, Joseph. "The Chambers Brothers: Their Time Has Come." *Goldmine*, March 25, 1988.

"Trial Opens for 7 in Disk Scandals." *New York Times*, January 15, 1976.

"Two Are Told to Testify on 'Payola.'" *New York Times*, February 17, 1977.

Vorda, Allan. "Archie Bell Interview." *DISCoveries*, May 1990.

Watkins, Mel. "Flip Wilson, Outrageous Comic and TV Host, Dies at 64." *New York Times*, November 27, 1998.

"WDAS Fires Georgie Woods; Jocko Henderson Moves In." *Philadelphia Independent*, April 2, 1966.

Weinraub, Bernard. "Here's to Disco, It Never Could Say Goodbye." *New York Times*, December 10, 2002.

Werts, Diane. "Isaac Hayes' Big Score." *Newsday* (Long Island), December 6, 1998.

Whitaker, Tim. "Cool at Last." *Philadelphia Weekly*, August 22, 2000.

Wickham, DeWayne, contributing ed. "Blacks in the Record Industry/Philadelphia International: Producing Philly's Sound." *Black Enterprise*, December 1979.

Wilder, J. Brantley. "With Georgie Woods in Vietnam." *Philadelphia Tribune*, February 19, 1966.

Wilson, Barbara L. "Rock 'n' Roll at Mastbaum." *Philadelphia Inquirer*, December 13, 1955.

Wilson, Brian. "The Rolling Stone Interview." *Rolling Stone*, November 4, 1976. Reprinted October 15, 1992, p. 81.

Wilson, Earl. "Alan Freed's Story." *New York Post*, November 23, 1959.

Young, Masco. "Nightwatch" (radio/TV column). *Philadelphia Bulletin*, January 22, 1982.

Interviews

Alexenburg, Ron. November 8, 2000.

Andrews, Lee. July 7, 1993.

Appell, Dave. January 20, 1994.

Bailey, Morris. September 12, 2000.

Bell, Archie. January 17, 2001.

Bell, Thom. September 30, October 2, 4, November 12, 20, 27, 2001.

Bendinelli, Frank. November 8, 2001.

Benson, Carla. September 25, 2002.

Benton, Evette. September 12, October 28, 2002.

Biggs, Cynthia. April 23, 2002.

Bosco, Robert. July 16, 2002.

Brunson, Frankie. October 8, 10, 2002.

Butler, Jerry. August 5, 2001.

Collins, Charles. February 7, 2003.

Dunn, Clifford. February 23, 1994.

Dunn, James. February 23, 1994.

Eli, Bobby. November 9, 10, 2000; October 21, 23, 28, 2002.

Epstein, Stephen. September 26, 2001.

Faith, Russell. October 26, 2002.

Gaber, Phil. September 18, 2001.

Genovese, Richard. February 12, 2003.

Hart, William. September 28, 2001.

Holman, Eddie. September 15, 1994.

Hurtt, Phil. August 19, 2002.

Jackson, Billy. November 9, 2000.

Jefferson, Joseph B. February 4, 2003.

Johnson, Jules "J.J." September 12, 18, 2002.

Joiner, Fred. February 7, 2003.

Kelly, Stephen. September 27, 2000.

King, Ben E. December 28, 2001.

Lipsius, Harold. October 18, 2000.

Lit, Hy. September 1, 1992.

McDougal, Weldon. July 27, 28, 1993; October 21, 2000; June 4, 2001.

Madara, John. September 19, 2000.

Mann, Kal. January 30, 1993.

Martin, Bobby. March 19, September 11, November 10, 2000; June 5, 2002.

Montana, Jr., Vincent. July 12, 16, 2002.

Nahan, Irv. July 13, 1993.

Pakula, Lenny. August 19, 2002.

Pritchett, Wendell. February 4, 2003.

Rawls, Lou. November 29, 2001.

Reed, Sam. February 5, 2003.

Renay, Dianne. April 25, 2002.

Ross, Jerry. December 11, 1993; September 15, 2000; October 30, 2003.

Sacks, Leo. September 12, 26, 2002.

Shively, Val. July 7, 1993; November 5, 2001.

Sigler, Bunny. November 14, 2001; October 9, 2002.

Slay, Frank. December 14, 1992.

Steinberg, David. October 8, 2001.

Swig, Rick. November 19, 1999.

Tarsia, Joe. September 27, October 7, 2000; September 27, 2002.

Terry, Joe. November 23, 1992.

Tindall, T. J. June 3, 2002.

Wilford, Win. July 11, 2002.

Wexler, Jerry. February 17, 2000.

White, Dave. September 13, 2000.

Wilson, Bernard. November 6, 2001.
Wisner, Jimmy. October 15, 2000.
Woods, Georgie. October 24, 2000.
Young, Earl. October 30, 2000.

Web Sites

Caruso, David B. "Kenny Gamble Living His Music's Message." (Associated Press, March 31, 2003). Available at http://www.projo.com/ sharedcontent/features/musicjazzblues/BI GAMBLE.b3a89843.html.
"Doing It the Old-Fashioned Way: Fighting the Good Fight." *Issues and Views*, May 5, 2003. Available at http://www.issues-views.com/ index.php/sect25000/article/25060.
Hunter, Al, Jr. "The Soundman of Philadelphia: Kenny Gamble." *Philadelphia Online*, 1998. Available at http://www.philly.com/.
John-Hall, Annette. "His Music Is the Blueprint" (*Philadelphia Inquirer*, posted August 3, 2003). Available at http://philly.com/mld/inquirer/ 6449592.htm.
National Advisory Commission on Civil Disorders (The Kerner Commission Report), March 1, 1968. Available at www.africanaonline.com/ reports_kerner.htm.
Olsen, Eric. "Billy Paul Wins $500K in Dispute with Gamble and Huff" (posted May 1, 2003). Available at http://www.blogcritics.org/archives/ 2003/05/01/104924.php.
Waller, Don. "Kenny Gamble and Leon Huff" (*Billboard*, December 18, 1999). Available at http://www.findarticles.com/m3018/51_111/58500494/ p1/article.jhtml.

Miscellaneous Items

Bendinelli, Frank. "The Intruders and Friends: Philly Soul Rarities—Volume 1." Liner notes to compact disc, Collectables COL-5771, 1997.
"Best of Melron Records: The Early Philly Sound." Liner notes to compact disc, Philly Archives, 2000.
Brown, David L. "Best of Del-Val Records: Vol. 1." Liner notes to compact disc, PH-6, 2000.
Brown, Geoff. "Greatest Hits of Philadelphia, 1976–1986." Liner notes to compact disc, UK Music Club MCCD 379, 1999.
Croasdell, Ady. "Ben Lee's Philadelphia Story." Liner notes to compact disc, UK Kent KEND164, 1999.
Dene, Lewis. "Archie Bell and the Drells." Liner notes to compact disc, UK West Side WESD 212/1, 1999.
———. "Billy Paul: Let 'Em In," "Only the Strong Survive," "First Class." Liner notes to compact disc, UK West Side WESD 211, 1999.
Fileti, Don. "Groups of Grand Records." Liner notes to compact disc, Relic 7113, 1995.
———. "The Castelles: Sweetness." Liner notes to compact disc, Relic 7114, 1995.
Galloway, A. Scott. "The Best of the Jones Girls." Liner notes to compact disc, Right Stuff 72435-27582-2-7, 2000.

Gamble, Kenneth. Address to Republican National Convention. Audio tape recording. Philadelphia, August 2, 2000.

Horace, Harboro. "Swan's Soul Sides: Dance the Philly." Liner notes to compact disc, UK Kent KEND 120, 1996.

James, Rollye. "Yo! Philadelphia: Look What I Found." Liner notes to compact disc, Heritage HYP 002, 1999.

"The Jamie/Guyden Story." Liner notes to compact disc, Bear Family BCD 15874-BH, 1995.

McCloskey, Jason. "Bobby Martin." A&M Records biography, 1978.

Marymount, Mark. "The Ebonys: Golden Philly Classics." Liner notes to compact disc, Collectables COL-5659, 1995.

———. "People's Choice: Golden Classics." Liner notes to compact disc, Collectables COL-5818, 1996.

Nathan, David. "Best of the O'Jays 1976–1991." Liner notes to compact disc, The Right Stuff 72434–99133–2–5, 1999.

"Philadelphia's Doo-Wop Sound: Swan Masters—Vol. 2." Liner notes to compact disc, German Dee-Jay CD55039, 1996.

"Philly Soul: Volume 1." Liner notes to compact disc, Philly Archives, PH-4, 1999.

Ridley, John. "Storm Warning: Philly Original Soul Classics-Vol. 1." Liner notes to compact disc, Jamie-Guyden JG4003-2, 1998.

Sacks, Leo, "A Mighty Love." Liner notes to compact disc, *The Spinners: A One of a Kind Love Affair: The Anthology*. Atlantic 82332-2, 1991.

Sacks, Leo, and Virginia Prescott, eds. "The Philly Sound: Kenny Gamble, Leon Huff and the Story of Brotherly Love." Booklet, included in the Sony-Legacy three-compact disc set of the same name, Sony-Legacy Z3K 647, 1997.

Vickers, Tom. "Teddy Pendergrass: 'It's Time for Love' and 'This One's for You." Liner notes to compact disc, the Right Stuff 72435-21969-2-0, 1999.

Index

Index